*living spirit, living practice*

Ruth Frankenberg

# LIVING SPIRIT, LIVING PRACTICE

*poetics, politics, epistemology*

*Duke University Press* DURHAM & LONDON 2004

© 2004 Duke University Press

All rights reserved

Printed in the United States

of America on acid-free paper ∞

Designed by C. H. Westmoreland

Typeset in Minion

by Keystone Typesetting, Inc.

Library of Congress Cataloging-

in-Publication Data appear on

the last printed page of

this book.

# CONTENTS

## ACKNOWLEDGMENTS

First and foremost I thank the individuals who were interviewed for the research upon which this book is based. For this work could not have been achieved without their willingness to share with me their time, their ways of seeing, and their understanding of their own spiritual and religious lives.

Also crucially important to this book and its completion has been my ongoing, multifaceted connection with Lata Mani. Her insights, both spiritual and intellectual, have been present through all stages of this project from its inception to the present moment.

Several institutions have supported me during the period of my work on this study. I thank the University of California, Davis Humanities Institute. Early on, a Fellowship at the UCDHI provided a context for me to begin analyzing and writing about these interviews. I also thank all at the Center for the Study of Culture and Society in Bangalore, India. During two extended periods of research leave based at CSCS, around two-thirds of this book were written. Finally I thank the University of California, Davis, for two faculty research grants.

This book could not possibly have come to fruition without the painstaking work of several women skilled in transcribing interviews. Stephanie Harolde undertook the greater part of this work as well as some emergency web research. Trena Cleland, Dora Ritzer, Janet Dawson, and Anne Savino were also patient, careful, and remarkably swift in transcribing this material.

Many colleagues have supported me throughout this work. I especially thank Jay Mechling, Kent Ono, Carolyn Thomas de la Peña, Michael Smith, and David Wilson, and as well Angie Chabram-

Dernersesian, Rosa Linda Fregoso, Herman Gray, Wendy Ho, Charles Hirschkind, Saba Mahmood, Judith Newton, Jacob Olupona, and Brenda Schildgen. Talal Asad, James Clifford, and Karen McCarthy Brown also offered assistance at key moments.

Beyond the groves of academe the following individuals were, in their different ways, crucial to my journey through this project: Navroze Contractor, Ambika Kathe Chambers, Deepa Dhanraj, Alison Frankenberg, Ammu Joseph, S. G. Vasudev, and Drs. Robert Zeiger and Sudha. I would also like to thank Ronald Frankenberg, whose presence in my life traverses the scholarly and the familial.

Ken Wissoker at Duke University Press was unfailing in his commitment to this book, and wise in his professional counsel. The editorial and production teams at Duke have been a dream to work with and Leah Stewart's copyediting of the text was exactly what I would have wished for.

To all named here as well as to the creative spirit, I remain ever grateful.

# INTRODUCTION

## *on rivers, mountains, and secrets*

RF Tell me what the word *spirituality* means to you in your life—personally what it means to you.

SADIQA When you first say "spirituality," I think of a word that's been seriously overused lately. It's marketing.

RF I've heard you say "spirit." Maybe *spirit* is a word that works better for you.

SADIQA Yeah, *spirit* feels better. Spirit is guidance, spirit is oneness, spirit is higher self, spirit is the all in all, which is Allah, you know. It is the uncomprehendable. It's bigger. Spirit is also right here. Spirit is the earth as well as the sky. But spirit in my life is—it changes its form. It changes or maybe it just grows. I don't know if it actually changes. It just starts to have more words I can understand or define it by. It's just a feeling. It's a feeling, you know. Because, as I was telling you over the phone, I've had, lately, lots of issues with spiritual teachers, or leaders. And so I've had this struggle, going back and forth. Does this mean I'm a nonbeliever? Does this mean I'm a Muslim? Does this mean I'm a Sufi? Does this mean I'm a Christian? Does this mean I've given up religion? So, spirit doesn't necessarily translate into religion, spirit just translates into the higher knowing, the higher self, which can include the religion or the religious practices that can help you go there, through the mantra or the *zikr*, the chanting, the spiritual, the phrase. You know, usually Allah's name, which is very common in Islam. *(Sadiqa, is a Palestinian American, 28, born Orthodox Christian, now a Sufi)*

SPIRITUALITY. Spirit. Religion. God. Life force. Interconnection. These are the concepts this book explores through the voices of fifty women and men, diverse in race, ethnicity, and national origin, socioeconomic status, age, and sexuality, as well as with respect to the forms taken by their religious and spiritual practice. Yet each answered in the affirmative my question, "Are you a person for whom religious or spiritual practice is a central aspect of your daily life, work, and identity?"

These are in many ways ordinary Americans, or as I prefer to call them, "United Statesians." They are, however, a group often ignored in our understanding of United States culture: people who combine a consciousness that is broadly liberal or progressive in ethical, political, or philosophical terms with deep and thoughtful spiritual and religious lives. As well, they are men and women who have never taken for granted either the sacred or the secular. All of these people, from Sadiqa, who starts this chapter, to Rabbi Alan Lew, who ends it, have found that spiritual life has shaped their secular lives, just as secular life has shaped their spiritual ones. Spiritual wisdom and religious traditions have made sense of life, whether in challenging periods or quiet times. Examination of the journeys undertaken by this group, and of the contexts that have prompted and made possible their travels, requires us to reevaluate United Statesian religious landscapes.

*Living Spirit, Living Practice* is about spirituality and religion as form, as method, as transformative force, and as historically situated life activity. Above all else, this is a study of the *practice* of religious and spiritual lives, and of the ways in which that practice is key to the making and remaking of everyday life, asking how interviewees themselves understand their own spiritual and religious worlds.

Spiritual and religious practices emerge as both processual and situated. They affect and transform—while being themselves touched, altered, or constrained by—other aspects of sociocultural context. Thus when the book asks how individuals "live spirit and live practice," it seeks answers to that question at the most intimate, local, and singular level, yet situates those answers on a broader canvas.

I use the words *religious* and *spiritual* throughout this text. In general, *religion*, for most interviewees, signaled specific form, history, and institution, and often a sense of belonging to a particular identity group. Confusingly enough, *spirit* and *spirituality* at times also meant all of that. But for many those words connoted also a sense of differentiation from the conservatism of many mainline or mainstream religious institutions. Moreover, the word *spirituality* for interviewees tended to convey that which was spontaneous and direct in the process of communing with divine and/or energetic forms—processes that might equally well take place with or without relationship to specific religious institutions.[1]

The extract with which I began this chapter, from one of the later interviews I conducted for this study, illustrates critical issues about religion and spirituality, ideas about time, place, tradition, and the unnameable force that interweaves and supersedes all of these. There was, for me, an irony in Sadiqa's caustic comment on the overuse of a term that had been at the heart of a question in my study, "What does the term *spirituality* mean to you?" It was ironic because I, too, had become troubled by the seemingly endless flow of new books, lead articles in mainstream magazines, even new lines in clothing and advertising, drawing upon the notion of spirituality. As Sadiqa remarked, "It's marketing."[2]

Yet, listening to Sadiqa I witnessed and experienced a shift in energy as Sadiqa expressed the meaning, to her, of the word *spirit*. Her narrative moved at that point into a multifaceted listing of the attributes of that which she called "uncomprehendable," an invented word that is hard to spell, yet easy to grasp. Here, Sadiqa signaled that which is common to most, perhaps all, spiritual systems—the recognition of a force beyond known semantic systems, but one that must almost inevitably be attached to form, name, and system in the context of the human spiritual journey.

Sadiqa next named some of the vexing processes that go along with that process of placing spirit, and one's belief in it, in a given calculus. As she made clear, there is the potential for both benefit and disruption to one's relationship to spirit in the presence of any mediating guide, teacher, or system. For, as she told me, the teacher/seeker relationship is so potent, so significant, in some religious systems that breaking with a teacher can call into question the very authenticity of one's spiritual journey, one's sense of belonging on a particular path. Here, in the teacher/seeker relationship, is one of the points at which spiritual practice meets the notion of religion. Thus, Sadiqa wondered whether, if she left her (Sufi) teacher, she would by default be returned to her birth (Orthodox Christian) religion. There was, then, the challenge to select a name for one's practice. (Am I Muslim? Am I Sufi? Am I Christian?) But Sadiqa resisted this disciplining, emphasizing that, with or without teacher, "spirit doesn't necessarily translate into religion"—insisting, in effect, on her right to her own "higher knowing, higher self."[3]

For Sadiqa, the dance between unnameability and naming continued as she considered the range of practices that "can help you go there"—to that unnameable place. Names are given even to the unnameable, and those names have histories, were one to seek them out. What histories, for example, undergird the naming of spirit as "higher," rather than inner, as "self" rather than external authority? Likewise the practices of chanting and mantra are connected with particular religious/spiritual traditions—why not mention hymns, or peyote? Then there was the eventual deployment of a name, *Allah*, for that which is "uncomprehendable." Yet Sadiqa still ended on a qualifying note, situating that name as "usual," as "very common" in Islam, but not in all places. The name thus remained both present and provisional in Sadiqa's depiction of that which is beyond naming. In effect Sadiqa had been speaking here of that which *she* might term *knowledge*, that which secular commentators might refer to as *belief*.

Philosopher and historian of religion Donald S. Lopez Jr. has examined the complex political processes that are a part of the naming of religious belief and, one might add, connected with its status as knowledge.[4] Lopez comments that it is, on one hand, difficult to place linguistic closure around religious and/or spiritual belief. Hence, he notes, many encyclopedias of religion will defer or displace the term *belief* to another text entry (rather than defining it, he says, such texts will, under the heading of *belief,* merely say "see 'faith'" or "see 'doubt'"). On the other hand, Lopez argues, provisional closures almost inevitably settle on belief, faith, and religious naming—closures whose provisionality is often obscured, rationalized, and naturalized.[5] Lopez frames his commentary with the words of philosopher Ludwig Wittgenstein: "The expression of belief is just a sentence . . . and the sentence has sense only as a member of a system of language; as one expression within a calculus."[6] Here the idea of *belief* (a term displaced in Sadiqa's discussion onto the word *spirit*) is returned to that which is in and of itself "uncomprehendable." For Sadiqa, like Wittgenstein, sets that which is spiritual (that which is belief) in a given linguistic calculus deemed by its speaker provisional and partial. Sadiqa is, as we saw, satisfied with this mode of belief, in effect deeming it "knowledge."

This book walks that line between the named and the unnameable, between "knowledge" and "belief." It explores the application of spiritual and religious epistemes (meaning systems) in daily life and in moments of crisis. By means of detailed life history interviews it examines the inseparably visceral, discursive, experiential, and practical dimensions of religious and spiritual life. It also examines the narrative structures of the interviews themselves, for I am interested in understanding something about the discursive traces—the ways of naming and their points of origin—that mark contemporary spiritual and religious languages. Yet, just as I wish to situate these voices in time and space, I am determined to pause long enough to encounter on their own terms the four realms of spiritual practice just named—visceral, discursive, experiential, and practical—before drawing them into contemporary sociocultural analysis.

"I like Geography best, he said, because your mountains and rivers know the secret" . . . It would be misleading to claim that all American religion at century's end could be captured with one metaphor . . . The lines drawn on the religious maps remain and have certain kinds of significance. But the metaphorical mountains and rivers have their own secrets, which are now being laid bare. All too visible are those features of the landscape and climate that do not show up on the maps where political and organizational lines have been drawn.

—MARTIN MARTY, "Revising the Map of American Religion"

WHERE ARE WE, and where in that landscape might one place the men and women I interviewed? Much has been written in the last three decades about the changed religious landscape of the United States.[7] As an interdisciplinarian trained in qualitative sociology, among other things, I take seriously the edict of Penny Edgell Becker and Nancy Eiesland: "Each scholar in the sociology of religion must eventually give her account of the American religious situation. What are the sociologically relevant features of religion in its diverse cultural and organizational manifestations?"[8] Yet I will not, here, seek to fully account for that field nor for the religious world of the United States. Rather I will, in this discussion, simply signal some of the key themes spoken of in the literature. Moreover, as I strive to name some of the lines on the maps, I will not forget the caveat offered by Martin Marty, that they may ultimately fail to reveal those rivers and mountains wherein the inner and intimate lives of religion and spiritual practice are lived.[9]

Frequently noted at the outset of discussions of religion in the United States is its sheer persistence, presence, and prevalence. Thus sociologist Wade Clark Roof points out the oft-cited poll statistics on faith in God: "The polls indicate that 94 percent of Americans believe in God, 90 percent report praying to God on a fairly regular basis, nine out of ten claim a religious affiliation."[10] Martin Marty, drawing on and quoting the extensive long-term data collection undertaken by John H. Gallup for the Princeton Religious Research Center, says:

> There has been surprising continuity in what can be measured . . . Gallup . . . compared the 1940s and the 1990s in the recent work. In 1944, 96 percent of those polled said they believed in God; in 1994, 96 percent said the same. In 1950, 39 percent of the people said they "happened to attend the church or synagogue" that week; after a high of 49 percent in 1955 and lows of 40 percent in 1970 and 1990, 43 percent made the claim about attendance in 1995. In 1940, 72 percent claimed church or synagogue membership; after a high of 76 percent in the 1940s and lows of 65 percent in 1988 and 1990, 66 percent avowed membership in 1995.[11]

One must also note, though, Roof's comment about the phenomenon of the "happen to be" religious affiliation:

> "I happen to be" religion is common in the United States (for example, "I happen to be Catholic") . . . [Such] religion is mostly a leftover: an ethnic or cultural past, preference for a particular food, family connections, inherited status or belonging . . . Such identities must be critically examined in contemporary society: in what ways are they important in people's lives, and more generally what is their place in the larger process of constructing religious identity?[12]

In a similarly questioning vein, sociologist Nancy Tatom Ammerman begins her study of Christian congregations' resilience in the face of sociocultural and demographic change by noting that "while there is a great deal of dispute about just how many Americans really attend religious services each week, for most of the last half century, more than forty percent have *said* they do."[13] It thus becomes necessary to move beyond statistics and actually *ask* individuals what religion means to them in terms of belief, practice, and daily life activity. This is something that was undertaken for both Roof's and Ammerman's texts. It is also central to the present study.

One sees in the literature discussions of both continuity and change. Yet it is apparent that change, rather than stasis, is the order of the day. This is reflected in the titles of contemporary studies of religion in the United States—Robert Wuthnow's influential *The Restructuring of American Religion*, Marty's "Revising the Map of American Religion," and Wade Clark Roof's *Spiritual Marketplace: Baby Boomers and the Remaking of American Religion*.[14] In 1955, sociologist of religion Will

Herberg offered a reading of U.S. religion as a Protestant-Catholic-Jewish triad.[15] Efforts to remap the U.S. landscape often return to Herberg in order to note that his is no longer an adequate framing.[16] Yet others point out that, in actuality, data proposes that there is still something to be said for that earlier triadic representation. Patrick McNamara, for example, says that "today's United States displays a kaleidoscope of religious groupings that goes much beyond the Catholic-Protestant-Jewish predominance simply presumed by author Will Herberg in the 1950s. Yet these three church traditions still embrace by far the majority of American churchgoers."[17] The assertion that although things have changed, much remains the same, is also present in the opening words of Ammerman's study. She first describes the earlier and long-lasting Christian presence and then—as though with a sudden realization that change has occurred—seeks (at the expense of both image and metaphor) to add some more items from the "kaleidoscope" brought forth in McNamara's depiction:

> One of the most enduring images of the American landscape is the steeple, a landmark signaling the presence of a congregation. Whether small and simple, or towering and ornate, whether soaring alongside skyscrapers or rising out of the rolling hills or subtly blending into the sameness of a suburban housing development, the spaces set aside by Christian crosses, Jewish Stars of David, Muslim minarets, and other religious markers are the single most pervasive public gathering places in American society.[18]

Ammerman's description signals the semantic or conceptual status quo in current depictions of the U.S. religious landscape. For, the challenge faced here is that of how to get from point a to point b, that is, from the "steeple" to the "other religious markers," or from the "triad" to the "kaleidoscope." Marty is perhaps the most frank (the most realistic, one might argue) in his assessment that he, for one, cannot provide a singular metaphor with which to cover the situation.

There has been much work characterizing the changed and perhaps still changing situation within the "Herberg triad" itself. Here there is discussion on a range of fronts. One of these is commentary on the presence of media in the promulgation and conveyance of religious thinking.[19] A second site of awareness is that of the emergence of the Christian "megachurch."[20] A third is the story of the nationalization and politicization of fundamentalist forms of Christianity.[21] A fourth is the chronicling of the processes of transformation facing many mainline Christian congregations.[22] In a similar vein there is discussion of the ways in which Judaism is undergoing renewal and transformation.[23] Scholars have also commented upon individuals' sense of "permission" in recent years to make choices as they build their spiritual lives. In telling the stories of this latter sense of permission, scholarship begins, at times, to step outside the "triad." For as a part of this process, Western-born individuals have felt enabled to move toward forms of religious and/or spiritual practice besides Judeo-Christian ones.[24]

Thus, if there is a problem in contemporary mappings of the U.S. religious landscape, it is the seeming incapacity to integrate the non–Judeo-Christian, beyond the naming of other religions as "and," "as well," "other," or—strangely—"new." (Exceptions will be discussed below.) Here I have in mind Islam, Buddhism, Hinduism, other East Asian and South Asian religious forms, African diaspora–derived religions, and nature-based religions. It is not that scholarship is unavailable—there are other reasons for this state of affairs.

One might argue that the number of individuals involved in other spiritual practices is too small to dislodge an abiding sense that the United States is primarily Judeo-Christian.[25] Yet, as is clear in the trade and scholarly literature, signs of non–Judeo-Christian forms and practices *are* present in the United States—hence the growing interest in striving to name and understand them. One might also propose that non–Judeo-Christian religious practices remain less visible in the public sphere, despite their presence in private and subordinate spaces. However, giving the lie to this idea are those many moments when non–Judeo-Christian voices *have* appeared in the public realm in recent years. To offer just two examples, the Reverend Louis Farrakhan reminded the public of the continuing presence of the Nation of Islam when he called the Million Man March to Washington D.C. on 16 October 1995. And some may remember a 1999 controversy about freedom of religion in the wake of U.S. military personnel being accorded the right to practice Wicca on military land.[26] Lastly, one might argue that perhaps transformations in the religious landscape involving "religious minorities" are still recent enough to be deemed "works in progress." However, no one in this field of study will deny that Islam, Buddhism, Confucianism, Hinduism, and Sikhism have been present in the United States for as long as have been their immigrant practitioners (which is to say since the second half of the nineteenth century).[27]

Two recent scholarly collections—Yvonne Yazbeck Haddad's *The Muslims of America* and Barbara Daly Metcalf's *Making Muslim Space in North America and Western Europe*—bring together work on Islam in the United States. Similarly, a text like Charles S. Prebish and Kenneth K. Tanaka's *The Faces of Buddhism in America* offers specialists and nonspecialists alike commentary and analysis of Buddhism in the United States. (Buddhism and Islam are of course not the only religions about which this kind of work is under way, nor are these the only texts on these two religions, although they are, of course, very significant ones.) When one reads such books, one learns quickly that the Muslim and Buddhist worlds share with the Christian one the very same interwoven strands of community, institution, and individual, and the very same processes of growth, transformation, and at times decline and even demise. One sees too that Buddhist and Muslim houses of practice contribute to the public realm, supporting towns and cities stricken by sudden disasters and ongoing challenges, and hosting public figures at institutional receptions.[28] Strikingly, Islam and Buddhism have had significant impact in the U.S. prison system, providing spiritual support and, it is argued, countercultural modes of discipline and order in otherwise challenging spaces.[29]

Lastly, non–Judeo-Christian religious sites bring with them, indeed require, literal, physical spaces. And now one returns to Ammerman's description, quoted earlier in this section, of the range of spiritual signs and signals dotting the contemporary U.S. landscape. But the question remains why it is that the *beginning* of Ammerman's paragraph, with its implication that the church steeple is the religious sign most easily recognized, most familiar, and most easily connected with a notion of U.S. religion, is the part that rings most forcefully true. One is reminded here of cultural critic Antonio Gramsci's argument that within a hegemonic system there will always be a range of mutually contradictory modes of interpretation, not to mention material experiences. Yet, given the dynamic (dis)equilibrium of forces and tendencies in play, that which is subordinate will continually appear, only to disappear into forgottenness (and simultaneous rememberedness) again and again and again.

There is, then, more that needs to be addressed. A recent collection—*Retelling U.S. Religious History*—argues that reassessment and revision are much needed. As its editor, Thomas Tweed, states, "the main problem with most surveys of U.S. religion is a lack of inclusiveness. To put this point differently, narrators and narratives have been positioned in ways that obscure important dimensions of America's religious past."[30] Tweed and the contributors to his collection are engaging with the past—albeit in the Foucauldian sense, with the present moments and spaces that those tellings of the past might conjure up. Historian

Catherine L. Albanese argues in the volume's concluding essay that, in fact, the United States has always been a country marked by religious exchange, communication, and mutual transformation.[31] Religions "old" and "new" have, from the beginning of the colonial period, given to and gleaned from one another. The problem, Albanese argues, is that this kind of blending "became, in America, a secret obscured. And religious exchange obscured and unrecognized as such became religious exchange denied, an ideology of purity and containment proclaimed in its stead."[32] While one might dispute the overly positive interpretation that Albanese seems at times to place on religious exchanges, I find very helpful her commitment to questioning the categories of "new" and "old" and, one might add, central and marginal.

Tweed notes that it is unrealistic to expect that the narrative of U.S. religion can be reconstructed quickly. Yet Marty is also correct in bringing attention to the "mountains" and "rivers" whose secrets are now "being laid bare." The interviews in this book make visible those religions now becoming a larger presence in U.S. public culture (Islam, Buddhism, Hinduism), while still giving generous voice and attention to women and men from within the Herberg triad of Protestants, Catholics, and Jews.

🖉

> When we cannot understand everything [healer Mabel McKay] says in responding to our questions about basketry, Dreams, or even about herself, if there are black holes of uncertainty, borders and obstacles that seem impossible to cross, we must . . . remember our own limitations and accept difference for what it is, an indication of the distance we have to travel by means of a sublime sensitivity to the Other and to the history, "either misrepresented or revealed invisible," that accounts for the world from which Mabel speaks.—GREG SARRIS, "A Culture under Glass: The Pomo Basket"

> Anthropological and folklore studies note that spiritual therapies are more effective for certain ailments, particularly those with psychological components. Elements within spiritual healing practice, and the typical signs and symptoms alleviated, suggest that hypnosis and placebos contribute to the efficacy of spiritual healing. Folklore studies provide a means to test hypotheses derived from this theory. Analysis of 85 accounts of folk healing collected in northeastern North Carolina support, yet reveal limitations regarding hypnosis/placebo explanations.—JAMES MCCLENON, "Spiritual Healing and Folklore Research: Evaluating the Hypnosis/Placebo Theory"

THE QUOTES FROM Sarris and McClenon signal fundamental issues that arise when one seeks to study religion and spirituality in an "rationalist" academy.[33] In beginning to contemplate the notion of communing and communication with or with*in* spirit, one can identify three, to my mind equally inadequate, modes of naming at work in the secular quarters of the contemporary United States. First, such experiences are sometimes written off as unreal, dismissed as "all in the mind," with *mind* standing in here for *imagination*. A second discursive move is the linguistic banishment of spiritual life and communing with beings and energies deemed "divine" into the semantic and sociocultural margins. This is achieved by the naming of such experiences and practices as *supernatural, extra-rational, paranormal,* or, more grandiosely, *otherworldly.* The very structure of these terms— with their prefixes *super, extra, para, other*—situates them outside the mainstream, serving to reemphasize extant conceptions of the normal rather than complicate or broaden them.

A third and related option compartmentalizes religion and spirituality into "special" sections, whether of bookstores, TV shows, or even at times special issues of major newsmagazines. But once again the very "specialness" of that which is other, super, or para means that the "normal," the "rational," and the "real" remain intact in the purview of public culture. This, despite the frequent appearance of such texts on the best-seller lists of even the most highly reputed newspapers. Any sense of the integration into daily life of spirit or spirituality remains sinister. It immediately signals the intrusion of the Other into the mainstream in some form, whether deemed "magical realist" (and therefore hemispherically misplaced), quaint, folkish, or old-fashioned, or, worse, dangerously cultish. It is then, perhaps, the effort to forge links, visibly or publicly, between sacred and secular worlds that is most threatening and certainly most semantically challenging. In this regard it is also striking that the *Oxford English Dictionary,* a gatekeeper of the dominant semantic terrain, retains that four-part tautological, mutual definition of the terms *reason, rational, sane,* and even *human.*[34]

In naming these three moves, that of dismissal, that of marginalization, and that of compartmentalization, I have begun with the popular rather than the scholarly. But there are points of connection between the two; in both realms, these strategies to contain the spiritual or to keep the sacred and the secular firmly apart are not always successful and tend easily to dissolve.

Ethnographer Greg Sarris emphasizes the need to renounce the academic all-knowing stance, accepting instead the "black holes of uncertainty," "*our own* limitations" (emphasis added), and proposing a recognition of "the distance *we* have to travel" (emphasis added) in order to engage with the subjects of our scholarship.[35] Notice that Sarris both calls on the sublime as our only recourse here *and* situates the crisis of understanding in historical process. Again, *misrepresentation* indicates that perhaps a complex, power-laden gaze is in operation, as we seek to engage "Other" ways of seeing. Sarris's radicalism lies in part in his refusal to legislate in either direction (for or against Mabel McKay, for or against the academy), but perhaps in greater part in his insistence on the necessity of living with, and simultaneously historicizing, uncertainty.

McClenon's psycho-medical analysis of spiritual healing is perhaps more familiar. Spiritual healing practices are recuperated and simultaneously repudiated by their revision or reduction into a psychologizing framework. Crudely, the inference here is that spiritual healing practices can be explained away. Perhaps the ostensibly ill body is in fact ill only "in the mind" after all. Arguably exotic practices of faith healing are brought home, geographically, by the location of McClenon's informants in North Carolina rather than, for instance, New Guinea. Let us note, though, McClenon's last sentence in this first paragraph: there are "limitations regarding hypnosis/placebo explanations." The end of McClenon's paper reveals the nature of these "limitations." He comments that "many accounts lacked features typically associated with hypnosis, such as a practitioner [of hypnosis]." Moreover, and equally challenging to the placebo or hypnosis hypotheses, he admits, "Four reports specified that infants less than two years old had been healed *anomalously*"[36] (emphasis added). McClenon goes on to conclude that "folk *hypnotic* treatment may be effective as an *adjunct to standard* medical care, particularly for *burn patients* in the emergency department"[37] (emphases added).

We may note that McClenon has translated and simultaneously subordinated healing practices he deems "nonstandard," as well as the cognitive frameworks within which they are, presumably, embedded. However, its practitioners do not conceive folk healing as "hypnosis," nor healings as "anomalous." They do not consider their practices "adjunct," but rather freestanding. Moreover, the juxtaposition of spiritually based healing practices to "standard" ones hierarchizes healing systems. But the conceptual and methodological chaos of McClenon's argument is dramatized in his proposal that folk healing might be especially beneficial in emergency room burn units. What, one might ask, is more visceral, less psychosomatic, than a burned body? This chaos is in fact symptomatic of the closed circuit of analysis that characterizes the concept of "rationality" itself, wherein the definitions of "reason" and "reasons" are never fully specified but rather taken as self-evident, and wherein elements of historically contingent argument are taken to be a priori truths. In relation to McClenon's work then one sees an only partially successful effort to explain away the spiritual and folk or faith healing. Here, Sarris's allusion to practices "either misrepresented or revealed invisible" takes on a concrete significance.

Processes in academia that are analogous to the compartmentalization and marginalization named above are sometimes subtle ones, but they can nonetheless be identified. One such is the kind of situation described by anthropologist Karen McCarthy Brown. Brown documents two experiences of traveling to speak at academic institutions with the subject of her ethnography, *Mama Lola: A Vodou Priestess in Brooklyn*. Brown explains that audiences were not certain how to react when Mama Lola, during both events, was "visited" and "ridden" by Ogou and Ezili Danto, both Vodou spirits with whom Mama Lola often worked in her priestly capacity. At one, the faculty in attendance were taken by surprise (although one might argue that, had the audience read the book that had occasioned the invitation, they would have been less surprised). In response, Brown says, most of those present either "medicalized" the situation, asking Mama Lola for the remainder of the visit whether she was feeling better, or repressed it from their consciousness, not referring to the event at all. At a different scholarly function, a similar turn of events led to Mama Lola being met with a wheelchair when she got ready to leave the podium and the stage.[38] Similar experiences greeted Greg Sarris and the subjects of his analytical work, Native American basket weaver and healer Mabel McKay and other members of her spiritual community.[39]

The physical presence of spiritual practitioners who refuse to adopt the rhetorical and behavioral protocols that are normative in academic settings exposes the compartmentalization whereby such subjects usually enter the academy as data, as description, as subjects or objects of analysis. It is important, however, not to present an overly homogeneous picture. For in the situations described by Brown and Sarris, there were students and faculty making efforts to bridge the apparently disparate worlds of academia and spiritual practice. Nor was this cultural clash one-sided. For as Brown and Sarris both make clear, the healers and practitioners found it as difficult and at times as unnerving to imagine entering the academic world as those invited to meet them found it to commune with theirs.[40]

Another kind of compartmentalization is made manifest when some scholars of religion feel it necessary to disavow, or at least distance themselves from, any belief or membership in the religious or spiritual communities that are their subjects of study. Again, this is not a simple situation, nor a univalent one. The craft and science of qualitative sociological, anthropological, and otherwise ethnographic research entail, by definition, entering the worlds of one's subjects of study. As a result, here the discussion opens onto a process in which separations between the academy and religion/spirituality, and at the same time between the rational and irrational, between the believer and the skeptic, begin to dissolve.

In general it is, or so it seems, almost impossible for the qualitative scholar to remain utterly separate from the research site. Thus, for example, at the start of his study of women devoted to Saint Jude in the United States from the mid- to late twentieth century, historian Robert Orsi tells his own story of an encounter with the saint, known to all as the patron saint of hopeless causes. Orsi is on a plane to New York. His plane has been circling the airport for forty-five minutes. He is late for a crucial meeting with a foundation. Orsi hears over the sound system the pilot telling the passengers that owing to inclement weather the airport is facing traffic problems. This plane, the pilot explains, will therefore need to turn back and fly to Philadelphia. Orsi will thus miss his meeting. The avowedly skeptical Orsi offers a prayer in desperation, or perhaps as the spontaneous result of his immersion in his data: "St Jude, I really need to land in New York—please, do something." Within seconds of his plea, the voice of the pilot returns to the passenger cabin. Surprised, even shocked, the pilot announces that for reasons he does not understand he has suddenly been given landing clearance and that the cabin crew should prepare the vessel for landing. As Orsi puts it, were anyone to ask him if he believed in the powers of St. Jude, he would say no. However, he adds, he had promised (as is the convention when one prays to St. Jude) to make visible his experience by way of showing gratitude. Thus, Orsi says, he tells the tale here. As he ends the story Orsi adds, "But what's belief got to do with it?"[41] Orsi's discourse asserts distance from faith in St. Jude, even while following the protocols of the faithful, thus failing to maintain a compartmentalized position. In one deft moment Orsi reasserts his disclaimer and simultaneously dramatizes the doubleness and thus in effect the compartmentalization of his discourse.

As is well known in the fields of qualitative research, that which is commonly referred to as the "reflexive turn" in ethnographic practice has made it possible, permissible, some would even argue essential, to account for one's own location in the research site. Here, the researcher's location is visible rather than invisible, a resource rather than an obstacle or distraction. This, I would argue, helps to undo some of the "compartmentalizing" processes named above. Thus, for example, E. Burke Rochford Jr., reflecting on eight years of fieldwork on the ISKCON (Krishna Consciousness) movement in the United States, said:

> While there were advantages to [the] participant role, there were a number of distinct disadvantages as well. Not only my family and friends, but also the university questioned my involvement and relationship with the Krishna movement. Was I after all a researcher-participant or a participant-researcher? . . . These experiences were themselves worthy of analysis, and I began to attend to how my involvement with ISKCON influenced my relationships in and outside of the movement. In sum I tried to maintain a reflexive stance toward the setting and my relationship to it in an effort to gain a deeper understanding of the Krishna movement, its membership, and the nature of fieldwork as a method.[42]

One must ask whether the university would have questioned Rochford's involvement had he been studying a mainline denomination rather than one at times named a "new religion" and "cult-like." For I would argue that it is less risky to undo the lines of separation between religion and the academy when the religious form in question is a more conventional one. In any event, it should be noted that Rochford does not deem a "confessional" necessary. For while he lists in detail the roles he performed in ISKCON chapters, as well as the kinds of initiation he underwent as an "observer-participant" (or was that a participant-observer?) he does not explain to his readers whether he is or is not a member of the ISKCON movement. From the rest of what Rochford says readers can draw their own conclusions. For Rochford, the particular benefit of active participation seems to be the building of trust. However, although he finds it of great benefit as a fieldworker to have experienced some of the same events as his research subjects, he at no time implies that he has on a psychological or psychic level experienced the same things as they have.

Anthropologist Susan Friend Harding takes matters one step further. She argues that by means of immersion into her field site a degree of discursive affinity became possible. Near the beginning of her book she tells the story of a near-collision between her vehicle and another one, as she left the site of a long interview-cum-conversion effort between herself and a pastor in the Reverend Jerry Falwell's church:

> Halfway across town, I stopped at a stop sign, then started into the intersection, and was very nearly smashed by a car that seemed to come upon me from nowhere very fast. I slammed on the brakes, sat stunned for a split second, and asked myself, "What is God trying to tell me?"
>
> It was my voice, but not my language. I had been inhabited by the fundamental Baptist tongue I was investigating.[43]

Harding's next step, analytically (although not necessarily in that moment), is to strive to comprehend this experience from within. She proposes that, in that moment, her discursive and psychic (the latter is *my* word, not hers) frame had become that of the individual greeting the possibility of conversion, or in fundamental Baptist language, acceptance of the word. For Harding (presumably in retrospect) explains that "the process [of conversion] begins when an unsaved listener begins to appropriate in his or her inner speech the saved listener's language and its attendant view of the world . . . At the moment of salvation . . . the Christian tongue locks into some kind of central, controlling, dominant place; it has gone beyond inhabiting the listener's mind to occupy the listener's identity."[44]

Harding's near-collision experience, which she considers a "near-conversion experience," might be understood in a number of ways. Some might explain it away as the effect of fatigue. Others might medicalize it as the effects of stress and overwork. And still others might rush in, fearing the onset of "decompartmentalization." Such analysts might propose that Harding was about to fall over the line from outsider to insider, on the verge of "going native."

Yet none of these is an appropriate reading of the situation. In Harding's view, it is precisely her willingness to allow her mind to enter the universe of her research subjects' discourse that enables her to comprehend that world and frame. And it is, Harding argues, the refusal to cross that boundary that prevents "social scientists and professed unbelievers" from fully understanding the meaning and process of conversion.

One might guess that Harding's theory of conversion might still not be congruent with that of some of those who have, as they would express it, heard and accepted the word of God. Her description of the emergence of an aspect of the self that is "dominant," "controlling" (of what? by whom?)—the idea that the convert's mind is now under "occupation"—is possibly more mechanistic and more coercive than many, during or after conversion, would term it. As Harding puts it next, "men and women convert to fundamental Christianity because they become convinced that supernatural reality is a fact, that Christ is the literal son of God, that he did rise from the dead and is alive today, that the Holy Spirit is speaking to them, that Jesus will enter their hearts if they acknowledge their sins, that they will have eternal life, that God is really real. To continue to think otherwise would be irrational."[45] Here Harding both baldly states aspects of fundamental Baptist belief and at the same time drops hints to her readers that she may not be in agreement with these views. Thus "men and women convert . . . *because they become convinced*" (emphasis added). And, Harding continues, "the appropriate question then is: How does this *supernatural* order become real, known, experienced and *absolutely* irrefutable?" (emphasis added).

Later in the text, Harding offers the reader a very direct reminder of her externality to this discourse and community, when she is one of an audience of several thousand listening to Jerry Falwell speaking:

> The men and women seated around me seemed to settle in for a delightful and edifying evening. Sometimes they amened and chuckled . . . sometimes held their breath as though watching a dramatic uplifting epic unfold. I on the other hand felt increasingly disappointed, headachy, irritated, lost and dismayed. I had hoped that . . . I would come to a better understanding of how his oratory produced his national moral authority in the 1980s. Instead . . . my mind went blank . . . I felt as outside the community of fundamental Baptist belief as I ever had.[46]

Placing all of this together, there are two sets of interests in play. On one hand, it is Harding's commitment to enter into, and engage directly with, the discourse of Baptist fundamentalism that makes her able to map it with a degree of warmth and intimacy. On the other hand her outsider status, and her commitment to signaling that status to self and reader, both marks her language and particularizes her reading of fundamental Baptism. Harding is operating firmly outside of the first two modes of separation named at the start of this section—dismissal and marginalization. But what she *is* doing is working with the option of compartmentalization, going into, and stepping back from, the discursive and experiential worlds of her research subjects.

Karen McCarthy Brown's approach is a different one. She has other modes of signaling both her otherness and her connectedness in relation to Mama Lola in particular and Vodou practice more generally. In moments of cultural disparity, as for example on college campuses, Brown is a transcoder. Here she simply explains what has happened, from Mama Lola's point of view, from the audience's point of view, and then from her own analytical vantage point.[47] In the (very many) moments when the differences in location between her own and Mama Lola's positioning in the world become nakedly visible, Brown engages them, so that they become occasions for analysis. There are points when Brown's relationship with Mama Lola becomes especially difficult. For example, Brown describes an evening when Mama Lola had refused to participate in the planned session of tape recording, during a long and at times tense trip to Benin. Brown says, "I walked out of her room, quietly closed the door to mine, and then picked up an empty suitcase and hurled it against the wall."[48] This occasion becomes a moment of contemplation about the construction and retention of memory, as well as about the ongoing, always subtle, relationships and investments between ethnographer and subject. (Brown adds that "twenty minutes later, there was a knock at my door." Mama Lola had come in search of Brown, who was by now not fully ready to cooperate either. In response, Mama returned to her own room and slammed the door. But in the end, as Brown tells it, "after all that acting out [we] had a good long talk—and it was all on the record.")[49]

For both Brown and Harding, then, engagements with the author/ethnographer's own positioning are a rich resource. Unlike Harding, Brown does not find it necessary to signal by means of linguistic hints her disagreement with Mama Lola's universe of discourse. This is, one might easily argue, simply because of Brown's allegiance with Vodou in contrast with Harding's more complex relationship with fundamental Baptist Christianity. And one might propose just as reasonably that Brown's and Mama Lola's differentness is so obvious (racially, economically) and Harding's so much less explicit, (again racially, economically) that it becomes necessary to flag the points of difference. Lastly, one might suggest that Harding's very strategy of entering and working from within fundamentalist discourse makes it necessary to signal forcefully the moments when she is ready to step outside of it. In any event, these delicate efforts to disrupt any strict compartmentalization of researcher and researched, and simultaneously with that which is religio-spiritual and that which is academic, generate creative and insightful modes of undertaking work in the academy on religious and spiritual questions.

The reflexive turn in ethnographic practice disrupted certain of its well-established categories and separations. But it also revealed some of those very separations as illusory. When the lessons of the reflexive turn are applied to the study of religion and spirituality, another set of binaries can be undone—those between the practitioner and the academician, the recipient of the miraculous and the commentator on it, and more generally that between the world of scholarship and that of religion. The point here is not that the researcher must "confide" in her readership about her religious location, nor even that her location must be univalent. Rather, researchers' relationships with their subjects vis-à-vis religion, as also with all other areas of research, are subtle, complex, and usually multivalent. Consciousness of this is of great benefit to researcher, to readership, and, no doubt, to research subjects also.[50]

JAY MECHLING's analytical meditation on the challenges—and the joys—of teaching about religion in the American studies classroom provides a new frame from within which to examine the meaning(s) in United States life of religion and spirituality.[51] Beginning with the notion of religion as subjective reality, and moving from there to its socialization within what Mechling calls "communities of memory," Mechling proceeds toward the public sphere/square. Finally he engages his end point, the remaking of the idea of "civil religion," a concept deemed problematic for years, given its enmeshment in exceptionalist and consensus-driven understandings of (or at least hopes for) the United States as a nation.

For me, Mechling's journey is important in an additional way. Placing it in reverse enables me to situate the locus, direction, and purpose of my engagement with fifty women and men whose lives center on religion/spirituality as subjective reality, with equal emphasis on both of those words. In part of his discussion, Mechling brings together the work of three scholars—William James, Peter L. Berger, and Clifford Geertz—in order to map religion and its journey from interior to exterior spaces. First, he reminds us that philosopher of religion William James defines *religion* by reference to "the feelings, acts and experiences of individual men [*sic*] in their solitude, so far as they apprehend themselves to stand in relation to whatever they may consider the divine."[52] He then moves to cultural analyst Peter Berger who in "Jamesian mode . . . stresses the 'supernatural,' what James meant by the divine." According to Berger, the supernatural "denotes a fundamental category of religion, namely the assertion or belief that there is *an other reality,* and one of ultimate significance for man [*sic*], which transcends the reality within which our everyday experience unfolds."[53] Next, Mechling says, and here he speaks in concert with Berger,

> Each of us has access to our own experiences (including emotions, moods and so on) with a transcendent reality, with a "sacred" reality posed against a "profane," ordinary, everyday reality . . . The phenomenological position asserts simply that all people have experiences that we might call ecstatic (as Berger notes, "in the literal sense of *ekstasis*—standing or stepping outside reality as commonly defined") and that for many people this ecstasy gives them a glimpse of a reality that transcends our own.[54]

Mechling turns then to the "communities of memory" in whose context experience is made intersubjectively available—these are not necessarily literal, "face-to-face" communities, says Mechling, but may be mass-mediated ones.[55] What Mechling calls (following Bellah et al.) "communities of memory" and what I call "networks of meaning" are critical in helping to make common sense and shared sense of spiritual practices.

Mechling now draws upon anthropologist Clifford Geertz, who, Mechling notes, enables one to shift gears from the internal, even interpersonal, to the structural level, albeit "slight[ing] the personal experiences so important to James and Berger."[56] As with James and Berger, Mechling draws directly on Geertz: "Religion is, [Geertz] writes, '(1) a system of symbols which acts to (2) establish powerful, persuasive and long-lasting moods and motivations in men [*sic*] by (3) formulating conceptions of a general order of existence and (4) clothing these conceptions with such an aura of factuality that (5) the moods and motivations seem uniquely realistic.' "[57] Here, Mechling proposes, it becomes possible to "subsume [James and Berger's] notion of a divine, sacred, transcendent reality under Geertz's general order of existence."[58]

Mechling's analytical journey brings into relief what it is that I strive to document in this text. Like James and Berger, I am particularly interested in describing, in as far as it is possible, the inner spiritual journeys of the men and women with whom I worked. And, like Mechling, I have learned that interviewees are members of "communities of memory," participants in "networks of meaning" that help to make sense of their experiences of what Berger calls *ecstasy* or *ek-stasis.*

And I agree with Geertz that religion, as with all other aspects of human life, entails the crafting of, and dependence on, symbol systems that help generate a kind of facticity and realism.

At the same time, I take issue on several grounds with the articulations of James, Berger, and Geertz, particularly in relation to what is, in effect, their "exceptionalizing" of the religious and spiritual spheres of experience in the social realm. First, I suggest that despite their interest in and commitment to making sense of individuals' inner spiritual lives, both James and Berger continue to work from within the binary mapping that I described earlier in the chapter. Thus the experiences that Berger seeks to describe are deemed *supernatural* ones. And in a similar vein, his sense of the ek-static is that it takes the experiencing subject away from, or beyond, the commonplace, away from, in Berger's words, the "everyday." Here, then, we encounter once more the marginalization and compartmentalization of the spiritual and religious realms.

As Mechling notes, Geertz is less interested in the inner lives of men and women than are James and Berger. Going further, I would add that Geertz's articulation implies that the religious, more than other arenas in life, needs to *assert* its factuality, rather than having been always and already factual. Thus, in his definition, religion as a symbolic system "*acts* to establish moods and motivations . . . *formulating* conceptions . . . *clothing* these conceptions with . . . an *aura* of factuality that makes [them] . . . *seem* uniquely realistic" (emphases added). Much as there may be to gain from Geertz's interpretive frame, it conceives religion, here, in purely mechanical terms. We thus return to the first of the three secular orientations to the sacred named earlier in this chapter, the one which simply explains away things religious or spiritual. I do not, I should emphasize, propose that the religious or the spiritual are *more* real than other arenas of social life (although some might argue that that is, in fact, the case). Rather, I merely suggest that languages and experiences of spiritual and religious matters are as much enmeshed in the sociocultural and the sociohistorical as are, for instance, constructions of sexuality.

I continue to find extremely beneficial Mechling's mapping of the religious via James, Berger, and Geertz. I would, though, add two things to it. The first, following from what I have just said, is a commitment to undoing the binaries that still dog our efforts to name and emplace the spiritual and the religious in contemporary culture. Second (and I do not assume that Mechling would dispute this), I would propose that for those whose religious/spiritual lives are central to their existence, all of the stages identified by him—internal, intersubjective, collective, historical, and public—are thoroughly intermeshed rather than easily separable.

From the standpoint of this group of interviewees (and I suspect they may not be alone), this was certainly the case. The internal, intersubjective, collective, historical, and public realms were also in constant dialogue with one another, at times harmoniously and at times in contention. The challenge is, then, to find language that does not remain entangled in secular discourse as usual. I am interested in turning my attention, through the stories told to me by fifty men and women, to the ways in which the ek-static constantly becomes everyday, commonplace. I am interested in reading and decoding discourses, because they help me to understand the making of meaning within, against, across, and beyond an array of "networks of meaning" and the "communities of memory" that nurture them. I am interested in seeing how it is that the ek-static commonplace gives form to networks of meaning, and vice versa. I am interested in understanding the ways in which histories and presents form one another and are at times thoroughly disrupted by the ek-static as it bursts in and then becomes commonplace. And I am interested in seeing how all of these things shape, contend with, and transform an array of competing public squares and spheres.

This book moves, chapter by chapter, from the inner and intersubjective to the public sphere. Yet, as might be imagined, inner worlds will shape the external world throughout. Languages of the internal realm will of necessity be marked, constrained, and/or aided by history or what has gone before, as well as by contemporary intersubjectivies and current public spheres. And the public sphere/square will be impacted by and will at times brutally repress the inner spiritual journeys of many men and women.

☙

THE VOICES of the men and women I interviewed are central to this book. All deeply committed to the recognition of spiritual practice as a living, transformative force, they provide a rich context in which to examine the place and potential of spiritual/religious practice in the contemporary United States. Closure and compartmentalization become ironic in this context, since the men and women I interviewed are living precisely by means of refusing such separations. For these interviewees, the "sacred" and the "quotidian," the so-called "otherworldly" and the "here and now" are interwoven, thus making problematic and even absurd that very semantic separation. Interviewees were also well aware of the hierarchies of meaning within which they live. Yet they were uniformly far more interested in living within their epistemic frames than in conforming to a dominant rationality. As interviewee Akaya Windwood said, "Somebody else would think I'm *nuts!* And I just laugh at that and let it go, you know. I derive too much strength and sanity from it. Let me say it this way—if my spirituality is a source of madness, I can live with it. I'd rather be mad than sane of another nature."

The men and women who are the focus of this book practice a range of traditions.[59] They include twelve Christians from Episcopalian, Congregational, Catholic, Lutheran, Presbyterian, Religious Science, and Orthodox Christian denominations. Another twelve had been raised in Christianity (as Protestants, Catholics, Baptists, Orthodox Christians, Pentecostals, and Protestant fundamentalists) but were now practicing other paths. The twelve Buddhists had practices centered in Zen, Theravada, and Tibetan traditions. There were nine women and men whose practices and teachers I would, as shorthand, name "Hindu," although that appellation is not one that most of these interviewees chose for themselves.

Of four Jewish interviewees, two practiced within the Reform tradition and one was a rabbi in a Conservative synagogue. The fourth was involved in the revival of Jewish mysticism. In addition there were four individuals of Ashkenazi Jewish heritage. Of these four, three were now Buddhists and one was involved in a Hindu-derived path of kundalini yoga. Two Muslims were born into and continued to practice Islam (one Sunni, the other Shia). Another was a Sufi. A fourth belonged to the Nation of Islam. And two interviewees who would not by any means identify themselves as Muslim were members of spiritual/religious movements with roots in Islam: Bahai and the Diamond Heart Path. One interviewee was a Wiccan, which is to say, part of the linked, European-originated traditions of witchcraft and goddess worship. Two women were involved in Twelve Step, the spiritual path of recovery that is a clustering of organizations emergent from Alcoholics Anonymous. The spiritual practices of four women are best described as extra-institutional and/or syncretic, although one of them is also involved in Twelve Step.

Interviewees from diverse racial and ethnic backgrounds practiced the traditions analyzed here—Christian, Buddhist, Hindu, Islamic, Jewish, and extra-institutional. Moreover, the religious and spiritual autobiographies of individuals cathected forcefully with key moments in postwar U.S. religious history. Thus, for example, Michael Yamamoto and Mushim Ikeda Nash, third generation Japanese Americans from different parts of the United States, both name Buddhism as having shaped their childhood communities. Neither remains a practitioner within those same forms of Buddhism, however. Rather, both, as adults, became students of Buddhist teachers who had not arrived in the United States until well into the second half of the twentieth century (Michael's teacher was a Tantric Tibetan teacher, and Mushim's a master of Korean Zen Buddhism). Both individuals thus benefited spiritually from the post-1965 opening of the United States to immigrants from Asia, just as their parents' and grandparents' religious lives had taken form in the context of earlier phases of immigration and community building. And both individuals had moved toward religious paths outside the ethnic communities of their birth, something increasingly common among all religious communities and racial/ethnic groups.

Meanwhile, Christian interviewees' lives were similarly marked by transformations in their religious and sociopolitical worlds. For example, the life path of Nancy McKay was shaped, for one thing, by the increasing openness of most Christian denominations to women entering the ministry. Thus she became a minister. Yet a second process of opening on the part of some denominations sent her out of the ministry altogether, when her own congregation refused her proposal that it consider an "open and affirming" relationship with persons of all sexualities. Episcopalians Margaret Majors and John Potts and Lutheran Nancy Nielsen all benefited from a different kind of openness that, many have remarked, touched Christianity in the later decades of the twentieth century: an openness to cross-denominational and even interfaith communing, work, and community building. Thus Margaret Majors studied healing by prayer and touch in an interdenominational setting, with a Presbyterian teacher. Fellow Episcopalian John Potts took courses and drew on the teachings of the Diamond Heart Path (a contemporary synthesis of Sufism and psychology) in his work as a trainer in "diversity issues." And Nancy Nielsen, herself Lutheran, offered workshops in building interfaith communities through the organization Catholic Charities of the United States.

The metaphors and names interviewees used for practice varied. *Spirit, spirituality, practice, faith,* and *religion* are terms that appeared frequently in these interviews, and so at times did Allah, Buddha, God,

Goddess, Higher Power, Jesus, Mother; church, congregation, guide, guru, lama, lineage, *sangha*, synagogue, temple, and tradition. Breathing, mantra, meditation, and prayer, "listening to the messages," and "receiving guidance" were key methods named by interviewees. At times the body needed to come into play as a cognitive resource to compensate for the saturation of mind and intellect with preexisting meanings.

Although diverse in terms of path and spiritual identification, these men and women were oftentimes strikingly similar in the kinds of experiences they reported, and the ethical codes in context of which they continued their practice. Spiritual practices of a range of kinds were indeed crucial to the capacity to communicate with divine form or energy. As such there is a delicate play, throughout, between spontaneity of experience and the possibility, perhaps necessity, of corralling such communing into some kind of semantic anchorage, by means of the cultivation of spiritual practices that in turn depend on surrender into spontaneity. This somewhat abstract discussion will become more concrete in the context of engagement with dimensions of interviewees' spiritual journeys.

Given the necessity of moving continually between meaning systems, language will remain a challenge in this discussion. That challenge is itself, perhaps, a constant signal of that which is beyond discursive control. Interviewee Zenkei Blanche Hartman, seventy-one years old, Abbess of the San Francisco Zen Center said during our meeting, "There is a koan that says, 'What is this?' And someone answered, 'Just this is it . . .'" Fortunately or unfortunately, Zenkei Hartman's admonition is crucial to this project, maddening as the impossibility of mastery feels at many moments, whether the mastery one seeks is scholarly or existential.

☙

THIS GROUP WAS DIVERSE in race, national origin, gender, sexuality, and age, as well as in economic history and current situation. With one exception, all of the interviewees lived within a 250-mile radius of the city of San Francisco.[60] However, only seven of the fifty interviewees were born and raised in this region. In addition, one was born in San Francisco but raised in Texas. Another was born in Oakland and raised between that city, San Diego, and Washington state. The rest were born and raised across the length and breadth of the United States and, in the case of immigrants, outside its borders. Most had moved to the San Francisco region as adults in pursuit of work, education, or, in a few cases, to join spiritual communities.

Twenty-six out of fifty interviewees were white. Of these, seven were Jews of European American ancestry. Seven men and women were African Americans and four were Chicana/o or Latina/o. Nine interviewees were of Asian ethnicity, among them East Asians, South Asians, and Southeast Asians. Three were from the Middle East. Only one woman identified herself as being of mixed heritage, Chinese and European American. Others, though, emphasized that their immediate familial heritage, and thus their own senses of self, were biracial—one African American woman described one of her parents as partly Native American; and two Cuban women noted their Afro-Cuban as well as Latina heritage. Thirty-seven men and women were born in the United States; the other thirteen were immigrants to the United States, having spent part of their childhood and/or adult life in Canada, Cuba, Germany, Great Britain, Hong Kong, Iran, India, Peru, Saudi Arabia, South Africa, or Vietnam.

Eighteen interviewees were male and thirty-two were female. Of the fifty, thirty-two described themselves as heterosexual, six as gay, ten as lesbian, and two as bisexual. The group spanned twenty-one to seventy-one years of age, with seven between the ages of twenty-one and thirty, eleven between thirty-one and forty, seventeen between forty-one and fifty, twelve between fifty-one and sixty, and three older than sixty-one.

Questions about race, ethnicity, national origin, age, and even sexuality were for the most part occasions for a simple exchange of information. This was not so for class or economic status, for several reasons. Having no direct access to "objective" economic data on individuals, and given a diversity of generation, geographical points of origin, and the complex sociocultural politics of naming class, I listened closely to individuals' economic self-naming, and sought details of material circumstances to enhance descriptions. On this basis, at least a comparative map could be generated.

Thus I would argue as follows: in childhood, twenty-three out of fifty saw themselves as having been middle or upper middle class. The other twenty-seven were divided equally between people who saw themselves as having grown up poor/working class or lower middle class. The adult picture was different. Here as before there was no access to "hard" data; nonetheless it was possible to comprehend their material situations by "reading" individuals' residences and employment, in addition to their self-descriptions. Generating, again, a comparative and qualitative rather than quantitative map, it was possible to conclude that eighteen out of fifty (fewer than in childhood) were upper middle or middle class. Fifteen interviewees were lower middle and upper working class, and of these several worked in the nonprofit sector. Five interviewees were poor. Of the remaining twelve, two were living on disability income. But a full ten were either living simply by conscious intent (four), or were resident renunciates in spiritual communities where they received little or no pay for the work they undertook (five), or working by *dana*—that is, receiving donations rather than wages in return for work (one). It should be noted that the individuals "living simply by intent" were not people who were once wealthy and could thus, as it were, easily "afford" downward mobility. Rather, these individuals originated from all points on the socioeconomic scale. Furthermore, the choice to "live simply" was not an effect of *white* privilege. Both white people and people of color had made this choice.

The ten individuals living simply by intent were only the tip of the iceberg, for others also commented on the relationship between their spiritual practices and their chosen means of earning a living. Two Buddhists, both white men, spoke in strikingly similar terms about their work. Nick Mueller was working class in childhood and remains so today. Tom Wagoner (Tibetan Buddhist) was raised upper middle class, but now lives more modestly as a middle-class building contractor. Nick Mueller was a car salesman when I interviewed him:

> RF How do you practice this in your workplace?
> NICK Well, it's kind of a fine line, I tell you, because of the trade I'm in, selling a car . . . When I went into this particular field, I thought to myself, if I'm going to sell cars I'm not going to turn into a "car salesman." That's not my function in life to be like that. So, now for better or for worse, and it's actually worse, I sell less cars because I'm not a typical car salesman.
> RF Is that right?
> NICK Because I won't push people into doing something. I don't lie to them. [Customers] ask me a question . . . They're stunned because I've just told the truth. And they're, "Oh, well I'm not going to buy this car." I say, "Well okay. But you asked me a question so I tell you," you know.

Interestingly enough, Tom Wagoner noted that his line of work and Nick Mueller's were often viewed in the same light. Tom said, "Building contractors, lawyers, and used car salesmen are the three apparently sleaziest professions. So I'm in a sleaze profession." To be exact, Nick sold new, not used cars. But Tom, like Nick, emphasized his commitment to revising the protocols of his profession:

> RF  So then how does your [religious] practice shape how you do your work?
>
> TOM  It requires me to be honest with people . . . There has to be kind of a fairness and understanding of karma. They've contracted you to do something, and you need to take as best care of them as you can . . . And sometimes I will do things in excess of what I said I would do because the job needs it. And sometimes often you're having to, you know, eat time or materials or whatever to do it right, whereas you could say, "Oh, I'm not paid for this and I'm not going to do that." Well, my inclination is more to do that, to just go ahead and do it. Does that—are you getting a feel?

For Tom and Nick, then, it was possible, and vitally necessary, to dissolve the separation between "working life" and spiritual practice, even if this brought with it financial losses.

Others also made work choices on ethical grounds. Mercedes Martin (thirty-five, heterosexual, Cuban American, extra-institutional spiritual practice) said, "My full-time work is doing diversity work. I have my own business. And the way that I balance that is, part of the time I'm doing work with non-profit community based organizations and the other half of the time, I work for corporations." Likewise, Birgit Wolz, (forty-three, white, heterosexual German immigrant) a practitioner of the Diamond Heart Path, devoted a considerable part of her working life to providing low- or no-cost grief counseling in addition to her private practice in psychotherapy. In short, interviewees found many means of prioritizing ethics above material gain. The Buddhist concept of "right livelihood" is apposite here, although as should already be clear the commitment to right livelihood was by no means confined to Buddhist interviewees.

🖉

THERE WAS for these men and women no real separation between "spiritual life" and other aspects of daily activity. This did not mean that religious and/or spiritual activity should conform with material life. Rather, when possible the converse was the case. Interviewees sought to bring all other dimensions of life activity into harmony with the ethical and practical codes emergent from the spiritual and/or religious frameworks with which they connected and in the context of which they lived.

Alan Lew, rabbi of a large Conservative synagogue in San Francisco, is heterosexual and fifty-five years old. He was born in Brooklyn, New York, into what he called a "densely, richly Jewish world." He went on, "One grandfather was an Orthodox rabbi . . . And then my other grandfather was certainly not Orthodox, but he led choirs and sang in synagogues—the leading synagogues in Brooklyn."

Although Alan's father and paternal grandfather were estranged, the older man still came to the house and taught Alan the Hebrew alphabet. Alan said he "showed up at the house with a little black satchel which had Hebrew letters in it and taught me to read [them]. I remember that as one of the really intense and magical experiences of my childhood. Those letters were alive. I looked into his bag and those letters were moving and dancing. And the principal meditation practice that I do now is meditating on the Hebrew letters. You know, I just think that that started back there." From the age of seven, Alan's growing-up years were completed in a rural setting "in an experimental community that had been founded by Frank Lloyd Wright." There, there was no religious activity at all, although, as Alan said, "my parents were passionate about being ethnically Jewish." Alan did not lose touch with spirituality—its form just changed. He said, "I have very early memories of doing strange things, like going out in the woods and making a circle of stones and sitting in the middle of the circle and feeling these really intense feelings. And so I had these very strong spiritual feelings, which only intensified [through college and graduate school]. And I came out to California in 1969 in part to seek a path."

Alan became a Zen Buddhist. He is clear that it was in part his many years of estrangement from Judaism that led him, at first, elsewhere than to Judaism itself. Yet, he said, it was his Jewishness that sent him to Buddhism rather than to any other non-Jewish religion. "Being alienated from the flow of Jewish spirituality for so long caused me to have a hunger for spirituality which I sought to satisfy in Buddhism and other paths." To become Christian would have been tantamount to treason against his religio-ethnic community, he said. It was thus, he noted, that he and many other Jews of his generation became Buddhists, or joined Hindu ashrams.[61]

In Alan's case, the period of intense Buddhist practice lasted about ten years. But that work, it turned out, led him directly back to Judaism. He said:

When I was a Buddhist, I practiced Soto Zen, the branch of Zen that stresses *shikantaza,* just sitting. You just sit with an awareness of your breath, an awareness of your body, an awareness of your consciousness . . . Focusing on my breath for ten years, I got a pretty good idea of what was carrying my consciousness away from my breath. And an astounding amount of what would carry my consciousness away from my breath was Jewish. It was Jewish material, Jewish unconscious material. I'm walking into a room, "Well, I'm Jewish. Is this guy Jewish? Does he know I'm Jewish? What does he think about this?" On a deeper level, I was also aware, ten years into this practice and being carried deeper and deeper into my own spirituality, that there was something intrinsically Jewish about that spirituality. So little by little I became very interested in this business of what Jewish spirituality was. I'm giving you a very short version. [Still] that's how I come to Judaism primarily as a spiritual practice and how Buddhism was the immediate preceding step in my life.

Here one sees not only Alan's life story, recounted step by step, but also his own analysis of it. As Alan names the mode of sitting meditation that was for him central to Soto Zen, he also tells his listener exactly what he learned both from succeeding at the practice, and, as it turned out, from failing at it. Alan found that when he could not sit in deep awareness of the breath as he "should" be able to within Soto Zen, he was shown why this was not happening and where he might need to go instead. This was how Alan moved from Soto Zen Buddhism back to his birth religion. To cut a long story even shorter, Alan explained that after several years "winding down," as he put it, his Buddhist practice, and several more entering into the study of Judaism, he entered rabbinical school. By the time I interviewed him Alan had been rabbi of a San Francisco synagogue for more than half a decade.

Alan's story brings forth several key themes, including the inseparability of religious practice from the rest of individuals' lives. Alan is clear that the familial and social contexts in which he grew up were critical to his journeys within, away from, and finally back to Judaism. He also comments that the sociogenerational context in which he grew up was significant to his path: he was not, after all, alone in leaving Judaism, not for Christianity, and not for no religion at all, but rather for one of two religious forms that seemed more acceptable as alternatives. As he added, in the late 1960s and early 1970s, he knew exactly where in the United States he might travel in furtherance of that quest. As he put it, "California was full of paths at that time. You could walk down the street in Berkeley—one house was a leading exponent of Zen

Buddhism, the next house was the exponent of some kind of Hindu meditation, the next house was the leading exponent of Tibetan Buddhism. Don't ask me why that was so, but it was so then." One sees here the interplay of context and agency in the crafting of Alan Lew's spiritual journey. He did not merely dabble in any and every practice. Rather, he investigated, chose, and then focused for a full decade on the path that seemed most apposite at the time.

Another aspect of Alan's story that must be noted is the crucial role of what Sadiqa called the "uncomprehendable." In this instance one may note the "inexplicable," the dancing Hebrew letters in Alan's grandfather's satchel; the unusual (to Alan) experience of sitting in a stone circle, feeling what Alan could only explain, tautologically, as "very strong spiritual feelings." Alan, even when fully anchored in Jewish life and theology, continued to benefit from his decade of immersion in Soto Zen meditation and philosophy. He said, "Engaging in meditation together with Jewish practice every day as I do—certainly the meditation has changed the nature of the experience of prayer, but prayer has also changed the experience of meditation. You begin to think of the various mind states that you experience in meditation in terms of the categories of prayer. And I'm just beginning—this is a very subtle process." He continued:

> Very often in awareness meditation, your awareness will reach a heightened state, a state where you begin to experience the world differently, where you begin to experience the world as an interconnected flow of energy. I'm not talking about hallucinating—I think you just really come to see that's what the world is. If you . . . spend one hour every morning meditating and then you spend the next hour addressing God, well then you come to think of that experience in terms of God. You apply the God language of the prayer service to this experience of this interconnected, energetic flow. You just spontaneously come to think of that as God. If you were simply a Buddhist and you were only meditating and not engaging in prayer, you might not have that feeling about it, or you might not give it that name. You might not understand that experience in quite the same way.

Alan's words signal something frequently encountered in this study: individuals' awareness of their subordinate location in an epistemic hierarchy. It is in this context that there is a striving for language adequate to one's experience. Alan's insistence that he is describing the *real*, not something he has imagined, invented, hallucinated, speaks to a presumed gallery of naysayers. At a certain point, Alan himself even adopts the stance of a skeptic, in recalling "early memories of doing strange things." Moments of this kind of self-questioning occurred frequently in the interviews. It is unclear whether Alan really believed his childhood experiences to be "strange," or simply thought that his listener might find them so. The experience of sitting in a circle of stones may also have been less easily reconciled with his current spiritual path—fitting into neither Judaic nor Soto Zen practice—and therefore more easily deemed "strange." The interview with Alan Lew illustrates a central argument of this book: that spiritual practice is structured by a dialectical relationship between spontaneity and cultivation. Spiritual experiences are neither naturally occurring phenomena nor the effect of conscious cultivation alone. Thus, as Alan practiced "just sitting," that which he named "Jewish material" took him on a path back toward his Judaic roots. Likewise, "just sitting" gave rise to spontaneous experiences of feeling the world as interconnected energy. In each case, the former was the sine qua non of the latter, even as the latter transformed the meaning and experience of the former. The interplay of spontaneity and cultivation has implications for the analysis of the agency and consciousness of the spiritual practitioner.

## TALKING TO GOD—AND GOD TALKING BACK

Historian Leigh Eric Schmidt, in beginning his masterful *Hearing Things: Religion, Illusion and the American Enlightenment,* remarks on a friend who "half in jest, described this project back to me as 'a book about religious wackos.' That mirrored reflection was troubling because it seemed to reverse so much of what I was trying to say. What I really wanted to offer was an excavation of my friend's assumption— the ready equation of 'hearing things' with deviance, illusion and insanity."[1] In like terms, philosopher of theology Nicholas Wolterstorff begins his book, *Divine Discourse: Philosophical Reflections on the Claim that God Speaks,* with the remark that he is fully aware that "most of my philosophical colleagues would regard the topic as 'off the wall' for a philosopher—or something that one would have to be slightly mad to take seriously." Both of these authors see the remarks just quoted as so important that they must be placed, prolegomena style, at the very beginning of their books.

These quotes, and the placement of them, make clear the difficulty faced by those who attempt to articulate what one might call "divine rationality"—the logic, the coherence, and the precision of a diverse yet comparable range of experiences of what one might for convenience's sake name extra-material communing, communication, and comprehension. The Christian and Hindu men and women discussed in this chapter were all involved in spiritual practices of communing or communication. These can be located in time, space, and spiritual/religious context and tradition. But my effort to situate their practices does not explain away such communing. Quite the opposite is the case.

I seek to make manifest the rationality and logic of practices often deemed extra-rational or illogical.

In his book, Schmidt traverses and analyzes the period in U.S. history wherein, as elsewhere in the Western world, vision supplanted audition as the mode of witnessing and encountering the world deemed most trustworthy. With this process, Schmidt argues, came "the dwindling of hearing as spiritual sense and the lost presence of divine speech."[2] More, this "dwindling" traveled alongside an othering of divine audition. As he puts it:

> [With] such a grand story of modern ocularcentrism, a history of modern aurality is hardly possible, especially a history of religious modes of hearing, since in this myth the very origin of modern culture is grounded on the exclusion of the "primitive" or "ancient" ecstasies of listening . . .
>
> Two of the larger twentieth century motifs around which the story of modern vision and hearing have been plotted [are]: (1) a hierarchy of the senses with sight vastly ennobled; and (2) a marked dichotomy between eye and ear cultures that has commonly drawn on racialized constructions of Western rationality and ecstatic primitivism.[3]

As a result, Schmidt adds, "The story of modern hearing loss . . . is always, finally a story of religious absence."[4] However, loss is not total; "dwindling" does not mean, here, an entire obliteration. For as Schmidt reminds his reader, "the religious complexity of modernity itself" means that "various communities—evangelicals and Pentecostals not least among them—have played by different rules . . . Within a broadened perspective, [John] Lockean ways of assessing divine speech look far more local and contingent than their pretense to universality suggests."[5]

Reminding his readership that for Locke, "reason is the ever vigilant judge over religious experiences of immediate inspiration," Schmidt argues with good reason that Locke provided philosophical means by which God's silence might be made normal and even, given other aspects of social context, desirable. Schmidt's purpose in the text under consideration is to name the localism and contingency of what one may describe as a Lockean hegemony. Schmidt analyzes its emergence in the American colonial context, and further into U.S. history. Here, then the normalcy, normativity, and universalism of refusals to hear or even listen for divine language is called into question.

Nicholas Wolterstorff challenges that same set of refusals precisely on Locke's own terms, terms critically important since, in Wolterstorff's view, "the general epistemology which Locke developed . . . has been profoundly influential in the modern West . . . [in particular its application to] the epistemology of religious belief." Wolterstorff reminds his audience that despite or indeed in context of Locke's framework, he both believed solidly in the divine and proffered methodology for discerning, by means inward and outward, the veracity or falsity of particular Godly utterances. One should in all honesty, Wolterstorff claims, bring "to the level of conscious self-awareness this part of our cultural inheritance."[6] Wolterstorff demonstrates at the end of his discussion that one can indeed, via the work of John Locke, but by means of emphasizing that his is a framework for situated knowledge-generation, determine which instances of "God speaking" are more believable than others.[7]

Like Schmidt, Wolterstorff reminds his audience that, for one thing, "countless human beings down through the ages, and on into our own time and place, have in fact believed that God speaks." He continues, "Let us, then, pose our question in full recognition of that fact; let us ask how such beliefs are to be appraised."[8] Wolterstorff and Schmidt, then, both strive to engage the idea of God speaking, utilizing the very means by which the possibility of God speaking has been, in recent centuries, made marginal or, in the language of these scholars' critics, "wacko" or "off-the-wall." Both authors, too, remind their readers that the "erasure of God" was not fully successful, philosophically, or socioculturally. Finally, both emphasize that modes of thought usually deemed outmoded or archaic (here in particular that of John Locke, for Schmidt also deeply connected with the rise of colonial thinking) are indeed still alive and well even in postmodern times. I too strive to challenge on their own terms modes of rationality at once old yet firmly present at the turn of the twenty-first century.

IN THIS CHAPTER, the term *Godtalk* acts as place-marker for a broad range of modes of communion with the divine in various forms. Talking to God—and God talking back—entails a discussion of three things. First, there is the contemplation of *who* or *what* one is talking with (or talking about). Second, we must ask *when* and *where* that *who* talks back. And third, we must examine the intermediary term, *how*, inquiring into the means by which communication takes place and/or is perceived. One must ask *how the cultivation of particular practices makes the space available for a spontaneously arising encounter with the divine.*

More broadly, the emplacement of an individual in a particular religious and spiritual frame *provides* language and/or *constrains* the language that that individual might use in experiencing, naming, valuing, or discounting a given set of events. (I use the word *given* advisedly here in both senses of that term.)

For almost all of the men and women I interviewed, three terms—*name* or *form*, *practice*, and *surrender*—organized the experience of communing with spirit. The three are, as will be shown, interwoven. For some there is a fourth term—*guru* or *lama*.[9] *Name* or *form* indicates, rather obviously, that word used to refer to a being or, for some, simply an energy. *Name* entails also inscription into a set of knowledges, formal and informal, written and oral, *about* that named entity. *Practice* refers here to the processes in which each individual is involved, making possible the cultivation of communing with spirit, however conceived. *Practice* is inevitably organized in part around *name* (that is to say, placed in time and space). Lastly, the goals and/or the outcomes of practice fundamentally entail *surrender*. More specifically, the cultivation of practice is connected with surrender to the name or named practice (zazen, for example), and surrender to an ethical frame.

For some interviewees, name, spiritual practice, and thence the process of communing with the divine were placed clearly within a single religious form. Surrender thus took place within that context, generating an ethical frame particular to it. Homer Teng was one such individual. Homer was twenty-eight years old. He had grown up in Hong Kong, and moved to the United States at seventeen. He is heterosexual, married, and the father of a son who was fourteen months old at the time of the interview. Homer was born into a Roman Catholic family that was, in the terms of Hong Kong Chinese experience, upper middle class. (Homer named himself upper middle class on the grounds that his family had a large apartment and his father worked for a U.S. multinational corporation—different and more modest criteria than one might demand in order to name a U.S. family upper middle class.) Homer remains a member of the Catholic Church. From childhood on, faith (his term of choice) and religious practice were far more important to him than to others in his family. He explained, for example, that only he had gone to weekly mass in his childhood years. His parents, while applauding his choice, had been happy to stay home and let Homer walk the several mile round-trip to church. Today, Homer says,

Faith . . . [enables] me to make sense of why I'm doing certain things. I believe everything that I do is a reflection of who I am as a person of faith. I don't see faith as simply something you do on a particular day of the week or a particular day of the year. I see faith as very much linked with everyday life . . . Like changing [my baby's] diaper. I know it is a duty of mine to do this because it's my child. But then I see him as a gift from God that I need to take care of. This is an individual created by God. I am his parent, but yet he's got a more powerful parent than I. That makes me think of this person, my child, in a different way, so I would never want to control him the way that some people tend to control others. Because I see [him] as a unique individual that is created not by me but by God. I obviously have a lot to do with it, but I mean, everything doesn't come without God having some kind of influence, either directly or indirectly. So everything I do, everything I think about, I try to think about in terms of, you know, what it means to me as a person of faith.

Here Homer speaks about his relationship with God as he conceives it. The relationship is comprehensible in terms of received teaching. But it is perhaps even more forcefully understandable as Homer Teng's own appropriation and application of that received teaching. For example, Homer's certainty that his child is not only his but also that of God might be shared by all Christians. Yet his corollary to that conviction, that therefore he should not control his son, diverges from much mainstream Christian thought, Catholic or otherwise. One sees therefore the importance of Homer's own work in the crafting and application of a spiritual practice or, as he would name it, a faith-based life. Practice can be identified as both philosophical orientation *and* physical application. One can connect practice here with name and form, and with application and rearticulation of received teaching about both of these. And Homer's surrender to an ethical frame, a way of being, is anchored in his relationship with the divine.

Ostensibly, names and forms of divine beings are received, rather than created by their users. After all, what is more widely known in the contemporary world than the name and form of the Christian God? But shifts in Homer's conception of the divine through his life demonstrate that both are in fact fluid and transformable. Homer explained that as a child, he had seen God very much as a disciplinarian. This was largely, he felt, because of the strictness and rigidity of the Catholic schools that he had attended. Later, around his time in college, he had come to "see God more as a compassionate figure in the person of

Jesus." Here, the name and form of God are in fact altered, as Homer turns toward recognition of Jesus *as* God. (Note that Homer turns to Jesus, not *alongside* God or as the son of God, but *as* God. As such he again diverges from the religious institution of his childhood.) We learn too of the institutions and teachings that make both name and form available—Homer names school, church, and college as key sites.

In the same way that Homer's sense of God had changed over time, so had his interpretation of the ritual of confession. For Homer, that which had once been a routine childhood monthly activity changed to a practice undertaken less often but with more forethought. Homer now thought long and hard before going to confession, asking himself "why I'm saying this, why I'm doing this. Am I really contrite, am I really feeling that what I did was wrong? . . . If I knew that something was kind of wrong but I wasn't exactly sure it was wrong, then I would wait, before I go in and confess that I did something wrong." Confession is, arguably, one form of speaking with God. Yet for Homer, at least in this point in the interview, confession seemed to be more about speaking *to* God than about God speaking back. It seemed, too, that Homer undertook the task of deciding whether he had sinned, rather than allowing God or another intermediary to do so. Surrender is, we can note here, a conscious and intentional process in which Homer contemplates and responds to his unfolding comprehension of religious institutions' authority.

Thus far, God, one might argue, is the absent presence in Homer's discussion. God's name, history, and sites of institutional location are known. Homer, as I have suggested, is well able to maneuver and work with all three of these. Yet, his dialogue with God seems one-sided. Homer asks the questions and provides the answers based not only on his faith in God but also on his "faith in his faith" and his faith, too, in his capacity to interpret God in the context in which Homer knows Him. This pattern subtly changed, though, when I asked Homer how he applied his relationship with God to the process of making difficult decisions (whether to leave a secure, career job and enter graduate school in theology, for example). Here, a back-and-forth communication was much more evident. He explained that at such times, he both prays to God and asks friends whom he trusts—sometimes Catholic and sometimes not—for support in decision-making processes. He added, "I think God will listen to me when I pray to Him. So that's how I seek for help." Pushing the question further, I asked, "Okay, so God will listen, but will God give you the answer?" In response, Homer explained that he did not feel the need to talk directly with God in a literal sense, in order to know that he *was* in fact communicating with Him:

> I believe God will give me the answer that He sees that's fit for me. And I see that answer coming in many different ways, perhaps through a person who happens to talk to me about certain things. I think that the so-called epiphany comes in the most undramatic moment. Maybe gradually it becomes, "Oh, that's really the right decision for me." As I said a while before, I didn't have a dramatic moment of religious conversion. Likewise I don't believe in some kind of dramatic vision, a dream or something like that. I mean, I'm not saying that that doesn't happen to people. But from my own experience, I come to my decision-making through just gradual talking to people and feeling what's right and constantly praying. And I believe God will provide the answer. It might not be the answer that I thought was right for me. But nevertheless, I have to trust in God because that's who I am, and I cannot imagine life without trusting in a higher power.

The cynic might argue that Homer Teng might just as easily invent "God's answers" as receive them directly and indirectly. Yet, in challenging the skeptic one must note that for Homer, God does not always offer "the answer that I thought was right for me." We can add, too, that whether cynical or not, the observer witnesses the precision with which Homer Teng proceeds towards his conclusions.

In this discussion Homer was clear about the form or forms of God to which or whom he felt connected. He was also clear about the ways in which his comprehension of a divine force or being had shifted over time. We learn too about the processes through which Homer's spiritual practice is cultivated. We see also Homer's knowledge about an array of practices—technologies of communication with God including prayer, conversations with peers, and visionary dreams. There was neither ranking nor differentiation among these. As he put it, while others might experience dramatic teaching and dramatic conversion experiences, for him there was an acceptable gradualism in the process of receiving guidance from God. And lastly, we see exactly how and to what effect Homer surrenders to name, form, and practice, in honor of the living of a faith-based life.[10]

HOMER TENG was confident that at times God might speak to him through the voices or actions of others—not unusual others at that, but rather ordinary peers. Derek Jones's spiritual journey was one in which the same kind of displaced presence was also in play, but placed alongside other experiences of "God talking" that are more explicit although still not literal. And both Derek Jones and Homer Teng have cultivated their own, faith-based philosophical thinking in order to interpret communication with the divine. Derek Jones was born into the Anglican Church (close kin to the Episcopal Church in the United States). By the time I interviewed Derek, he was a deacon of the Episcopal Church, and an active member of a church in an upper-middle-class, mainly white town in the San Francisco Bay Area. Yet what might be mistaken on the surface of things for a direct road from childhood faith to adult faith, from a youthful involvement in the church to an adult one that was almost identical, was in fact by no means a straightforward journey. In a sense, Derek Jones has traveled through all three of the stages Robert Wuthnow identifies on the spiritual path. These are "dwelling" (in a secure, geographically stable religious community); "seeking" (once the first is no longer available or now unsatisfying); and "practice" (meaning the more mature establishment of a restored, or new, mode of religious or spiritual belonging).[11] But a close reading of Derek Jones's journey complicates all three of these stages. It also makes possible exploration of the subtle and not-so-subtle means by which communication with the divine may take place.

Like Homer Teng, Derek Jones is an immigrant to the United States. Born into a white, working-class family in London in 1939, Derek moved to Canada and then to the United States as a young adult. Derek is now well established in the upper middle class (a degree of class mobility that he strongly feels would have been impossible had he remained in Britain). His own business enterprises are successful enough for him to live very comfortably on them while no longer himself working in them. He is the unpaid, full-time director of a meals service program for homeless and impoverished persons in a large Bay Area county. ("We have three dining rooms; we do about 140,000 meals a year out of those three dining rooms.") Derek is married and has five children of whom one, born in Korea, is adopted. Like Homer Teng's family, Derek's was not much involved in the church during his childhood years. Derek said that the primary reason that he remained in the church up into his teens was that he was a member of the choir: "I enjoyed that—I got paid for it, which was also nice. But it obviously steeped me in a lot of church traditions and history, even though I may not have recognized it at the time." (Derek explained that although a fortune to him at the time, payment for choir participation was modest—ten shillings for every three months of service, with an extra half crown for weddings. In U.S. currency this translates to approximately $1 per three months and a quarter for each wedding.) As a teenager Derek left the church entirely, not for any dramatic reason but rather in context of what he called commonplace teenage rebellion.

In the years leading up to and after his marriage, Derek joined his wife's family denomination, the Anglican Church of Canada. On the couple's migration to the United States from Canada, both became Episcopalians. But Derek told me that up to his late thirties he was a churchgoer in name only. At that time, Derek was in the midst of a crisis. Asking himself questions about the meaning of life, he began to experiment with what he named "black magic" (something that, in speaking to me, he very consciously distinguished from Wicca). At that point (although not because anyone at church knew about his explorations with witchcraft) he was invited to a *cursillo* or spiritual retreat at his church.

The cursillo experience radically transformed Derek's sense of God, and of himself. As Derek said, it "put me in touch with God, convinced me that there was God, and that God was manifested in the world through love. It obviously killed any desire I had of being involved in witchcraft of the type I was looking at, and just became a starting point of a new journey." Derek told me that the cursillo had a major impact on his marriage. While his wife had always been more connected than he with the church, and with her faith, "I came back so changed that I think for her I was a different person."

Among the changes emergent from the weekend retreat was a period in which Derek found himself drawn to "what I would call more fundamental religion." If this sounds like a gentle way of naming "fundamentalist Christianity," it was in fact just that. As Derek explained, the newness of his faith led him to wish for a very firmly bounded version of that faith:

DEREK  I couldn't easily accept any challenges to my faith at that time, which was very, very new and very tentative. I think that [at such times] one puts barriers up to protect oneself. Some of those barriers for me at that time were the fundamental belief in the Bible, that it was entirely written by God and that nothing could be altered. It provided everything that one needed—that type of approach to things. My wife and I went through some of that together.

RF  That's different from the Episcopalian interpretation of the Bible, isn't it?

DEREK  That's right. That's right. I was going to an Episcopal Church [then, but] I don't know if I could honestly call myself an Episcopalian at that time.

One witnesses here the degree to which an individual's relationship to a form of faith can alter. Derek was, in name, an Anglican or Episcopalian from birth up until the present. But this meant several different things at different moments. As a child and young adult, Derek's connection to the church was literally a matter of form—at most a context for singing and for building family and community. If this was the period that Wuthnow would refer to as "dwelling," the shelter provided was minimal. Later, in the period of crisis that began in his thirties, while experimenting with "black magic," Derek was still in name an Episcopalian. Again, when after the cursillo, Derek took refuge in literalist or fundamentalist interpretations of the Bible, he was, again, still in name and membership an Episcopalian. Yet later Derek became an Episcopalian in a fuller sense of the word, as an educator within the church and as an activist in its name. Regarding Wuthnow, we may notice that "seeking" did not entail a complete departure from the "dwelling place." And "practice" did not in any sense lead either to a new place of dwelling or to a "return" to the original one in an unchanged form.

It is interesting that while the cursillo was presumably intended to invite participants into a broadly (though not coercively) Episcopalian form of connection with the Christian God, it actually, at least for a while, had the effect of sending Derek Jones to a different way of seeing God. The individual's journey of contemplation of the divine is inevitably uncontainable by institutional forms. Thus Derek, for reasons almost beyond his control, found himself moved to subvert and revise the goals of the cursillo, traveling toward a fundamentalist reading of the Bible well beyond the parameters of Episcopalianism.

As with Homer Teng's journey, Derek Jones knew himself to be moving within and among a range of discourses on religion, spirituality, and spiritual practice. Thus Derek knew clearly that Episcopalianism is not fundamentalist or literalist in its reading of the Bible. He also knew that so-called black magic is even further away from either Episcopalian or fundamentalist Christianity. Yet Derek was equally clear that Episcopalian and fundamentalist Christianity have some things in common: both are frames from within which one can connect with a Christian God. Here, at least at that point in Derek's explorations, that loving God was almost by definition a Christian one, rather than any other kind. And the inevitability of this was under-scored by Derek's temporary turn to a literalist reading of the Bible.

It is crucial at this point to return to the structure of feeling evoked in Derek's description of his experience at the retreat: It "put me in touch with God, convinced me that there was God, and that God was manifested in the world through love." Here one moves past that which is explicable by reference to form alone. Indeed, it is striking that having been convinced that "there was a God," Derek felt the need to turn toward a more forceful form than that offered by the cursillo. One might argue that for Derek the cursillo is a form of Godtalk. In it, God speaks through one particular structure, and Derek, apprehending that structure, needs to go to another place in which, perhaps, God talks in a louder or more firmly containing voice. As Derek said, "my faith at that time . . . was very, very new and very tentative. I think that [at such times] one puts barriers up to protect oneself." Derek, in sum, encoun-ters God in a form familiar to him—the Christian form with which he grew up, and the institutional form with which he remains socially if only minimally connected. This form is able to speak to him ("con-vinced me that there was God"). Yet Derek needs to order up a change in the form in which God speaks—still Christian but now literalist, now fundamentalist.

This story is not yet over. Time passed, and Derek reconnected more firmly with the Episcopal Church. He began assisting at cursillos, facili-tating discussions, giving talks, helping in the kitchen, and, as he put it, doing whatever was needed. Later, he said, "I eventually ended up being what they called the rector of a weekend, leading a whole team for a weekend, which was a great experience." At the training period for one such event, Derek met a deacon of the church, although as he said, "I had never come across a deacon; I couldn't have told you what a deacon was [or even] . . . how to spell it." But at the end of the training period, the priest invited those ordained and "anyone so moved to do so" to come up to the front of the room and help him as he offered the final blessing. Derek said, "I didn't join in, *but* my heart started beating at a high rate. I almost started hyperventilating. I couldn't understand what was happening. It was just a very strange experience."

As Derek told this story, its structure *as* a meaningful story became more forceful. The narrative begins with the ordinary, an event—the training period for cursillo staff—whose like Derek had experienced before. Within it, an encounter soon to become meaningful brings into the foreground a person and a word never before paid attention to. Derek dramatized the unfamiliarity by saying "I couldn't have told you who a deacon was [or even] how to spell it." Next, and again as the priest does something that is ostensibly ordinary, inviting others to offer the blessing, a visceral reaction, a physiological event, demands that the ordinary be rearranged: "I couldn't understand what was happening. It was just a very strange experience. But—" As Derek said, he did not go forward and help lead the blessing. Nonetheless, signaled by the bodily trauma of a high heart rate and difficulty breathing, chaos was made out of order.

After Derek went home that evening, a new order began to be made. Again, his mode of telling the story reminds the listener that the events being represented are dramatic, significant. The word *but* with which the story continues lets the listener know that clarification is at hand: "But what happened was that when I got home that same night, the rector of my church phoned me and said, 'You are one of the people that I would like to consider becoming a deacon.' And of course that shook me up completely. I said, 'Okay, I need to think about that . . . I'll let you know.' *Synchronicity:* the ordering, sequencing, and simultaneity of events make meanings where there were none before. In this instance, Derek hears and pays attention to the word *deacon,* is invited to go up and help lead the blessing, experiences strong physical reactions to the invitation, and then goes home to an invitation to be that entity whose name he has never thought about before. For Derek, something that I will name divine cause and effect is seen to be in play. Certainly one might argue that it is Derek who tells the story, and therefore Derek himself who has made meaning of this sequence of events, as indeed we all do, about our lives as we live them. Nonetheless, these events *did* happen. Derek did have difficulty breathing, and the rector *did* telephone him that very same evening. It is in part the density of meanings emergent here that lends force to Derek's account. As Derek finished telling me this story, he described yet one more synchronous event, saying:

> I got back Sunday night and, what I was doing at that time was reading a Daily Bible Study series by Berkeley. He's an English theologian and priest. I picked up the Bible Study that I was using. I had put [it] down for about a week because of being involved with the cursillo. [I] turned to the very next one that I was going to read. [It] happened to be in First Peter, and it started talking about "you are a royal priesthood." [It] goes through a number of different things, but basically it ends up stating that "Once you were nothing, now you are everything," and that "You are called into relationship with God," and

so on. And I realized that my answer had to be yes. So then I started on the journey of studying to be a deacon, which was about three and a half years. I was ordained in 1978.

Here Derek himself emphasizes synchronicity as signaling significance: the text had been set aside for a week and was now picked up; the section on the call to the priesthood appeared in the very immediate text, not the one for the next day nor the day after. For Derek, as for Homer, the message is clear. As he said, "My answer *had to be* yes" (emphasis added). Here as for Homer, we witness Derek's surrender to Divine instruction as seen by him.

In fact, the story Derek tells here is a classic tale of divine intervention, one whose like I encountered in interviews with Christians, Hindus, Wiccans, Sufis, Tibetan Buddhists, and non-institutionally situated interviewees. While the divine did not arrive and speak in Derek's description of events, for Derek the unfolding of events, their synchronicity, and their temporal density made clear their status as an instance of Godtalk. As with others, name, form, practice, and surrender may be mapped out easily here. The institutional structure (form) in which events take place is clear, from the deacon, the rector, and the priest, to theologian Berkeley, and his citation from the first letter of Peter in the New Testament. Derek Jones's capacity to make institutional and cognitive sense of all these is a part of the salience of form. It was also an aspect of his practice. Both form and practice meant that he went to the cursillo as a staff member in the first place, and meant that he opened Berkeley's book in order to "catch up" in his studies, on his return from a weekend workshop. Surrender here meant that his answer "had to be yes"—Derek had in other words to take seriously and act on the sequence of events just named.

It might be noted that in Derek's telling of his invitation into the role of deacon, the literal presence of God was not named nor commented upon. Given this, once Derek seemed to have finished the story I asked:

> RF How you just told the story—you meet someone who's a deacon and you don't know what that is. Then a day later you have a very strong physical response to being invited among others to join in leading the blessing. Then you go home and you turn the page and you read a passage from the Bible—or rather, then you go home and someone asks you to become a deacon and you read the passage. How do you interpret that? Many of the women and men I've interviewed would very clearly interpret that as divine guidance, very explicitly. They would say, "My guru made this happen like this to tell me this in

that moment" . . . But would you interpret that as divine guidance, as explicit direction?

DEREK  Oh, I think so, yeah. That's very explicit for me. It was little prods, and then a couple of two-by-fours. But yeah, very definitely, very definitely. It's not something I've experienced to any degree like that since, but I was *very* aware of it at the time.

In the experience just described, Godtalk is made possible—one might say, made recognizable—by the existence of a particular set of formal and contextual arrangements. In the events unfolding in that context, divine guidance is recognized as such—as Derek said, "That's very explicit for me . . . Very definitely"—despite the absence of any literal data-derived presence of a being that one might name God or divine.

Here one begins to see what I would call "sacred reason" or "divine rationality," for this is one instance in which Godtalk is made sensible, is made rational. The protocols of divine rationality are very clearly marked out in Derek's telling of events and his interpretation of them. First, there is the capacity or willingness to note synchronicities of events. Second, there is an acceptance (again part of a recognition of synchronicity) that events emerging via mixed media may be connected with one another. Thus for Derek a social encounter at the cursillo training can be seen as related to a forcefully physical response to an invitation to lead prayers. And again an invitation from a living human to become a deacon can be seen as related to the encounter with a text written by someone long dead.

Third, there is the sense of familiarity with the protocol itself, for when Derek said, "It was little prods, and then a couple of two-by-fours," I had the sense that he was describing something conceptually familiar to him although not personally so, either before or after. Thus, just as Homer Teng had said of forceful divine interventions, "I'm not saying that that doesn't happen to people," Derek Jones's interpretation of his invitation to become a deacon was patterned in part by his familiarity with similar events happening to others. It did not, then, matter nor invalidate his interpretation that, as he said in finishing up his story, "It's not something I've experienced to any degree like that since."

The fourth and critical aspect of divine rationality is that it can only be made sense of in connection with divine will. Divine will was, after all, the punch line here—the range of events deemed synchronous meant that Derek "had to say yes" to the invitation to become a deacon. And in fact it is only given a force namable as divine will that a set of events may be sorted and linked together as, in Derek's phrasing, "prods and two-by-fours," so as to be deemed the manifestation of divine will. Again just as Homer was able to trust and make sense of human speech and intuitive thought in relation to his own decision-making processes, Derek's decision about taking on the deacon's training was made logical on grounds of faith in a divine form deemed ever-present and omnipotent.

⌇

> The very first night after the diagnosis—I didn't think I was ever going to go to sleep again. I was going to die and perhaps by Christmas. I lay down and I heard a voice. "Come unto me all ye who are heavy laden and I will give you rest." Straight out of scripture, Jesus says this . . . And I began to relax a little bit. But a day or two later . . . I thought, "Rest? What kind of rest? Eternal rest? I don't want that. No, thank you. I want to live."—NANCY MCKAY

NANCY MCKAY is a European American, has been married for thirty-seven years, and has two adult daughters. She is fifty-nine years old, was born in suburban southern California and currently resides in a mixed-class, mainly African American and white, Berkeley neighborhood. Her husband is a now-retired high school teacher. She described herself as currently lower middle class.

Ordained as a Protestant minister, Nancy is now employed as a teacher at the San Francisco Theological Seminary, and is a spiritual director. She is also a health counselor. (Previously, Nancy ministered for over a decade at a United Church of Christ congregation in the San Francisco Bay Area.) Listening to Nancy, one notes very clearly her familiarity with the New Testament of the Bible, her love of Jesus as guide and teacher, and her awareness of herself as a member of the Christian world, albeit one committed to creatively challenging that world. In contrast with Derek, for whom explicit divine guidance was a one-off event that happened in a moment of transformation, Nancy's self-description brings forth an individual for whom conscious and literal communication with the divine in a range of forms is a central aspect of spiritual life.

If any single life literally entails "talking to God, and God talking back," it is Nancy McKay's very detailed interaction with Jesus. As is discussed elsewhere, Nancy's work with the female aspect of God and with a Reiki master, as well as her work as a poet and health counselor, are crucial examples of Godtalk.[12] The professed familiarity of Homer Teng and Derek Jones with the possibility of direct communication with God, Jesus, or the divine suggests some acceptance of that communication in the Christian world. But Nancy interrupted my use of the terms *vision* and *visionary* in relation to her, because she perceives her own part of the Protestant community as uncomfortable with those words. For while some students at the seminary were excited by her experience of, as she and they put it "getting images," Nancy emphasized, "I tend to not use [the word] 'vision' because . . . my tradition [has been] very afraid of visions and discounted them."

Nancy was very conscious of where she fit, and where she fitted less well, within Christianity. Nancy has been challenged by some Christians in response to her efforts to bring the divine feminine into the weekly liturgy. She was indeed forced to resign from her congregation when she sought to create loving spaces in it for people of all sexual orientations. Regarding direct communication with divine beings, Nancy was clear that her experience of receiving "images," while unusual, was not unique. She cited in this regard the Abbess Hildegard of Bingen, and the ecstatic, visionary Desert Fathers, as well as their now recognized female counterparts. It is her knowledge of these antecedents that made her experiences of hearing from Jesus normal and believable rather than questionable or marks of insanity.

In reading the narratives of Homer Teng and Derek Jones, I demonstrated how an intimate knowledge of the form of Christianity, of Jesus, and of scripture made relevant or "believable" each individual's experience of Godtalk. I suggested that form or name and practice came together, providing the context in which "divine rationality" or "sacred reason," made sense. This is equally true for Nancy McKay. Yet for her, a decision to thoroughly cultivate particular practices made conceivable a far richer and more ongoing set of processes.

Nancy's capacity to participate in Godtalk was founded in practices that began with Christianity yet extended more widely than it. Nancy described to me the centrality in her daily spiritual life of "focusing" techniques. Nancy drew in particular on BioSpirituality, a method developed in the early 1970s by Father Peter Campbell and Father Edwin McMahon, both priests and psychologists of religion, who were in turn drawing on the work begun in the 1960s by University of Chicago psychologist Eugene Gendlin. "Body learning," Campbell and McMahon proposed, "comes as a spontaneous gift or surprise. It is not a byproduct of logic and reason. It cannot be predicted or controlled. There was a transcendent or 'graced' quality to meaning in the body."[13]

Describing the effects of BioSpirituality in brief, Nancy said, "the spirit and the body really work together. It's . . . going inside, paying attention to whatever is present. Not a denial of it, not trying to change it or fix it, but a trust that if you really pay attention in a nonjudgmental way to whatever you're experiencing, and if you really are in the truth of the moment, then the spirit comes in and works and you get a felt shift. You can feel something change within." She also said, "I think my basic spiritual practice is in listening and is in awareness, and in that sense I tend toward the Buddhist practice of mindfulness. I find Thich Nhat Hahn very, very helpful. I also find [very useful] the work of psychosynthesis and [its] guided visualizations, in the trusting what comes up when you go inside and get centered, and letting visualizations just move. So, I listen and I watch. Those are real practices for me." What one might call "listening within" was for Nancy an ordinary activity, rather than an extraordinary one. Also, writing had for many years been a tool Nancy used for connecting with self spiritually as well as emotionally. This made natural her turn to pen and paper in the context of a crisis that was first and foremost a physical and emotional one.

Nancy described in detail at my request her journey through metastatic melanoma. Nancy had been diagnosed with advanced cancer in September 1993. (Thus, four years prior to my interview with her Nancy had been given the prognosis of six months to two years to live.) While her direct communication with Jesus and the skills that she drew on to facilitate it preceded that moment, her description of the communication with self, body, and the divine were, in context of my interview, closely interwoven with her story of the healing process. One of the early moments in that healing journey was clearly marked as a tale told to others besides me: Nancy is a minister and has shared this account in sermons. This telling was customized, though, to make it more accessible to an interviewer questioning her about her religious and spiritual life.

As noted above, Nancy heard a voice immediately after her diagnosis. Telling me about the voice and the words that she heard: " 'Come unto me all ye who are heavy laden and I will give you rest,' " Nancy added, "Straight out of scripture, Jesus says this." As with Derek, the sudden presence of a divine form was made comprehensible and identifiable by means of familiarity and identification with a particular text, set of institutions, and histories.

Two weeks later, the conversation with Jesus continued. Following "surgery to remove the lymph nodes under my arm," Nancy rather understandably experienced intense rage and frustration about her condition. Less predictably but perhaps drawing on the methods for self-awareness and of attentiveness to mind, body, and emotions that had for many years been central to her practice, Nancy took up a pad and pen, and wrote down her feelings. And in yet another moment signaling the situatedness of her path, Nancy explained to me that as she took up the pen a voice said, "Be angry, but don't let it lead you into sin." The voice continued, "Nancy, ground these feelings by writing them down." She continued telling me about the unfolding of events, moving back and forth between a literal reading aloud from her notes and journals, and looking up to supplement and contextualize what she had on paper. Nancy told me that she had written: "I am so sick of this. My life has been taken over by this disease. I can't even wash my own hair. I have no control over my life. The cancer controls me. I hate it . . . I hate hurting and being tired. I hate hurting [my husband and daughters]. I am grieving my own life as I've known it. It can never be the same, even if I'm in remission for 30 years. Now I have dreams of dying, even if they are comforting dreams . . . I can't cook or clean or garden." Nancy added, "I have this in a sermon. At that point [when I'm preaching] I look up from the reading and I say, 'Now, I never used to really like to cook or clean, but I would have given my eye-teeth to be able to do it again.' And there's always the laughter [from the congregation]." Nancy continued, "In fact, what I had written that night was 'I can't stop crying. Jesus, Sophia, help me.'" And looking over at me again, she emphasized, "That's an important piece of who I am, is the Sophia." She went on:

> "Help of the helpless. I don't want to be helpless." And then I heard, "Cast your burden, yourself, upon him. He cares for you." And my breathing changed and it became like swells in the ocean, those deep swells. It flashed through my mind that one can get dehydrated from crying and I asked myself, "What is going on? I'm overtired, I know that. Is this a warning to just not get over tired or everything will come crashing in?" And after asking that question, I heard, "Come, follow me." Which is the Jesus statement of all time as far as I'm concerned . . . And then a dialogue developed that I wrote down.

An immediate question that arises for the listener or reader is this: who and what are the voices that Nancy names here? As we have seen, the presence of Jesus was made very clear to Nancy by means of continual references to the New Testament, through the enunciation of terms and phrases such as "Help of the helpless," and "Come, follow me." Yet when Nancy finds herself writing, "Be angry, but don't let it lead you into sin," and hears "a voice" that addresses her directly, saying, "Nancy, ground these feelings by writing them down," we are not told who the speaker might be. Is it Nancy herself, perhaps, or Sophia as a female manifestation of divinity? Here is a discourse whose subject, Nancy, is divided into several distinguishable aspects. There is the Nancy who narrates this story. There is Nancy present as a witness— she who, in Nancy McKay's own terms, watches and listens to the unfolding of events.

As well, one sees a questioning or even skeptical mind who asks herself whether in fact all that is unfolding here is dehydration and an ensuing disorientation. Yet as though in a response to that moment of doubt, someone says, and someone else hears, another forcefully clear "Jesus statement"—a call to follow. Again here, while there is a clear connection between Nancy as narrator and Nancy as listening subject—as she says, "*I* heard" (emphasis added)—there is an equally clear separation between Nancy and what is spoken: "Come, follow me."

Nancy told me what happened next:

> Jesus says, "Follow me," and I say—and I'm still angry—"Well, you're the best thing in sight." And that's really key because it's being—not suddenly going into a pious stuff, it's staying with what is real. God works in ways real, has been my experience. And Jesus says, "That's more like it. I like your tough humor. Come on, walk with me a little while. Shh, shh, just keep breathing." "That's exactly what I'm trying to do!" And then he says, "You love life?" "Yes, I do. It may not have sounded like it for the last half hour but I do love life and I want to live, even with this cancer." "Shall I give you your life?" "What do you mean? I'd have to be all the way responsible for it? Not without you around but with you, yes, I want my life." "Then you shall have it. Take it." "Just like that?" And then you get this, this sense that I have spent some time with the Bible. "Like Paul says about the mind of Christ, 'Just take it'?" "Yes. Take me, my body and blood. Take your body, soul and mind." "And you will walk with me?" I ask. "Yes." "Always?" If you've got Him there, negotiate. Get as much as you can. "Yes, always." "Okay, here I am."

Looking up from her journal, Nancy said, "I date my healing from that point. The next night, I was in the same mess emotionally. I was overtired, upset, angry, scared. I lay down in bed . . . I started pounding on the mattress saying, 'Jesus I need you, I need you here, I need you right here, right now.' And I got this sense of a face with a twinkling eye and a bit of a smile, just a sense of it, and I heard, 'Yes, ma'am.' And of course I burst out laughing. But it's been that kind of a journey. Kind of an amazing thing."

This long extract from my interview with Nancy is worth discussing in detail because of its richness. And one must note in beginning that several different agendas may be summoned up by the retelling of this dialogue. For Nancy, of course, the conversation was critical as the inauguration of a journey into healing from a life-threatening illness. Moreover the story as told here is deeply moving, reminding those open to faith in any form of an ever-present, sheltering force, here named Jesus. And for those more specifically Christ-focused, the dialogue and description might remind the reader of the tender, compassionate presence of Jesus, available to those who call out to Him. But in the present context I seek to do something different in relation to Nancy's words, asking what gives her experience meaning, actuality, and form. For it is not enough to view this as only a spontaneous event, nor only as a "natural" event, nor for that matter "only" as a miraculous manifestation. On the other hand, I do not seek to "explain away" Nancy's experience, but rather to ask what makes it possible.

First, both the content and conceptual frame of Nancy's conversation, and the named being, Jesus, with whom it took place, merit exploration and comment. On a purely philosophical level one might argue that Nancy did not actually need to know that there is a being called "Jesus" in order to hear from such a being. However, I suggest that it was Nancy's detailed knowledge of the New Testament that meant that she could readily identify the presence *as* Jesus, on the three occasions described above. Further, of course, Jesus was not only recognized. More, in context of Nancy's longstanding devotion to him, his arrival on the scene brought immediate relief and inspired a sense of safety, with the sarcastic tone that only loving familiarity can permit— "Well, you're the best thing in sight," and later, "If you've got Him here, negotiate!" In the dialogue that ensued, we see the marks of Nancy's familiarity with the New Testament of the Bible (her enthusiasm as she identifies the words "Come, follow me" as the Jesus statement of all time; and her question to Jesus, "Like Paul says about the mind of Christ, 'Just take it'?"). Additionally, her many years of study, contemplation, and worship within a Christian framework made it unsurprising that her inner voice warned her in decidedly Christian terms. Thus, while the inner voice drew on her commitment to being present to her feelings and therefore urged her to call up and honor her rage, the same voice admonished, "But do not let it lead you into sin."

One cannot, it must be emphasized, see Nancy's relationship to the content and frame of Christianity as static, nor as "received teaching" in any simple way. For in her words we see signs of some of the struggle and debate of which Nancy has been a part. One example of this is her calling on Sophia as a name for the divine feminine, her linkage of that name to the name of Jesus, and her pause in the narrative to tell me that the invocation of the name, Sophia, is "an important piece of who I am."[14] Likewise, when Nancy says that it is in her view appropriate and necessary to "be real" with God, rather than, as she puts it, "going into a pious stuff," we are reminded that Christianity is a dynamic and plural space, not a singular nor a static one.

Second, one must consider the place of particular practices in making possible this extended dialogue between Nancy and Jesus. As already noted, Nancy had intentionally worked with a range of modes of meditation, visualization, and witnessing, drawing on bodily, emotional, and mental means of cognition. As I suggested above, the result of this is a complex consciousness. Thus, we hear in this extract from a Nancy that witnesses or listens. We also hear from a woman who is engaged in a different kind of cognitive processing. She comments almost as an outsider on her capacity in the moment to draw on and ask about Biblical references, and even, as she put it, negotiate and argue with the being who is speaking to her. We see also Nancy's awareness of a body breathing in different registers. Finally we see the outsider/commentator who both deems this the beginning point of her healing from cancer and then remarks on this as "kind of an amazing" (rather than an ordinary) set of events.

It is critical, also, to return to Nancy's own citation of the history of female mystics within which she places herself, as well as her citation of her cultivation of work within a range of more contemporary psychospiritual practices. As Nancy said, this work entails "trusting what comes up when you go inside and get centered, and letting visualizations just move . . . Those are real practices for me."

Given the limitations of space, I have not been able in this context to discuss the ways in which Nancy's work with both Reiki healing and experimental allopathic oncology were interwoven in the story of her journey with cancer. But we must notice that, as mentioned above, Nancy had at the time of my interview with her outlived a terminal cancer diagnosis by two years, and was in very good health.[15]

This extract from Nancy's interview makes possible further steps toward the development of the notion of "divine rationality." It is true that for Nancy McKay as for other mystics (*not* her term for herself), any encounter with the divine in any form must be recognized as spontaneous and as beyond the control of the recipient. Yet again one must ask what makes Nancy's experience possible. In this sense the experiences of the three interviewees named thus far cannot be defined *only* as spontaneous ones. For example, I would argue that it is in the context of an exact balancing of attention to form, name, practice, and after considered contemplation, negotiation, and surrender, that it is possible for Nancy to undertake and participate in her work with Jesus.

These interviews with "mainline" denominational Christians make clear, I hope, the degree to which Godtalk is first a "local" rather than "foreign," "exotic," or "Other" phenomenon. Godtalk must be seen as situated within particular religious or spiritual histories. These individuals communing with the divine are aware of the situatedness of their experience, and that of others. While on one hand the experience of Godtalk is spontaneous, it must also be understood as emplaced within a set of what one might call protocols of comprehension. Thus for Homer Teng divine guidance was seen to arrive serendipitously yet strategically. For Derek Jones divine guidance was understood to be that because of a density of appearance of visceral, human, and textual signs. And for Nancy McKay, receptivity to divine guidance was consciously cultivated. And each of these interviewees was aware of a continuum of Godtalk, from the implied to the literal—a continuum along which each knew his or her own place, as well as the places of others. Finally, for all three of these Christian interviewees, divine guidance was seen as having been received spontaneously, yet as comprehensible only within a known history of divine spontaneity.

Again, *form, practice,* and *surrender* are the three terms within which Godtalk can be witnessed and described. At times, the name of the Christian God and his son (or mortal form) Jesus are so familiar that they need not necessarily even be uttered. This was so, for example, in some of Derek Jones's narrative. The parameters of practice were on the one hand familiar and thus deemed normal. "First Peter," "Paul," and "Come, follow me!" are sites of enunciation that, for these interviewees, did not need to be explained and which, it was presumed, would be familiar to me, their listener. As noted already, practice was not homogeneous, and was at times contentious enough that each of these three interviewees could, and needed to, name the ways in which they had moved within and between, subverted, or found themselves marginal in particular branches of Christianity. Yet I suggest that all three, though personally unknown to one another and denominationally different from one another, would have recognized one another very easily, had I sat down with them as a group. Lastly, despite divergent practices, in each case *surrender* meant faith, belief, and acceptance of the idea that once one had comprehended the signs of Godtalk, one should follow its direction. This was so despite the possibility that, as Homer stated, God does not always offer "the answer that I thought was right for me."

🌿

I TURN NOW to a group of individuals whose spiritual practices are closely connected with the religion most simply named *Hinduism*. A mode of Godtalk comes to the fore that is distinctive yet startlingly connected to the Christians' experiences just discussed. At the outset it is important to comment briefly on the term *Hinduism*. In fact, only one of the nine people I have in mind here used the word *Hindu* to describe himself. When I asked Aditya Advani what factors had shaped his spirituality, he answered, "My being Indian. I'm a Hindu. I would probably not be one if I wasn't born in India."

Complicating Aditya's linking of his nationality and his religion are the two other interviewees of Indian descent included in this research. Enigma, born in Hyderabad, is Muslim. She thus gives the lie to the majoritarian and indeed the contemporary fundamentalist claim that India is a Hindu country and that all "true" Indians are Hindus. For of course, not all Indians are Hindus either by birth or by practice. It should be noted that Aditya did not himself argue that all Indians are Hindu. Rather his claim is that his access to Hinduism, and the fact that his spiritual hungers have been given form by Hinduism, are explained by his having been born and raised in India, a country whose majority religion is Hinduism. In fact Aditya's own family is of mixed religious affiliation, Hindu and Sikh. There is a complicated and variously politicized relationship between the word *Hindu* and the nation-state India.

The other interviewee of Indian descent practicing in this tradition gives further force to this point. Darshan was born in Canada, was not born a Hindu, and did not use the term *Hindu* to identify herself. Born into a Sikh family, for Darshan God and spirit were above all formless forces, as is the case in Sikhism. Yet the embodied spiritual teachers most important to her were Satya Sai Baba and Mata Amritanandamayi, spiritual teachers in present-day India connected with Hinduism even if not exclusively self-identified with it. Her choice not to identify as Hindu points to the sense in which the term *Hindu* connotes not merely religion but also ethnicity. It also speaks to the syncretic history of religion in the Indian subcontinent, one instance of which is Darshan's birth religion, Sikhism, which sought to synthesize Hinduism and Islam.

There are seven other interviewees, Westerners, whose practices, gurus, and the deities associated with them are closely connected with the history of Hinduism. Yet these men and women did not choose to identify as Hindu. Rather, they connected their practice with particular teachers and their teachings. In these individuals' histories one hears the names of the Indian spiritual masters who have brought to Europe and North America modes of teaching and practice that some might in fact name *Hindu*. These were/are at times transcoded into ecumenicism and at other times simply transliterated into English. But in all cases they bear the marks of their origin points in India, in the form of named deities, philosophy, episteme, epistemology, practice, and language.

It must be noted that these teachers did *not* seek to convert Westerners to something called Hinduism. Nor did they necessarily name their teaching *Hinduism,* although some do, or did, at some moments name their practice precisely that. More commonly, these teachers emphasize(d) that the philosophy and teaching that they offer(ed) might be followed without renouncing one's birth religion, or that the path offered would lead the practitioner to the place wherein all religions converge into one. As we will see, though, the road to that place of convergence is close in form and philosophy to that which in India and its diaspora is named Hinduism.

Hinduism is not an "American" religion. It is perhaps unsurprising, then, that for most non-Indian United Statesians, the route into Hinduism and Hindu-related religions is via those gurus and spiritual teachers who carried these practices to the West.[16] It must also be emphasized that the Indian gurus or teachers discussed here do not simply work with Westerners. In some instances many—in other instances *most*—of their devotees are Indians based in India, in the United States, or elsewhere.

It should be clarified too that the "guru path," which is to say a spiritual path centrally organized by means of a learning, student, or devotee relationship with a particular teacher, is in general neither cultlike, in the colloquial sense of that term, nor only a Western phenomenon. Rather the presence of a teacher—whether deemed "Avatar" or embodied, deistic being, a highly evolved but fully human teacher, or simply a man or woman seen as wise enough to be spiritual adviser to many—is a longstanding dimension of Hinduism as practiced in India.

Daniel Gold, in an article on some of the Indian and non-Indian devotees of Swami Chidvilasananda, begins his comments by suggesting that there is an increasing turn to teacher over temple in modern India. He says that as city life and science-driven education systems make some aspects of Hindu tradition seem time-consuming and difficult to feel connected with, many have moved toward modes of devotional and yogic practice "grounded less in ritual and myth than in direct personal experience." Here, he suggests, the teachers or gurus providing such resources offer "streamlined forms of old Indian internal practices that can be carried out by large numbers of people under modern urban conditions. Because neither the practices of these gurus nor their spiritual authority depend on acceptance of the whole complex of Hindu tradition, their religious influence has also been able to spread among Westerners in search of religious alternatives."[17]

Gold's discussion reminds us of the importance of the guru/devotee relationship in Hindu spiritual paths. He notes that developing a meaningful spiritual path and guru/student relationship without engagement with theological Hinduism "lock, stock and barrel" is very possible, and is a mode of practice undertaken not just in the West but in India also. (On a point of clarification I note that this text engages with Hinduism and Hindu-derived practices almost entirely in relation to guru paths rather than temple communities.) I do not accept Gold's argument, however, that this is a new orientation within Hinduism. Nor do I think that the guru stands autonomous from "the whole complex of Hindu tradition," although as Lata Mani has argued, contemporary Indian spiritual teachers do, at times, seem to gloss over or disavow their relationship with older traditions.[18] It is true, in any event, that the individual practitioner or devotee is offered access to much of the guru's teaching and even her spiritual powers *without* needing to know of or even concur with Hinduism in general. The situation is complex, though, since in effect the individual will be provided with Hindu-derived ritual, tradition, and practices "as needed" by the guru and her close devotees.[19]

Whether individual practitioners hail from the United States, from South Asia, or elsewhere, the teacher or guru is a crucial point and site of meaning for them.[20] At times and for some individuals, the guru's status is that of intermediary between individual and deity. At other times it is that of one who assists the individual in a journey toward communion with the divine. Simultaneously the guru is recognized as, for want of any better terms, a spiritually and supernaturally empowered being in her own right. This means that the relationship between deity as "God talking," guru as "God talking," and individual as witness and participant in a triadic conversation between self, God, and guru is a subtle one. Moreover, given the recognition of the guru as spiritually empowered, and the dynamic relationship between guru and deity, it is perhaps not surprising that gurus currently in the body and currently not in the body are in many ways comparable, even equivalent. All of this is not, in fact, as exotic as it may seem at first glance: after all, is not Jesus seen diversely and variously as a divine being in his own right, as God's son, as teacher, philosopher, or wise man, and even as all of the above? And was Jesus not also seen as spiritually empowered both before and after he left the body?

In these interviewees' experiences and modes of Godtalk, there is a kind of interweaving and kinship among spiritual houses or congregations, practitioners and practices. This interweaving is made more explicable once one is aware of the triadic deity/guru/practitioner relationship just named. The Indian-descent interviewees have already been named. Among the Westerner devotee group are Sita and Archana, both renunciates (nuns) in the house of Mata Amritanandamayi. Sita and Archana are both European Americans who were given Indian spiritual names by their guru. The late Happy Carol Winingham (European American) was a minister at the Ananda Center for Self-Realization. That community is dedicated to the teachings of Paramahansa Yogananda (no longer living), and is the establishment where Sita had lived and practiced prior to her move to Mata Amritanandamayi's ashram. Anna Gamboa (Latina American) had also taken Mata Amritanandamayi to be her guru, although she continued practicing the Buddhist teachings of Thich Nhat Hahn. Michael Bell (African American) affirmed that Gurumayi Chidvilasananda was his guru. Gurumayi is the youngest (and still living) spiritual master in the lineage of Kashmir Shaivite master Nityananda—the same lineage of which Stuart Perrin, David Jacobson's teacher (*not*, it must be clarified, his guru), is also a student and teacher. (David Jacobson is European American). Gloria Williams (African American) is a student of Sri Sri Ravi Shankar (living), but had for twenty years been a student of Maharishi Mahesh Yogi (also living), teacher of Transcendental Meditation. Sri Sri Ravi Shankar is himself a student and former *pujari* (priest) in the spiritual house of Maharishi Mahesh Yogi. As it happens, Archana had also, earlier, practiced and worked in the house of Maharishi Mahesh Yogi. Despite this crisscrossing, these interviewees are not known to each other, except that Sita and Archana are nuns at the same ashram, and Sita had known Happy Winingham while at Ananda house and thus given me her name as a potential interviewee.

For many of the interviewees the guru is a crucial fourth term of spiritual practice—indeed one could argue that for some in that group the guru is in fact the *first* term, as the center and motivating force of spiritual life. This despite or perhaps because of the status of the guru, as one who is (probably? possibly?) not a deity, but is nonetheless a spiritually empowered being. An exchange between Archana and myself about Mata Amritanandamayi very forcefully addresses this ambiguity:

> RF Do you think she's God or do you think God is coming through her but she herself isn't God? Or do you think that's an impossible question?
>
> ARCHANA Yeah. [*Both laugh.*] What I think probably doesn't matter, number one. But number two, I couldn't even think of what God is anyway. I don't even know what God is, because I guess you'd have to be God. I think it's a matter of semantics, because how can I say anyone's God? I don't even know what God is. It's like saying, "Oh, I think she's something, I don't know what she is." And that's what it is. I don't know what she is. Because—and even if she isn't God, I still don't know what she is, you know.

The subtlety of Archana's response is striking. Here, in a few words, Archana takes us to a complex philosophical examination of human subjectivity and its relationship to the divine. First and foremost, Archana insists on humans' incapacity to name or know the divine ("I couldn't even think of what God is . . . because I guess you'd have to be God [to do that]"). Yet this incapacity is not incapacitating. Rather it sets clear epistemic and analytic parameters within which Archana continues her naming of Mata Amritanandamayi as she sees her. She sticks by a particular conundrum that names her not knowing and her acceptance of not knowing: "I think she's something, I don't know what she is. And even if she isn't God, I still don't know what she is." Critical to note here are the simultaneous affirmation, "I think she's something," and the acceptance that "I don't know" what that something is.

But a set of protocols of knowing in fact enables Archana and others to know far more about what Mata Amritanandamayi and other gurus are than is implied in these words. Archana says: "[One] night I was shelving the books in the library and all of a sudden I felt Mother at my feet. I just knew she was there, putting anklets on my ankles. The next day, I backed off so she wouldn't do that."

At that time, Archana was working at the college in Fairfield, Iowa, founded by Maharishi Mahesh Yogi, having spent many years practicing Transcendental Meditation (TM) as taught by him. But by the time of our interview, Archana was a devotee of Mata Amritanandamayi (addressed and referred to as *Amma, Mother,* or *Ammachi* by her devotees), living as a renunciate at Mata Amritanandamayi's California ashram (MA Center). On the night just described, Archana was in fact in the process of making the transition out of her involvement in Maharishi's house toward a connection with Ammachi.

In the context of guru paths, a very specific set of practices and experiences comes to the fore, one recognizable across gurus as well as within the houses or lineages of particular spiritual teachers. In the incident Archana described, Mata Amritanandamayi was not, of course, actually in the room. I say "of course" since the guru's tangible presence despite her physical absence is part of the point of the story. Mata Amritanandamayi or "Mother" is known to be able to create physical sensation from long distance. When Archana "backs off" she is, again, not describing a physical so much as an emotional or cognitive response.[21]

With a different guru, but on a comparable path, Michael Bell, a thirty-nine-year-old African American gay man, raised upper middle class in the Episcopal Church, told me of an incident whose structure is strikingly similar. I asked him if Chidvilasananda, referred to more popularly as Gurumayi, was his guru. (This was not exactly a leading question since when I went to interview Michael I discovered that his offices were a suite in a back corner of her ashram, filled with images of her and the teachers who precede her in the lineage of which she is a part.) Michael answered:

> Yes, yes, she is. I had an amazing—I mean, I think everyone—I don't know if everyone has a Gurumayi story, but about a year before I met Gurumayi, I was at one of my first group meditations, and the swami was there to lead the meditation. And as we began—it was a stormy, windy, San Francisco evening. We were high on a hill in a living room where there were these huge panels of window and the sky was dark purple and black and crimson and the wind was blowing and it was chilly. And we came inside and there was a stillness that was kind of growing in the room. As we went into meditation, the swami leaned over to someone sitting on the other side of him and said, "Do you

feel it coming?" And as he said that, I felt this kind of rising wave of stillness coming up my body, and I went into the meditation, and as I was in the meditation, I began to smell a gardenia—as though it had just been placed under my nose. And I said, "How strange. I don't remember any gardenias when I came in." And I remember thinking, "I'll have to look for them when I'm done." And of course there were no gardenias. There were no flowers anywhere. And I said, "How interesting." And so, a year later, when I came up to meet Gurumayi, she looked at me and she said, "I think you've been waiting for this," and handed me a gardenia. A year later.

As was true for Archana, one of the points of this story for Michael is that the guru is able to have significant impact on physical environments in which she is not present—the scent of a gardenia, the feeling of stillness.

In both of these incidents—Michael's and Archana's—the body and bodily sensation play critical roles. For Michael there is the capacity of olfactory sensation and the even more subtle sensation of ambient stillness. And for Archana, there is physical sensation, the feeling of being touched. The body becomes the site wherein and the means by which the guru reaches around the commonplace world. Simultaneously the body becomes the processor, the witness, for the presence of an efficacy not visibly proximate. Lastly, and connected to both of these points, the body becomes the archivist and analyst, providing information that links guru to devotee, and documents the presence and practices of the guru per se. As such, the body is the authorizing witness for the guru's presence and force, and also provider of data then analyzed, commented on, and shared with others.

When Michael feels "stillness" it is crucial that he is not alone in doing so, hearing the swami (himself a figure of authority) remarking upon it to another person in the room. But he was alone in smelling a gardenia. This singularity is in fact crucial to the experience, since when Michael meets Gurumayi again, it is to *him* rather than to someone else that she hands the gardenia flower. As he emphasizes, the guru not only altered his physical environment, she remembered having done so, and finished making her point a year later, with that capacity to remember and to do something specific *for him* a crucial part of the experience.

We might also remember and compare the tenderness and intimacy of the two gestures—the proffering of a flower, the placing of jewelry upon the ankles. Here, both gestures are part of a larger process, for in each case the individuals are new to these gurus' paths and communities. As Michael comments, the first "gardenia incident" takes place at one of his first experiences of group meditation and the second when he finds himself in the presence of Gurumayi for the very first time. And Archana is being assisted in her journey toward Mata Amritanandamayi when she feels the touch of anklets on her legs.

What is the effect of these incidents on those who experience them? And what makes them salient in the consciousness of individuals talking to me about their spiritual lives? First, the "extreme" character of each of these events signals that something "other," something out of the ordinary, is underway. Yet this otherness is, in a sense, marshaled into the ordinary, or at any rate into a category of that which is the "known" by those close to the guru. What happens through the experience of the miraculous is, then, the crafting of a community of recognition or comprehension around the guru—one that lives *within* the miraculous as ordinary yet simultaneously not so.

For Michael the experience just described was formative to his relationship with Gurumayi. Immediately following his affirmative response to my question about whether Chidvilasananda was his guru, the "gardenia incident" was proffered as demonstration of this fact. At the same time, the story was offered as proof positive of Gurumayi's efficacy and of Michael's membership in a collectivity of persons who have experienced her force. For as Michael said, "I think everyone has a Gurumayi story." In a markedly similar way, Archana, continuing her description of the journey from Maharishi Mahesh Yogi to Mata Amritanandamayi, emphasized, "It was a miracle, you know. There are so many miracles around Mother, it's not really unusual." Godtalk here is as much about the "ordinary human's" capacity to name and interpret the workings of divine power as it is about the raw, simple, and direct witnessing of divine intervention.

Godtalk in these instances, then, is recognized by its recipients as the working of a being to alter and impact the physical world, in order, to simply convey the message, "I am here to communicate with you." Godtalk is noticed via its impact on the physical environment and experience of the individual. And it is identified *as* Godtalk through aural/oral communication among persons who have also experienced it, rather than only or primarily via written history (like that of Christian mystics) or even written scripture (the New Testament). But it must also be noted that, although to my knowledge a gardenia does not feature in any particular way in Hindu text, culture, or folklore, the anklet does. For example, religious music that describes the Divine

Mother as Kali (with whom Mata Amritanandamayi is described in her mission's literature as being closely associated) often signals her arrival by the sound of her anklets jingling as she moves. Thus, for Archana to be given anklets connects her specifically with Mata Amritanandamayi as Kali, and conversely, signals that it is Mata Amritanandamayi as Kali that is communicating with her.

AWARENESS OF the guru's efficacy is not associated only with the building of a particular form of consciousness, nor with individuals' spiritual journeys to the guru's side. Sita (white, lower middle class, forty-eight years old), for example, described feeling the presence of Mata Amritanandamayi as she struggled with the difficult task of organizing a shuttle service to bring devotees onto the San Ramon Ashram grounds during Ammachi's ten-day-long stay there in November 1996.

There were multiple problems to address. First, because of the impact of traffic on the ashram's neighbor, a horse ranch, the parking space on the ashram was to be replaced by a borrowed off-site lot. Second, because of off-site parking, a van shuttle service had to be arranged. And third, on this occasion Mata Amritanandamayi was to make only one stop in the United States, at the San Ramon Ashram. Because of this, as many as fifteen hundred men, women, and children might be expected to converge on the ashram, needing to travel to and from the parking lot in the morning, evening, and in between.

Faced with all this, Sita said, "I realized that the job, essentially, could not be done . . . There's something wrong with these numbers. And I thought, 'Oh, well, you know, if God, in this case meaning Mother, is giving us this situation, I bet she's planning on pulling some miracles here.'" Sita needed to recruit volunteer drivers:

> I knew in the end that with people wanting to do a little bit here and a little bit there, it wasn't going to be enough to do the whole job . . . There's no way that you can go out and ask someone, "Would you like to drive for the next 15 hours, taking cat naps periodically?" But that's essentially what it boiled down to for many people. Like I said in my [thank you letter to volunteers after the event], we can't recruit heroes, but with someone as powerful as Mother, they just naturally come out.

One intriguing aspect of Sita's discussion of this situation was that her confidence in Mata Amritanandamayi was bolstered by her experience at a different ashram, in the lineage of a different guru, Paramahamsa Yogananda. Sita said:

> I'd seen that happen before when I was at Ananda. There'd be a project and so often there'd be impending disaster, and I would get upset about it. But always, somehow at the last moment, there'd be a miracle. [*She laughs.*] Something would happen and it would save the day. And after seeing that happen a few times, I thought, "Okay, I'm not going to be worried about this kind of thing any more. If it really turns out to be a disaster, then okay, we'll have a disaster, but I don't believe it. I think there's something else that's trying to happen." And Mother really came through in a very big way.

For Sita, it was striking that in fact part—but not all—of what was "trying to happen" was the creation of "heroes." Here, Sita suggests that in fact when the guru "comes through," she does so in part by means of the transformation of individuals. Sita reemphasized this idea when she said, "Whenever people extend themselves or they push beyond what we consider to be reality, then you can tune into a larger reality . . . Nobody could see how [the tour] was really going to work . . . This picture just wasn't working. [*She laughs.*] But only because Mother was coming did we feel that it was possible." For Sita, Mata Amritanandamayi would determine the outcome of events. One can argue that perhaps some of the parking and shuttling achievement might be laid at the door of humans (the willingness of some volunteer drivers to drive for long hours, for example). However, other factors (such as the possibility of parking twice the vehicles in an area of reduced size) were less easily attributable to individual accomplishments alone. And in fact one could well argue that human cooperation and goodwill under pressure might just as easily be seen as divinely achieved than as arrived at by simple good fortune. I would also suggest that here some of what was "trying to happen" was a dramatic demonstration of the guru's power. Here the devotee was asked and enabled to alter her entire sense of cause, effect, possibility, and efficacy. This was emphasized by Sita when she said "only because Mother was coming did we feel that it was possible."

For Sita, Mata Amritanandamayi's ability to bring about the transportation of fifteen hundred individuals was analogous to the aversion of another near disaster at her former home, the Ananda Center. Sita said:

> One lady, a nun, was sleeping in a little tiny trailer one night. She woke up in the middle of the night and she felt Divine Mother's presence.

[*"Divine Mother"* here does not refer to Mata Amritanandamayi but rather to the feminine aspect of God, nonembodied.] And the nun said, "Oh, it was such a sweet feeling to know that Divine Mother was right there with me." But then she was thinking, "But I wonder why Divine Mother woke me up right now." And just at that moment she could smell the smoke [from the cook stove]. The trailer was starting to catch fire. So she had enough time to put it out.

For Sita, outcomes such as the ones just described are most effectively attributable, as a collectivity, to divine will broadly conceived. Thus Sita says that "God and *in this case, Mother*" (emphasis added) would be able to address the enormous vehicular crunch that faced the ashram. Similarly God averted minor and major catastrophes at the Ananda Center. It is the juxtaposition of these incidents, ostensibly very different from one another, that depicts for Sita the capacity of the guru or deity, embodied or not, to guide, to teach, to provide humans with "superhuman" capacities, and to influence cause and effect as needed. Sita's experiences can be easily connected to those of Michael and Archana.

Sita's understanding of what one might name "divine efficacy" demonstrates how, in these interviews, instances of divine action were, in fact, interchangeable in ways that crosscut among embodied gurus still living (Mata Amritanandamayi), embodied gurus long dead (Paramahamsa Yogananda), and deities recognized within the Hindu pantheon (Divine Mother). We are reminded of Archana's lack of concern about whether Ammachi is God or something else. Linking these is recognition that almost the same protocols and powers may be made manifest in embodied and nonembodied beings deemed divine. All of this is less surprising once one remembers the radically decentered and plural character of the Hindu pantheon and Hindu religion themselves.[22] And as Sita's, Michael's, and Archana's voices are analogized with one another, one sees that in fact a metanarrative is in play, one in which divine cause and effect via the medium of the guru is made visible, normal, and, simultaneously, remarkable.

NOTING FURTHER THAT the very same structures of knowing and of efficacy may come into play with or without the presence of a living guru, we return now to an individual whose experience both parallels and differs from that of his Western counterparts. One witnesses here Godtalk in the form of "God's actions." Aditya Advani, an Indian gay man and an immigrant to the United States, was thirty-four years old at the time of the interview. Visiting his homeland, Aditya was distraught about long delays in the completion of the process of obtaining a green card, that is, permanent residence in the United States. He was invited by relatives in Delhi to visit with an elderly gentleman, known affectionately and respectfully to the relatives as *Baba* (a term meaning variously and at times simultaneously "father," "respected elder," and "religious man"). Baba, the relatives thought, might be able to give Aditya advice about his situation, not because he was an expert in immigration issues but rather because, as the family said, "He's not particularly religious, but you should talk to him and he can tell you everything." Aditya added, "My brother's wife's family is a very orthodox Hindu religious family . . . into strong religious practice."

As soon as the discussion with Baba began, Aditya told me, he was intrigued as the gentleman volunteered, without anyone having given them to him, facts and dates about Aditya's immigration problems. As Aditya said: "Baba said in Hindi, 'You're a very bright guy, but you don't have any *vivek*, no [discernment]. Your problem started three years ago, in January of '94. You made a hasty move.' Aditya told me that he concurred with Baba, telling me, as he had told the gentleman, 'Yes, I did, because I chose a bad lawyer as a hasty move.'

We should notice here that it was not, in fact, Baba who named the immigration lawyer and Aditya's selection of a "bad" attorney as the site of Aditya's problems. Rather the Baba named a specific *time* as the beginning point of Aditya's current problems. Aditya put that named time together with his own sense of what he had done and what had gone wrong regarding immigration to the United States. Thus for Baba the problem was never really immigration but rather Aditya himself. Thus Aditya's sense of his difficulty—lack of a green card—was translated by Baba into lack of good judgment.

As the discussion between Baba and Aditya continued, Baba did not propose that Aditya get a new lawyer. Rather he suggested that Aditya's problems should be addressed by an improvement in his meditation practices. For when Aditya told Baba that he had been meditating and praying to the god Shiva, Baba told him that his prayers and meditations were incomplete. He proposed that they be complemented by prayer and meditation to Parvati, the deity named Shiva's consort, and also Ganesh, the deity named as their son. As Baba put it, "How can you pray to Shiva and not to Parvati?" Aditya responded, he told me, "That's true." Baba continued, recounted Aditya, "You have to get a little photograph of Shiva and Parvati . . . the Parvati with the baby

Ganesh in her lap. The whole Shiva family." Were he to do this according to Baba's specific instructions, Baba told him, "in six months your problem will be solved."

After returning to the United States, Aditya followed these instructions. Again as Aditya tells the story one can see two different narratives unfolding. In one, Aditya's relationships to self, world, and spirit change in a way that one might propose is in line with the Baba's sense of focusing in on Aditya rather than on his immigration status. For Aditya said: "I came back and I started saying this mantra, and immediately I felt this sense of—what's the word for it?—not electricity, but tightness, as if my inner being was kind of tightened inside, and focused. Focused is the word. It's like a lamp being focused." Although Aditya did not, at least in the interview, make this connection, I suggest that a tightening of the inner being and the notion of "a lamp being focused" seem strikingly close to an increased capacity for discernment and good judgment. Aditya continued:

I started praying and I got all these experiences. You know, this place where my third eye is would often throb as I would say the mantra. I started being able to get up [in the morning], which I never could. At six in the morning I would get up, I would pray, I would do the practice, and just deep belief in God. It was like this feeling of surrender that I hadn't had before I just started having. I said, "I surrender to whatever you wish. I'll live wherever you want."

Again one sees Aditya's priorities altered in context of these practices. Likewise he and his partner began visiting the local San Francisco Bay Area temple to pray and make offerings to Shiva, with the help of the swami (priest) but following Baba's instructions. At the temple, in addition to a sense of peace and with renewed energy from daily meditation, Aditya said, "I just changed." He added that he had also thought, "I'm not going to be here very much longer. I'm just going to live life for the moment, be happy while I'm in America."

Yet at the same time, Aditya did not set aside his immigration-related goals and as he said, "meanwhile, the green card thing started happening really fast." Aditya explained to me that whereas once the Immigration and Naturalization Service (INS) had taken six months to reply to a single letter, now they would respond within a week. When they had once refused Aditya and his employers' approval for Aditya's immigration status, they now responded positively to an appeal so that his case could be reassessed.

As would-be immigrants will know, one key step to an employment-based green card application is the demonstration that the job has been advertised and no qualified citizen or permanent resident has applied for it. In this instance, it looked as though Aditya was about to be out of luck:

> Someone applied who was totally qualified for the job, but I just kept praying. I was like, "It will work out. It's God's feeling." And then he [the applicant] wrote to us to say that he had found another job. So you know, we had offered him the job, because he was qualified, but he refused it, which was just this incredible thing . . . And the next day we were supposed to send the letter back to the government saying, you know, "We did a search and we found one person qualified and he refused the job. We offered him the job." And so, we mailed that letter off, and that was six months almost to the day after I met the Baba.

Just two weeks before the interview discussed here, Aditya had received word from the INS that he had been granted a green card or permanent residency of the United States. As Aditya said, "It was just this intense *sadhana* . . . it was just intensely spiritual practice."

For Aditya, an array of guides and practitioners were involved in the process just described. These included the Baba, the local priest, Aditya himself, and his partner, and, of course, the deities Shiva, Parvati, and Ganesh. For Aditya, process was almost as important as product, or rather a range of unexpected products and byproducts were as important as that of the green card. As I suggested above, Aditya was, in a sense "riding two horses" throughout this process of, as he names it, "intense sadhana." As the Baba had suggested, his "problem" was lack of discernment as much as it was lack of a green card. And also as the Baba had suggested, his prescription would address both of these issues. Thus we see Aditya simultaneously finding himself surrendered to any outcome as long as it was God's outcome ("I'll live anywhere you want me to live") and also continuing to feel strongly that faith would see him to the green card. As he put it, "I just kept praying. I was like, 'It will work out. It's God's feeling.'"

An intriguing aspect of this story is the interweaving of the term, *God,* named so to speak "generically" with the named deities, Shiva, Parvati, and Ganesh. I did not pursue this point with Aditya. However, I suspect that here, *God* refers to Shiva. For one thing, Aditya had meditated and prayed to Shiva before meeting the Baba. Secondly, Aditya's mantra referred most directly to the god Shiva. Third, the genderedness of language suggests that unless marked otherwise, *God* is male. Lastly it is critical to notice that for Aditya deities from the Hindu rather than any other tradition comprise the unmarked category. Thus a Hindu deity can be named, simply, *God*.

By the end, when Aditya was informed that he was to receive a green card, he viewed it as the direct result of spiritual practice. This might suggest that a direct line of cause and effect is being proposed. We must note also that Aditya viewed his attainment of a green card as what God wanted, "*God's* feeling," not Baba's feeling, not Aditya's feeling, and not necessarily that of the INS either. Again we witness here the assertion that divine efficacy is in play. Moreover, for Aditya the role of each of those involved was clear: the deity or deities were the active agent; Baba and perhaps the local priest assisted in guiding Aditya in the process. Yet differently from the others named thus far, Aditya saw himself also as playing an active role. Thus his morning meditation was critical, and the green card a reward for that daily work.

It was perhaps in that context that Aditya insisted that the arrival of the green card should not be seen as a miracle. In his view:

> A miracle is something that just happens without your doing all the *tapas* [hard spiritual work]. Maybe it's a miracle, I don't know. I would be a little shy to say a miracle's been done for me. It wasn't such an important thing. It didn't need a miracle. I wasn't struggling, I mean, I wasn't going to Lourdes on crutches and walking away. I would have survived. It wasn't such a big deal. But the turnaround was, um, was interesting, so, things just worked out.

Here Aditya's own "turnaround" is as "interesting" as his discussion of what counts as a miracle. Aditya views the morning meditation as very hard spiritual work (in actuality less challenging than that which many would consider to be tapas, although this is of course both a relative and a subjective assessment). Thus he suggests that perhaps a miracle was not "done for him." Yet it is unclear whether the causal relationship between tapas and the green card is the only thing at stake here. For his insistence that his immigration status was not "such a big deal" may be either an effect of the peace of mind that comes forth after the catastrophe is over, or an effect of the surrender to "God's will" that he had earlier described. Further, his comment that he was "shy" to suggest that a miracle had been done for him presents another, different line of interpretation, in which he feels, perhaps, that a green card *is* "no big deal" in comparison with the challenge of a physical disability. And lastly, his use of the word *interesting* mirrors that of several other interviewees whose language has revealed sudden moments of doubt in their own telling of the tale. (Nancy wondering whether she was dehydrated is one example here.)

In several ways Aditya's story appears as a classic tale from within the Hindu tradition. The protagonist prays for one thing, performs spiritual practices in order to seek the granting of his prayer, and finds that his prayers are answered. But simultaneously he finds that circumstances change and so do his goals. These processes are both clearly present as Aditya recounts the events that took place in the six months following his meeting with the Baba. Further, although Aditya does not himself say this directly, reading between the lines makes clear that there are very specific reasons for the Baba's meditation and prayer instructions. For Aditya, by praying to Shiva, is praying to the principle of "stillness" but not to that of *shakti*, dynamism or movement, represented in all forms of the Divine Mother, including Parvati. Thus as the Baba pointed out, it was not surprising that Aditya's immigration status was not moving. As Baba said to Aditya, "How can you pray to Shiva and not to Parvati?" Moreover—and again Aditya does not note this, or at least did not comment upon it in the interview—Ganesh is not only seen as the son of Shiva and Parvati but is also the deity understood as the remover of obstacles within Hindu tradition. Thus one might note that once a Shiva/Parvati/Ganesh altar has been established there is movement, the removal of obstacles, and surrender—a holistic outcome. As with other interviews, Aditya's signals the ways in which any religious form is multifaceted, as well as the ways in which an individual's relationship to that form may change over time.

Here one reaches an interesting point, analytically, in which an interviewee's experience might easily be mapped onto processes of which he or she does not appear to be aware. On one hand, this is not unusual—it is after all the task of the scholar to build bridges unavailable to individual subjects of research. Yet, commenting on the ways in which Aditya's experience of Godtalk exceeds that which he himself describes, I am using other interviews and wider resources to argue for the veracity of "divine rationality," "sacred reason," and "divine efficacy"— that from which Aditya himself backs away when naming his experience an "interesting turnaround."

᯽

I HAVE USED the word *Godtalk* to describe three things: the potency of the divine in a range of forms; the process of individuals naming their experience and comprehension of divine efficacy; and the possibility of mapping and theorizing divine power. It will, I hope, have become clear that first, "God" does far more than merely "talk" in the lives of these interviewees. Interviewees are in a range of ways adept in describing, explaining, and cultivating their fluency in Godtalk. Their stories make visible an interlocking set of aspects of Godtalk as praxis, one that holds across the traditions that have been worked with here.

There are ways in which one can easily connect the Godtalk of those whose practice one might link with Hinduism with that of the Christian interviewees. In all cases, form and name were critical to recognition of God or guru talking. Indeed, knowledge of the relationships between forms and names was centrally important, whether the god, guru, or teacher was Jesus, God, Sophia, Paul, and Peter, or Mata Amritanandamayi, Paramahamsa Yogananda, Gurumayi Chidvilasananda, Shiva and Parvati and Ganesh.

Interviewees are able to speak with confidence about their experience in part because of the histories of others' experiences. Thus Homer can comment on how his epiphany fits along a continuum of other Christians' learning processes, and Archana, Michael, and Sita are aware not only of their current teachers' capacities, but also those of other gurus understood to be broadly within their spiritual world. Likewise, Aditya is fully familiar with the names Shiva, Parvati, and Ganesh even though, as I noted, he did not comment on their qualities and relationships to one another.

If there is a difference between these two groups of interviewees, it is that the Christians, because of the normativity of Christianity in the Western world, feel able to count on their and my awareness of a written tradition. By contrast, interviewees whose gurus emanate from within or around Hinduism drew more on oral than on written sources in order to explain their experiences to me and to confirm and exchange witness of their experience with one another. Yet this distinction barely holds up. One may note, for example, that verbal as well as written testimony is critical to the communities around saints in the Catholic world.[23] Conversely, the recounting of the extraordinary and enormous actions of Hindu deities, sages, and teachers is a part of Hindu religious texts, as well as something spoken of. One thus realizes that these differences are local and contingent rather than formal ones.

Christianity, as I have stated, might be seen as a relatively contained, centered, and particular religious form wherein God and Jesus are the key names and sites in relation to which Godtalk might be enacted. Having said this, however, I have also commented on the flexibility and at times the contentiousness of Christianity as these were expressed and experienced by Homer Teng, Derek Jones, and Nancy McKay.

In contrast with Christianity, Hinduism and its close cousins (once again retaining for convenience a name not chosen by most of this group) practice within a framework that is radically plural and decentered. This is so in terms of its institutions, its history, and thus in the modes of identification and knowledge that it offers practitioners. In this mode of practice there is room for the play of a triadic conversation between self, God, and guru. The term *guru,* too, as I pointed out, might refer to a range of embodied beings, living or deceased. And as we saw, the guru could be comprehended in a range of ways. Likewise, unlike within Christianity, the term *God* is a plural rather than a singular one within Hinduism, so that particular deities could signal importance to one interviewee yet be less salient in the life of another.

However, any assertion of the decenteredness of institutions and practices in the Hindu tradition must be countered by a comment on *its* opposite, the consistency of these interviewees' spiritual practice and religious world. For even though interviewees had different gurus, the ways in which they described those gurus were strikingly similar. And even for those who, like Aditya, did not name a guru per se, his articulation of the relationships between an embodied teacher (the Baba), practice, and deity could be identified as making sense within the same universe of discourse as that within which Gurumayi and Ammachi were described.

Thus, just as recognition of the centeredness of Christianity must be counterbalanced by a comment on its converse, a kind of harmonious or inharmonious diversity, awareness of Hinduism's decenteredness must give way to an acknowledgement of its consistency. And in both cases interviewees were to varying degrees knowledgeable about similarity and diversity within their traditions. That is, interviewees were conscious about the particularity, the variance, and the boundaries of the religious forms in context of which *their* Godtalk took place. And they had also moved around within the discursive and institutional worlds in which their practice unfolded. Thus Derek had moved while still within Christianity into "black magic" and back again, as well as in and out of Christian fundamentalism. And in a different way, Aditya and other practitioners of Hindu-related spiritualities moved among both gurus and deities.

What, though, is Godtalk for these men and women? We might emphasize at the outset that all of the men and women on whom I focused in this chapter were cognizant of the actuality of communicating with the divine. They were familiar with the demonstrable presence of "divine efficacy." And they were conscious of the involvement of both divine presence and human practitioner in keeping open channels of communication. (As Nancy McKay put it, "Those are real practices for me.") We should also note, though, that although I focused neither on all the Christian interviewees, nor on all those involved in Hindu-related practices, a key difference between these two groups must be recognized. While I could easily, space permitting, have named the meaning and practice of Godtalk for all but one of the latter group, this was not the case for the former group. For while some Christian interviewees had much to say about forms of Godtalk, for others the spiritual center of gravity in their practice seemed to be elsewhere.

For those to whom Godtalk is important, the similarities between Christian Godtalk and Hindu Godtalk are far more compelling than the differences between them. One can list those similarities under the following headings: first, viscerality; second, synchronicity; third, and connected to the second, the density of multiply mediated events. Fourth, the recognition of material efficacy both in the moment and across time and space was part of what made Godtalk understandable. Fifth and lastly, individuals' familiarity with particular religious/spiritual traditions, oral and written, enabled both the expectation and interpretation of Godtalk. These five features are, I suggest, mutually reinforcing. Together they make Godtalk knowable, and together they provide the framing for that which I am naming here "divine rationality."

Viscerality: as we have seen in context of a range of experiences, Christian and Hindu, bodily experiences make possible the recognition that the guru or deity is present and is taking action of some kind. Here for example we might remember the touch of bangles on Archana's ankles and the scent of a gardenia in Michael's first experience of group meditation. Likewise, Derek's suddenly racing heart and lungs and Nancy's unexpectedly *slowed* heart and deepened breath signaled the presence of a being knowable as divine. Although in each of these cases the actual form of that being is different—Mata Amritanandamayi, Gurumayi Chidvilasananda, a God known in Christian terms, and Jesus, respectively—the nature and form of "divine intervention" is the same. Teachers and beings significant in these interviewees' lives communicated via the body, rather than via, or only via, the thinking mind. The body's experience thus intervenes in the ongoing flow of events, signaling that something new is happening. Thus as Archana does her librarian's work at the house of one spiritual teacher, the presence of *another* teacher, Mata Amritanandamayi, visits in the midst of her activity. Similarly Derek is an audience member at the end of a workshop when his body pushes him to notice his hunger for a change of status. In both instances, the body, used as a resource by a divine form, does the work of altering the status quo. The body thus becomes an "alternative cognitive processor."

*Synchronicity,* a term coined by Carl Jung, is defined in the *Oxford English Dictionary* as follows:

> The name given by Swiss psychologist C. G. Jung (1875–1961) to the phenomenon of events which are coincident in time and appear meaningfully related, but have no discernable causal connection. "Synchronicity, he explains, is not synchronousness. In a 'synchronicity phenomenon' as he uses the phrase, two contemporaneous events are linked together in a meaningful manner." 1953, Jrnl. Soc. Psych. Res., XXXVII. 28; 1955 R. F. C. Hull, Tr., *Jung and Pauli's Interpretation of Nature and Psyche,* I, 27, "I have picked on the term 'synchronicity' to designate a hypothetical factor equal in rank to causality as a principal of explanation."[24]

Synchronicity as just defined is critical as maker of meaning in the context of Godtalk. The concept of synchronicity, indeed, makes possible the emergence of a distinctive rationality, as well as making normal or at least normative the process of living within that rationality. It was the synchronicity of a set of events that made Derek Jones sure that Godtalk was in progress. Derek's story in fact made most obvious the transition from synchronousness to synchronicity, for a set of events proceeding simultaneously or in quick succession, all of which might have been meaningless alone, made new sense as a collectivity. For Derek, that new sense was clearly Godtalk or, in his words, "quick prods" followed by the physical thwack of a "two-by-four."

Yet for others *synchronicity* was also a critical term, without the simplicity and directness of all relevant events taking place simultaneously. Thus for Michael one can note the first incident—meditation with Gurumayi's spiritual community plus scent of gardenia but with no actual gardenia visible—and the second incident—an encounter with Gurumayi in the flesh accompanied by gardenia in the flesh. And were Michael to be unable to put these ostensibly unconnected events together, Gurumayi does this for him, by saying, "I believe you've been looking for this." Gurumayi here names the synchronicity and takes personal responsibility for it. Thus again synchronicity is connected with Godtalk.

Attention to the density of multiply mediated, connected, or connectable events affirms the necessity of the idea of synchronicity. With *multiply mediated* I refer simply to the appearance of a page of a text, a scent, a physical sensation, two or more similar or coincident events, all deemed salient to a single incident. Here, as before, one can see the remaking of simultaneous yet ostensibly unconnected events or occurrences into a set of causally connected events. And as those multiply mediated events are now seen to be connected, this is deemed to be via the efficacy of a divine form and/or force. Sita's many descriptions of what she named "miracles" provide good examples. A nun wakes up in the night for no apparent reason, and discovers herself to be thinking of the Divine Mother. Wondering why the Divine Mother has arrived in her consciousness at that moment, she realizes that it was good that she woke up, since her home was ablaze. Here, then, two instances of "no apparent reason" add up to the "reason" of divine force. The possibility of coincidence is rejected, and exchanged for that of God talking. Further, the repetition of incidents that can be understood within this same structure and form themselves contribute to the density of multiply mediated events associated with Godtalk. Thus we saw Michael, Sita, and Archana all comment on the normalcy of events of this kind once one is within the ambit of a particular guru or of God in general.

Material efficacy is, as we have seen, crucial here. Godtalk is not just talk. It is critical to all of these individuals' understanding of their relationship with guru, God, deity, or other spiritually empowered being that the divine has material efficacy in the moment and across time and space. Michael's gardenia story makes clear what I mean here. Homer's experience of receiving necessary advice when faced with a dilemma also exemplifies divine efficacy, albeit from within a different tradition and more subtly. Yet also, Aditya's story dramatizes the symmetry of Godtalk and the material efficacy of the divine. The Baba gave Aditya a set of instructions and promised that his problems would be resolved in six months. Six months later, there is an event across the globe that makes it almost certain that Aditya *will* be granted a green card.

Individuals' knowledge of salient traditions, be they learned orally or textually, are critically important as individuals engage in Godtalk. Knowledges both Christian and Hindu circulated within these interviewees' worlds and helped them make sense of what they experienced and interpreted. Yet it must be emphasized that in naming the importance of these knowledges I do not suggest that received traditions or expectations account for individuals' experiences, much less explain them away. It is possible that received tradition helps provide the name or explanation of an experience. As such it offers the possibility of categorizing that experience as residing in a particular discursive history, and associating it with a particular form (Jesus, Parvati). What *is* important about immersion in a received tradition is that it provides a context in which to make Godtalk a commonsensical rather than nonsensical aspect of daily life.

## MIND EMBODIED

*spiritual practice and consciousness*

Embodiment is a fundamental, indeed definitional, aspect of humanness. As such, it is a critical site for spiritual experience and practice. It is also a centrally important location in relation to which to comprehend the formation of spiritual experience, whether spontaneous and episodic or more consciously cultivated. For the men and women I interviewed, the body may be understood to operate in three ways, distinct yet comparable with one another. In one the body is an activating force, capable of cognition in its own right. In a second mode, the body is very simply the site for actions and operations clearly beyond the control and at times even the comprehension of mind. As in the first mode, the body is the site for relatively autonomous cognitive activity. At times body and mind work together. To put this another way, cognition may be (re)conceived as taking place across interconnected pathways. In a third mode of bodily operation, the body is a crucial resource, a site that leads the mind to reassess itself, and/or provides the context in which the mind is reoriented, rerouted, and remade. These three modes were very often simultaneously or sequentially in play in individuals' lives and practice, although one or other predominated in given instances.

As one witnesses and assesses the role of the body in the cognitive processes of this group of people, it follows that the meaning and functioning of minds (at least in relationship to bodies) will also inevitably be engaged. The term *consciousness,* in its sense as the terrain of cognition, locatedness, and subjecthood, needs to be reexamined, given the kinds of bodily cognition the interviewees experienced. For in light of bodily cognition, the terms *mind* and *consciousness* can no longer be seen as coextensive in any simple way. However, despite the need to rethink its terrain, it is nonetheless true that the mind as storehouse of knowledges and discourses—that is, *mind* in the most old-fashioned sense in which we understand it—is necessarily engaged. For individuals draw on the mind in that sense as they seek to comprehend and work with what the body is doing. Thus it becomes possible to ask how minds and bodies in relation to one another, or embodied consciousnesses, work in spiritual practice.

Interviewees were often conscious of their emplacement within a hierarchy of ways of seeing. They at times represented their own practices by means of dominant discourses on religious practice, transcoding, that is to say translating between meaning systems, in conscious and unconscious ways. In addition, they described their experiences at times alongside or despite dominant discourses on the body and consciousness, at other times assertively in relation to or forcefully against these ways of naming spiritual practice and embodiment.

Rather than being able to present an existing theoretical framework within which to situate my analysis of questions of embodiment and consciousness, I strive to articulate elements of a theoretical frame emergent from the interview data and from my analysis of it. My hope is that these elements may contribute to a wider rethinking of relationships between body, mind, cognition, and practices both secular and sacred. Particular descriptions of particular bodies situate bodies (at least *some* bodies) as entities more forceful, more intelligent, more meaningful than is usually proposed. In these instances bodies provide the foundational a priori for minds' thinking *about* bodies and further, about minds, and selves also. Unusual as this might sound in the context of most contemporary work on bodies, these claims are, in fact, not entirely without precedent, either in the Western or Eastern Hemispheres.[1]

Key questions such as "What are bodies, personally and socioculturally?" "How does the construct, 'body,' connect with its consort construct, 'mind'?" and "What is done to, with, and by bodies?" are large ones, so large that indeed an effort to engage them is daunting. As William R. LaFleur puts it, "We humans cannot exist without representation, including that of the body itself. The number and variety of such representations are immense . . . To write it up would be impossible, a fact recognized when such a project reached 1,500 pages and ended by being titled 'fragments for' such a history. And even that enterprise was less a history of the body itself than of how bodies have been represented by the mind."[2] It is perhaps inevitable for one to be restricted to analyses of the body by the mind when one seeks to analyze bodies. However, I focus as much as possible on (1) depictions of the body and bodily activity and (2) bodily disruptions to, and contributions to, mental processes and practices.

One might note, with Bryan S. Turner, that "the first and rather obvious comment is that we cannot take 'the body' for granted. The body has many meanings in human practice, and can be conceptualized within a variety of dimensions and frameworks."[3] Turner proposes the following categorization of approaches to at least some of those frameworks:

> There are basically four views of the body in modern social theory. First, following Foucault the body is an effect of deeper structural arrangements of power and knowledge. Second, the body is a symbolic system which produces a set of metaphors by which power is conceptualized. Thirdly, the body can only be understood as a consequence of long term historical changes in human society . . . The fourth approach . . . is concerned to analyze the body in context of the lived experience of everyday life.[4]

In practice, these four approaches need to be viewed as interwoven rather than as separable from one another. In a similar vein, Nancy Scheper-Hughes and Margaret Lock, in their effort to develop a framework for critical medical anthropology, argue that one must engage with "three bodies." These are "the representational *body social;* the controlling bio-power forces of the *body politic;* and the not unrelated but self-conscious, more or less alienated, attribution of meanings to the individual and existential *body personal.*"[5]

In fact none of this tells one what the body is, so much as how it is constructed, how one might go about identifying it in a given setting. While all four of Turner's identified orientations to the body, and all of Scheper-Hughes and Lock's "three bodies," are important, the center of gravity in this chapter rests near Turner's fourth site and Scheper-Hughes and Lock's third one. For I am interested in how the men and women I discuss inhabited, worked with, and were, indeed, worked by and through, their bodies, in the arena of spiritual practice and religion. Here the body social and the body politic are of relevance, certainly. But both of these, as well as the body personal, are at all times in communication—and at times utterly disrupted—by yet a fourth body—one that by extension of Scheper-Hughes and Lock's terminology, would need to be called the *body spiritual*.

Medieval historian Caroline Bynum has argued that one must take seriously "dozens of discussions [in medieval texts] of both body (especially female body) as manifestation of the divine or demonic and of technical questions generated by the doctrine of the body's resurrection . . . as well as the mass of texts in which they spoke directly about the place of physicality in human nature and in the divine economy."[6] In relation to Bynum's work one could readily apply the analytical frames named by Turner, or those of Scheper-Hughes and Lock. It must be noted that Turner's effort here was primarily to map modes of analyzing bodies, and that Scheper-Hughes and Lock sought to revise and "customize" them for the development of analyses of health and ill-health. Yet that task is more delicate than it might appear at first sight. And indeed Bynum's essay is in part precisely designed as a corrective to some applications to the medieval period of the approaches Turner names. For, Bynum argues, contemporary concern about embodiment, gender, and sexuality "written backwards" on the medieval period has focused on what has endured forcefully into the present (sexuality, excoriation of women's bodies). But this has happened, she argues, at the expense of what is now marginal or all but forgotten, bodies connected in positive terms with the religious and the spiritual.[7] Perhaps even more important than a simple substantive correction process, however, is that as one reads Bynum's examination of medieval bodies and what she terms the "somatic miraculous," one sees in effect bodies unexpected and inexplicable by present-day standards.[8]

In a similar vein, while asking how Marcel Mauss's work on bodies might be of use in contemporary scholarship, Talal Asad discusses his own research into "medieval Christian monastic discipline":

> I deal there with how bodily attitudes are cultivated, but also with how sexuality (libido) was differently managed among Benedictines (who recruited children) and Cistercians (who recruited adults only) in the education of Christian virtues. In the one case this involved trying to direct the body's experience; in the other to reconvert the experienced body. My suggestion was that not only the force and direction of universal desire but desires themselves (specific Christian virtues) may be historically constituted.[9]

Asad draws here on the experience of given bodies in order to interrupt a sense of bodily universalism. To do so in the arena of sexual desire indeed challenges a kind of normativity deemed beyond disruption in post-Freudian U.S. culture. And as he does this work, an irony strikes the reader: even as poststructuralist scholarship asserts its commitment to anti-essentialist and anti-universalizing approaches, a brief detour into other or "Other" territory demonstrates the abiding normativities by means of which our scholarship often proceeds.[10]

One learns from all of this, moreover, that any specific substantive area of study will demand that theoretical and analytic frames be adopted but also that they may need to be revised. One detour from the contemporary normative, both analytical and substantive, is, then, that into a historical period far from one's own. But another is to take the risk of traveling far afield spatially, by means of what Sarah Coakley has called "'magpie' raids on Eastern religious bodily practice."[11] Coakley is correctly concerned about such excursions inasmuch as they often appear to serve "consumerism" or other kinds of "narcissistic quests." Yet there are several good reasons in the current project to engage—although more from an external than internal standpoint—approaches from traditions beyond those of the contemporary West. First, such materials are salutary as resources by means of which to defamiliarize the status quo. Second, a good number of interviewees included in this book, and indeed some of those focused on in this chapter, are long-standing practitioners of Eastern-originated religions. And lastly, some of what one can learn from, and about, Eastern paths is also applicable to Western practitioners of Western forms.

Yuasa Yasuo, in a comparative study of Eastern- and Western-based philosophical approaches to embodiment. demonstrates that there are indeed differences between them. For, he argues, the inseparability of "body-mind" has been presumed in the East for as long, indeed longer, than the struggle to reunite the pair has been an abiding issue in the West.[12] Yuasa points out that a specific relationship between body, mind, and the cultivation or training of both, are crucial in the greater part of Eastern philosophical thinking about body and mind. This has implications for how bodies are understood—as necessary to intellectual and spiritual growth rather than ancillary or irrelevant. It also has effects on the meaning of knowledge—making embodiment and the effort to know inseparable. As Yuasa puts it, "personal 'cultivation' (*shugyo*) is presupposed in the philosophical foundation of the Eastern theories. To put it simply, true knowledge cannot be obtained simply by means of theoretical thinking but only through bodily 'recognition' or 'realization' (*tainin* or *taitoku*), that is, through the utilization of one's total mind and body."[13]

It is all too easy to overwrite one's own location onto all other locations, thus to universalize local and contemporary, even epochal, depictions of embodiment and cognition where other interpretations might be needed if only as additions. Thomas P. Kasulis begins his *Self as Body in Asian Theory and Practice* by noting that both Eastern- and Western-originated individuals are aware that there are relationships between mind and body. As he wryly notes, "Many teachers of introductory Western philosophy courses could testify that a large proportion of a class period has to be spent on explaining the mind-body problem before the students will be ready to consider the various attempts at a solution of it." The issue is then, not whether there are relationships between mind and body (as it would be named in the West) or between/within body-mind (as more likely named in the East). Rather the issue is what those relationships are, and how constituted. And relatedly (something that is a historical question as much as a purely philosophical one) how certain ways of seeing and knowing have come to be marginalized while others are normative.[14]

My experience of life is very sentient being, very visceral. I register a lot of sensations, gut instincts, God whooshing over my head will turn my stomach. A lot of times something I pray is, "God if you want me to do this, either increase my desire or decrease it," and I feel the physical sensation happen.—PALOMA TAN, 28, Chinese American/European American, Twelve Step and extra-institutional spiritual practitioner, temporary office worker

PALOMA TAN EXEMPLIFIED the first of the three modes of bodily operation named above—that is, the body coming into play as a relatively autonomous presence capable of cognition. Paloma was born in 1969 and was twenty-eight years old when interviewed. She was born and raised in New Mexico, in an upper-middle-class family. Her father is a research chemist with a major corporation and her mother a "housewife" (Paloma's term). Paloma is biracial, with a Chinese immigrant father and a white mother. Paloma's spiritual practice was not based on anything provided for her by her family. Nonetheless, she asserted that there was an Americanness to her spirituality: "The basic thing that influences my sense of spirituality is the fact that I'm an American . . .

I'm not nationalistic at all. But the reason that—for me—[being American] shapes my sense of spirituality . . . is the sense of freedom that we have here, freedom of ideas. And as I get older . . . I [see] . . . how much that shapes my belief system . . . my desire to explore, and my lack of belief in rules, a lot of times." I would argue that Paloma is both right and wrong in this depiction of Americanness and spirituality (one that she made in common with a good number of interviewees). On one hand, the notion that the United States offers its subjects freedom of ideas is questionable. On the other hand, Paloma's access to a degree of autonomy from natal family and community, as well as the multicultural and multifaith character of the parts of the United States where Paloma has lived have, perhaps, given her access to a diverse range of spiritual paths.

Ironically, Paloma also emphasized the Americanness of what she called her "spiritual disease," eating disorders. As she put it, "I think that that experience is very contextual, of the late twentieth-century American girl." Eating disorders had shaped her life since she was around six years old. At the time of the interview, Paloma continued to grapple with eating issues in part through a Twelve Step program, Overeaters Anonymous (OA), and in part through about a year of work, terminated just before the interview, with a spiritual counselor unaffiliated to any particular tradition.

Paloma defined *spirituality* as "the practice of my relationship with what I believe is the force that is all things. And I use the terms *God, universe,* and *life* to all mean the same thing, and to identify that force." This conception of spirituality is a priori in two senses. First, it is not "provable" in terms external to itself. Second, it founded and made comprehensible all else about Paloma's relationship with God. But as an a priori conception, it had a history that, when asked, Paloma contextualized in terms of three separate knowledge streams. I asked, "How did you get to that place, that sentence that you just said? Where did that come from for you?" Paloma responded:

> It's something that's been developing slowly, over the past seven to nine years. That specific sentence I just said is what I've come to believe in the past year. I might be simplifying it a little bit, but this is the best I can answer right now. I think it's a combination of—I worked with a spiritual guide person, for lack of a better term, until a few months ago. That was the conception of life that he presented to me. And I found it to be true—thinking back on experiences that I

had, that was like a conversation that I was having with life. And, I think, being in a Twelve Step program and dealing with spiritual principles rather than a specific religion . . .

Paloma positioned her definition, then, in a framework of knowledges prior to and after experience. She accepted the conception offered to her by her spiritual teacher but not without also testing it by means of "thinking back on experiences" that she has had. The other conceptual frame in relation to which Paloma "cross-checked" her teacher or guide's depiction of spirituality was that of the Twelve Step movement: Twelve Step, among other things, proposed that she characterize eating disorders as "my spiritual disease." It also offered Paloma a relatively nonsectarian framework of belief, one founded also in the dense inter- weaving of empirical personal experience with a rigorous set of spir- itual practices. Like others interviewed here, though, Paloma's own practice and her empirical experience both far exceeded the frames offered her from outside herself, and indeed made it possible for her to craft her own mode of spiritual practice.

Something that Paloma did not mention as she defined *spirituality* was that her body and bodily experiences had figured as a crucial, relatively autonomous resource throughout the period of life that she described to me. This is the third strand around which her practice was articulated. At a key moment the body literally stepped around the thinking mind in order to draw attention to itself as in struggle. In that moment the body inaugurated, one might argue, a more conscious conversation with "God, the universe, and life." Later, the body became a different kind of cognitive processor, one that could communicate with the divine.

Paloma's sense of God, universe, and life may be historicized in several ways. First, she explicitly names the context for *her* relationship to these. Second, she names that relationship as something that has *developed* rather than something that was always there. And one must also note the externality of origin of her vision of God—it is something that "has developed," not something that *she* has developed.

It is striking that the two external contributory streams to her spir- itual path were nameable to very different degrees. On one hand, she lacked a proper name for her "spiritual guide person," calling him that, as she says, "for lack of a better term." This illustrates clearly the ab- sence of "proper names" for large numbers of spiritual practitioners in the contemporary United States, something I frequently encountered through this project. On the other hand, Paloma had ready access to the name of a well-known institutional framework when she positioned her conception of spirituality within Overeaters Anonymous and other Twelve Step programs. Within this statement were indeed the traces of another history: the transformation of the Twelve Step movement from a primarily patriarchal and Christian-focused one into one that has over time been increasingly syncretized and feminized by groups and individuals.

As noted above, Paloma named disordered eating as her "spiritual disease." When asked about this, Paloma elaborated as follows:

> PALOMA  Obviously I don't have any scientific study to back this up, but I guess [that] I'm all one thing. Like, my physical body and my spirit and my emotions and my mind is all one thing as I walk around. And so, if I have a physical malady, to me it's an expression of the entire organism. And so the eating disorder is no different.
>
> RF  Okay, yeah. So, the body is commenting on what's going on—the physical body is responding to what's going on in the emotional or the psychological or the material?
>
> PALOMA  It's responding to it and it's expressing it. And it's also—I also believe it's trying to heal me.
>
> RF  Um, okay. How does it try to heal you?
>
> PALOMA  Well, I don't know a lot about it. I read a book on homeopathy recently, and I believe that the symptoms that the body produces is its own way of trying to bring me back towards health . . . The physical symptom is bringing your whole being into health. Because it's some other part of your being that's participating in the situation that's toxic, and the physical symptom brings you out of that, because it will be generated if you reside there . . . [If] the symptoms [get] bad enough [they will make] me choose healing for the whole being.

Here, Paloma offers a reading of the body both *in* consciousness and *as* consciousness. This linking of body with mind is very different from that conventionally associated with late-twentieth-century Western rationality, although it is becoming increasingly familiar in the contemporary United States. The phrases *I guess* and *this is just my own belief* signal the a priori status of the conception that orders her further comments, although they overstate her individuality in this regard.

At several points Paloma compares and contrasts her rationality and method of knowing with others: "I haven't read up on this"; "I don't have scientific study to back this up," and then her suggestion that her "belief" parallels homeopathic theory. Paloma specifies her interpretive framework *and* its substantive and methodological relationship to other paradigms, as well as gesturing toward her awareness of how knowledge-systems are ranked in the contemporary United States. But in any event, Paloma proposes a holistic image of the body, and offers a clear analysis of the relationship between symptom and, in her words, "the whole being."

Paloma said that (1) the bodily symptom leads the way to a healing of the whole being and that (2) in looking back over past experience she is able to confirm her present understanding of God. An event that brought these two ideas together took place many years prior to the interview, when Paloma was an undergraduate and severely ill with bulimia, undiagnosed as such at the time:

> I was sitting . . . this is February 1989, and I was sitting in the student union building at UNM [the University of New Mexico]. I was waiting for my class to start and I was sitting there writing in a notebook, 'Help! Help! Help!' over and over and over. I looked down at the paper and I was like 'Whoa!' So I knew I had an eating disorder, so it was like, well, I can go there for help. It was like an excuse to get help.

Here, Paloma further articulates a conception of the relationship(s) between mind and body. One sees, to begin with, separation and dialogue between different aspects of the self. Paloma writes "Help!" and then looks at her writing and is shocked and surprised. One wonders who, so to speak, was writing, and who was noticing the written text. Was the body writing? Was the mind seeing? Is the mind multileveled? Does the body have a "mind" that talks to another part of the mind? The notion that "I'm all one thing" is developed here into a multifaceted, complex intelligence.

As Paloma explained to me (now many years into her journey with eating disorders and spiritual practice) she conceives her eating disorder as a symptom that provided her with a means for healing "the whole organism." She also views it as a "symptom" that began her spiritual journey. Like many participants in Twelve Step whom I interviewed, Paloma did not view OA and other Twelve Step programs as sites for identification with the "disease," whether addiction to food practices, alcohol, or narcotics. Rather these were seen to be powerful contexts for spiritual work. As Paloma put it, "that program is designed to help me get out of the way so that I can pursue a spiritual path."

One might argue here that the body "initiated" Paloma onto a spiritual path by means of putting into language ("Help!") her physical distress as well as manifesting the symptoms that signaled that distress. Here one can argue that the body is both source of knowledge and site of cognitive processing. For the body is more, here, than the site of phenomenal data, undigested and unordered. Rather, in ways that are not yet fully clear, body seems to be a site of agency and intelligence.

I will not detail here Paloma's first meditation experiences with a support group at UNM for women with eating disorders, nor her long-standing, ongoing work with OA and brief but intense and focused work with an extra-institutional spiritual teacher. But the body was not finished with the role of agent and communicator after sending out the "distress signal." For as Paloma told me, her body continued to be a key player in her spiritual life long after she had "gone there" for help and became well established in a journey of self-inquiry and recovery from bulimia. Speaking about her current spiritual practice, Paloma described the crucial role of prayer in her life: "Pray is the first thing I do when I'm conscious. It's the last thing I do before I let go of my mind. I pray in the bathroom at work, several times a day, I pray in the bus. I pray when I'm standing still . . . Prayer is my half of honest interaction with that which created me. So a lot of times that involves breathing, too, because it gets me into my physical body . . . And I feel the physical sensation happen." When Paloma described the physicality of her communication with God, perhaps because of its uniqueness, it was difficult for me to grasp. When I asked for clarification of the process that she had spoken about, Paloma further described the experience:

PALOMA  The physical sensation? God shakes my head and then the "no" happens.
RF  And that's like an energy drop? [Here I'm reading her body language.]
PALOMA  Um hum (i.e., "yes").
RF  If you say to God, "Okay, now reduce my desire for this"—
PALOMA  [Interrupting me] "If it is your will for me to do this, increase my desire. If it is your will for me not to, then decrease it." And there's like a physical—it's like, almost—if it's decreased, almost like my stomach turns, but it's not quite that exaggerated. If it's increased, there's like a lightness and a sense of moving forward. And sometimes I don't get a message, because I'm not ready to hear. Sometimes that is the message.

It is important to notice in passing Paloma's correction of my description of what she is doing. When I suggest that she asks God to "reduce her desire," she reminds me that actually she is asking to be guided toward, as it were, *God's* desire. This in turn reflected another key moment in Paloma's spiritual journey, when she realized that "basically I was saying to God, 'This is what I want,' and I didn't ask, 'What do you want from me?' And that's a different choice. So then I went 'Shit!' And then, so I chose. You know, I chose what life wants from me." But whether or not Paloma is asking God to meet her desires or, more accurately, asking to be shown the will of God, one sees in Paloma's description the enactment of a particular relationship between body, mind, and an entity named "God/universe/life." Here, the body is a critical intermediary between the second term, *mind*, and the third term, *God/universe/life*. While of course much everyday language conjures a relationship between body and mind—"my heart sank" or "leapt," "I had a gut feeling"—here we are introduced to a different, or perhaps just more precise, bodily conversation. In it, God is present, body and mind have developed their own means of communication, and mind is the interpreter of the body's message. In this description, particular sensations are associated with straightforward yes/no or do/don't directives. The process of body-centered communication was only one part of what Paloma called the "conversation that I was having with life" (and it should be remembered that for Paloma, *life* also means *God*). One may note also how for Paloma breathing—that very fundamental aspect of embodiment most often practiced without conscious attention—is here a consciously deployed aspect of Paloma's capacity to commune with that which she deems divine.

Moreover, the body worked in at least two ways, not just by means of physical sensation but also by means of that which one might call inner audition. And the content of what the mind learned via the body was, strikingly, not always predictable nor what its recipient might have desired. Thus Paloma told me about the arrival of her current partner, Alejandro, in her life. This was, she said, an instance when "God told me to do something which was out of my realm of what I conceive of as being right for me." This despite the fact that, she emphasized: "I have a pretty clear channel. You know, it can get muddled [but] I can clear it out and I can hear pretty well, and so I know what it sounds like. And I was like, 'What?' " Paloma said it happened like this:

> I was taking salsa dancing lessons. And this guy started asking me to dance all the time. This guy, who is six inches shorter than I am, Mexican, dark, and at the time barely spoke English. He's a little rough-looking. He's stocky. He looks—and this is my own prejudice

coming out—he didn't look well-educated. Not that I would know . . . He kept asking me out. And I kept saying no, because it just didn't fit my picture at all. I usually date tall, white, well-educated men who get mistaken easily for being gay, and who are well-dressed. And are slender. So finally one night I walked out in the parking lot and he had just asked me out for how many times, and God said to me, "Why don't you go out with him?" . . . And I said, "What? Are you kidding me?" And God said, "Why don't you go out with him?" I said, "No, I don't think so. I don't know." And so I stood in the parking lot for a while and hemmed and hawed, and almost went back in, and could not bring myself to do it. And went home, prayed about it . . . The next time I saw him and he asked me out, I said, "Yes." So we went out, and of course, I'm in this "I'm up here and he's down here" thing. What can this person possibly give me, right? So we go out and I had a great time. We could barely talk to each other. I speak a lot more Spanish now, he speaks more English now.

The body thus becomes the site for a complex set of awarenesses and methodologies. It is clear, above all, that for Paloma there is a separation between, on one side, the one who hears, and, on the other side, that which is heard and understood to be what God/universe/life wants to accomplish. Yet in order to name the relationship between Paloma as narrating subject and that which is heard, one needs to skillfully parse out subjects and objects, while containing all of them within the same bodily boundaries. The statements, "I *have* a pretty clear channel . . . *It* can get muddled [but] *I* can clear it out" (emphasis added) is rather like the sentence, "I have near-perfect pitch." It suggests that there is a subject or owner who is the guardian or perhaps possessor of a particular capacity. But the "it" that gets "muddled" refers not to an "Other" who gets muddled, just as a singer who falls flat or sharp does not call into doubt the nature of the notes themselves. Rather, "it" is there to be grasped in its exactness—the hearer knows what it "sounds like" and therefore knows when it is accurately articulated.

What, then, might one claim at this point about the body *in* consciousness and *as* consciousness? In general terms, one can, by means of engagement with this interviewee, begin to identify some of the methodologies of the body associated with spiritual practice. First, the body is present as a relatively autonomous site. Second, in recognition of some kind of mind-body separation, there is a narrating consciousness able to witness the body's actions. The hand writing "Help!" for example, is separable from the voice that, years later, tells me the story.

Third, the body does far more than obey what one might deem the mind. Thus it is mind that answers the call of the body to seek help for an eating disorder. Fourth, here we see body as an agent. Fifth, there is actually a coordination of effort between mind and body in Paloma's life experience, one that, as her life unfolds, is increasingly multi-layered. Thus, in the student union incident, mind responds to the call of body for help. And Paloma's mind later interprets that distress call as the signal to inaugurate a larger healing of "the whole being." And we should notice that body's cry is far different from a simple "call of nature." For here body is using one of mind's tools—writing—rather than merely manifesting physical pain or even crying out nonlinguistically. Of course, even the clichéd "call of nature" is in reality a call of culture, therefore signaling the inevitable, ongoing dialogue between the encultured mind and the encultured body.

One witnesses in Paloma's story a rearticulation of the relationship between mind as intelligence and body as intelligence. One sees, too, a remaking of the terms of enculturation. For Paloma connects all of this with a sense of self as "all one thing." And in her description of more recent experience, Paloma names her body as a dependable conveyer of information from God/universe/life. But one also sees as agent something external to both mind and body: in this instance God/universe/life, or that which uses or works with the body for purposes of communication. And we see again the relationship between agency and surrender as the body and mind are drawn into the cultivation of spontaneity and practice.

⁂

PALOMA'S EXPERIENCE was a singular one. But she was by no means the only interviewee for whom the conscious, self-knowing mind was sidestepped or challenged by the emergence of alternate ways of knowing. Avram Davis, 46, is heterosexual, the father of two young daughters, and the founder of Chochmat HaLev Center for the Study and Practice of Jewish Meditation. Avram Davis might on one level be seen, like Paloma, to have experienced the body as a relatively autonomous force. But his experiences also signal the second and third dimensions of bodily action that were named above—the body as site for events beyond the control or comprehension of the mind, and the body as a crucial resource that leads mind toward reassessment, reorientation, and revision. Avram said, "As a teenager, I spent a lot of time by myself, in nature. And I had very strong experiences—*enlightenment* is too big a word, *illumination* experiences is a better word, where I felt very closely, very much inside, the presence of the divine. That moved me in a very, very deep and profound way as a young boy."

It is important to note here Avram's grammar and choice of words. *I had very strong experiences, I felt,* and *that moved me* signal a clear experience—something happened. Moreover this "something" was forceful: Avram uses the word *very* repeatedly here, together with *strong, closely, deep,* and *profound.* In the way Avram tells this story it is evident that he does not view himself as the author but rather the recipient of what occurred. But who or what the author might be and from whence that author arrived is less self-evident. Avram is clear that this experience must be named as "the presence of the divine." But the divine might be singular or plural, perhaps more a force or state of being than an individual entity. Also the journey from inside to outside is less clearly accounted for: Avram feels the divine "very much inside." He has no means of naming how that presence arrived within him, yet it is clear that this presence was not generated by Avram but arrived from without. And lastly, one must reiterate that the experience was neither the product nor in the control of the self-knowing mind.

When I asked for clarification, Avram said:

> In terms of the experience itself, the strongest was probably when I was thirteen. It was not like choirs of angels. It was more me being in a place in nature and feeling a place of great light, hearing many, many voices. [They were] not stern voices and not saccharine sweet voices, but really just more voices of great compassion, great love, advising me to study more within the tradition, to relax a little bit, to open. And with that auditory vision also came great physical or somatic feelings, which at the time when I tried to write about it or speak about it, I described as being soaked in honey. It felt like I was inside and outside soaked in honey. Which, you know, if you think about [it] now is kind of faintly disgusting, but the way that I felt about it at that point, [that] was as close as I could come to it.

Enlightenment, illumination, light, choirs of angels, voices neither saccharine sweet nor stern, compassion, love, honey: Avram's description offers (in order to assess, sort through, and select from them) a range of images of the presence or experience that he is striving to describe to me. For the most part these namings emerge from the Judeo-Christian world, not surprising given that Avram was raised in Judaism and is even more deeply rooted in that tradition as an adult. But in this careful sorting process, Avram rejects some terms as too strong—*enlightenment, choirs of angels*—and notes that others may slide toward the clichéd—*choirs of angels* again and also *saccharine sweet* voices. In the end he does settle on very particular language choices. *Illumination* rather than *enlightenment,* he proposes, names most effectively the level of learning that he was offered by the experience. *Compassion* and *great love,* he says, best characterize the emotional temperature of the voices and their message. But at times he needs to comment further on the paucity of language to explain what happened. Thus *soaked in honey* sounds, he notes, "faintly disgusting" but is still the best turn of phrase available to him. And to categorize the multifaceted nature of the event he resorts to what one might call a compound neologism, *auditory vision.*

Once again, then, the mind as "master of all it surveys" is hardly in control of the event. But the mind is very much in play as Avram seeks to clarify to an outsider and possibly for himself, too, the meaning of this moment in his past. Yet even thirty years on and as an adult now in a leadership role as a spiritual teacher, Avram cannot find language with which to fully convey what happened to him on that day. And this underscores the inadequacy of the speaking subject alone to articulate and account for this experience.

The voices Avram heard, he said, had encouraged him to study the tradition more closely—Avram does not say so, but context makes clear that the tradition in question is that of Judaism. It is noteworthy in this regard that the teaching from that day is still significant to Avram. He said, "The innocence of that kind of experience has not repeated itself very much past that era, but what has gone deeper are psychological clarities and psychological dropping away moments. And those have been very instrumental in continuing to move me along a spiritual endeavor and a spiritual teaching path." Avram explained that "psychological dropping away moments" are again not "high falutin'" but rather moments that may occur either in meditation, prayer, *or* when one is stuck in gridlock traffic: "quite cliché things, but where the cliché becomes realized for a moment [or even longer]." He added that it's "a kind of 'What the hell?' or 'It don't mean a thing if it ain't got that swing.' Clichés that we learn from movies. We know them to be true—"Dancing in the rain"—but it is much harder to realize them in ourselves . . . And on that level, very few of the sages say different things. I mean, they all say more or less the same thing on that simple level."

As Avram grapples with the task of transcoding that which continues to move him, he is caught between, one might say, that which is conventionally labeled *popular* and that which is conventionally labeled *sublime,* juxtaposing, as it were, "sages" of popular music and cinema with those of earlier times. But as he points out, commonplace and even comparable as the utterances of the religious and cinematic "wise men" might be, they are very difficult to realize and to live by. Thus, the notion of a "dropping away." For Avram proposes that what drops away is the dailiness of one's self and perhaps of one's sociocultural identity, in exchange for a recognition of "our deeper selves, our essence selves . . . There are times I have, and we all have, fallen through that, uh, hole, that place, and then we're in that place. So that's really what I mean by more psychological, rather than lights, and lightning bolts, and voices from heaven. It's just more of a realization space." Language gives way once again as Avram describes that "realization space." As he repeatedly rejects images he deems both clichéd and reductive, "lights," "lightning bolts," "voices from heaven," he is left with two options: recourse to the "psychology" of one's essence or recourse to tautology—"we fall through that place, and then we're in that place." But what remains is his sense of the criticality of going to "that place" and the possibility of many rather than few individuals journeying there.

❧

MISHA I'm very, very strong in dreams. Any event in the world that happens, exactly one day before that, or a week before that, symbolically I have a dream. My spirituality started with dreams.
RF Maybe you can give me an example?
MISHA I have a lot of examples. My mother's death. I'll tell you. My mother was in United States, I was in Persia at that time. I dreamed that I'm sitting on a carpet in my room and all of a sudden I saw my mother open the door. And she stayed exactly under the door. She didn't come in. And I was so happy, I told her, in my language, "Mom, come in. Why do you stay there?" She said, "No son, I cannot come in. I have to go." I said, "Mom, you just came. I want to see you. I didn't see you for a while. Please come here, I want to talk to you." And she said, "No son, you cannot talk to me. I have to go." And I just got up and I went to take her in, and all of a sudden she shut the door and I start screaming and beating on the door. I said, "Mom, come on, I want to see you." And her voice just faded little by little, little by little, little by little. And all of a sudden I woke up with tears on my face

and on my pillowcase. The bishop that we had here, he called me. He said, "Misha, your mother passed away." The same night. The same night. *(Misha Ashoorian, interview)*

PALOMA TAN's body took the lead in initiating a journey toward health and also toward a spiritual practice. Later the body was a crucial resource as her spiritual journey continued. She did, as we have seen, engage with the philosophical and analytical questions raised by her practice and by the part her body played in it. Yet there was no question that the body remained for her a site that must be understood, indeed honored and depended on, as a significant resource in its own right. Avram Davis's "illumination experiences" and more recent times of "psychological dropping away" did not arrive in crisis. Rather, the early experience offered him direction for his coming adulthood, and the later experiences helped him to stay on that path. But what Paloma Tan and Avram Davis have in common is that their bodies proffered experience, information, and, one might argue, kinds of wisdom that were not forthcoming from their minds, prior to particular bodily experiences.

Misha Ashoorian's process was at once different from and similar to these individuals' journeys. Misha was sixty-nine years old at the time of the interview. He is an Assyrian Christian by ethnicity and by religion. He remains active in his ethnic group as a folk song lyricist. Misha is an accountant in semiretirement. Married and the father of two grown children, he was born in the country that he consistently called Persia, known today as Iran. He and his wife and children came to the United States in 1980, as he put it, "After [the] revolution, when those religious people took over and shove us out of Persia, Iran."

Most significant in Misha's view of his own spiritual journey is that from early childhood on he has lived with the capacity for prophetic dreaming. Although even as a child he was well aware that his experience was "other" than that deemed ordinary for most people around him, he seemed not to need, as a youngster, to "explain himself to himself." Misha's dreaming was not taken as a symptom of something amiss with him, as was true for Paloma. Because of the longevity of his dreaming experience, there was no sense of "a prior worldview" interrupted by prophetic dreaming. As he said, "At eleven years, I started spirituality. If you want, I—let me tell you." He said, "In the beginning, I was so very confident and very happy. Sometimes it made me cry. It made me cry when my dreams were coming. But now I'm used to it. Because I know the nature of how it happens. Now when I see things happening, I don't care. Not I don't care, it doesn't excite me like before." Misha remarked that often, then and now, friends teased him and "demanded" dreams about themselves, and that his wife (sometimes and unsuccessfully) sought to convince him that if he would only forget about particular dreams, they would not "come true."

Yet as an adult Misha *did* strive to understand the phenomenon of prophetic dreaming. As he said, "I participate in so many seminars and classes. I really wanted to search, to see, what's all about spirituality. Probably at home I have six hundred books—good books, not bad books—about philosophy, meditation, Sufism, Hinduism, astrology, astronomy . . . Sometimes I ask myself, 'Where these dreams come from? How they can inform me? What kind of force is that, that gives me exactly the things that are going to happen next day?' " Misha's research had led him toward a means to answer these questions. For him the capacity for prophetic dreaming might be understood in the context of three ideas. The first of these is, as he put it, "a formless essence or universal consciousness that we call God." The second, he said, is a phenomenal world that is fully interconnected because of that "universal consciousness." Third, Misha said, "If you have an open mind, or if you have—not trained yourself—[but] if there are those elements in you [and] you are open to those types of energy, it's just like broadcast and receiver. [Like] TV, they send all the things and you can see them on your TV. It's very difficult to describe but I know that this is happening in this way." What did it mean, though, to be that "TV"? How might one be open to "those types of energy"?

Like Avram, Misha struggled at times to find clear language—"it's very difficult to describe." And like Paloma, he was committed to telling me his sources. He cited a teacher whom he felt would prefer not to be named, with whom he had studied theory and philosophy of religion and spirituality. This was not, it should be noted, training in spiritual practice, and took place in the United States well into Misha's middle age and senior years. Particular texts studied with this teacher helped Misha place prior experiences in context. This work thus helped explain Misha to himself rather than enhancing or altering his skills. Again in a similar vein to Avram and Paloma, bodily and cognitive experiences, in this case the dreams, were the a priori.

But although helpful to him personally ("I really wanted to search, to see"), externally available apparatuses seemed—even more than the dreams themselves—to signal Misha's own sense of alterity, at times endangerment or fear of being misunderstood. Thus as I encouraged him to share that learning process with me he resisted, saying, "Sometimes, to be honest with you, I don't dare to tell everything I know. Because sometimes people immediately put a label on you that you are this and that, especially these days." I asked, " 'This and that' meaning they think you're a very special person? Or maybe they'll think you're crazy?" He affirmed, "Crazy. Mostly crazy." As he shared with me the conclusions he had reached about how prophetic dreaming was possible, he repeatedly admonished, "Don't get me wrong," "Don't misunderstand me," and even, regarding the ever-present spirit guide in his dreams, a Sufi master, "I don't want to be very fanatic." Here the sociogenerational differences between Misha on one side and Avram and Paloma on the other come to the fore. The two younger individuals, clearly marked both by a post-1960s sense of what one might call "spiritual permissiveness" and as well, perhaps, by their nonimmigrant status, felt far more comfortable to explore, to experiment with language and theory about their practice, and to name those activities. (Returning here for one moment to the "three bodies" listed by Nancy Scheper-Hughes and Margaret Lock, one can see the interplay of changing *bodies social* and *bodies politic,* and their complex and at times discordant relationships with the *body personal* as well as with my own addition, the *body spiritual.*)

However, Misha's depictions of actual dreaming and of dream interpretation were an entirely different matter, less a site of anguish or discordance. For there, it seemed, Misha's ability to name and explain the process of dreaming and interpretation was unhindered by concern about what I might think. And while it was still clear to him that he was living within a conceptual hierarchy he was also emphatic that it was fully possible to empirically demonstrate the veracity of his experience and practice.

I asked Misha, "Do you remember how [it] began, or when it began?" He replied that at ten or eleven years old he began to see, prophetically, his grades in school. He explained,

> [Grading] in Persia is not like the United States. It goes from one to twenty. So twenty is excellent. Ten is not that good. If somebody gets less than ten, it means he has not passed the test and has not passed the class. So, I was a kid, around ten years, twelve years. When I was doing their test, I didn't know how many mistakes I had. I was not scared, but I was so [eager] not to make my mother sad, because I loved my mother. She had only one child and she gave really her life to me. I mean, she spent all her money just to make me to go to school . . . I didn't know anything about meditation. I was sitting like

this and closing my eyes, and I said, "God, help me. I want to see what number I will get" . . . Or sometimes [at night] I was concentrating and I fell asleep, [and] when I was falling asleep, I would see symbolically something.

He offered an example of this:

I dreamed that I was in an elevator. All of a sudden the door opened and I saw a number thirteen, the thirteenth floor. But then I woke up and I said, "What's thirteen?" I said, "Oh, God, I was asking for a number." For that lesson, I got thirteen. Honestly. Honestly. The next day I went to the school and the teacher said, "Misha, this time you didn't do good. Your number is thirteen." And I was crying. He said, "Don't cry. Thirteen's not bad. You have passed the class, but it's not [a] good number." But I didn't dare to tell him that I dreamt that this is thirteen, see? And I will tell you hundred of this stuff. It happens exactly, exactly that.

As Misha looks back he is able to speak from the purview of an adult—"I didn't know anything about meditation"—and emphasize the spontaneity and noncultivatedness of the process of sitting, concentrating, and praying, or alternatively concentrating, sleeping, and dreaming. He added that from his study of dreaming as an adult, he has learned that, in particular, prophetic dreams happen after midnight, and also that his dreams can and should only be understood in symbolic rather than literal terms. Be all of this as it may he was at the time and now remains conscious of the reason that he sought information: his concern about disappointing his mother. One notices, too, that he "dared not" tell his schoolteacher about his dream: even at ten or twelve it was clear to Misha that prophetic dreaming was not "usual" and therefore not something to be readily shared with another. And lastly Misha's repeated affirmations—"Honestly. Honestly," "I will tell you hundred of this stuff. It happens exactly [like] that"—underscore his recognition that as in his childhood schoolroom, here in the contemporary United States the information that he is offering me is atypical and therefore may not be believed.

While Misha did not tell me a "hundred of this stuff," it is well worth revisiting some of the dreams that he shared with me. Explicating the multiple symbolic fluencies on which Misha, and Misha's dreams, draw as they are experienced by him, it becomes possible to begin to ask how prophetic dreams "work." Already one sees that the body seems somehow to be involved as an instigator here, moving Misha from concentration to sleep and thence to an image relevant to what he was seeking at the start of the concentration process. And the mind is also involved, setting the agenda, in this instance that of learning what Misha's grades might be. As an adult Misha's bodily and mental process of preparation for dreaming simply formalized that with which he had begun: morning and evening meditation, not necessarily to receive answers to particular questions but rather to, so to speak, make way for any prophetic dream that might be forthcoming. For of course Misha had not requested a dream about his mother's death, nor on any of the topics that will be described below. Yet when Misha did seek to dream on a particular topic, he prepared for this with more meditations. And in any event, as he explained, he always kept a notepad at his bedside to record a few words about particular dreams. What was at first spontaneous is now cultivated—yet, as should be clear, what is being cultivated here, in the body via the mind's intention, is really only the space for further spontaneous experience.

One dream that might be particularly meaningful to many, including those who were resident in the United States in the early 1990s, took place at the start of the United States's military engagement with Iraq, named "Desert Storm" by the U.S. administration. Misha said about this:

> I saw—I was walking with a master. He was a Sufi. You know, because I know a lot about Sufism . . . [As] a kid, I used to go to their temple, sitting and reciting, repeating their mantra, even [though] I was a Christian . . . I was with one of them, walking. I saw thousands and thousands of doves dead in the desert, on the walls, in the buildings. And I was taking this body of the doves and crying and asking this master. I said, "Why all these doves dead here and there and all over this place?" He just looked into my eyes and he said, "When you wake up, you will see the reason was because the wind blew from the west." Can you believe that? From the west. I mean, the United States is a Western country, right? And when I woke up—I used to do some accounting [for a tire company]. And I was just doing my things and all of a sudden my son called me and he said, "Are you watching TV?" I said, "No son, what's—" He said, "Now United States attacked, and fight between Iraq and United States," where we saw that all these thousands of people were killed.

Paramount as one examines Misha's succinct summary of his dream is the recognition that for him the waking and sleeping worlds are not firmly bounded. Rather, they are spaces between which transfers can easily be made. This becomes clear as Misha tells me not only what happened in the dream and after waking, but also how he interpreted it. Thus Misha has not finished with his description of the dream until after the point when his son informs him that the bombing of Iraq was reported on TV. And in order to make clear to me, his listener, what has transpired, he transcodes, telling me something about why events happened like this within the dream and outside it, in terms of their content and symbolism. Lastly, he lets me know how he learned that his dream was accurate, so that I will understand that it is, indeed, no simple dream, but rather a prophetic one.

The words, *I saw, I was walking, I said [to the master], He said [to me]*, and lastly *I was doing my things* and *My son said* position Misha on equal terms in two worlds. One is the time/space of the dream. The other is what the popular spiritual teacher Ram Dass once memorably described as "zip code." It should be noted that Misha does not bother to explain to me that there are two separate times and spaces at issue here. He does not, for example, say, "I dreamed that I was walking with a master," but rather just "I was walking with a master." But it should also be noted that, in the dream, there are signals that this time/space is a dream, is separate from Misha's waking life although connected to it. For within the dream, the Sufi master says, "When you wake up, you will see the reason . . ." The dream, in other words, signals its status *as* a dream, as well as its authoritative relationship with the world into which Misha, in the dream, knows that he will wake up.

The context for the crafting of the dream is a straightforward one: Misha is with a Sufi master because he is familiar with Sufism from yet a third time/space, that of his childhood in Iran. He is in the desert because the country and the events about which (it turns out) he is dreaming are situated in a climatic desert. The presence of dead doves must be taken, I suggest, to stand for the death of peace and the onset of war, with the dove a peace symbol whose salience is now nearly universal.[15] The immediate locale of Misha's work as translator and interpreter is made clear in his presumption that he need not add much by way of explanation of "the wind blowing from the west." Here, Misha assumes that the United States's position, geographically and geopolitically, in the context of this dream and this war, will not be lost on me.

In Misha's recounting of these events the transition from dreaming time/space to waking time/space is achieved by means of his conversation with his son, who in turn tells him what has been presented on TV. TV and the dream are then equivalent sites of truth. Both tell Misha that the United States has declared war on Iraq. But the news on television authorizes the news in the dream, rather than vice versa. And Misha's remark to me in the middle of his dream narrative, "Can you believe that?" underscores the hierarchy of knowledges in which Misha knows himself to live.

One could, of course, assert that, in any case most news-watchers in the United States were fully aware in the fall of 1990 that the United States was about to bombard Iraq. This might thus raise the question of whether Misha's dream was a prophetic one or rather merely an anxious dream that turned out to be on the mark. Likewise, one may argue that "everyone knows" that the San Francisco Bay Area is an earthquake ridden one and that therefore to be living in the San Francisco Bay Area and have a dream about an earthquake is nothing special. However, another dream that Misha described to me was, arguably, far too close to an actual, severe earthquake to be dismissed as only coincidental. As before, Misha begins his story with a protestation:

> Honest to God. I dream about the earthquake of '89 in San Francisco, okay? That I dreamt. I was in the desert that day. I saw million[s] of dragon[s] flying in the sky. And I was so amazed. I said "My goodness. Dragons cannot fly. What kind of dragon are that?" . . . In those days most of the time I had lucid dreams. Do you know what lucid dreams are? You are dreaming but you know you are dreaming. That's a lucid dream. It's very difficult to dream lucid dreams. Anyway, I have many, many book[s] to interpret, and I have a lot of friends that we work together with dreams. We went to the books and we saw that they say that "Misha, dragon is the symbol of energy. Flying dragons a kind of flowing energies." And the same day that I dreamt, I went to visit a friend of mine in hospital. He had cancer in his stomach. Twenty days—every day I went to visit him. The day that I had that dream, I went to him, I talked to him. I didn't even remember what dream I had. When I was coming out of the hospital, I said, "My goodness, if one day an earthquake happened, what these people will do with these patients? How can they save [them]?" And just like a crazy guy, I was just looking all around like this and that—how they wheel the bed out and, honest to God, I didn't go to the elevator. I went to the stair door and I opened the stair door and I said, "Let me see, if they bring the beds, can they take all these beds from people down?" And [only after] I did that, I went to the elevator. I went down and got in my car. After four minutes I was home. I took my jacket off and then it started. [*Makes noise like shaking*] Just imagine. The same night I had dreamed the dream of moving dragon, which is the moving of energy,

all right? And for twenty days I went to visit my friend in hospital. I never thought about earthquake. Why the same day? And the same day, not twenty minutes even, probably ten minutes or fifteen minutes before the earthquake started, I asked myself, "If earthquake comes, what will happen to these people?" You know, things like that I have a million of these things. Million.

Here, as before, Misha is at pains to point out to me the ways in which what happened in the time/space of the dream and what happened in his waking hours are multiply connectable with one another. The concept of multiply mediated events pointing in the same direction is useful here. So is that of synchronicity. Thus Misha emphasizes that it was on the very day—indeed within ten or twenty minutes—of a major earthquake that he suddenly panicked about what would happen to hospital patients in the case of such an eventuality. Moreover, he points out, not only did this happen the same day, but Misha's dream of "flying dragons" or "energy movers" happened in the early hours of that day. As in the dream about the bombing of Iraq, in short, Misha makes certain that I will understand that this dream is firmly connected with events in the waking world and that this is, again, not only a dream but a prophetic dream.

This dream, like the ones described earlier, is readily interpretable. But on this occasion, rather than the dream being interpreted only within the dream, Misha lets me know that he is part of a network of meaning, one that draws on texts and collegial interpretation. He is thus not alone in his interpretation but rather intentionally turns to peers for assistance. Still, as before, as Misha tells the story, he demonstrates his full awareness that he inhabits a context in which there is a hierarchy of meanings—"Just imagine!" and "I never thought about earthquake. Why the same day?" And again he nonetheless insists on the normalcy, for him, of this kind of experience: "You know, things like that I have a million of these things. Million."

Misha describes the concept of a "lucid dream," and one must assume that the dream about doves dead in the desert would also be classified as one, given Misha's exchange in dream-space with the master who said, "When you wake up you will understand." Misha says that a lucid dream is one in which "you are dreaming but you know you are dreaming." One must ask here, though *who* it is that knows she or he is dreaming. Here mind is challenged, or at least made more complex than it previously understood itself to be. And the body is a crucial intermediary here. For one cannot, by definition, have a "lucid dream" unless the body is in a very particular state—the sleeping state. Thus once again causality cannot be emplaced fully in the "hands" (using a bodily metaphor!) of mind but rather must at the very least be understood by reference to bodily states beyond the control of the mind. This is, then, an example of my second proposal about the body and the mind—that at times the body is very simply and straightforwardly the site of cognitive results that are beyond mind's control or comprehension.

Body, mind, and consciousness are in a subtle relationship with one another in the processes that Misha describes. Clearly the waking, conscious mind is not in control of the dreaming mind. Dreaming, per se, is different from the waking state as such. Yet the conscious waking mind is, in very interesting ways, in dialogue with the dreaming mind. To begin with, as Misha has said, an awareness of the waking mind is present in the dream state. Indeed the concept of lucid dreaming proposes precisely that it is possible for the waking mind to be aware of itself in relationship to the dreaming mind. Misha says, "It's very difficult to dream lucid dreams." But the waking mind communicates with the dreaming mind in a different way, by means of efforts to interpret the language of dreams from the standpoint of the waking state. In this regard, Misha and his peers draw on a range of materials that will help them analyze particular symbols. "I have many, many book[s] to interpret, and I have a lot of friends that we work together with dreams." As well, quotidian and contextually specific languages and symbols make interpretation feasible as in, for example, the presence of Misha's "actual" mother (not a symbol of her) in a dream and the appearance of the "actual" number thirteen on a wall rather than a symbol of "thirteen-ness" as a concept.

What can one say about the body, here? It is simple enough to note that the body sleeping is different from the body waking, and that the conscious mind relinquishes control of the body, at least partially, when the individual human being is asleep. Misha also suggests that the body and mind are more amenable to the dreaming of prophetic dreams at certain periods of the sleep cycle. Here the body is not in any obvious way "speaking" as was the case when Paloma wrote, "Help!" Still, the body is a critically important resource in the process of prophetic dreaming. What these experiences share is the necessary role of the body as that space or site that enables the subject to move, or be moved, to a way of seeing or experiencing that is other than "status quo," other than "normal," other than previously to be expected.

One might conceive Misha's life with dreams as a body/mind dialogue. In this regard, one must note that the process of prophetic dreaming is one in which the mind is absolutely not "masterful." It is not that mind is absent or uninvolved—the mind is of course in action in the interpretive process. And in another set of cognitive processes, one must note that Misha has by now developed a framework within which to explain the fact that he has prophetic dreams. Yet, one must remember that the dreams come with or without that framework. Moreover the dreams do not for the most part arrive at Misha's mind's instigation.

At the same time, however, Misha is committed to a regimen of practices to support his prophetic dreaming, organized by the mind if not undertaken by mind alone—meditation, a notepad by the bed, books that might help interpret some of the dreams' symbolism. One might suggest here, though, that rather than taking the lead the mind supports the body in its activity. In the final analysis, I would argue that by definition the body must have the last word here. For one cannot dream when one is awake, and one cannot really choose when to be asleep.

LIKE PALOMA TAN, Blanche Hartman told me of an experience led by what one might name "bodily consciousness." It made necessary a radically new way of seeing self and world. And like Avram Davis, Blanche described to me an event that led, ultimately, to the position she held when I interviewed her. For Blanche Hartman was now Zenkei Blanche Hartman, abbess of the San Francisco Zen Center. Like Misha, Blanche was able to describe the framework within which to make sense of her experience. And finally, as for all three of those individuals, Blanche's body-led experience was for her the foundational a priori that called for all else to be reordered in relationship to it. But in a way different from the experience of Paloma, Avram, and Misha, although clearly religious and spiritual in its content, Blanche Hartman did *not* see the divine in any form as relevant to her journey. Blanche said this about the key event in question:

> I was in the front, face-to-face with a riot squad policeman, who was closer than you and I are, in his full riot gear. And they were kind of shoulder to shoulder. It was interesting . . . At a certain moment I

made eye contact with the policeman in front of me, and I had an overpowering experience of identity. With . . . with me. It was not anything for which I had any intellectual preparation. It's really hard to talk about it. But it was a very direct experience of identity, with this—what I would have said was the epitome of "not me." In Zen language, you know, self and other are not two. Fine! I'd never heard Zen language. I had never had any preparation for what that experience was. However, the experience was totally, completely more real than any idea I had ever had . . . That night I was elected chairman of the students' commission to support the strike . . . But actually, my political career as I had known it died at that moment. Because what actually happened was, "The world is not the way I thought it was. It's different. And I have to change my life."

Blanche Hartman was seventy-one years old, married with children and grandchildren when I interviewed her. She was born in Birmingham, Alabama, the daughter of middle- and upper-middle-class Jewish parents. When she and her sister were still young children, the family's trajectory was altered forever when Blanche's father became involved in civil rights work, effectively driving him out of employment in his home state. As an adult, Blanche also committed herself to radical political activity. As she put it, "for twenty-five years, it was the center of my life." But the incident recounted above contributed to the demise of that life: "my political career as I had known it died at that moment." By the time of her face-to-face encounter with the policeman in riot gear, Blanche was already in her forties and the mother of four children, one of whom was a student at San Francisco State University. Indeed it was partly on account of her son that Blanche Hartman found herself at SF State on that day, for in the context of student protests and police abuse, community members had been invited to "interpose themselves between police and students to prevent further violence." Blanche was not at that time, as should be clear, a practitioner of Zen Buddhism.

Now, though, when she says, "I had an overpowering experience of identity" in relation to someone whom "I would have said was the epitome of 'not me,'" she *does* make sense of that moment by reference to Zen Buddhist philosophy. As she explains, in "Zen language, you know, self and other are not two." But still she makes it forcefully clear that her experience was, in fact, a priori, with her tone returning perhaps to the moment of strong emotion that came with the incident: "Fine! I'd never heard Zen language." In Blanche's description of the events of that morning, it is striking that indeed for her experience actually overrides any preexisting theory or explanatory framework. As she puts it, "I had never had any preparation for what that experience was. However, the experience was totally, completely, more real than any idea I had ever had."

As is often true of origin stories, this one has antecedent and ancillary incidents surrounding it. For Blanche these included some disappointment with the left tradition of which she was a part ("I don't want to go into ancient history [but] I began to be disillusioned [with] the Soviet Union, and socialism as it was developing there . . . [My husband and I] continued our political activity, but somewhat differently. And somewhere along the line I became a pacifist"). Equally significant, or perhaps even more so, a dear, close friend died suddenly. Blanche said of this:

> Up until then, death was . . . "Ah, sure, everybody's going to die," but sort of out there and very, very separate and distant from me. This made it very personal and immediate. Pat and I were the same age. We'd had the same small children, and she was my best friend. And that same year, I got a severe infection and also almost died. I went into septic shock and was hospitalized for some time. So I say that as a background, although I didn't notice till ten years later this sequence of events.

Lastly, Blanche told me, in the moments prior to her "close encounter" with the police officer, she witnessed an incident involving three students that gave her pause for thought: "The [student] pickets were jostling students going to class, and there were jocks. There was a jock there, taking a photograph of a picket jostling a student. And the picket grabbed the camera and smashed it on the ground. There's this whole thing. I'm standing there saying, 'Where is my side? This kind of thuggish picketing is no more my side than this thuggish jock confronting the pickets.' You know? I mean, I was a pacifist."

What is the place of the body in all of these incidents? To begin with, of course, the body is as always present throughout. But more importantly, one may note that the sudden recognition of the frailty of the body, its impermanence, is part of what disrupts Blanche Hartman's, as she named it, "linear thinking." Secondly the moment of the "camera smashed on the ground" is physical, visceral, and it is interesting that even thirty years on Blanche describes the incident in stark terms. It is the jarring character of the incident that interrupts Blanche's prior certainty about who fit where in her personal and political landscape. And lastly it is significant that it is a bodily encounter that overwhelms prior thinking. For it was eye contact that catapulted Blanche Hartman into a different way of seeing.

In these incidents, to be sure, the mind is also present. For an intellectual and political process was underway as Blanche and her husband begin to practice left politics on new terms. Likewise, mind was present as Blanche's body registered the camera thrown violently to the ground and asked herself, in shock, whether she had any allies, and if so, where they were and how she might recognize them. But the engagement with the policeman answered that question in terms that were entirely experiential and non-linguistic. It did so by disrupting the question itself, eradicating not only the distinction between ally and enemy but also that between self and other. In that moment, Blanche sees the experience as primordially "real." As such Blanche's choice of words emphasizes by multiplication the hyperexperiential character of the event ("the experience was totally, completely more real than any idea I had ever had"), and insists that ideas, and therefore mind, are not in the lead here. Yet mind returns, both in the immediate aftermath as Blanche realizes that an experience that was *not* created by mind as sovereign subject means that mind must now think about how to live differently—"The world is not the way I *thought* it was. I have to change my life" (emphasis added). Then, later, as Blanche comes to translate pure experience into the language of Zen Buddhism, the relationship between the experiencing body and the mind is rearticulated.

Just as the body led the mind at San Francisco State University, it was the event just described that led Blanche Hartman to Zen Buddhism rather than Zen leading her toward the kind of experience that she had on that day. It was in this context that I asked her:

> RF From the point of view of Zen Buddhism, how do you understand [what] you said on the phone to me, kind of jokingly, [was] your conversion experience?
> BLANCHE The event with the policeman. I consider that, yeah, a conversion experience. If I understand what conversion experiences mean. Just to see that the world is different than I had conceived of it, up until that moment.

The process of making sense of the "conversion experience" was both slow and fast. Blanche said "At that moment, I was just stunned. I was just stunned. [I felt,] 'I don't understand this, but this is more real than anything I've ever known in my life. And I have to find someone who understands this. I have to find out what . . . who knows about this.' So, that's when I started doing a lot of reading. It was in there that I got this book on Zen, among others. And I read it, and I said, yes, yes!" She continued:

> But still, this other part of me, my lifelong habit, said, "Zen Buddhism, that's weird. Religion is the opiate of the people, blah-de-blah-de-blah." But—the experience was more real than any of that. And I had to come to some understanding. I had to find someone who understood a world in which I and a riot squad policeman could be identical. I mean, how I talked about it at the time was [to say] "he was defending all that he thought was right and good from these evil people facing him who were going to destroy it, and I was doing the same thing." But that's just trying to put some idea on it. It was much more fundamental than that.

Several things are worth commenting on here. First, Blanche emphasizes once again the irreducibility of the experience involving the police officer. Thus she sought "someone who understood" that experience as real. The necessity was to learn how to align a knowledge system with that experience, *not* to align the experience with a knowledge system. (Here, then, body led and mind followed rather than the other way around.) Next Blanche described something of the battle over ways of seeing that took place in this process. Her response to a book on Zen had been "yes, yes!" and yet her leftist history had argued that "religion is the opiate of the people." Meanwhile her "relativizing" explanation of the incident to herself, the proposition that both she and the policeman were striving to defend good in the face of evil appeared to her insufficient, "just trying to put some idea on it." Blanche's choice of the word *fundamental* underscores her insistence that any analysis follow from the encounter in its essence rather than challenge or even transcode it. Thus the mind grapples with an incident that refuses to be reduced to anything besides or outside of itself, an incident that took place phenomenally, viscerally, and then triggered a search for cognitive realignment.

Blanche's journey toward realignment took, she said, "the better part of a year. Because it was September '68 that the strike happened. And it was July 3, '69, when I went to the zendo in Berkeley and had meditation instruction." It is striking that Blanche remembers the exact date that she received meditation instruction. And it is interesting that here once again there is a sense in which the preexisting rationalist frame both battles with and gives into a subtle multisensorial experience that simply says "yes," despite mind's questions and concerns. Thus Blanche commented, in regard to her first visit to the Zen center and the meditation hall:

> Something about the meditation hall and the meditation and the whole atmosphere there, just went . . . "Yes." And I began going to meditation on a daily basis from that day on. Uh, still not knowing what I was doing. Still thinking, "This is weird and strange, and these people [are] sitting on these black cushions and chanting in Japanese, and this is really crazy." And still I kept . . . it seemed like exactly what I had to do. Then when I met Suzuki Roshi, the first thing I ever heard him say in a lecture was something like, "you're perfect just as you are." And my immediate response was, "Well, he doesn't know me." But he kept saying things like that. "You're perfect just as you are. You have everything you need. You're already complete." Finally I think, "He is talking about me. He's talking about everybody. Nobody is left out." And when I saw him, person-to-person, the way he looked at me, I . . . "He understands that experience I had. He understands there's no difference between self and other." Because that's the way he treated me. He seemed to have the capacity to meet everyone with total, unconditional acceptance. Which was, in the kind of adversarial world that I had lived my whole life, quite startling. And felt right to me. It felt like, "I would like to be able to live like that." I haven't got there yet, but I'm—that's my aspiration. So. That's enough of that. That particular question.

Thus, in the end, the mystery is resolved. Blanche does find a framework, the rationality of Zen Buddhist philosophy, wherein her experience with the riot squad policeman is explained, is rational, is real. Suzuki Roshi, indeed, on the basis of his conscious, cultivated practice, treated Blanche Hartman in the same way that she had met the riot policeman and spontaneously encountered her identity with him. Thereafter, the challenge, as Blanche said, was to "live like that," to make that which had suddenly happened on the San Francisco State University campus into an ongoing state of affairs.

How, in Blanche's process, are the concepts of body, mind, and self of relevance? First, it is the body that repeatedly sidesteps mind's pre-existent frames of reference throughout the journey described here. Body, one might say, hosts the foundational a priori that then leads Blanche toward a commitment to reshape mind's ways of interpreting self and world. But mind is a critical player here, too, sorting and engaging a range of competing explanatory frameworks before saying "Yes!" to the framework that can welcome, accommodate, and embrace Blanche's viscerally experienced encounter with nondualism.

In comparison with earlier discussions in this book, a striking absence is, of course, God in any form. As was discussed in chapter 2, for many, visceral, multiply mediated, synchronous events were understood to be signs of divine efficacy. This reading of life experience was made sensible in part thanks to meaning systems associated with specific religious traditions. In addition to all that has already been said about Blanche, as it happened, she and her husband began a practice of sitting meditation simultaneously, without prior communication or consultation, on opposite coasts of the United States. Her husband had gone east, partly to care for his ailing father and partly because of marital stress so serious that "it was not clear to either one of us whether he would come back or not." At the same time that a friend gave Blanche's husband a book on Zen, Blanche received personal instruction in sitting zazen at the Berkeley Zen Center. As Blanche said, "So it's one of those interesting circumstances." Curious about the parallels between this sequence of events and those described by interviewees who practiced deistic religions, I remarked:

> RF Now, some of the people that I interviewed would really address both of those moments as a kind of divine intervention. But I don't know how a Zen Buddhist would think of that.
> BLANCHE I would certainly not think of it as divine intervention. I would think of it as two people who [were] both searching for a way to live, searching in a very turbulent time for how to live that felt more true. Or—[that] satisfied some inner feeling of, of living appropriately on the earth.

Clearly, then, for Blanche, no divine hand was a part of any of this. What then, can account for the nondual experience, and the two moments of "Yes!" on reading a book on Zen Buddhism and on entering the Berkeley Zen Center? The only answer to this question that might be deemed correct within the terms of Zen Buddhism is, I suggest, that of the "realness" of nonduality, its, so to speak, "per se-ness." For as Blanche argues, her experience of "not-two-ness" was real in a way that threw all preexisting language aside.

However, accounting for the simultaneity of Blanche's encounter with Zen and that of her husband is a different question. It can perhaps only be left in the hands of Blanche Hartman herself. For the question remains of whether there is, within Zen Buddhist philosophy, an explanation for *that* fact that is as elegant and economical as the one that accounted for the "policeman incident." Otherwise one must decide whether one of Blanche's three comments—"It's one of those interesting circumstances"; "Two people . . . searching for a way to live"; and "quite surprisingly"—or even my question to her, "Could this be explained as Divine intervention?" is anything other than (using Blanche's language) "just trying to put some idea on it."[16]

🌿

AS BLANCHE MADE CLEAR, as important as her life-changing, sudden, and spontaneous encounter with "not-two-ness" may have been, it was daily practice that might make it possible to cultivate rather than "only" experience that state of consciousness. Yet it is also significant to note that, from within the perspective of Soto Zen Buddhism, practice is not a site where change happens. Rather it provides a place wherein *that which is already true* can be experienced. Thus Blanche had emphasized at the beginning of our conversation:

> [The] very fundamental understanding in Soto Zen Buddhism is [that] there's nothing to get by practice. We have everything we need. We're complete as we are . . . And so our fundamental practice is, in Japanese, *zazen*, which means "just sitting." Just sitting doesn't mean "merely sitting." It's more like "only sitting," not doing something else. Not sitting with some aim in mind. Just sitting upright, right where we are, being here. Being willing to be. Just being willing to be this one as it is. And finding that not only enough, but very full and rich and including everything.

Recognition of that which already is is important within Buddhist practice, and its salience will become even clearer below. But for now I focus on the relationship between body and mind in the cultivation of that recognition. For I would argue that although the body per se is not the focus of Zen philosophy, it is nonetheless centrally necessary in that practice. For it is *both* mind's willingness to "just sit" *and* the body's capacity to cooperate that make possible the process just summarized by Blanche.

The journey from "just sitting" to "finding that not only enough, but very full and rich and including everything" sounds straightforward enough. Yet it is a journey that entails many steps and takes diverse forms for different people. The relationship between body and mind for interviewees whose practice came close to that described by Blanche was a complex and subtle one. (It was in particular practitioners of Soto Zen Buddhism and of Vipassana, the mindfulness meditation emergent from Theravadin Buddhism, that fell into this category. Other forms of Buddhism and indeed other practices within Soto Zen Buddhism entail different configurations of the relationship between body, mind, and practice.)

As I learned in interviewing Blanche, much of the daily routine at the San Francisco Zen Center entailed the cultivation of bodily practices with the end of (1) stilling the mind and (2) creating a bodily environment steady enough for the mind to contemplate *its* location in time and space. And it should be noted immediately here that the assertion that something is done "to the end of" accomplishing something else in fact sidesteps Blanche's insistence that in zazen one is "just sitting," not "sitting with some aim in mind." Thus a different way to make this statement might be to propose that when one undertakes certain bodily practices, the mind may become still enough to witness its location (not contemplate it, for that might also be deemed an action with an intent in mind).

Blanche described at my request the daily, weekly, and annual rhythms of the Zen Center. She told me of the morning period of sitting meditation, walking meditation, chanting, and breakfast eaten in silence. She explained that there were weekend practice and study periods which nonresidents might attend if they wished. And she described the weeklong, monthlong, and even three-monthlong periods of intensive practice. On one level all of this might appear repetitive, mundane: sitting, walking, sitting again, chanting, eating in a formal and carefully planned manner, sweeping, and otherwise cleaning the zendo (meditation hall). But all of this provided the opportunity, one might even argue the alibi, for the cultivation of a deepening self-knowledge, a deepening capacity to meet self and other just as they are. Thus Blanche said:

> An awful lot of Zen practice is just trying to meet each experience as it arises, without preconceptions . . . to facilitate seeing our habitual tendencies, and loosening our grip on [them]. Or just seeing how our habitual tendencies cause suffering. And then it's up to us whether we want to hang onto them or let them go . . . Partly that silence helps you to not be continually caught up in this endless thought stream. Maybe begin to experience some spaces between thoughts. Perhaps see some

things directly. As, for example, I saw this policeman directly, rather than through some idea of who he was and who I was and how we were different.

There is then a very particular relationship between body and mind as the mind calls on the body to do things that, it is expected, will in turn create room for the mind to witness, as Blanche says, "its habitual tendencies." And, making another critical link, Blanche points out that from the standpoint of Soto Zen Buddhism, "habitual tendencies cause suffering" which one can choose to relinquish or not. Thus one might suggest that in Soto Zen the body is used to facilitate recognition of that which, for *all* Buddhists, not just Zen Buddhists, is fundamental: there is a relationship between first, embodiment; second, human wishes, hopes, dreams, or, to use the all-encompassing term, desire; and, third, suffering. The body, here, is the site and/or tool that provides an opportunity for mind to witness human suffering and thus choose to relinquish it. For there is another a priori in Buddhism— desire is not necessary because, drawing once more on Blanche's language, "We have everything we need. We're complete as we are." Unlike the moment when Blanche witnessed her "not-two-ness" with the riot squad policeman, and indeed unlike the events and practices named by Paloma, the body cannot be considered directly an agent of change in this instance. However, it is coaction of mind and body that, in context of intensive practice, gives rise to the sense of "fullness," "richness," and "see[ing] things directly" named by Blanche.

The journey from habitual tendencies toward realization of one's true nature involved bodily microprocessing. As Blanche explained, even the quite frequent shifts from one activity to another had a purpose:

> Part of practice is to stop what you're doing and do the next thing. And you notice this sort of stickiness. You know, really enjoying sitting zazen, and the bell rings and it's time to do walking meditation. And there's this little stickiness that says, "Oh, I'm enjoying sitting, I don't want to stop and do the next thing." You just notice this throughout the day—how we tend to cling to whatever we're doing. It's typical of Christian monastic practice as well as Buddhist monastic practice, to have these frequent transitions through the day and to work with that stickiness. Okay, time to stop this, and do this. [*Fingers snapping*] Working with this attachment we have to the idea that, "it's really important what I'm doing, whatever it is." [*Laughter*] This sort of self-clinging that goes with what I'm doing. So, in a way these are

devices, to help you see yourself, and see your tendencies, and see how you cause yourself suffering by the way your mind works.

One might argue that here a kind of social psychology of mind, of habit, is crucial to Soto Zen practice. That is what makes it possible to bring to consciousness what is for many habitual. However an area of difficulty and indeed contention emerged in discussion with some practitioners related to these very crucial notions of "suffering" and what is considered "habitual" about it.

If this mode of spiritual practice sounds rigorous, it was in fact a source of great joy for many. Diana Winston is forty years Blanche Hartman's junior and also of Jewish ethnicity. Born in 1966, Diana has practiced Vipassana meditation since she was twenty-two years old—that is, for eight years at the time of the interview. Diana was the founder of Buddhist Alliance for Social Engagement (BASE), an organization that generates placements and organizes support for individuals who, in Diana's own words, "want to bring their social action or service together with their Buddhist practice." But in the present context I focus on the place of meditation practice in Diana's life. She said:

> At this point, I don't see anything outside of my practice. Because I'm always thinking in terms of mindfulness and nonmindfulness, in terms of the teachings that are going through my head, in terms of the Buddhist precepts, in terms of all these things. It's the filter [through which] I see the world. And it's not from—I do a lot of study, but I've also done a lot of practice, and for me that's the foundation of what I do. Like if I didn't practice, it would all be bullshit, really. I was about two years in Asia—but I've been doing three-month meditation retreats pretty much every couple of years since then. And that's a really significant piece of my life . . . I'll be leaving to go to Asia in another couple of months to practice for up to six months in a Burmese monastery with a teacher [in] the lineage that I practice in.

Diana added that she also did one- to two-day retreats every two months, but that they were, in comparison with long retreats, "really not that helpful." She meditated once or twice daily, and in addition to the precepts sought to "pay attention to my mind all the time. What am I doing? Where am I caught? Where am I attached?"

Diana uses the word *practice* in two distinct ways. In one, *practice* means adherence to the Buddhist principles of "nonharming" (a shortened naming of a longer list of modes of thought and action that are central to Buddhism) and mindfulness in a daily, second-by-second manner. As she puts it, "It's the filter [through which] I see the world." But in a different use of the term *practice*, Diana emphasizes methodologies like those Zenkei Blanche Hartman described: daily or twice-daily sitting meditation; and longer periods of sitting, at times as short as two days but at other times (preferably, she says) between a month and half a year.

Diana emphasized that mind alone can neither achieve nor replace what takes place in the process of meditation: "I do a lot of study, but I've also done a lot of practice, and for me that's the foundation of what I do." And she used some of the same language as Blanche, asking herself, "Where am I caught? Where am I attached?" For Diana to, as she terms it, "pay attention to my mind" she actually needs to use her body, transferring body *and* mind into a meditative place and into a meditative state. And stating the case strongly, Diana views this kind of work with the mind as more useful than study and quintessential to ongoing application of the principles and philosophy that are interwoven with *practice* in this latter sense of the word. As she puts it, "if I didn't practice, it would all be bullshit."

As noted, Diana was deeply committed to meditation in general, and to long-term meditation retreats in particular. This was so much the case that, until communication with the Berkeley-based Buddhist Peace Fellowship led her to relocate to California and help found BASE, Diana had even set aside any quest for paid work of inherent interest to her, in exchange for the possibility of regular long-term meditation retreats. She put it this way: "I felt a real rejection of worldly life. I just felt—what happens in retreat is so sublime, and all the rest of the stuff is just—it's like biding my time until I can get on the next retreat. During my early years of doing retreat . . . I would support myself doing like really junky jobs, like waitressing, that I hated, but just to make the money so I could go on a retreat." Whether or not the work of a waitress is "junky" is of course a matter of subjective judgement. But Diana's point, here, is well taken: she was more interested in meditation retreats than in undertaking waged work that was meaningful to her. And her other point is made equally clear—to Diana, "what happens in retreat is sublime."

Diana explained that she had participated in retreats mainly at the Insight Meditation Society, in Barre, Massachusetts. Such retreats take place in silence, except for a ten-minute interview each day with a teacher, and a lecture in the evening. Depending on the somewhat customized schedules of individual participants, there might be two or three meals during the day. She went on, "Basically you do a sitting meditation for an hour, walking meditation for an hour, sitting for an hour, walking, eat lunch, sitting, walking, like that, through the whole day, and there's some time for shower and all that kind of stuff . . . You end up not sleeping very much, like somewhere between four and six hours a night, and just meditating." The structure of the practice is thus marked by a particular, repetitive set of bodily actions, undertaken with no particular privation as part of the goal or context— eating and bathing are, as Diana says, part of business as usual. And as at the San Francisco Zen Center the object here has little to do with disciplining the body for the sake of any effect on the body per se. Rather, the effort is to have particular experiences in relationship to the mind. Diana put this clearly:

> The object of the practice is to be observing my moment-to-moment awareness. Generally, you start with watching the breath. You're aware of the breath, you're aware of the sensations of the breath. And when things come up, like a sound or a thought or a sensation in the body, when it becomes predominant, you pay attention to that until it goes away, or changes and does something else. And then you pay attention to whatever's predominant and then you can return to the breath. So it's just this process of being aware of whatever's happening in the moment, and really learning to develop that as a skill, essentially. It's kind of like boot camp in mindfulness. You go for a long time and you just do it.

Body and mind might be seen as coactors here—"you're aware of the breath" signaling precisely that teamwork. Likewise, awareness of sound, sensation (bodily experiences and mental tracking of them) becomes a complex polyrhythm, overlying a more stable rhythm that is more bodily than it is mental, that of the breath. Diana's last metaphor hints that this exercise, with or without meals, is no picnic: "It's like boot camp in mindfulness. You just do it."

From here, Diana offered more detail about the effects of this bodily/mental process upon the mind as such. She said:

> Through the process of this practice, the mind quiets down. It stops being so distracted. It gets more concentrated. It gets more calm. It gets more equanimity and joy . . . Insights happen . . . psychological insight, or what's called a dharma insight, which is an insight into the nature of reality, for instance. The main thing with this practice is there are three characteristics of existence, that things are impermanent, unsatisfactory, and [there is] no eternal self, you know, no lasting self. So you actually begin to see that for yourself by doing the practice . . . and you're seeing it on a deeper and deeper and deeper level.

At this point, it seems, body has been set aside, no longer the focus, no longer even the object of interest here. Yet, one must remember Diana's opening words, "through the process of this practice the mind quiets down." Body is, then, the tool or enabler here. And one must also note that "dharma insights" as Diana characterizes these—impermanence, unsatisfactoriness, and the absence of a lasting self—are also facts of embodiment as much as they are facts of the life of the mind. Lastly one can note that Diana's mind does not "try" to make any of this happen, and nor for that matter does her body. Rather, one can log or track, as it were, what mind does and what happens to mind. Similarly, although this seems to be less of a focus from Diana's purview, one can name what the *body* does and what happens to it. In addition to all of this, one can note Diana's sense that this is not something that happened only to her but somehow was to be, if not expected, certainly not greeted as though it were utterly unknown or unexpected. Yet the cause-and-effect relationships between body, mind, and all else are, it seems, unknowable except by reference to the "is-ness," the "per-se-ness" of the events as described. Thus Diana refers to these experiences of mind while in cultivated body states as glimpses of "aspects of truth," and as "classic Theravadin teachings."

When I asked Diana, "Why do you do [retreats]? Why do you go every year or two years for three months?" Diana responded as though this should have been obvious to me, "Because it's totally amazing. I mean, there isn't anything like it. One of the Buddhist teachings is that worldly pleasure . . . is good, but compared to having a mind full of concentration . . . loving-kindness . . . mindfulness, it's nothing." She continued:

> There's the stuff that's obviously fun about it. Your mind starts resting in a place that's—really sublime. I mean, most of my mind when I'm not on retreat is generally just like [*makes grinding sound, laughs*]. But after practicing and concentrating the mind, you're aware of each moment in this really deep way. The way it feels in the body, the way it is, is so amazing. And then you get "goodies," if you want to call them that . . . Rapture, or experiences that feel blissful, exciting.

At this point it becomes almost impossible to classify what Diana describes as separably mental or physical. What does it mean, for example, to "be aware of each moment in a really deep way"? And is "rapture" mental or physical, or both? Should one most accurately say that the bodily process of sitting and the mental process of cultivating mindfulness eventually alter mind states as well as physical states? Neither? Both? One more than the other? In any event Diana quickly called a halt to this line of thought, saying, "But the thing is, any of these experiences, it's fine if you have it, but you're not supposed to get attached to it." While one might be forgiven for assuming that what one is not "supposed to" attach to here is bodily pleasure, a more usual Buddhist interpretation is simply that *any* attachment will lead automatically to the very same suffering/desire nexus that the practitioner seeks to eschew.

Overarching Diana's description of retreat is the insistence that something *different* takes place within meditation from what one might experience outside of it, or without benefit of it. Moreover that difference is not simply a quantitative but a qualitative one. As she put it, "There's nothing akin to it, even the greatest sexual experience or even the greatest chocolate." Again here, body and mind merge. For while Diana describes this process primarily in terms of states of mind—*equanimity, loving-kindness*—her comparative images are bodily—the best sex, the best chocolate. And Diana returns briefly to the body as a topic when she names the experience of deep meditation: "You're aware of each moment in this really deep way. The way it feels in the body, the way it is, is so amazing."

Language with which to communicate her experience was not readily available to Diana. Besides comparing the effects of the practice with the incomparable ("there's nothing akin to it"), and commenting on it as "more than" (worldly pleasures, the best chocolate, or sex), Diana simply names her experience within its own discursive terms (*dharma insights, Buddhist teaching, Theravadin teaching*). Part of the difficulty is that the practice takes the practitioner beyond the purview of "rationality as usual," and likewise of mind/body binariness. As Diana links the retreat experience back to the precepts that she seeks to embrace away from retreat time, the challenge to name the process remained: "On retreat, essentially you're building wisdom, compassion, loving kindness. I would say that probably one of the best experiences is equanimity, which is when your mind is so completely unmoving that anything can go through the mind. It can be like intense fear and your mind is just right there with it, and it's witnessing everything, but it's not caught. So equanimity's really powerful." Here again the mind/body separation is blurred. Is "fear" only a cerebral state? And what of equanimity? The ideas that your mind is "right there," "witnessing," and "not caught" are defiant of any clear separation between mind and body. For that matter, the process of Vipassana meditation, just like that of Soto Zen practice, also challenges the "control/chaos" binary inasmuch as it seeks to *not* strive or make effort, to witness without attachment, rather than control or alter that which arises.

As for all the others whose experience has been described, clearly both body and mind are in play here. Mind is not in control despite the involvement of mind in arranging for both body and mind to find themselves in the space of a meditation retreat. In Vipassana, then, mind is not fully in charge. But neither, for that matter, is the body. Moreover neither body nor mind can be deemed in full control of what transpires once the practitioner is in a meditation retreat. For arguably the body does not control the onset of fear, rapture, or equanimity, any more than it writes the scripts of dreams or of relationships between men and women whose "matchmaker" is God/universe/life.[17]

FOR DIANA as for Blanche Hartman the body appeared as a site or resource that could offer a point of stability and anchorage, but the mind, not the body, was the focus of attention. For them the body is a tool or an enabler engaged with in a conscious manner. Granted, as has been seen, the body at times stepped well beyond the bounds of mind's control. Moreover the body is, in Soto Zen and Vipassana meditation practice, efficacious in ways that mind cannot control and indeed does not seek to control. I would propose that body and mind are co-actors in the processes of Soto Zen and Vipassana meditation.

However, all of this presumes that the body may be seen and experienced as a transparent, neutral term. What happens when the body in culture and in its physical being is itself marked rather than unmarked, challenged rather than not? Now the body becomes a site in relation to which the practice itself may need to be transformed. And as well, the body may become the subject of practice, rather than only the ground for it. The experience of interviewees who were living with disability or addiction, and/or in racially marked bodies brought to the fore this set of issues.

Judy Smith was thirty-seven years old and had been a practitioner of Soto Zen Buddhism for fourteen years. She had received lay ordination at the Berkeley Zen Center several years before the interview, and remained an active member of that center. She is white and lesbian. Judy is program director of Axis Dance Company, a dance company made up of disabled and nondisabled performers. She teaches self-defense and also offers workshops on disability and diversity to corporations and community organizations. She has been a wheelchair user since the age of seventeen when, as she told me, "I was driving drunk and I lost control of [my] car. I went down a mountainside. I didn't have a seatbelt on so I got thrown out. I have a neck injury." She explained that she now has limited hand use, and no functioning from the chest down. She also has some spasticity in her lower limbs. But no matter how dispassionately Judy seemed able to describe her injury to me, its impact on her life was, of course, enormous. Thus she said with equal bluntness, "Primary to my issues and to what I have been dealing with over the last twenty years is my disability, and how do I live in this container I'm in?"

For Judy, Zen Buddhism has been crucially important to her ability to live with disability. She said, "Being able to hold really contradictory feelings, which Zen is incredibly good at . . . It's about how we see things. The way we see things is not always the way they are, and it's not always *not* the way they are. So, yeah, my disability is a tragedy, but is my disability really a tragedy? Or is it just an event in what is called my life? And how, then, do I look at that and work with that and live with that?" And she added later, "Finding Buddhism was an incredible turning point in my life. You know, that it's okay to be different."

Yet if Zen has been critical to Judy's journey with disability, disability has also been central to her journey with Zen. As she put it: "I wouldn't say that my involvement in Zen has been without pain and without the whole disability issue following me along, you know, like this big wagon . . . Some people would just get so put out that they even had to deal with this. There were other people there who really advocated and pushed, but I felt a lot on the spot. Which I think flavored my practice to a degree."

Judy was born in 1960, and grew up in a tiny town in the mountains of Colorado. She described her family as lower middle class: "My mother was a housewife—a full-time, *over* full-time housewife. She had five kids by the time she was thirty-four. My father worked for [the telephone company for that region]. Started out as a lineman and worked up to a supervisor with his own crew . . . I don't ever remember a time when money wasn't an issue. That's why I say we were probably *lower* middle." Regarding religion, Judy said, "I was raised Catholic until I was seventeen when I broke my neck and my mother got furious at God, and decided we weren't going to go to church anymore." Judy added, "My mother's alcoholism came out of the closet at this point in time. She was very depressed and very angry. She died three years after [my accident] of difficulties related to lung cancer and chemotherapy."

For Judy as for her mother, the injury was an utterly life-changing event. She said, "My identity was very much tied up in horses and in riding. I was very successful in competition. And when I got hurt, my whole sense of everything was totally shattered. I can remember lying in the hospital for about the first three weeks, praying nonstop [to be healed]. Then I realized that wasn't going to work, so I just stopped. And I stopped believing." Prior to the accident, Judy had hoped to go to veterinary school. But, she said, "when I got hurt that put a rather large damper on that plan. So I continued in the horse business in the aspect that I could, which was managing the stable, and teaching, buying and selling." Thereafter that business fell apart. Simultaneously, Judy's mother was dying of cancer. This was, she said, a time when "all illusions were shattered."

After her mother's death, Judy went to college, but not because she had an inherent interest in doing so: "It was at the time the only thing available. They needed to find some place for me to go where I could get attendant services, have housing, etc., etc. So I ended up in Boulder, Colorado . . . I kind of had to go wherever and do whatever." Judy lived, she said, in survival mode for several years. The move from a town of only fifteen hundred people to the University of Colorado was a difficult although ultimately a positive one. Judy said, "I met some wonderful people and I got my mind opened up to different belief systems, different ways of looking at the world."

Somewhere along the line someone in Boulder told Judy about Berkeley as a place that was and is "very disability friendly. It's really kind of the Mecca. It's where the whole civil rights movement for people with disabilities started. That's why I came here, actually." As things turned out, although Judy transferred from the University of Colorado in Boulder to UC Berkeley, she never graduated "because I got involved in other things that kind of took priority." But meanwhile she entered therapy, participated in AA and other Twelve Step meetings, and began learning martial arts and self-defense. It was her martial arts teacher who suggested that Judy try meditation. And, while Judy said Catholicism had never fully "taken root" in her, the loss of at least "the illusion of a framework" had meant that she "definitely felt a vacuum for a number of years."

By the time of the interview, Judy said, "spirituality is how I try to live my life." Like Diana, Judy emphasized the value of Buddhist precepts as guidelines by which to live. And like Zenkei Blanche Hartman she stressed that the practice both created an order for her own life and provided a framework within which to honor all other beings and indeed the planet itself. However, neither Blanche Hartman nor Diana

Winston described the specific ways in which their own bodies might be a place in relation to which Zen Buddhist practice might be helpful. In contrast Judy said, very specifically, "In terms of dealing with my own issues around disability and my own limitations, it's a great venue for that." When I asked her what she meant by that she began by describing one of the key facts of her disabled body as she saw it:

> [Like] anybody who has a chronic illness or a chronic disability, I deal with a lot of things that are out of my control. Control is just such an illusion anyway, when we think about it. But, it's also relative and, relatively speaking, I have a lot less control in my life than somebody who is not disabled. You know, my wheelchair breaks down in the middle of the street in the rain and I'm stuck. I can't just go grab a cab and go home. If my body messes up in whatever way it does, I have to deal with that. So, in a very, very direct way I'm stuck with myself. And stuck with my situation.

My next question was, what does Zen Buddhist philosophy say about or do with that situation? Here again Judy had some very specific answers. First among these was that Zen Buddhist philosophy had offered her new ways of looking at, and living with, her disabled body. She told me of a meeting with the abbot of the Berkeley Zen Center. In it she had expressed to him her pain and frustration that, as she put it, "I had gone to AA, I was meditating, I was doing martial arts, I was in therapy, I was trying to be a good person, and, you know, shit still was happening." The abbot had surprised and shocked her at that point by asking her "Did you ever think that it has nothing to do with you?" Judy told me that, in fact, "No, I had never thought that, you know." Judy did not develop this idea further. But reading between the lines, one may guess that the abbot was in that moment challenging her sense that what she did might change the external facts of her situation. For when Judy said in effect, I've done all these things but I am still suffering ("shit is happening"), a crude but commonplace interpretation of Christianity ("If you are good you will be rewarded and if you sin you will be punished") was evoked. Likewise, a more general late-twentieth-century presumption ("If you take care of yourself in a holistic fashion, you will stop suffering") also suggests that what one does, how one "is," and how one acts might change things for the better.

This same "cause-and-effect" logic was disrupted again when Judy had a realization one chilly morning at the zendo: "I've been in places in my life where I have thought, 'Why Me? And, my God, I must be doing penance for something bad.' And I was sitting there in the morning, and it was dark, and it was a little bit cold, and it was early, and all of a sudden I thought, 'Well, why not me?' Bad things happen to people all the time all over the world. You know, parents are losing babies, people are being tortured, hearts are being broken, so, why not me?" Again Judy's description of this is subtle. But it is clear, first, that she is shifting from one frame of interpretation to a different one. Second, she is setting aside a mode of seeing her own life history that one might connect with the Catholicism with which she grew up, and turning instead to a reading of self, body, and history emergent from Soto Zen Buddhist philosophy. Of this, the following dimensions have already been named: the possibility of holding contradictory ideas in one's consciousness without seeking their resolution in any simple way; acceptance of the universality of suffering; and the refusal of any presumption that suffering must be explicable and/or one's own fault. It also becomes clear that the questions raised by other Buddhists, "Where am I caught? Where am I attached?" are being forcefully articulated in relation to Judy's body. And the words with which I began this discussion of her, "Primary to what I have been dealing with over the last twenty years is my disability, and how do I live in this container I'm in," are made concrete in their application.

Questions of "caughtness" were further examined in relation to Judy's body when she sought to participate fully in the spiritual practices of the Zen Center. For one thing, when she first joined the center, it was not accessible to her as a wheelchair user. There was no ramp leading into the zendo, and there was no wheelchair access to the bathroom. But whose "caughtness" was at stake here? Judy said,

> The bottom line when I met with [the abbot] the first time was, "Well, we don't have a ramp." The stance was that nobody had showed up who needed one. I said, "Well, I have a ramp." And it was really inconvenient. It was an ugly ramp and people decided that it was so unsightly that they'd rather have it put up and taken down when I came. It took up a lot of room, blah, blah, blah. So, I had to call ahead and make sure there was somebody to put the ramp up and then somebody to take it down. And then, you know, that really pushed my, "Oh my God, I'm a burden" button.

Judy's enmeshment in an idea about herself as "a burden" thus ran head-on into Zen Center members' "stickiness" (to use Zenkei Hartman's term) in relation to the status quo and their "attachment" to particular aesthetic arrangements. In the event, Judy said, "after a little while of doing that, the [building] got ramped." But not, as we have seen, before all involved were given the opportunity to engage in questions about bodies and Zen practice in ways different from those raised by practitioners who are nondisabled and whose bodies are thus encoded "normal" or "unmarked."

For Judy, struggles were ongoing about how to practice Soto Zen Buddhism in a way that was authentic to Soto Zen Buddhism itself. On one hand, authenticity might be seen to entail conformity to the status quo. In this regard Judy said, "I really put a lot of effort into making the form work, participating in the form as much as I could. In as similar a way as possible. And with some degree of success." ("The form" here refers to sitting and walking meditation, formal eating ceremonies, and cleaning the zendo, for example.) Yet there were times when this effort led to a sense of inadequacy, such as when she feared spilling or dropping something at a formal meal. Similarly, when Judy was ordained, a significant part of the preparation for that ceremony entailed making one's own robe. But Judy said: "You get this tiny packet of material. You cut the material up and then you sew it back together. And you chant while you stitch and it's this big deal. And I couldn't sew, so the woman who was teaching the class actually sewed my [robe] for me. So again, [I was] coming up against not only what I couldn't do, but [also] how I couldn't quite do the practice and the form the way everybody else could do it."

On the other hand, authenticity might equally involve meeting fully with all that arises and making it the site of inquiry as one engages in the practice. For Judy that process time and again entailed self-questioning about her body and her relationship to the practice. She said:

When I first started, I thought that the way I had to do it was to sit every day, go to every [sesshin, intensive retreat]. I got up at a quarter to five almost every day and rolled to the zendo, which was fifteen minutes away, unless it was pouring rain. And then I'd try to go back in the afternoon. I kind of set this precedent of perfection for myself. You know, I'd sit [for hours] even though it would totally wreck my body—it's just not good for me to sit still for that many hours. For a couple of years the community room wasn't accessible so I spent the whole time outside. It was, you know, pretty inclement to be sitting in the cold all day . . . As I got older I started realizing, "God, I'm so hard on myself. How can I lighten up?" . . . I guess I was trying to prove something to myself or to somebody—probably that I could do more than I thought I could do, or more than most people thought someone in my position could do. Now I find that my best meditation is when I'm lying down. I practice at home much more [now] because it's just not easy for me to lay down in the [meditation hall]. It means transferring out of my chair and I hate making scenes.

Clearly there were ways in which sitting zazen—rigorous for anyone—was considerably more challenging for Judy because of her injured body. The interface between zazen practice and Judy Smith's body was, then, first, specific, and second, arguably different from the interface between zazen and a nonparaplegic person's body. Thirdly we must note that the particularities of Judy's body, rather than lessening the benefits of zazen, became the occasion for the kind of self-inquiry that zazen practitioners seek to experience at the very best of times.

Judy proposes that in the way she undertook Zen practice in the beginning she was, perhaps, seeking to prove something to "herself or somebody." In other words she demonstrates clearly how it is that, and here I borrow Blanche Hartman's language, "these are devices to help you see yourself, and see your tendencies, and see how you cause yourself suffering by the way your mind works." Yet one must note too the double sense in which this is the case: zazen itself is the site of the suffering in relation to Judy's body. At first, Judy's response to that suffering was counterproductive and added to the suffering, so that it is now both physical and emotional. She sat for hours "even though it would totally wreck [her] body," persisting so as to prove that she could do more than she or others thought possible. As she recognized this, both mind and body reaped the benefit—Judy now experiences her "best meditations lying down" and recognizes that she was previously being too hard on herself. Yet the story is clearly not over—Judy does not meditate at home only because it is easier on her body but also because she "hates making scenes" at the Zen Center by transferring out of her chair and lying down. And one must recognize here that it is precisely the social construction of disability that makes of this "a scene."

As Judy went on, it was clear that the body remained a fecund site for, as it were, practicing the practice. She said,

> Part of my quandary with finding a way in Zen has been resigning myself to the fact that I can't sit full lotus. I always have these ideas about what it means to be really doing something the right way. So that to me has been an ongoing source of dialogue and questioning. I can't sit full lotus so, what does it mean to me? I don't have good posture because I don't have trunk support. I don't sit up with a straight back like a lot of the people in the [community] do. What

does that mean to me? I think I'm starting to let go of that kind of stuff more, but it was kind of a source of torment and torture for a number of years.

One does not need to search far to discover how the body is involved in spiritual practice in this instance. And it hardly needs to be said that Judy here offers what is almost a textbook case of answers to the questions, "Where am I caught?" "How am I attached?" Yet in ways that seemed not to have been planned by the philosophers of Soto Zen Buddhism, the body is, here, subject, object, *and* ground for this exploration. As should be clear, when I spoke with her, Judy's story was far from over. Judy says only, "I *think* I'm starting to let go" (emphasis added). And this is hardly surprising for, as before, Judy was not alone in this kind of "attachment." She said: "I think a lot of people—and we talk about this—confuse doing the forms well with being a good Buddhist. It's really easy to get so into the forms that you forget why you're there, and that the practice becomes doing everything perfectly. And then I think sometimes it's easy to miss the point." Judy makes it clear that she is speaking of herself as well as others as she suggests that attention to the form of practice might at times suffocate the actual purpose of the activity. And indeed one might argue that Judy's attention to form had more recently, in a new way, benefited her. For her willingness to accommodate her practice to her body had, as stated above, enhanced her practice rather than detracting from it. But one might note again that if Judy rethought her practice from the vantage point of her disability, her example might also offer her fellow community members the chance to reconsider their own relationships and attachments to form.

Judy demurs and claims that she only "thinks" she is starting to let go of some of the shame and self-judgment that had traveled with her injured body. Yet it became clear as we continued talking that the impact of her practice upon her sense of self, body, and spirituality now traveled well beyond the Berkeley Zen Center. The transition from an outer (crudely articulated Judeo-Christian) to an inner sense of transformation (here associated with Soto Zen Buddhism) was dramatized finally when Judy went to renew her driver's license, seeking for the first time, thirteen years after the accident, a disabled driver's permit. She said:

> So I go to take my driving test and at the end of the test the guy, who is from Romania or Czechoslovakia, asks me if I found the Lord. I said, "No, I haven't found the Lord. I have a spiritual practice that I feel

really good about and attuned to." And he said, "If you prayed, you'd be healed." I looked at him and I said, "Well, how do you know I haven't been healed?" And so I think sometimes the definition of healed is really narrow . . . For me it's being as much at peace with my situation, my life, as I can be and doing my best to promote peace, in my life, with my friends, with people I work with. To me, that's what being healed is. Beyond that, in some ways it doesn't matter anyway because we all end up in the same boat.

Here Judy summarizes beautifully the fruits of her practice. As before she does not erase nor sidestep the realities of "the container [she's] in." Rather she seeks peace with her situation. And she emphasizes once again that this does not entail completion or physical transformation, so much as being "as much at peace as [she] can be." And again the challenged body is only one site in her life, not the whole of it. Thus she speaks of finding and promoting peace with friends, coworkers, and the world in general, not only of focusing on her own self and body. As she had said, one might see the disabled body as a tragedy or as just one event in her life. Lastly, Judy reminds one that her injury is not unique, that even if it *were* most appropriately seen as a tragedy, "in some ways it doesn't matter anyway because we all end up in the same boat." Here she in fact universalizes her situation, not by reducing it but by contextualizing it. For she replied in the affirmative when I commented, "Yeah, the whole idea that some people are temporarily able-bodied." Thus Judy is able to draw on her body as a resource in the practice and on her practice as a resource vis-à-vis her body. And the body is neither only local nor only global but, in fact, both of these things.

It is all too easy, when one is discussing someone whose body is "marked" rather than "unmarked," "different" rather than "normal," to focus on the significance of the body while ignoring the mind. And as has been seen, Judy's body has indeed been a site wherein, on the one hand, Zen practice has supported her, and on the other, Zen practice has painfully pushed her, in both physical and emotional terms. Likewise her body has been one that has challenged her spiritual community to think, rethink, and, at times, adjust, albeit, it seems, far more slowly than one might have hoped would be the case.

One cannot, though, forget that mind has been critically involved in all aspects of Judy's journey with and within Zen Buddhist practice. To begin with, indeed the body has been a place of steadiness—a steadiness different from that anticipated by many other teachers and practitioners, but a point relatively unchanging nonetheless. However, we have witnessed Judy's mind being challenged and altered by the encounters between her body and Zen practice. For example she has described a movement from a self-imposed demand for bodily conformity to something other than that. She has described elements of an ongoing self-inquiry about the ways in which she was wounded by her inability to conform. Moreover she commented on some of the apparent inconsistencies between Soto Zen philosophy in theory and Soto Zen philosophy in practice. Thus she said:

> I'm going to say this about the Buddhist community at large, and the spiritual community at large, although I think churches have been much further ahead. It seems so contradictory to be preaching about spirituality and compassion, and then to have such an incredible resistance or lack of somehow seeing the importance of accessibility and accessibility issues. Because I think disabled people, probably as much as anybody could use a spiritual path . . . So that always, to me was, you know, an example of human failing.

Clearly then, Judy's work within Soto Zen practice engages mind as well as body. As for the two other Buddhists discussed here, Blanche Hartman and Diana Winston, the practice at its best will engage self as mind, self as body, *and* communities as well as individuals. And for Judy this practice is a context in which to skillfully interweave all of these dimensions.

⚘

THE TWO MEN AND FOUR WOMEN interviewed in this chapter are not alone in their practice or in the part played by body and mind in its crafting. Rather they were chosen because they exemplified the themes I sought to examine here. The group was diverse in many ways. They were members or participants in several traditions: Twelve Step and unaffiliated spiritual practice; Orthodox Christianity and unaffiliated (although "networked") prophetic dreaming; Judaism; Soto Zen Buddhism and Vipassana practice. They ranged in age from twenty-eight to seventy-one. One was an immigrant and the others native-born. They were ethnically varied, and came from childhoods of poverty (Misha); or they were lower middle or working class (Avram and Judy); mixed or middle class (Blanche, Diana); and upper middle class (Paloma). With the exception of Judy, they were heterosexual.

Paloma Tan and Judy Smith named serious physical challenges as centrally important to their spiritual journeys. And indeed it may be remembered that Blanche Hartman's own brush with death and her best friend's unexpected demise were in hindsight understood by her as contributing to her spiritual "conversion" (her term). Misha and perhaps also Avram might be considered persons whose spiritual experiences began at a young age. All six, though, shared a deep and (relative to their ages) longstanding commitment to their spiritual practice.

There is, arguably, one significant line of differentiation between the traditions within which these men and women have made their spiritual homes. In particular, one might suggest that the three Buddhists shared a great deal, but their practices were much different from the deistic frames within which Paloma, Avram, and Misha locate themselves. Yet I would suggest that the six had much in common: for all of them the body proved critical in the context of their journeys into and through spiritual practice. The body emerges here as a relatively autonomous terrain in relation to spiritual practice. Listing that which happens in that terrain, one must include automatic writing; inner audition and visioning; dreaming; visually encountering another as "not other"; transformed consciousness via meditation; and having a disabled body. All of these lead the way toward both spiritual practice and revision of spiritual form. But making an even stronger claim, I propose that in all of these individuals' spiritual journeys the body is the site of a foundational a priori in relation to which all else about their practice is organized. Thus, for example, Paloma's encounter with a body that wrote "Help!" initiated a quest for "recovery" (in the sense the word is used in Twelve Step). But there is more—Paloma's body in suffering was also at the center of her capacity to develop and act on a conception of self and what she named "a conversation with God/universe/life." Paloma's body provided the resources by means of which that conversation proceeded in two ways. First, there is a literal involvement of the body in interactions between Paloma and the divine, through prayer. Second, the effort to heal the body (or the body's effort to heal) entails in the end a journey toward recovery not just *through* but also *into* that conversation with God/universe/life.

Avram's body, as he explained, took him to places wherein he would receive guidance about present and future. And it was, he said, "psychological dropping away moments" that reminded him of his purpose and his path. Here I would argue that Avram was in effect describing a kind of "letting go" of mind not intentionally but as an effect of bodily interruptions to the mind's "business as usual." And it is, I suggest, these "dropping away moments" that reminded Avram how and why his practice should be organized.

In a different way Misha's dreams are the foundational a priori of his spiritual life. And a bodily experience beyond the control of the mind is the sine qua non of dreaming. Blanche Hartman experienced a bodily encounter—eye-to-eye contact—that demanded of mind that she radically revise her sense of self and world. Here again, then, the body was the site for the foundational a priori of Blanche's spiritual journey.

Meditation is, it may be argued, an activity of mind seeking to "set itself down," or "set itself aside." Yet in fact one might propose that body is receptacle or host, and also witness, to that process and its effects. The traumatized body of Judy Smith, and all that mind and body had to face in the wake of that trauma, was the foundational a priori of Judy's spiritual journey. As was the case for Avram, Misha, and Paloma, the body did not merely make one single appearance in the drama. Rather Judy's body remained a critical point in relation to which her practice was measured and refined.

It should be emphasized that I am not arguing that the mind is absent in these processes. For, as discussed throughout, the mind is absolutely present. Mind is at times that which must be revised (Blanche, Diana, Judy, for example). At other times it is that which works "in dialogue" with the body (Paloma, Misha, for example). And yet again it may be that which sorts, classifies, and chooses between ways of interpreting what is underway on a bodily terrain (this was so for all six of these interviewees). However I *am* arguing that the body and bodily processes per se are critical in disrupting, sidestepping, superseding, or acting autonomously from, processes of mental cognition. And further, I am arguing that these body-led and/or body-situated processes emerge here as fundamental to spiritual life.

These bodies are encultured. And this enculturation was at times obvious to interviewees. Thus for example it was precisely the shame that surrounds the disabled body, and the denial of its particular needs by self and by others that challenged Judy Smith and others members of her community. Likewise, Paloma felt that her "spiritual disease," bulimia, was comprehensible in part by reference to her nationality and her gender. But in fact the experiences and practices described here had precisely the effect of "stepping around" enculturation. Blanche and the two other Buddhists in particular named the ways meditation practices were intended to bring practitioners' attention to their habits (or to put this another way, their enculturation). And in a different way Avram proposed that his "dropping away moments" took him within that which appeared clichéd to something "deeper." In short, there is a complex process underway here that served to disrupt and reorganize the encultured body and mind, moving both in particular—and particularly spiritual—directions.

I do not, then, essentialize the body. The body functions, as I have argued, in a variety of ways. And that functioning is at times spontaneous and at times cultivated. Further, the body as described here is of necessity to be named, classified, and talked about by mind, in whatever ways are available to those who speak about it. Thus these men and women struggled at times to find language with which to describe bodily experiences ("soaked in honey"; "almost like my stomach turns, but it's not quite that exaggerated"). They named the modes of description that did or did not work for them ("cliché"; "Fine! I'd never heard Zen language") and their relationships to those modes of description ("I don't have any scientific study to back this up"; "I have a lot of friends that we work together with dreams"). They also named their fear about what others might think of these experiences ("Don't get me wrong") and what they ought to feel about them ("it's fine if you have it, but you're not supposed to get attached to it").

Nor did these interviewees essentialize the body, which was indeed far less the focus of their own conscious discourse than it was my focus in analytical terms. Yet there were ways in which the body could not be challenged as final arbiter, witness, or resource ("I can hear pretty well, and so I know what it sounds like"; "I [did not] understand this, but this [was] more real than anything I've ever known in my life"). The body was for them, in the final analysis, a site or resource wherein things took place whose truth could not but be accepted ("It's very difficult to describe but I know that this is happening in this way").

All of this suggests that the term *consciousness,* in its sense as the terrain of cognition, locatedness, and subjecthood, might be reexamined. The body is a site of cognition, and not only in the literal sense that the brain does, of course, reside within the parameters of the physical body. In addition, processes whose focus, reference point, and center of gravity are "below the neckline," at least if only in the terms of conventional, metaphorical bodily geography, were in play here. And these, as much as the more conventionally (again metaphorically) cerebral processes of assessment and classification, must be deemed "processes of cognition." Likewise ways of experiencing and modes of perception not simply or obviously either "cerebral" *or* "physical" need also to be taken seriously and into account.

One must thus seek to embark on a new bodily geography, asking, for example, about the effects of sitting meditation and the cognitive processes associated with it; about the visceral communication between Paloma and God/universe/life and how that is also a mode of cognition. And again the process of prophetic dreaming is one that entails a number of practices and experiences that one might deem bodily and cognitive in all of the connotations I described.

On entering this new terrain, it is necessary to set aside easy notions of mind's exclusive agency when it comes to cognition. At the same time one may ask how and what to make of the agency inherent in other processes that seem to result in cognition—if the phrase *process of cognition* can be understood to mean that which leads toward knowledge of some kind. What has been seen here is a rich and dynamic cognitive processing, in which the body and the mind are involved, and wherein modes of classifying experience, both received and new, are present throughout spiritual practice.

Locatedness is also transformed by the processes discussed in this chapter. First and foremost one must note the number of calls upon the "infinite" and the "universal." In addition, the "a priori" is, more often than not, not located. For example, when Zenkei Blanche Hartman says that "in Zen Buddhism, self and other are not two," it is unclear *where* self and other are located, and *where* they are not two. Likewise when Paloma Tan says, "I'm all one thing," Paloma does not claim that she is "all one thing" in any particular place or time. Rather, in her view, she is "all one thing," in general, as she moves in the world. And to cite Misha once more, this time alongside Avram Davis, it is hard to locate either the space of Misha's dreams or the "auditory vision" of Avram's teen years in any particular place or space.

On the other hand, very obviously, all of these experiences are located, by means of their embodied recipients' locations in zip code, and the languages and discourses used by them in the effort to describe and transcode what has happened and how they practice. Thus Blanche did say, "*In Zen Buddhism,* self and other are not two" (emphasis added) not "In the American Marxist left, self and other are not two." Likewise Avram was told to cultivate the practice into which he was born rather than another one. And Paloma drew on homeopathic theory in making sense of her experiences. These statements are, in short, located ones.

But clearly these individuals' senses of their location were of necessity transformed. For they now needed to accommodate a multiplicity and/or simultaneity of locations—meditation time in contrast with nonmeditation time (Diana); a conversation with God in the parking lot after a dance class (Paloma); a "psychological dropping away moment" while stuck in rush hour traffic (Avram).

The question of subjecthood, and how that is transformed, is a more subtle one. Clearly these men's and women's sense of self was thoroughly marked by their spiritual experiences, both spontaneous and cultivated, and shaped also by the fact that as practitioners they were in some sense full-time "guardians," witnesses, and recipients of those practices. And all of these individuals literally name the practice as having altered their lives on a fundamental level. They are, then, subjects formed and marked by their practices.

From here it is a short step to the proposal that the consciousness, the sense of self, world, and location is distinct and nameable for this group. And going further, I would argue that this group has much in common despite their religious/spiritual diversity, and despite also the deistic/nondeistic divide that separated in this case the Vipassana practitioner and Soto Zen Buddhists from the three others discussed here. The necessity and the capacity to shift through temporal and spatial registers; the difficulty of finding language(s) adequate to describe their experience; and the frequently expressed sense of alterity in relation to other ways of seeing deemed more "normal"—these were among the commonalities.

But more than that, the significance of the body as critical site, resource, and "shifter," and the absolute commitment to an a priori idea in relation to embodied experience make these practitioners more like than unlike one another. These men and women have at times striven to support, even "defend" their a priori statements, by reference to particular systems and symbologies. But perhaps, over and above that, one must note their commitment to those a priori statements with or without defense, with or without any sense of public or even personal comprehension or acceptability. Here is the place at which deistic and nondeistic frames may be seen to be united. For it is the commitment to that which I have named the "per-se-ness" of bodily experiences—whether seen to be deistic in origin, or universal but not deistic—that connects and transforms the consciousness of all of these individuals.

# PLACE AND THE

# MAKING OF RELIGIOUS PRACTICE

Religious and spiritual lives are inevitably located. It thus becomes necessary to investigate the place of "place" in practice. In this chapter, *where* at times refers to a place of origin, whether that of the religion, the practitioner, or both. At other times it signals the remaking of a religious form in relation to the national culture of the United States. *Place* also means the internal rather than external: that which is key to self and identity, or that which resides in the literal and imaginative memory of self, family, or community. At all times, *place* refers to the interweaving of religious and spiritual life with all else about daily life in the present, such that even what is apparently about "the there and the then" is equally about "the here and the now." Individuals interviewed here were not passive but rather active and adaptive as they received, transformed, and created distinctive religious and spiritual places.

This chapter focuses on two religions, Islam and Buddhism.[1] It draws on discussion of four Muslims (two immigrant and two native-born) and four Asian American Buddhists (one immigrant and three United States–born). Both Islam and Buddhism are in distinct ways marked "marginal," "minority," or "other" from the standpoint of contemporary mainstream U.S. culture, religious and secular. This alterity meant that all eight of these men and women needed, in more or less conscious ways, to be theorists and tacticians of their religions, and to some degree *bricoleurs* of religious and spiritual practice.

turned out, the places in which these interviewees practiced
_gion and spirituality were not stable. For all, there was an original
"old place" wherein religion was first encountered. This place was usually childhood. Yet for none of these eight individuals was adult religion
the same as that experienced in childhood. Memory was thus key in the
telling of their stories. Questions about what was remembered, how,
and in the aftermath of which trauma, transition, loss, or even imagined
reconstruction, were at times part of the investment in adult identification with specific religious names. *Place* here refers to inner and outer
locations of self. Individuals carried within them an array of tools by
means of which to craft and structure their religious lives.

For some, a key transition was from childhood in a place where one's
particular religion was the majority one and thus unmarked, to a new
situation in which the adult was now practitioner of a marginal and
thus marked religion. Here the challenge to configure one's practice
with the mainstream—cultural or national—was especially clear. Transitions from a childhood with no particular sense of religious belonging to an adult entry (now possibly nameable as *re*-entry) into a religiously marked sense of self raised almost the same questions of how
one could be of x or y religion and still deemed "American." As well,
and conversely, religious identity was at times connected with the rein-
forcement of a sociocultural or socioethnic identity.

Ultimately, *place* conjures "old" and "new" sites. A place deemed
new may bear the imprint of the old. Thus the old and the new are not
necessarily separate or separable. However, they are not inexorably
fixed together in a nostalgic frame. Movement to new geographical
locations might limit religious or spiritual identities/identifications
and/or give rise to transformations that, whether positive or not, certainly alter the form and at times even purpose of spiritual practices.[2]
The interconnection of location and the relationships between activities considered spiritual and those deemed secular is inevitable.
Place structures the secular; as such it also provides the context for the
enactment of that which is felt and hungered for in spiritual and
religious terms.

Discussion of the ways in which religion or spirituality were present
in daily life raised two related questions for practitioners. On the one
hand there was the issue of finding language to express the value of
religion in and of itself. On the other hand, it was often challenging to
name Islam or Buddhism in environments that were primarily secular
and/or Judeo-Christian in socioanalytical terms. The challenge to
"translate" required interviewees to make conceptual distinctions be-

tween the religious and the secular when, for them, such distinctions were meaningless or themselves misleading.

As a result, the question of which activities and behaviors should be coded "religious" and which secular was at times difficult to answer. The more apposite questions here included how the "religious" or "spiritual" was interwoven into aspects of daily life, and when and why the use of time in daily life involved religious or spiritual activity. It was not as though these interviewees did not know what they were doing, or could not distinguish between acts that might be deemed spiritual or religious and other activities. Rather, there was a commitment to consciously draw on the spiritual to enhance what one might call the "practical." And as well, there was recognition that the "practical" might need to be redesigned to make room for the practicalities of spiritual life.

⚘

OF THE FOUR MUSLIM INTERVIEWEES, one man and one woman were immigrants raised, respectively, in an Islamic Shiite or Sunni sect. The others (both women) were adult converts, one a member of the Nation of Islam, and the other a student of one of a very few female Sufi teachers. Whether born into Muslim families or having turned to Islam as adults, each had in meaningful ways *chosen* Islam, made it her or his own. Religion was inseparable from other aspects of daily life activity. It generated routines, and helped to form things as fundamental as diet, language, and dress. It also gave rise to particular practices and codes of behavior in relation to others, to selves, and to the very religion of Islam itself.

For Enigma (self-chosen pseudonym), born into and still connected with a particular Sunni sect, Islam entailed daily prayer and meditation, and participation in a range of study groups and courses organized by local Muslim teachers. For Tariq Naficy, born Shiite, Islam had come to mean daily meditation, contemplation of scholarly works on Islam, and study of the Koran. For L'dia Omari-Mohammad, member of the Nation of Islam, religious and spiritual practice entailed daily prayer and meditation. For Sadiqa, Sufism meant daily meditation, the chanting of particular texts, and carrying with her the texts of those chants. All four of these individuals eschewed alcohol and other recreational drugs, and fasted at least during Ramadan, and at other times during each month. Two of these women (L'dia and Enigma) wore the kinds of clothing and head covering associated with their own branches of Islam. Sadiqa did not cover her head except on occasions when she attended a traditional mosque.

Enigma was twenty-four years old, born in India, raised in Saudi Arabia from one to twelve years old, and from then on in the San Francisco Bay Area. As a child, Enigma's entire community had been Muslim, so that the practice of Islam had seemed ordinary, to be expected. As she put it: "Over there [in Saudi Arabia], everyone is a Muslim. You tend to do things because you're so immersed in that culture—it's almost like second nature. You're just used to it . . . Everyone's wearing a headscarf, so you don't really think too much. Over here, because when you go out, you are the only one wearing the headscarf, you realize, 'Oh, I'm different from other people.'" As a young adult now living in a country where Islam is a minority religion rather than the majority one, Enigma's practice of Islam was more conscious. As well, she said, being a U.S. university student and participating in communities of Muslims from around the world meant that she had become aware, without judgment, of the differences between forms of Islam across cultures. These included, she said, issues as complex as different interpretations of Islamic law, and as mundane as different gestures during prayer. On this latter point she said: "When we come together, we are often confused with each other. But little by little, we begin to understand that, 'Hey, it's actually acceptable that in Islam there are these four schools of thought, and that they actually have different ways where you can—you can pray with your hands down or you can pray with your hands up.' And once you know that, then you're like, 'Oh, okay, that makes sense.'" In fact, she added, her peers' status as part of a minority religious community meant that "whenever we get together, we end up talking about religion—about what's happening to the Muslims around the world and some of the sciences of Islamic jurisprudence, and learning about Islam and, kind of, bonding together, you know. Because like hey, you know, you're connecting together. We're the same. So, and it's stronger, I think."

From a childhood in which Islam had been so normative as to be unmarked, Enigma experienced a transition that both marked her religious identity and at the same time anchored it in a new framework. New intrareligious connections needed to be made. Along the way, religious and intrareligious lives both changed.[3] Thus Enigma and her Muslim peers found themselves discussing their religion consciously rather than simply taking it for granted. Further, their conversations were translocal, and the discussion of Islam was political as well as spiritual.

Tariq Naficy, thirty-four at the time of the interview, was born in Iran and had immigrated to the United States in his early teens. Tariq's telling of his story made clear that, like Enigma, travel and place had been critical to his sense of self as Muslim.

Raised Muslim, Tariq said that "before I left [Iran] as a twelve-year-old boy, I was quite devout in what I tried to do—I tried to fast, I was praying, I did it because I wanted to try it out. But I think as a twelve-year-old, I wasn't really aware of the implications of what I was doing." He continued, "Coming to America, I wanted to be more American." But, he added, "Of course, Islam is not part of America." In the United States, Tariq said, "I had the good experience or, according to some people, the bad experience, of going to a Catholic school." His religious education in Islam, part of the school curriculum in Iran, thus ended at that point.

However, he explained, later a college professor and mentor inspired him to continue informally studying a diversity of religions. This habit came to good end after college when, posted to a research laboratory in Japan and facing a two-and-a-half-hour daily commute, Tariq returned to the comparative study of religion. He said, "I took probably thirty or forty books [to Japan], and some of these were very heavy-duty scholarly books on religions." Having made his way through texts on Hinduism, Christianity, and Buddhism, he turned to Islam. He found that "I did not feel any association with Shiism [*the tradition in which he was raised and, as will be seen below, still a reference point for him*]. I felt more association with Islam. I decided I really wanted to go back to the Koran and look at that and figure things out for myself." Simultaneously, he returned to experimentation with fasting. While the experiments were not entirely successful, particularly on those occasions when he skipped the pre-sunrise meal and then went a full twenty hours without food or water, this was nonetheless a period of looking closely at Islam as "a viable alternative." As he put it, through reading he contemplated "not just a superficial day-to-day, uh, going and praying—although some people consider that the core of Islam—but what more it offered me as an individual, and how it could, maybe fulfill my needs. I mean, it was quite strong. And I really started going back towards it much more strongly than I would have if I was just doing it because I was born in Islam." He concluded, "I really became more appreciative of what we had. And I guess since then, slowly I sort of became a lot more Muslim, whatever that means."

Again place was critically important, both in establishing Tariq's childhood sense of self as Muslim, and disrupting it as an immigrant, but also in enabling Tariq access to a broader and more comparative space by means of which to reconnect with Islam on new terms. By contrast with Enigma, community was not, on the face of things, a necessity as Tariq returned to exploration of Islam. Yet his description of the journey belies that first impression. His sense of belonging set aside identification with Shiism but turned to a broader connection with Islam and with the Koran itself. Similarly, when Tariq said that he became appreciative of what "*we*" had (emphasis added), a sense of inclusion was further emphasized. Tariq, several years after his return to the United States, articulated his sense of authenticity as a Muslim:

> One of the great things about Islam is something that I couldn't have understood if I just stayed in Iran. And it made a lot more sense to me having lived in this country and gone to Catholic school, and having a range of ideas available to me, a lot of them being anti-Islamic. [It is that] the basic tenet of Islam is that there's no God but Allah, and Mohammed is his prophet. And if you accept this, then people can call you a *bad* Muslim, or a Muslim that doesn't do their duties, but nobody can say you're not a Muslim, right? So that's sort of the binding force. And [this] allows a lot more divergence in ideas. One could even go in and argue that women don't need the covering.

Like Enigma, Tariq felt that his sense of Islam had changed, not for worse but for better, as a result of leaving a childhood setting in which Islam was the norm. As well, again like Enigma, Tariq found it necessary, and in his view beneficial, to learn about Islam outside of the restraints and particularities of any single Islamic sect. Thus, while Enigma found herself discussing Islamic jurisprudence with her friends, Tariq studied Muslim texts and decided that there is just *one* basic tenet of the religion—there is no God but Allah, and Mohammad is his prophet—rather than the five that most would insist on. For Tariq, it was thus his own examination of the religion, rather than community membership, that gave him the sense of his own interpretive authority, or at least interpretive capacity.

Examination of the importance of place might be taken one step further by noting the distinctly United States–originated ways in which Tariq contemplated his relationship to Islam. As has been widely noted, many in the United States, across the religious spectrum, feel enabled to draw their own conclusions about their traditions rather than depending fully on the established hierarchies of religious institutions.[4] In addition, within and beyond religious participation, the belief that residing in the United States confers a clearer purview on things is a well-established United Statesian idea, in and of itself. And lastly, Tariq's quest to find out what Islam "offered for me as an individual, and how it could, maybe fulfill my needs" fitted well with an ideal that is very much a part of contemporary U.S. religious culture. For in this context a key idea is that one deserves to, and indeed should strive to, settle only for that which serves one's own needs as well as, or even instead of, the needs of the religious institution at hand.

Enigma shared in some of this "Americanization," striving to work with lay peers as well as learning from established teachers. Yet the prayer that she told me that she had offered before this interview proposed a wider set of goals. Here, it seemed, her practice was not for her benefit alone but rather for Islam, and for all U.S. Muslims: "I know that I have this responsibility . . . you're going to be using this for research and you're representing the Muslims in America. Thus I have to be very careful and I have to make sure that what I say is reflective of all the other Muslims . . . And so, you know, I did a prayer, like I'm very anxious, 'Oh my God, please, please just let the words come.' "

Interviewees found it difficult to keep the sacred distinct from the secular whether in describing their daily practice or in living it. Tariq said that for him "mysticism is really part of daily life. It's not something that's separate, because it's very hard for me to meditate in the morning and then come and have a screaming match with my coworkers." And again (gauging his practice by reference to Shiism): "Shiites tend to be more flexible about particular times of day [for prayer]. But what I realize is that [sometimes] as I am doing my morning prayer my mind is some other place. I'm thinking about work and I'm thinking about what I'm going to say to this person, or all sorts of things. And I'm thinking, 'This is not right. There's something wrong with this.' "

Here, obviously enough, was ongoing traffic between Tariq's working life and his routine spiritual activities. But where in the first instance he spoke of the ways his "spiritual practice" has a positive impact on his working life, in the second he expressed regret about traffic in the opposite direction. His tendency to think about the workplace during morning prayer was deemed "not right."

In any event, there was, for Tariq, a relationship between spiritual life and work. At the best of times, the former should, he suggested, have an impact on the latter. When the reverse was true, Tariq said later, one might expect, if not applaud, this turn of events. As he put it, "I guess I try—and of course, I fail constantly—to apply what I've learned, whether it's just being more patient with people and having more understanding, or not getting angry."

A second example, from Enigma, demonstrates in a different way the difficulty of separating the sacred from the secular, the spiritual from the quotidian. Here the impact of depicting one's life in a sociolinguistic context that is mostly secular comes to the fore. For there was actually no way to articulate simply, except by listing it in detail, the interwovenness of daily activity with spiritual and religious belief and practice.

Enigma told me of prayers offered at regular intervals during the day, at the start and end of mealtimes, before sleeping, on waking, and before leaving the house. She explained her commitment to wearing a head cover or *hejab*. She also noted how Islam helped structure her diet. In this last instance, she explained to me that *halal* meat was like kosher meat. Place was key once again here as, drawing on a Jewish concept, Enigma connected her own religio-spiritual culture with one that she felt would be more accessible to a non-Muslim U.S. interviewer. However no such listing of practices could ever be sufficient, nor complete. As Enigma grappled with the challenge of describing her life and religion, she said: "Islam is such a complete, comprehensive way of life that there really isn't any separation between the spiritual or the physical or the virtual, I don't know. Everything is just so—so symbiotic, you know?"

The "religious," "spiritual," "physical," and "virtual" spun in her discourse as she sought to explain an event that is rather ordinary for a practicing Muslim:

> You know, we have the five daily prayers, and I guess you could call them spiritual practice. But at the same time, it's very physical as well, because you're moving your hands, you're washing with water before you pray so that you're in a state of purification physically, cleaning off the dirt, at the same time purifying your mind. Before you start praying, you make the intention that, "Okay, I'm going to pray to God now." And then once you stand facing Mecca and you pray, you're completely thinking of God—"Okay, I'm praying to you, God." In your head, you think, "Okay, God is watching you," and you bow down and make those movements, kind of submitting to God, which kind of goes all the way back to Abrahamic faith, when you bend down and you go on your knees and all that. So I guess, my answer would be just that it's a complete way of life rather than just a spiritual [one].

This clear articulation of one event out of an ongoing practice was offered to me extemporaneously as I sought to learn what Islam meant in Enigma's daily life. In it, she stepped smoothly into a mode of description reminiscent of ethnographic rhetoric yet thoroughly disruptive of it.

Enigma's description was explicit, almost frame-by-frame or second-by-second. Yet it contradicted, by means of its gaze and its location, those very stock representations of Muslim prayer in which the camera pans across a hundred or more rear ends, usually male, facing away from Mecca so that the forehead touching the ground can face toward it. Enigma placed the event of prayer in an interreligious history, noting its connection to "the Abrahamic faith." As above, in her comparison of halal meat with kosher meat, and indeed elsewhere in her interview, Enigma made a point of linking Islam with Judeo-Christian discourse, affirming, perhaps, the ways in which Islam is closer than is often noted to the dominant religious culture of the United States. She also disturbed ethnographic convention by placing Islam in the Western familiar rather than in the realm of Eastern alterity, in an historical unfolding that positions Islam within, rather than outside of, United Statesian normalcy.

Moreover, Enigma made the moment personal even as she described it from the witness's point of view. For she took her listener inward as she described the outer actions—she described what one feels and thinks when one acts. The thinking being is in fact the first person, *I*, generalized as the second person, *you*. Thus *you*, the listener, might be that praying woman or man. This tracking between the internal thought process and the external actions also makes inseparable the notion of the "spiritual" (colloquially associated with the inner journey) and the "religious" (colloquially deemed the institutional) in her description. Her words challenge any wooden, outsiderly classification of Islamic prayer as "religious," not "spiritual."

One sees here the richness of this five-times-a-day process of prayer. One sees also the ways in which it is, as Enigma pointed out, an event that is simultaneously spiritual, religious, physical, internal, and external. And beyond that it is an event that must be consciously placed in a U.S. time/space in which it is deemed unusual. Enigma said,

> [In Saudi Arabia], everyone does it. You know when the call to prayer comes five times—everyone goes to the mosque and they pray . . . Over here . . . you have to make sure you get excused when the prayer call comes. You have to cut class sometimes just to go and sneak away for about five minutes, do your prayers, come back into the class. You have to kind of go around with the secular schedule, I guess. But it's kind of like holding on to your identity.

Several points can be made about the process of practicing Islam in the United States, drawing on the words of Tariq and Enigma. First, as Enigma connected the challenge of negotiating the "secular schedule" with "holding onto [her] identity," an effect of the transition from unmarked to marked religious affiliation becomes clear. Once one's religion is marked, one's very sense of self becomes marked too. In response to the mainstream's flow (in Enigma's words, the "secular schedule"), explicit efforts need to be made to preserve one's socio-cultural *and* religious identity. Second, when lived in a context that makes it marginal to the larger culture, spiritual life might need to be named and performed in ways that refer to the context that surrounds it. And lastly, one can make the general observation that both spiritual and secular lives are lived differently because of one another.

🌿

IF IT WAS DIFFICULT AT TIMES for Enigma and Tariq to move in the world as immigrants and members of a marked religion, the same was true for United States–born convert to Islam, L'dia Omari-Mohammad. At the workplace, L'dia said, religious and secular modes of thought and speech had at times clashed explicitly. She said, "When I go and teach pregnant moms in the community, one restriction that they put on us is that we don't mention the word God or religion. That was difficult for me, because I always give praises to Allah for everything." L'dia did, though, find ways around this stricture. She explained, "I don't mention God, but I do mention inner strength and spirituality in a different way so that people aren't offended. And really, the clients *aren't* offended. It's the funding sources. There's the separation of church and state." Although this problem might have come up in relation to any religion, L'dia faced some distinct challenges in relation to her dress code. She said:

> It was hard at first. I was on the job. I accepted Islam maybe five months into the job. Of course, my clothes changed almost instantly. That was hard for them to take, at first. Until they understood that I was still the same person, you know?
>
> When I left that job to find another one, the interviews went fine as far as the resume, my skills, and my experience were concerned. But I do feel that I spent most of each interview trying to make the other person feel at ease. Trying to relax them because they were visibly uneasy about seeing me dressed in my garment, in my garb.

Self-employed by the time of the interview, L'dia has found her clients comfortable with her long robe. She commented, "They seem to feel 'Oh, well, she's teaching something holistic anyway, so it just kind of goes along.' The dress goes along with what I teach."

Reading L'dia's experiences tells one several things about the discursive environments in which she lived and worked. First, her own religious practice made it essential and even habitual to thank God or Allah in the context of her work, thus abandoning any separation between sacred and secular spaces. Second, in response to the reimposition of that separation, it turned out to be possible to at least nudge its edges, still invoking a spiritual belief, but one that was lacking in any kind of deism and in fact replaced the divine with the "inner self." What one sees here is that there are kinds of spirituality or quasi-spirituality permissible in the public realm. Third, distinctions may need to be made between official and popular discourses. For L'dia finds that, in her view, it is institutions rather than clients who are disturbed by L'dia's explicit invocation of Allah. It is entirely possible that some of her clients were also Muslim and/or also members of the Nation of Islam. It is equally conceivable that some were not happy as L'dia called on Allah or any form of the divine, yet did not feel empowered to express this. Still, L'dia's experience demonstrates the non-homogeneity of her workspaces, and the interchangeability of languages for calling on the divine.

L'dia's workplace challenges in relation to dress brought forth some similar issues. To begin with, obviously her dress as a Muslim was striking given her primarily non-Muslim places of work. More than that, her marked dress called into question, for some of her colleagues and potential employers, her status as familiar, as known, as coworker and as potential employee. L'dia, as she explained, had to do the emotional work of calming down others in her workspaces. But again, L'dia found that she had a diversity of clients—perhaps clients whose fluency or imagination in transcoding are more creative—as she traveled on the basis of her own authority into work settings as a self-employed practitioner. In this new situation, it appeared, her clothing no longer signaled the unknown, and therefore the lacking, in relation to needed work skills. For while her clothing still signaled the unknown, now it carried the promise of greater riches in relation to those skills ("She's teaching something holistic . . . it kind of goes along"). L'dia thus found ways to make her spiritual practice congruent with workplace protocols. She effected this by shifting from modes of signaling religion or spiritual commitment deemed unacceptable to ones with other, more acceptable connotations. However it should also be remembered that L'dia at times needed to change from one work site to another rather than from one mode of presentation to another in order to retain the spiritual integrity of her work.

L'dia, forty-two at the time of the interview, had joined the Nation of Islam at around the age of twenty, as the result of an intentional spiritual quest. She said, "I had been looking for a formal religion; also a religion that had to do with helping black people build their self-esteem." L'dia was also, she told me, a "universalist spiritualist," something that, she said, was compatible with the Nation of Islam rather than at odds with it. Near the start of the interview, and after I had asked her how she viewed popular conceptions of that organization, L'dia made it very clear that she was not speaking "for" or even "about" the Nation of Islam, but rather as an individual. She said, "I am not a spokesperson for the Nation of Islam. It's my religion and it's part of my culture. [But] in speaking with you, I'm basically talking about me, and my practice."

It was indeed easy to recognize the traces both of the Nation of Islam and of an array of folk healing practices in L'dia's approach to her work. While the Nation of Islam provided her with formal religious training and discipline, the spirituality that she deemed "universal" and thus equally present in Islam, Christianity, and all other religions, had to do with "treating people right, and treating people the way you want to be treated." This latter aspect of her spiritual self-description gave rise to a much broader canvas of resources. As L'dia put it: "It's like I'm in God's classroom. God directs me where I need to go at the time . . . What this means for me is listening to my intuitive nature. Which often times does not make sense to other people." In this regard L'dia was able to describe for me the serendipitous process by means of which she had progressively enriched her orientation to birthing and parenting education.

L'dia had at first been a community worker. She then became a *douala* or labor coach. In *that* context she had learned skills in massage, music therapy, naturopathy, and aromatherapy to ease women's labor pain. Developing her skills further, she had undertaken midwifery training so that she could assist those who found themselves pregnant with no medical resources or prenatal care. Lastly, the circle returned to the community, counseling potential parents, female *and* male. As she put it, women "aren't happy about creating children and then taking care of the children, so a lot of my work is about mothers understanding their value to society. Not just as a woman but as a mother as well." L'dia's commitment to actively connecting her spiritual practice with community empowerment, building self-esteem, and self-reliance fit well with the stated goals of the Nation of Islam.

As elsewhere, one can draw on the notion of "place" to analyze and comment on L'dia's religious and spiritual journeys. Religion and spiritual practice, and sociocultural context, were mutually constitutive. On one side, L'dia's religious practice within the Nation of Islam, and her broader sense of a "universal spirituality" provided resources that inspired, supported, and enhanced L'dia's work in the area of childbirth. On the other, it was her knowledge of the particular needs of her clients—male and female—that had helped give form to her work, in the beginning and as it evolved. And in turn, once those needs were known, L'dia's religious beliefs, the tools they provided, and the harder-to-name pathway of "God's classroom" enabled L'dia to craft spirit-driven approaches to her work. Meanwhile, the commitment to what one might term "spiritual authenticity" led L'dia to transcode her practice so as to ensure that it fit well enough into the religiously diverse settings in which her work took place.

⚜

LIKE L'DIA, SADIQA ENTERED ISLAM as an adult. She was the child of Palestinian immigrants. Her mother immigrated to the United States at the age of fifteen and her father when he was several years older than that. Sadiqa spent the greater part of her childhood poor, given the ups and downs of her father's life as a small business owner, and her parents' divorce when Sadiqa was thirteen.

Sadiqa had rarely lived near other people of Arab descent. Despite this Sadiqa felt strongly that her parents' place of origin had traveled with her. This shaped her life in the two U.S. cities where she grew up and gave her a sense of being from the "old place" despite the fact that she had actually been born in the "new" one. She said, "What happens to the Arabs in the Middle East is—you're surrounded with an Islamic society, so we're kind of brought up Islamically without knowing it. My father would have my brother wash his feet all the time and, you know, no pork in the house and all sorts of interesting things." Sadiqa's naming of place and space were confusing, here: one almost felt that Sadiqa had, in *her own* childhood, been raised in a Middle Eastern, Islamic context, even though this was actually not the case.

Moreover, Sadiqa's family had, in fact, not been Muslim, but rather Orthodox Christian. However, she said, her family had remained connected with their own religion more in cultural than in institutional terms: "I grew up in an Orthodox Christian family, but we were not really religious. I've read a tiny amount of the Bible. But we were socialized Christians. You're just proud you're an Orthodox Christian because you're a minority and your family is." Given (or perhaps despite) all of this, Sadiqa was emphatic as she told me that she had, throughout her childhood, felt intuitively connected with the divine. She said, "I've always felt the presence of God in me. Or, I've known about it, whether I've chosen to ignore it or not. Unspokenly, I've had my own intense private relationship with God. And I continue to ask God to show me the way."

By the time she reached adulthood, Sadiqa's difficult childhood, her ethnicity, and her nascent sociopolitical beliefs had come together with a spiritual practice. Thus, speaking not just about her family but rather invoking her community as she saw it, she said:

> We've had the choice to decide, do we want to heal or do we want to stay in the dark with our pain and not deal with it? I see constant abuse issues with other Arab friends of mine. This is why I feel like I need to do something in the community. My lifework is, hopefully, mainly going to be through spirit, actually making things happen, raising the consciousness through film, doing work as a sociologist, doing political work, because it's the time. We have no place in America. We have very little acknowledgment.

In ways that are reminiscent of Enigma's telling of her story, Sadiqa's sense of place, identity, and point(s) of geographical and cultural origin are tightly interwoven. Thus Sadiqa began to see herself as one of a group, rather than a lone individual. And as part of that process spirituality became a resource for supporting that cultural group.

Sadiqa's transition from an Orthodox Christian community to Islam, and in particular to the Jerrahi Order of Sufism, came about through a man who was, at the time, Sadiqa's domestic partner. This man, no longer in her life at the time of the interview, had been Sadiqa's first Sufi teacher. They had founded a business together, selling and demonstrating uses of henna. For Sadiqa, a personal and spiritual relationship that had at first seemed to herald a lifelong connection had turned sour, leaving Sadiqa with no choice but to leave her partner, dissolve the business, and try to start it, and all other aspects of her life, afresh. The broken links between spiritual practice and an intimate personal relationship had left her struggling to make sense of both.

The process of dismantling the East Coast branch of her business had called Sadiqa to New York. While there, she had visited a *masjid* (place of worship) of the Jerrahi order, in Manhattan. In it she met a new teacher who was, unusually for Sufism, a woman and also French American. At that point, Sadiqa said, "things just kept falling into place and feeling right. I would go back to the masjid and I would kind of be in it but also keep my eye [*that is, her critical and intuitive faculties*] open. And then I surrendered into it."

Welcomed into this order, Sadiqa received a spiritual name (*Sadiqa*, meaning "truthful"). Still, she emphasized, she continued to ask questions, both about her own lack of formal religious training and about the contemporary religio-spiritual scene. She shared some of her questions with me: "Am I being a hypocrite because I have my issues with the Koran? I have my issues with sexism, with classism, with modern-time promotion of spirituality, with why are the people running the show wealthier people? They're giving their life to God, but they still have a maid, they still have this, they still have that." As far as could be determined in the interview, Sadiqa did not receive answers to these questions. However, it is important to note that for her there should be no separation between the religious and the secular, and that, in fact, any relaxation of her expectations about ethics in secular life would in fact call into question the religious institution itself.

That being said, however, it seemed that Sufism provided Sadiqa with the framework within which to pursue spiritual practice and the logic with which to make sense of her efforts to support her community.

SADIQA Sufism helps me go deeper into a practice and into a community . . . It's almost the more I give, the more God gives me. It's like a sponge of love, you know. But I'm not giving to receive, I'm giving to give purely . . . I don't know what it is God has, but it's always been interesting. Never boring. And I know what's right. I get the feeling of what's right, what's supposed to happen. I just have to fine-tune my being more.

RF "Fine-tune your being," so that you can be more conscious of what you're hearing God telling you?

SADIQA Yeah. Exactly.

Sadiqa, like L'dia, makes clear that a way of knowing that is spiritually framed is key to her life and her practice. As such, a bridge is built between her work within and outside of her religion. To this extent one might argue that, as for others, the separation between spiritual and secular life begins to dissolve. Further, one must note that for Sadiqa the effort to dissolve that separation is an important part of spiritual life and a means of enhancing her work for her larger community.

☙

HOLDING THESE FOUR INTERVIEWS TOGETHER is, first and foremost, the practice of Islam. As both Enigma and Tariq had learned, the diversity of Islamic practice, evident in the United States, need not be cause for concern. Thus, we saw Enigma, Tariq, *and* Sadiqa making explicit their commitment to supporting Islam in general rather than in sectarian terms.

As has been seen, these interviewees' spiritual and religious practices had at times been remade in order to fit in with non-Muslim and/or secular environments. As well, practices had been redescribed by them, in order (they hoped) to make them more accessible and more acceptable to outsiders. Further, all four found it appropriate at times to examine and draw on religions beyond Islam, whether as tools for comparison, contextualization, and translation, or simply in recognition of their own positioning in multifaith and multicultural worlds.

However, while they needed to be open to creatively living and working in a religiously diverse and oftentimes secular world, they also needed to come to terms with Islam's status as almost always marked and almost always low in the U.S. religio-cultural ranking system.[5] In addition to the adaptivity that these persons had developed in this context, a strengthened sense of identity as not just religious but also racial/ethnic, and not just spiritual but also politically and culturally meaningful, came to the fore. The converse was at times also true. L'dia, for example, drew on the spiritual in order to heal or ameliorate cultural wounds, but also at times needed political and cultural analysis in order to make space for her religious and spiritual practices.

Examining questions about place made clear the significance of the United States's own religious and political landscapes. As noted, all were aware of the religious diversity of this particular place. The very nature of all four individuals' journeys—the capacity to travel into religious realms different from those of their birth communities; a sense of permission to examine and rethink their religious worlds— were signs that these individuals shared much with their non-Muslim contemporaries in actively examining their own religions.

Yet as we have seen, focus on the United States alone does not enable one to fully understand these individuals' spiritual and religious lives.

To begin with, of course, both Enigma and Tariq started their Muslim lives outside the United States. Both were aware that travel across national borders led to travel across religious lines, and entailed transformation of the latter. Enigma and Tariq in effect carried both places in their consciousness, working within and against the differences, at times benefiting from these, and at times working around them.

As well, Sadiqa's life story made clear that migration across national borders does not always complete families' transitions. Thus Sadiqa saw herself—at times consciously and at times almost unconsciously and reflexively—as having been raised Muslim and Middle Eastern. This was so despite the fact that her family was Orthodox Christian, and it was her parents, not she, who had grown up in a predominantly Muslim society. Likewise, Sadiqa was readily able to discuss the challenges faced by Arab Americans as a large category, recognizing again the way that one's place of origin, whether literal, cultural, or merely metaphorical, had an impact on one's treatment in the United States.

Only L'dia, raised in the United States and in fact converted to a form of Islam created here, presented no sense of geographic transition in her discussion of living with Islam. Yet, like the others, L'dia faced the local treatment of Islamic practice as not normal and thus potentially disruptive of secular working life. Indeed as noted above, L'dia was conscious enough of the controversial status of the Nation of Islam to balk at my questions about it early in the interview and make clear that she should be treated as a member of the Nation but not as a spokesperson for it.

Work was interwoven with religious and spiritual practice in several ways. First, all were clear that spiritual practice and religious discipline gave rise to an ethic that must be applied at all moments, including the time spent at work. Second, as has been seen, it was often necessary to skillfully adapt the workplace to fit well with religious timetables and needs. Thirdly, for all, (but especially L'dia and Sadiqa) the goals and content of work connected closely with spiritual and religious goals. Very often, work content was not only assisted, but indeed guided and directed, by spiritual inquiry.

For all four Muslims discussed here, the relationship between place and religion was clearly related to the national as well as the local, with the former influencing the latter in obvious ways. For example, the setting of Saudi Arabia (the national) shaped Enigma's (local) experience of daily prayer in a way different from her experience of the same in the United States. The literal, visceral, and experiential meanings of *place* were very much at issue. And, as follows from this fact, the content of spiritual and religious practices was shaped by the particularity of place.

⚘

THIS CHAPTER NOW TURNS to four Asian Americans, all practitioners of Buddhism. Place and practice intertwined in the lives of all four, none of whom practiced a form of Buddhism directly related to their immediate ethnic and/or geographical roots. Michael Yamamoto, Japanese American, had practiced Tibetan Tantric Buddhism since his early twenties. Mushim Ikeda Nash, Japanese American, had been initiated into a Korean Zen Buddhist lineage in her late twenties. Richard Chu, Chinese American, and Liên Shutt, Vietnamese American, both primarily practiced Vipassana meditation as developed in the United States from Theravada Buddhism, whose primary centers are Burma, Sri Lanka, and Thailand.

All four Buddhists, like the Muslims, had remade Buddhist practice in the context of their own lives. Political and sociocultural events key to Asian American history, and to U.S. history more broadly, had marked their own journeys, spiritual and otherwise. As such, the Buddhist lives of these four people were stamped clearly by the particularity of national location and transnational process. *Place* must also be understood by relationship to complex temporalities. For these four people, conscious *and* unconscious memories of the past turned out to have been crucial to the making of spiritual lives in the present.

There have always been, and remain, Buddhist sanghas (practice communities) in the United States situated within single ethnic and/or language groups. At times, Asian immigrant communities' efforts to assimilate to the United States have involved some steps toward making Buddhism look more like mainstream (that is, Christian) religious forms. An example here might be use of the term *church* for the place of practice. As well, immigrant Buddhist establishments have felt at different times the racism and/or anti-Japanese policies and prejudice of U.S. government and culture.[6]

Meanwhile, through a history somewhat interwoven with the establishment of Asian American Buddhist religious institutions in the United States, but primarily separate from it, there are now also considerable numbers of "mixed" sanghas. Some of these have predominantly white membership. Others are more complexly interracial. Some began with Asian immigrant teachers. White practitioners who had themselves studied with Buddhist teachers in Asia started others. Both have at times also been part of efforts to transform the practice, to make them congruent with or culturally accessible to a U.S. population.[7] One unintended consequence of all of this has been the recapitulation within many sanghas of the racism of the wider United States culture.[8] As will be seen, these four interviewees' lives bore the traces of different moments in these histories. However, none of them belonged in adult life to one of the single-community sanghas described above.

Like the Muslim interviewees, this Buddhist group at times commented on the "marked" status of their religion and its differentness from the U.S. mainstream. However that "marking" took a different form and thus gave rise to different language strategies than it had for the Muslim interviewees. The latter group, as discussed above, had at times striven to transcode their practices to non-Muslims, and made clear their sense of its noninclusion in the national scene. By contrast, as will be seen, this group of Buddhists commented in different ways on the "Americanness" of their religion, whether appreciating that fact, decrying it, or merely observing that relationship. This difference may well be because, albeit a marginal and numerical minority religion in the United States, Buddhism does not suffer the hostility, even demonization, faced by Islam in the present-day United States. Yet the need to name rather than take for granted the "Americanness" of their religious practice still signals its location on the borders rather than at the center of the U.S. religious landscape.

It was striking that, as these interviews began, this group of four all found it important to situate themselves temporally as well as in ethnic terms. This too reflects the history of racial/ethnic mapping in the United States. For, as has been widely recognized and criticized, despite the longevity of their presence in the United States, Asian Americans have been repetitively positioned discursively as "outsiders" or "newcomers."[9] Ultimately this also "marked the marking" of Buddhism in the United States. For on one hand, it was significant that as these men and women named themselves as long-standing "Americans" (or in Liên Shutt's case, the opposite), these practitioners also needed to describe Buddhism at times as "not a new immigrant" and thus part of the U.S. religious world. Yet on the other hand it was at times critical to describe the religion as distinct and different from the mainstream and its religious frames.

Michael Yamamoto, forty-nine, sharing the commitment to temporal self-naming just noted, described himself as "Japanese American, third generation." Mushim Ikeda Nash, forty-six, did the same, and also explained the reckoning system. Thus, she said, "I'm third generation in the way that Japanese Americans count, so I'm a sansei. All four of my grandparents, who were the immigrants to come from Japan, were the first generation, the issei. My parents, born in the United States, were nisei. My son is *yonsei,* or fourth generation."

Richard Chu, forty-five, described himself as "bicultural"—"Chinese by heredity and Chinese American by identity." Although there is no generational identification name that he could offer me, Richard felt it important to state that his parents were both immigrants.

Finally, Liên Shutt, thirty-five years old at the time of the interview, also spoke of her temporal relationship to the United States and the complexities that had come along with it. Liên was born in Saigon to Vietnamese parents. At eight, as her mother faced death from cancer, a European American couple had adopted her, together with her elder sister and a much younger Thai boy. ("That," she said, "was our family.") She felt, she explained, at times like the "one and a half" generation Asian Americans brought to this country by adoption or by immigrant parents. Yet at other times she felt more like one of the third generation members of Asian American communities who strove to reconnect with the cultures that their parents had found it necessary to leave behind. In any event, she said, "At eight, I became an American," losing access to her birth religion and her language as well. She added that her adoptive parents, U.S. government employees at the time of the adoptions, had made the effort to return to the United States as quickly as possible "to Americanize us kids."

The temporalities of immigration and its associated processes of assimilation, at once chosen and imposed, were, then, significant in the Buddhist lives of all four of these people, not just as individuals but as members of extended families and communities. None of them could say that they had been raised in unambiguously Buddhist settings. Still, none could say that they had been raised entirely apart from that religion.

*Americanization* was a key term here. And as Tariq said about Islam, Buddhism was not, for these individuals, for their communities, or for that matter for U.S. culture in general, considered a part of "being American." As noted, Liên's parents had made efforts to "Americanize" her. This had included baptism in her adoptive mother's Presbyterian Church. Likewise, Richard said of his parents: "In order to assimilate in the Midwest where they first lived, they became American Baptists.

They joined the nearest available church and just did what everybody else did around them. I went to Sunday school for the first twelve years of my life. In American Baptist practice, the child is given the choice of baptism in early adolescence. I refused, so it was clear that I wasn't going to continue that practice. Then my parents discontinued as well." Richard's parents were on their own complex journeys with regard to religion, both before and during their time in the United States. His mother, he said, had been raised Buddhist, but after a deep sense of the failure of her religion in context of her own father's death, she had taken the opportunity upon arrival in the United States to entirely set aside all involvement with Buddhism.

By contrast, Richard's father, raised a Confucian Taoist, had not abandoned his beliefs. Still, Richard said that while, in hindsight, he recognized his father's efforts to convey key Taoist concepts like the "middle way," he could now see clearly that his father felt constrained to share this philosophy through telling anecdotes, offering, as Richard put it, "spiritual teachings in a secular context." Richard concluded, "It was the only way he could bring that information to me. He felt that he had to sort of do it in a way of maybe not being too Chinese, because as a kid growing up in a white middle-class suburb, I was trying to be white."

Mushim's parents were not assimilators by intent. Nonetheless, Mushim could state clearly how the "Americanization" process had forcefully disrupted her parents' religious upbringing, and thereby her own, too. She said: "My maternal grandparents in Hawaii were very devout Buddhists. My mother was not, because she was a kid at the time of World War II." At that time, the U.S. government in the context of its war with Japan had closed the Buddhist temples in Hawaii. Thus, Mushim said, her mother "was of no religion that we knew of during her lifetime. But my aunt, her older sister, is a very devout Soto Zen Buddhist. So when I became interested in Zen Buddhist practice, my aunt said, 'This is your karma, because Grandpa and Grandma were such strong Buddhists.' So even though my particular practice lineage is Korean, connecting to this religious tradition has been significant to me. It has felt like connecting with my family roots." Lastly, while Michael's nuclear family was not religious, they were unusual in that respect. He said: "In retrospect I've always felt like my affinity for Buddhism grew out of my upbringing and broader family . . . Social lives revolved around either the Christian church or the Buddhist church. The majority was the Buddhist church. And that went for most of my relatives, my cousins, aunts, uncles, and grandparents."

As Mushim and Michael's last statements suggest, if the four could tell me how it was that their upbringing was *not* Buddhist, they could also tell me how Buddhism *was* nonetheless present.

Michael speculated about the impact of childhood memory on adult practice: "For all [my relatives] Buddhism was very important . . . When I was really young, for a time my grandfather lived with us . . . I still can remember, he was retired and he just did a lot of practice. At the time it was very mysterious. But now I can relate to it real well. I think it made a kind of an imprint." He continued: "It goes beyond just an observational thing. [There was a] subliminal or unconscious tran—you know, communication that I became aware of actually in the course of [my adult] practice." It is striking that, before drawing back and substituting the word *communication*, Michael goes so far as to toy with the idea that he might have received transmission from his grandfather of commitment to Buddhist practice. *Transmission* is the giving and receiving of spiritual wisdom from an elder to a younger practitioner in Buddhist lineages. It is a formal process that entails recognition and authority of the elder and, afterwards, of the younger as well. It is an exchange not offered to all practitioners, and deemed a high honor. Given all this, it is perhaps not surprising that Michael withdrew that word from his description of the childhood encounters with his grandfather. Yet, as he stated, what did happen was that he received unconsciously as a child, and more consciously in retrospect, the "imprint" (his word) of Buddhist teaching.

Michael struggled to find appropriate language for what was given and received, and the means by which the exchange took place. The word *retrospect* is key here: the gaze from the present toward what was there before. He said: "In retrospect you recognize it in [your current practices]. They connect with these memories. There's a kind of atmosphere that you might associate with certain kinds of experiences. I recognized them as familiar because they were associated with these memories of being in the presence of these people." Michael could now make present-based sense of past experience, realizing that, indeed, it had helped to create the present. Past and present communed as Michael witnessed states of consciousness (whether in self or in older relatives is almost unclear) that he can now—as a practitioner—connect with particular spiritual practices. Michael was, in short, describing the sameness of his own and their practices, and the results of these.

Challenged by the difficulty of explaining he concluded: "They're not the kind of thing that we're raised to be able to verbalize. They're more—what? Visionary or atmospheric or something like that. I don't know quite how to put it. But, I really feel like that was a big influence on me without my realizing it at the time." Connecting Michael's experience with the comment made by Mushim's aunt about karma, and remembering Sadiqa's temporal confusion about who was raised in a Muslim society—she or her father—one can make yet another link between these Buddhists and Muslims. For we may note that religious memories seem to travel through families, within and even at times across communities, in the making of religio-spiritual consciousness.

Liên, too, remembered fragments of a Buddhist childhood, despite a parting from her birth family traumatic enough for her to refuse, at first, to discuss the transition with me. She shared with me an article written about her childhood in which she states: "Though temple visits were not a regular practice, I still have vivid memories of my mother lighting long sticks of incense and bowing before an altar.[10] Continuing this line of thought, she told me that in the United States, "I started sitting and going to groups and it really resonated. It's a cultural base too. It's kind of like rice. You know, we all eat rice, but I think, for a lot of Asians, Asian Americans, we're all raised on white rice. You know that brown rice is better for you, but white rice just tastes a certain way that you can't get past. That's kind of like how I think about Buddhism, for Asian people who have it in the family history." Religion and other aspects of daily life, childhood and the present, and Asianness and Asian Americanness, were interwoven as Liên explained how Buddhism remained meaningful in her life. Just as Liên's most direct memories of religion included her mother's daily, home-based worship, so she connects that with another daily act, that of eating. Religion was recognized as something as mundane, as quotidian, and as necessary as the staple food of one's diet. Meanwhile, Liên's senses of present and past were deeply connected with one another. Rice, probably key to her diet pre-adoption but not afterwards (given her parents' commitment to "Americanization" of the children), was revealed to be fundamental, "basic" (her word) to her sense of self. Further, "rice" and "Buddhism" occupied analogous places in her consciousness and sense of self. Lastly, as Liên counted herself among "Asians, Asian Americans" one is returned to her discussion about generational belonging. For here Liên clearly names herself as "Asian American" and yet, as well, still unalterably "Asian" in a non-hyphenated way.

Given the circumstances in which Liên was parted from her birth mother, it was perhaps not surprising that another moment when Liên's Buddhist past merged with her later life in the United States was that of her adoptive father's death. Liên had spent a long period with her father, nursing him before his death. But when it actually happened, "I was kind of frazzled because it came really fast at the end. I was thinking, 'Oh, I need to pack for the funeral. Do I pack white or do I pack black?' I've always worn black since I've been in this country. But then I went to this place where it was like 'I always wore white before.'"

As Liên explains her thought process, her use of the word *place* is important, signaling both the literal separation between locations—geographical and temporal—and also the figurative intensity of memory. In fact, its use bridges what has been divided, for despite Liên's location now in a different place, it was in that moment very possible to return to the previous one, indeed, from memory's standpoint, insistently so.

In Liên's birth community, it was conventional to wear white for funeral services. Liên had prefaced the story of her father's death with a different one: a description of wearing white as a child at her mother's funeral, and being sent away from the gravesite with her sister as the coffin was lowered into the ground. While nursing her father, Liên said, she had been reading Sogyal Rinpoche's *The Tibetan Book of Living and Dying*. In it she learned that:

> One of the traditions is that—when a person is moving from this life into the next, their family can't be around because it might make it hard for them to move on. So when I read that I was like, "Oh." That explained a lot to me . . . It's a vivid scene. I was wearing all white, these cotton pants. We walked through tall grass. Then we came back and, honestly, I don't remember, was there dirt on the coffin or was it already a mound? I have no memory, but reading that explained to me why I wasn't there. Because nobody said to me, "This is our culture based on Buddhism, so at this point you have to go away." I think they just said, "Go away. You can't be here." So—that's what I'm saying. I read things where I go, "Oh, that explains my culture and explains how I do things or how I have ideas about certain things."

Memory merged with present crisis as Liên, preparing for the death of one parent, came to understand more about the death of another. In the newer crisis, the now-remembered behaviors for the earlier one seemed correct, although they were simultaneously known to be different from the practices of the present. Hence her questions, "Should I pack black? I always wore white before."

Past events become marked as specifically religious or spiritual ones. As Liên learned from a book about what is, arguably, someone else's religion (*Tibetan*, not Vietnamese, Buddhism), her own memories came to make cultural sense. There was of course no reason why, in the moment, her then-family should have named *religious* or *Buddhist* their insistence that she leave the gravesite. For one thing, Buddhism would have been taken for granted, unmarked. For another, the explanation might have been learned as she grew older, and perhaps witnessed other deaths.

Yet, plucked from that cultural context, she then never moved to the next stage, at least in that context or by those means. In its stead there was a serendipitous route whereby grieving another's death, in a different cultural setting, led her to unexpected comprehension of one more piece of her earlier life, religion, and culture. This earlier life now returned to a more present status. For Liên did not qualify insights of this kind as "past" or even "new" when she said, "I read things where I go, 'Oh, that explains my culture, and explains how I do things or how I have ideas about certain things.'" Sogyal Rinpoche writes of Tibetan, not Vietnamese Buddhist practice. Yet for Liên, national specificity was, at least in that moment, less significant than a broader notion of Buddhism as a simultaneously cultural and religious site.

🌿

THE JOURNEYS FROM CHILDHOOD to Buddhism in adulthood were not simple ones. Once again, issues circling around "Americanness," "Americanization," and the politics of location were important. As already noted, none of the four practiced, as adults, what their parents or extended families had practiced before them. For all four, any straightforward return was impossible, whether because the point of origin no longer existed, or because the "old place" no longer seemed fully adequate in spiritual or religious terms. Yet all were drawn to Buddhism in adult life. Each moved toward whatever forms of the religion were available and spiritually appropriate. Buddhism was remade, or entered on new terms. Each had his or her own story about that process. All four continued to grapple with spiritual questions about their situations.

Liên had been stymied by her inadequate knowledge of Vietnamese. She said, "There are several Vietnamese Buddhist temples in the Bay Area. I don't go to them because I don't understand it at all. I've taken some lessons but it's not anywhere—and to me that's part of having been assimilated." The idea of "having been assimilated" rings bluntly and painfully here. Liên continued that it had been a source of deep pain to turn to white teachers of Buddhism, and to need to read the texts of authors like Vietnamese Zen Master Thich Nhat Hahn in translation from his native language, also her own.

However, Liên corrected me when I suggested that as a result of this part of her spiritual challenge was not having a sangha (spiritual community). She said, "Yeah, I would say that that's a piece. But, I wouldn't say that I don't have a sangha because I consider the people of color sangha to be one that I'm a part of." Liên then explained that she had joined a group for people of color and served one term as its "caretaker" or administrator. As well, she said, "I also sit every Thursday with a people of color weekly sit, at [the San Francisco] Zen Center." Moreover, she had a twice-daily sitting practice at home, and reading Buddhist literature was a significant part of her daily life.

Yet her response to a call for submissions to the journal for Thich Nhat Hahn's spiritual community raised the continuing question of where and how she did (or did not) fit: "I wanted to submit something. [But] I said, 'Well, I'm not sure that I can say that I'm in that tradition. Because I don't feel like I've "congealed."'" In general I sit Vipassana. But I get all these new, different kinds of teachings from the different places I go, and then from my reading and so—I haven't really found one that I would say that I was. I could say 'Buddhism' and that's about as finite as I can get."

As an outside witness, however, one might propose that Liên *did* have a sense of where she was; if this seemed unclear to her it was, perhaps because she was walking (drawing on her words) "new, different" ground. Liên had a clear map of the local Buddhist landscape. She knew well enough who she was *not,* and where she could not belong. In this last category were traditional Vietnamese temples. As well, she knew that one consequence of these "new, different" alternatives included the painful irony of needing to accept Buddhist teaching from people who had received it from the very community from which she had been estranged as a child. Yet, as her sociopolitical and sociocultural identity had been recast, so too new possibilities for spiritual community building had emerged. Thus she rejected, yet still partially acknowledged veracity, in my description of sangha in her present. In a way that was quintessentially United Statesian, postmodern, and practical, Liên was the author of her own Buddhist path, drawing on a range of resources and working with them. In sum, Liên had, one might say, no fixed place in the Buddhist world. Yet one might say, equally, that her place in it was capacious rather than confined. Her own words express this doubleness when she says, "I haven't really found one that I would say that I was. I could say 'Buddhism' and that's about as finite as I can get."

For Richard Chu, as for Liên and indeed for the Muslim men and women discussed earlier, the form of spiritual practice owed much to the particularities of U.S. life in the late twentieth century. As well (and again like the others) his sense of socioethnic identity was a part of making his participation in Buddhism meaningful. Richard's spiritual practice was as much as anything motivated by his need to deal with three very secular problems. The first of these was the racism of the world that he grew into as an Asian American boy. The second was his distress when, from early adolescence, he became aware of his attraction to other men. As he put it, "Until I came out I had always said to myself, 'If it's this difficult to be a person of color in this society, there's no way I'm going to be a person of color *and* gay.'" The third issue was his turn to drugs and alcohol in response to the first two challenges.

Thanks to participation in Twelve Step programs (often feeling isolated as one of a few gay Asian Americans in his meetings), Richard did achieve the goal of sobriety. There were also, he said, nine years of therapy, with a hiatus midway while he returned to graduate school and qualified in social work and counseling. Finally, he said, while "there was no major sort of pathology going on, there was still this anxiousness and these issues of self-esteem that kept coming up." At that point his therapist suggested that he look into meditation. In responding to this suggestion, Richard said, "I encountered this aspect of Western convert Buddhism in the Theravadin tradition, Vipassana. The way that it's being framed and taught right now incorporates a lot of Western psychological concepts. And because I was already in psychotherapeutic training the concepts really were congruent. I felt that this was something I could understand." This bridging of Buddhism with psychology and with specifically Western (in Richard's view) ways of analyzing selves and worldviews began a process of connecting Richard's spiritual life with the issues that had, thus far, confronted him only in apparently secular contexts.

For example, he was able, in that context, to incorporate his sexuality into his thinking about spiritual questions. He said, "The first dharma gate [moment of spiritual opening] that I had was a gay and lesbian, day-long retreat . . . I immediately connected to that . . . Connecting one piece of identity with spiritual practice, and using it to deepen my experience of just being, of just sitting, of just walking. It allowed me to listen to the teachings in a different way . . . It was from that experience that my practice accelerated fairly quickly." Place was, once again, a critical concept in this moment. But here, rather than referring to a literal geographical location, generation, or memory, conscious or not, *place* now refers to an aspect of identity (here sexuality) and the consequences of that in a particular temporal and/or spatial location. As Richard stated, it was now possible to begin from and still remain within that place, and to engage its spiritual meanings.[11]

However, if this opportunity to bring a part of his identity together with spiritual inquiry had been positive, his encounter with racism in the sangha offered learning of a different kind. Richard said:

> Each community has it's shadow, and Spirit Rock certainly has its shadow. One of them is that it is primarily Caucasian. So, this major issue around race and diversity came up when I sat a seven-day retreat, in which I was one of two or three practitioners of color. It was a very difficult time, painful. I tried asking teachers for guidance. The response I got was "Okay, I will talk to you on the sixth day of the retreat. Please remind me." This was the second day of the retreat. I did, and the teacher said, "Oh, something came up. I'll have to see you sometime later." And by that time, it was kind of too late. I had spun myself out of control and I was very upset, so I left. I was in such discomfort and suffering.

Again, Richard had traveled to the place of this retreat bringing (as is to be expected) all aspects of his identity with him. Extending the metaphor of place, one might suggest that two places crashed into one another. Better, the place of race for Richard Chu as an Asian American man felt threatened and overwhelmed by the presence of a large majority of white people. The place of the meditation retreat no longer felt safe. The meditation teacher did not provide the support, as had the gay and lesbian retreat teachers, to connect this "piece of identity with spiritual practice."

Richard's phrase, "I had spun myself out of control" referred, he explained, to the consequences of finding himself in the "place" of Asian Americanness in a majority white situation. In the quietude of the meditation hall, it was all too possible to remember his very many negative experiences of that juxtaposition on previous occasions. As he explained it, "spinning out of control," meant that the "core issue" (his words) of racism cane to the forefront of his mind, leading him to think over "how painful it is. It totally consumes me. There's nothing else that I can feel. Even though intellectually I know that there are other things going on, I just can't get off of it." As before, Richard had traveled from within the place of his identity. Yet on this occasion, his practice community was *not* a place in which to safely investigate and sit with the issues of racism that he had carried in with him.

Fortunately, or unfortunately, Richard came to learn after the event that he was not alone in his sense that the sangha was not providing adequate support for practitioners of color. He was thus able to discuss the process with others and, better, join with them in seeking to transform the sanghas themselves. It was not, of course, that simply naming the problem was enough to resolve the issues. Still, beginning to connect this aspect of identity with practice and with a practicing community supported rather than drained him. Ultimately, he said, "I have found that working concurrently on this sort of day-to-day practice around diversity has deepened my sitting practice. Even in long retreats in which I'm one of a few people of color there's some equanimity in my experience even though the issue hasn't gone away." With an increasing dissolution between issues left outside and issues to be safely brought into the meditation hall, one might suggest that the "place" within the self and the "place" of the meditation hall become more accommodating, more in synchrony with one another. Reflecting on the difficulties inherent in that process, Richard said, "I'm seeing value in using identity as an opening. It's such a doorway question for me. Who am I? Yet, sitting in a completely Caucasian sangha at least in the beginning didn't do it for me. It brought up too many issues that were reflective of the social/economic culture of our times."

Richard's practice seemed in the end to begin to transform his sense of self as well as his capacity to practice as that self. Thus when I asked Richard, "Would you name yourself a Buddhist?" his response interrogated the question itself: "Yeah. The only caveat that I would have is that I'm hesitant to say that I am anything these days. I mean, even if I am gay, I'm Chinese, all of those labels have some kind of use but they're all limiting in so many ways." Richard did not consider the process of setting aside identity to be complete. However, the ability to integrate into one another Vipassana practice and aspects of his racial and ethnic identity offered him resources by means of which to transform not just the pain of racism, but his relationship to the question of identity itself.

☙

DESPITE OSTENSIBLE DIFFERENCES between them—one a practitioner of Tibetan Buddhism and the other a Zen Buddhist—Michael Yamamoto and Mushim Ikeda Nash had some things in common. To begin with the obvious, both were Japanese American, third generation or sansei. They were close in age, with Michael forty-nine and Mushim forty-six. Both had arrived at forms of Buddhism quite different from those of their kin. Finally, both grappled with the processes through which Buddhism was being transformed to settle into its U.S. home.

In both cases, "place" was a stable physical referent. Neither Michael nor Mushim was an immigrant, nor were their parents. Moreover, Buddhism had never been far away from either one, conceptually or spatially. For, while neither had grown up in a Buddhist nuclear family, each could, as an adult, draw on childhood memories (at times reconfiguring these) to examine the ways in which Buddhism was a part of their extended kin networks. This meant that Buddhism was not strange, exotic, alien, or even new to either individual.

Neither had needed to travel far to begin their adult practice. Michael even remarked that unlike many of his generation—he had begun his spiritual quest in the mid-1960s—he had not traveled to Asia, or even left his home state of California, in order to meet his teacher. And although Mushim had crossed the United States for university and work, prior to initiation into a Korean Zen order in the Midwest, she had met her teacher by reading a notice board close to her workplace. Instead, it was their teachers who had moved their locations, since Mushim's was a Korean monk and Michael's a Tibetan one.

However if something *had* changed, it was the United States itself. Mushim and Michael both connected their own turn (or *re*-turn) to Buddhism with the "counterculture" of the generation in which they came of age.

Thus Mushim said: "In the American interpretation of my generation . . . [Buddhism] really blended in with the counterculture's motto of 'question authority.' " Mushim cited the oft-stated admonition of the Buddha that his students must not take any teaching for granted, including his own, but rather should test all ideas for themselves. This, she said, fit well with the questioning of "givens" (her word) provoked by the Vietnam War and the Watergate scandal, as well as by young United Statesians' travels East and their experimentation with drugs.

It was the last of these factors that had led Michael toward Tibetan Buddhism. In this, he was clear, he was not alone. He stated: "It wasn't a really unusual phenomenon at the time. Frankly, everybody acknowledges that for a lot, if not the majority, of Tibetan Buddhists in the West, drugs had a lot to do with their initial impetus." However, he quickly added, "I'd hate for people to focus on that fact. It would lend disrepute to the tradition that it doesn't deserve. And, as you probably know, all teachers are uniformly clear about the fact that they totally disapprove of any drug use whatsoever." For Mushim and Michael to describe their entry points into Buddhism in a way that felt authentic to them, it was critical to make connections with place and history, and with events not directly religious in their meanings. Yet, especially for Michael, it also seemed important to stress that times had now changed, with drugs no longer relevant to United Statesians' Tibetan Buddhist practice.

By contrast, Mushim felt that in certain ways times had *not* changed since the 1960s and 1970s. For just as she felt that her generation's entry into Buddhism was connected with cultural criticism, she was in the present still committed to a form of Buddhist practice in which political and cultural issues were not set aside. Mushim said:

> My spiritual practice has taken me on a very long journey through monastic practice. Traditionally that style is not concerned so much with social issues at all. It's you and your meditation cushion. And coming out on the other side, now I'm a layperson, a householder, a family practitioner. And I'm also a person who's dealing with the community that I'm in. Issues of race, gender, and class are always in my mind, and have led me to be involved with the Buddhist Peace Fellowship, which is an Engaged Buddhist group.

In actuality, Mushim's monastic years had connected her with far more than her meditation cushion. Joining a Korean Zen Buddhist temple in its beginning years in a Midwestern city, Mushim said that she had spent four years of her life helping to literally build that temple and its community. For while meditation and chanting were crucial to her practice, as she explained, "we were basically living in a construction site. A lot of our practice was manual work. If something needed to be done, we were the work force. We did incredible things. We took this funky old house and we made it into a very beautiful Zen temple." Sacred and secular worlds were, by intention, placed together in the early days of the temple's coming into being. For as he created a religious community, Mushim's Korean teacher was committed to asking how the United States's social and cultural context might alter the meanings of religion and spiritual practice for entering practitioners. At stake, Mushim said, was "the form of community and style of practice most conducive for Westerners—acknowledging the Korean roots [of the lineage], but also that we weren't in Korea, we weren't Koreans." As things turned out, this teacher's system did not work for Mushim. Mushim said that any questions she raised were answered with advice to meditate more, and to look more deeply within. She was not, though, given support to ask whether any of her challenges might have to do with the institution and not simply her own spiritual understanding. Ironically, this approach seemed at once to push Mushim toward the Buddha's insistence on spiritual self-inquiry and yet also to refuse dialogue to assist in that process.

With a degree of concern about discussing that period still palpable in the interview, Mushim said that it had at times been hard to discern where the boundary line fell between rigorous practice and "workaholism" (Mushim's word). Thus it was that after four years Mushim left that temple, not to leave behind Buddhism or even Zen practice, but rather to discover whether there was a different way in which one might practice that religion. At that point she began visiting other Buddhist institutions across the United States, seeking answers for the questions she faced with respect to the temple, its plusses, and its problems. As she put it: "Was this just us? Was this Buddhism? Was this monasticism? Was there a lay form? I really wanted to find out what was out there and actually test my faith, my practice, my beliefs. And I wanted to be happier, frankly."

A means of addressing several of these questions came when Mushim, five months pregnant, spent a rigorous period of meditation at a Zen monastery far away from the one where she had previously lived. She said: "When the teacher found out that I was pregnant, he geared my entire practice to having this child coming. The bridge between the monastic practice and a lay householder's practice was the koan or question that [the teacher] posed: 'How do you manifest oneness with baby?' " This koan or presiding question was, Mushim said, still relevant "every day. All the time . . . It's a good question, one that leads me to live my life in a certain way, and to set my priorities according to—I guess you call them spiritual priorities." She elaborated:

> This has been my practice, to be with my son as he's growing up and to enter into his experience. He's very much like me in temperament yet he's different from me in gender. I am raising an American man. He has his own personality. I cannot mold him into some thing that I'd want him to be. He molds me and I mold him. It's a dialogue. It's a way of my trying to really understand, when I look at him, "Who are you as a person in the world? How can I help you become a happy person, a helpful person, a fulfilled person? As your mother, how can I help you become a spiritual person in the world?"

Mushim's practice is thus applied to her parenting, indeed *is* her parenting. Explaining how this is a spiritually based approach to parenting is a subtle endeavor. Her process of self-inquiry began with and drew on Buddhist philosophy. Hence her recognition of her and her son's separateness and yet connectedness, of the particularity of his and her essence, and also of the values by reference to which she chooses to raise him. One must note, too, the continuing presence of "place" here. For with or without Buddhism, personality, gender, or temperament, Mushim emphasized that she was raising a located individual, an American one.

The relationship between the sacred and the secular, the application of the former to the householder's life, and indeed the social and geographical particularities of all of this were also present for Mushim as she explained how monastic discipline remained beneficial to her activities as a parent. She said:

> Even physically, [that practice] gives me a reference point . . . When I feel nervous and dispersed, I can look at my thoughts and I can see they're unfocused and they're scattered. Then I do whatever I need to do at that time to try and bring myself into focus. What am I doing here? What's really important here? . . . For example, if I'm in a rush, say, to get to the grocery store because I have my list in hand, but my child isn't cooperating and I'm yelling, you know, "Get in the car! Get your shoes on!" If everything's becoming tense and kind of distorted, I really have to ask myself, is this demanded by the situation or is this *my* problem?

These goals are not, at first sight, necessarily spiritual ones. Indeed, they connect well with some psychologically or therapeutically based ways of thinking about the self as a parent. But that, in turn, may be seen as related to the conversation that has developed over the last thirty or forty years between United Statesian forms of Buddhism and United Statesian forms of psychology.[12] Once one recognizes this, one can see in Mushim's discourse the traces of her Buddhist practice in her work as a mother. Among these traces is the very idea that one might have developed the capacity to notice and question one's state of mind ("dispersed," "nervous," "unfocused"). Linked to this capacity is the possibility of recognizing that one may be behaving in a certain way and striving to control all around one simply because of one's preexisting plan and presumptions about how the future should unfold ("I have my list in hand"). Furthermore, tools by means of which Mushim situates herself as other than the center of time and space, other than the acme of value and wisdom ("Is this demanded by the situation?" "Is this *my* problem?") emerge, certainly in Mushim's case, from Buddhist practices of witnessing the mind, and are being applied to daily life far away from the "meditation cushion."

Lastly, while linking Mushim's Buddhist practice to psychological analytics, one must also note the ways in which these differ. Most importantly, when Mushim asked herself, "Is this my problem?" she strove to answer that question in a Buddhist way. Thus she asked herself about habits of mind and the possibility that she is simply attached to particular outcomes. From within a psychological framework, one might instead investigate one's emotions, childhood experiences, or incomplete oedipal dramas. In short, Mushim's Buddhist engagement with the question was premised on a particular understanding of selfhood, of how selves are made, and how they might be challenged for the better.

Mushim's application of Buddhist teaching remained, throughout, linked to a sense of place (American man, supermarket, car). And although she did not say so, it also connected with what she had described, earlier, as fundamental to a United Statesian interpretation of the Buddhist idea that one must examine for oneself all modes of thinking, even Buddhist ones. Thus, her sense that Buddhism entails not just self-examination but also examination of all aspects of context and teaching. So, while committed to passing on to her son the values that emerged from Buddhism, she was also committed to the (quintessentially United Statesian) idea that her child was a self-governing individual. And this was, as Mushim had found to her chagrin back in her early days as a monastic practitioner, a different view from that taken by her (non-American) teacher.

This same set of connections, and more, applied as Mushim spoke of a Buddhist teacher with whom she now sought to build a relationship, as her son grew old enough for her to return to formal practice. Mushim felt that her national status (and, I would add, her membership of a particular sociogenerational community of thinking) shaped the qualities she admired and required of any Buddhist teacher: "As an American, I feel that my teacher should be someone I respect because he or she is worthy of respect. Because of his or her conduct, their practice, the way they treat other people." She continued: "I would ideally expect my Buddhist teacher to be my friend. Not that I could call that person at any time of day and say, 'Hey, let's go out for a movie'—not that kind of friend. But the kind of friend who knows my husband, my child, the way I live, and who cares about me and my family in the sense of not wanting to separate me from things that are important to me."

As Mushim made this argument, it turned out that she had in her mind other, earlier modes of Zen Buddhist practice in the United States: "In the early days of American Zen, parents who were completely devoted to Zen practice and who loved their children very much nevertheless, from my point of view, neglected them in favor of the practice because they were told that was the superior and more noble thing to do. I would want my teacher to be my friend in the sense that if, say, I were signed up for a retreat and my son became ill, I might alter my plans." There is here a revisiting of Mushim's early questions on leaving the monastery, as to whether rigorous practice might have given way to workaholism. In seeking in the present to bring together practice and parenting, indeed to make parenting the practice, Mushim inverts what she perceives as the received hierarchy, arguing that, for her, staying home with her child—"manifesting oneness with baby"—was "superior," as "noble" as attending a retreat.

Mushim was at the time of the interview excited at the plans of one well-known American Zen teacher (whom she had known and worked with in past years) to begin a program designed for experienced Buddhist practitioners who were (her words) "raising families, very much in the world." Providing office visits and even phone consultations as well as family-oriented retreats, this had the potential, she felt, to meet her needs: the integration of practice with family life and open dialogue with the teacher.

As one contemplates Mushim's thinking about all of this, one must note that, in actuality, not all Zen teachers and priests are unmarried. Moreover, as noted earlier, Buddhist teachers, arguably by definition, are open to the Buddha's insistence that even his and their ideas must be subject to discussion and interpretation. At stake, perhaps, then, might be rather the *kinds* of intersection between family life and practice deemed appropriate, or the *kinds* of reinterpretation in play in a given situation. Thus in the final analysis what might have been at issue here was the reworking of practice in relation to place and culture.

MICHAEL YAMAMOTO, practitioner of Tibetan Tantric Buddhism, had also thought a great deal about what it meant to be American and Buddhist. He, too, was conscious of some of the issues raised by Mushim. Among these were the relationships between Buddhist students and teachers; the idea of the United States as a democracy; the meaning of U.S. values in relation to Buddhist practice; and the challenge of combining a busy working life with rigorous spiritual practice. (In Michael's case the latter meant a twice-daily schedule of chanting, meditation, and ceremonial prostrations; reading and contemplation of Tibetan tantric texts, and thrice-weekly participation with his sangha.) As will be seen, Michael's approaches to these questions were both similar to and different from Mushim's.

Michael, like Mushim, was conscious that the process of creating distinctly United Statesian forms of Buddhism was well underway. In response to a question from me, Michael said: "To my mind, there are two poles of Buddhist practice or attitudes towards Buddhist practice [in the United States] right now. And those are, on the one hand, people who are fixated on the problem of Americanizing Buddhism, and people who are hardcore traditionalists. And then there's everything in between. But it's a dialectic that's being worked out. I think that that's one of the big questions about the whole tradition going forward." It is striking that, in the current debates as Michael depicted them, being "traditional" as a Buddhist and being "American" as a Buddhist are at odds with one another. There is a semantic challenge since his discussion is about the primarily European American "Americanizing" pathways rather than other aspects of U.S. Buddhism. This, it should be noted, conceptually situates Buddhism as an "outsider" rather than an insider among U.S. religions.

As his language implied, Michael was less positive than Mushim about Americanizing Buddhism. Indeed, he put this clearly elsewhere in the interview: "In the whole scheme of American Tibetan practice my teacher is very traditional. I'm attracted to that. The more traditional the better as far as I'm concerned. [*Laughs.*] I'm a traditionalist." In any event one received the impression that Michael was concerned about the future of his religion in the United States. Possibly his sense was that, while Buddhism in some form might "go forward," the tradition might not. This line of thought was given fuller content as Michael continued. He said:

> Resolving the dialectic between traditionalism and Americanization basically focuses on the issue of the teacher/disciple relationship. There are other issues as well. But this is one of several big symbols. In fact, it's key. There are a lot of paradoxes involved. I have no idea what the answer is and I don't think anybody does. A lot of people are trying to figure out how to view it constructively. I've heard a lot of strong opinions in various directions.

As Michael spelled out the "paradox" as he saw it, it became clear that the issues of "Americanness," student/teacher relationships, and the notion of democracy were thoroughly interwoven. He said: "Traditionalists—from a very traditional standpoint there's a problem with democratization because there's the whole issue of transmission. I mean, you can't get transmission from anybody, you have to get it from a qualified person. And, you know, if you're in that tradition you believe that's real. But on the other hand, from a Western social standpoint it looks like a cult!" How, one might ask, do the terms *democratization* and *transmission* come to appear at odds with one another? The issue at stake here is that of how any individual is seen to have achieved authority, or to deserve it. In a functioning democracy the path to authority usually entails some process by means of which those over whom that individual will in the end have authority would have some input, whether by voting or similar means.

However, within Tibetan Buddhism the path to authority is a different one, premised either on long years of monastic training or on recognition of an individual, in childhood or adulthood, as the reincarnation of a now-deceased spiritual authority. While this is not the path to recognition in Zen or Theravada Buddhism, it too entails input from seniors in the lineage. Mainline (i.e., Christian and Jewish) religious institutions in the United States vary in the means by which individual teachers, priests, rabbis, and so on are selected and put in place—whether this is done by local congregations, or by their denominations' regional or national structures. Yet when Mushim says that she is choosing her teacher "as an American" she is, I suggest, thinking not so much as a member of a religious group, but rather as an individual, exercising her constitutional right to choose or to vote.[13]

As noted by Mushim, and as emphasized widely by Buddhist teachers and leaders, the Buddha's own teaching insisted that individuals think for themselves rather than blithely accepting teachers' authority. But still, the very road to authority itself was at stake here, and especially so in the Tibetan Buddhist tradition. Perhaps with this in mind, Michael added: "The whole problem about transmission is interesting. Those are things that just have not been conceptually resolved in more traditional Western terms. Well, they can't, because they don't exist! You know what I mean? There's no translation." Michael sets out, here, the impossibility of transcoding. As he put it above, "If you're in that tradition you believe that's real." And as he now states again there is, literally, no direct route and no direct translation between the pathways to legitimate authority in effect in Tibetan and other Buddhist forms, and those recognized (in principle at least) in the contemporary, secular United States. He concluded: "There is no simple solution. How people have resolved that in their own lives is kind of subtle. When it does get worked out it's not a very easy, formulaic sort of thing." Thus, although Michael was able to name the problem, and even begin to account for its points of origin, he nonetheless had no simple resolution to the question of whether and how authority might be restructured in the practice of Buddhism in the United States.

As we saw, Mushim at the time of the interview was committed to consideration of a Buddhist teacher on very specific grounds. Among these were his long experience in Buddhist practice, as also in the job of Buddhist priest and leader. He was, then, respected and had received authority on traditional Buddhist grounds, from his lineage and his Zen Buddhist seniors.

However, for Mushim, other factors in his favor seemed to be points of similarity with her beyond his teacher's status: like her, he was a parent, and like her, he was interested in building new bridges between practice and daily life. She had then depended on a mixture of the traditional, and some of the methods of choosing a teacher, representative, or guide familiar from secular U.S. life.

By contrast, Michael had worked with one teacher since his early twenties. Interestingly enough, he had approached him at the suggestion of a friend, after a few visits to another teacher had left him (and many others) feeling that a "cult of personality" was developing around that individual. In response to my question about his now long-standing commitment to his teacher, he said: "Gee, I don't know how to answer that question. I just felt a real strong affinity with him. I had immense respect for him and I liked what he was saying. The situation seemed to be working for me. That's the superficial way to describe it, I suppose." It is significant, perhaps, in light of the foregoing discussion, that Michael had, in fact, chosen his own teacher after encountering and assessing another one. He had remained with the current one because of feelings of respect and affinity. As well, he said, his teacher had on no occasion told Michael what he must do. Rather, Michael said: "Our teacher makes absolutely no demands whatsoever. He gives guidelines, he presents his point of view about what he thinks is good and what's bad. It just has a very voluntaristic sort of character." Again, Michael sounds in some ways like Mushim and in other ways different from her. He chooses this teacher after "looking around," albeit very briefly. He expresses strong affective commitment to his teacher, as well as respecting him in terms of the spiritual guidance he offered. Also, he is clear that his teacher would not force teachings on him so much as offer them to him. In his own words, his relationship with this teacher was a "voluntaristic," not a coercive one.

Yet in the end, Michael returned to his insistence that at stake here was not so much the content of the teaching as its origin and that of the teacher's authority. Thus he told me:

> MICHAEL Everybody draws their own boundaries. To me the definition of a cult is when people become enslaved by the teachings of that other person. But that doesn't include saying that I can't accept this person's voice as a voice of authority. So I draw the boundaries at a different spot than some other people would. I don't think—the people I practice with don't view it as a form of Quakerism or something. [*Laughs.*] I have no problem with Quakerism but that's not how it works.
>
> RF "Form of Quakerism" meaning a radically democratic space where everyone's voice is equal to everyone else's voice?
>
> MICHAEL Right. And somehow the truth that you're trying to learn is going to spontaneously come out of, you know—I mean, it does but— the teaching doesn't emerge in that particular way, I don't believe.
>
> RF So for you, the teaching emerges—
>
> MICHAEL From the tradition.
>
> RF And from the teacher?
>
> MICHAEL And from the line of transmission.

Here one sees a little more, finally, about the logic of spiritual wisdom as Michael conceives it. It is, as he stated earlier, a subtle framework. For while he concedes that "the truth that [one is] trying to learn" will in one sense be made manifest spontaneously, the *teaching*, or perhaps the structuring and analysis of that truth nonetheless need to be contained or at least tended by the teacher. And the teacher must in turn, Michael argues, be tended and contained by the tradition, with the teacher's capacity made possible through a line of transmission.

☙

LIÊN, RICHARD, MUSHIM, AND MICHAEL shared not only the religious frame of Buddhism but also the context of the United States in relation to which all undertook their practice. The relationship between place and practice was complex. At times, practitioners worked to do something that seemed like hauling the practice into line with its geographical context. At other times it seemed as though the effort was to "retrieve" a Buddhism that was about to drown in that context. Interestingly enough, all four did some of each. Making things even more complex, each at times seemed to be doing the one when they thought that they were doing the other. Thus, for example, while Michael described himself as a traditionalist, as has been seen, some of his decision-making strategies had more in common with what he described as the contrary Americanizing tendency.

There were readily identifiable moments when each named and lived by the core aspects of Buddhist practice: chanting; meditation; membership in a sangha; engagement with Buddhist teaching; application of that teaching in daily life. There were other moments when practitioners brought into their spiritual life pieces of their secular worlds. Identities formed in the secular world made necessary particular struggles over how to practice, as in the formation of sanghas, and the place in them of one's identity. Identities needed to be simultaneously nurtured and transformed, and possibly even renounced in those very sanghas as part of one's spiritual work. On one hand, as was seen, for example, in Mushim's case, the social context of practice, put "up for grabs" the meanings of the very teachings of the religion. But on the other hand, as Richard concluded, Buddha's very insistence that the human self be brought whole into the world of practice, and then transformed, made out of the religion itself a "melting pot" of a distinctive kind.

It might, in fact, be impossible in real terms to disconnect practice from context when one contemplates the structure of Buddhism, whether in the United States or elsewhere. Indeed a statement often made about that religion is that it has always been revised whenever it is geographically transplanted. Yet still up for debate in the United States is what stage has been reached in that process—has it begun in any meaningful way, is it in progress, or is there already a new phenomenon called "American Buddhism" by means of which (some? all?) United Statesians will be able to practice their religion? While I will not presume to answer that question, what is clear is that these individuals' practice of Buddhism was thoroughly shaped by the location in which it took place.

*Place*, for these interviewees, has meant several things. One of these has been sociogeographic locations and the histories that have crafted them. A second has been the travel of interviewees between such locations. A third has been the exploration of temporal and spatial shifts and layerings in individuals' consciousness, and the relationships of these to history, travel, and geographical stability. Yet what has made any of those dimensions of place meaningful has been their impact on the making of religious practice.

At issue for all eight of these men and women, immigrant and long-standing residents, Muslims and Buddhists, was the importance to them of practice as goal, method, and outcome. Place was complexly figured and reconfigured around practice. What has been discussed, then, was *not* how interviewees used spiritual practice to make place coherent or meaningful. The line of significance and purpose was something different. Religious and spiritual practice was not the ground for negotiating cultural, ethnic, national, or racial identity. Rather, while religion provided tools and resources in this regard, spiritual practice was, in the end, deemed meaningful in and for itself. And it was for that reason, I would argue, that these men and women strove to integrate, connect, and revise, as needed, the relationships between place and practice.

Place at times modulated and inflected practice. As well, practice had a key "place" in the life of each individual. These interviewees moved spatially, geographically, between and within traditions in dynamic and self-reflexive ways. Their locations did shape their practice. But what they were seeking from the practice, of the practice, and within the practice, was in the final analysis the motivating impulse and connecting thread of their spiritual journeys. It is thus as true to say that they were striving to make place for the practice in their lives as it is to observe that they were endeavoring to make their lives the very place of their practice. It is in this process that one saw the dissolution of firm boundaries between the secular and the religious or spiritual.

# THE SPIRIT OF THE WORK

*challenging oppression, nurturing diversity*

The three men and two women who are the focus of this chapter were engaged in work to create just environments open to the diversity that is a fundamental characteristic of the human world. Each earned part of their income through work oriented to—and here I draw on their own language—"working with organizations on how to value difference," "unlearning internalized racism," " 'untraining' white liberal racism," or "doing social justice work, around leadership, diversity, and anti-oppression."

The group was religiously diverse. As well, all five had sought and/or experienced spiritual change and growth in their own lifetimes. And while this might appear nothing more than coincidence, one might argue that this change had relevance to their current anti-oppression and pro-diversity activity. Indeed, individuals' religious change traveled alongside the emergence of their anti-oppression work.

John Potts (European American, fifty years old) was raised Presbyterian but later joined his wife as an Episcopalian. He had also gained much from recent (and ongoing) training in the syncretic Diamond Heart Path developed by the Sufi mystic A. H. Almaas. Michael Bell, (African American, thirty-nine) was raised Episcopalian, but left that church on recognizing himself to be a gay man and suspecting that he would not be supported as such in that denomination. At the time of this interview, Michael was a devotee of the female Hindu guru Swami Chidvilasananda, of the Siddha Yoga Meditation foundation. Robert

Horton (European American, forty-one) had grown up in a Unitarian Universalist household. Yet by sixteen he was drawn to the Tibetan Buddhist teacher Chogyam Trungpa. He remained connected with that lineage.

Ryumon Zenji (her spiritual name) was Afro-Cuban. She was forty-four years old. She had grown up in the Catholic Church. Simultaneously she had lived with and learned from her grandmother. Her practice was, Ryumon explained, spiritualism or in Spanish, *espiritismo*. It brought "together Catholic Christian prayers, the New Testament, Jesus, the parables, with actual medium work, mediums who would go into trance and spirits would come through them." The memory and logic of that practice remained with her in the present. But as well, and centrally in the decade leading up to this interview, Ryumon Zenji was a practitioner of Soto Zen Buddhism.

Lastly, Akaya Windwood (African American, forty-one) was the only one of this group raised with little to no religious teaching. This, she said, had been the conscious decision of her parents who had wished to separate themselves from their own conservative Christian upbringing. As a result, when Akaya sought a spiritual practice she was, as she saw it, both free to choose and lacking guidance or direction. However as this text has shown, spiritual direction frequently presented itself when needed. This had been the case for Akaya.

In a range of ways, spiritual and religious resources were key to these individuals' work against oppression and for diversity. This at times entailed the literal deployment, revised or in whole cloth, of tools already developed within a religious or spiritual practice, as individuals created their own approaches to this work. Spiritual frameworks were also drawn on to help shape or support interviewees' "secular" analyses of oppressive systems, thus giving rise to specific orientations to their work and particular understandings of "success" in it. Likewise, spiritual/religious practices offered analytical and philosophical resources that made believable the possibility of positive outcomes in an oppressive, hierarchical world. In yet other instances the spiritual path was a "sacred container" able to provide human community and spiritual sustenance for the practitioner, the practice, and the recipients of it. Taking this last notion yet further, for some "spirit" or "grace" was consciously recognized as a force or a presence in their work. For these five individuals, the link between forms of spiritual practice and their application in context of work against oppression was demonstrable, and had generated approaches that were distinctive and creative. The purpose here is not necessarily to posit the superiority of anti-oppression work that is spiritually based over that based in a secular framework, so much as to draw out the logic and particularity of the former—the spirit in which it is undertaken.

🌿

JOHN POTTS, married and father of two, had, for the last two years been self-employed as a consultant striving to help workplaces transform into more open and welcoming places—open, that is, to a diversity of employees, and welcoming, even enthusiastic, about the differences between them. This interest and area of work had come about rather recently in John's life. It was the result of a broader process of personal self-examination and led him to take early retirement from a very successful, two-decades-long career in management and planning in a major pharmaceuticals corporation, so that he could begin anew.

John told me that he had grown up in a conservative Presbyterian family. This childhood experience was followed in his college years by the rejection of him by the (even more conservatively Christian) family of his intended bride. All of this had driven him away from religion in any serious form for two or more decades. For although marriage to a lifelong Episcopalian woman had meant that he did, from time to time go to church, he did this only "if [my wife] was singing at church, or at Christmas. Once in a while I'd go with her family because that was the social thing to do. I was a good husband and I would go." Then, he said, about nine years before this interview, a vivid dream had had an enormous impact on his sense of self, church, and all else. He described it like this:

> [My wife] and the two kids and I are in a green wagon pulled by four white horses. The front horse gets away, goes into a big pond, and gets his head tangled up in copper tubing. I can't go in and untangle it. I'm shouting to the driver of the wagon who's on the other side of the pond, "You've got to go in and untangle this tubing or it's going to strangle the horse." The driver just stands and watches. The tubing gets tighter and finally cuts off the horse's head. He bleeds into the pond, and the blood falls into the water.
>
> A year later I'm hiking—I'm leading some Boy Scouts in the Sierras—and the vision comes back to me. And I say, "Oh, this is all about my soul, which is the blood spilling onto the water and being wasted. And I can have my soul back any time I want to take up the blood." A year after that, one Sunday morning I get up and say, "Hey, I need to go to church today." I go to church [with my wife], and when commu-

nion time rolls around, I get it. I tell myself, "Oh, this is a chance for me to come every week to church and symbolically take out the blood and have my life and my soul back."

Although John ended his telling of the dream by offering his own interpretation of it, I suggest that one might add to his observations. As John states, this dream was, for him, about his soul or lifeblood going to waste. I would add here that as he watched the driver *not* helping the situation, John was in that moment not seeing himself as active agent. This altered a year later when he recognized that he *could* save the horse (his soul) as soon as he decided to do so. However, at that moment, as he tells it, he does not bother to act on that realization.

Whether, in the dream, John was the horse, the driver, the narrating observer, or all three is another question. As John moved through three stages—the dream, his interpretation of it a year later, and his return to the church another year after that—there was an increasing integration between John as narrator, John as wagon driver, and John as the horse, or his soul or lifeblood. Thus in "stage one" John is passive and separate from the driver and the horse. In "stage two" he sees the horse as himself. Also in that moment both driver and narrator are deemed, at least potentially, active agents in the situation.

In "stage three" on the Sunday morning when John woke up (literally and symbolically) and took himself to church and communion, John the observer was (re)integrated with the horse and his, or the horse's, blood. One must recognize too, a different kind of integration present here: John saw the blood of Christ, symbolized in the wine of the communion ceremony, as not separate from or different from his own. Thus as John received wine ("the blood of Christ") he saw himself as retrieving his *own* blood, and perhaps his own neglected soul.

At this point one can recognize that John was not just restored but also transformed. For during the two stages of interpretation that followed the dream, the events in it moved from individualized to collective ones. The (re)turn to the church was by definition a communal one and a repeatable one also. The same was true of the connection between John as an individual and "the Body of Christ" in all its symbolic and literalist interpretations.

The dream and its aftermath were, then, crucial to John's religious and spiritual life. What, though, one might ask, did the return to church have to do with John's work toward the creation of diverse and welcoming workplaces? There was, it turned out, a connection. But rather than being explicable by itself, John needed to describe for me the relationship between his return to the church and other events unfolding in his life. For these, as it turned out, altered the very meaning, for him, of "the Body of Christ" in its sense as a human collectivity.

Two events, ostensibly unrelated to both church *and* John's soul, happened around the same time. One of these was his participation in a program to which he was sent by his company, "a five-day, residential, total immersion, multicultural awareness workshop." There, he said, he was pushed to revisit and contemplate the ways in which, as he grew up, he had been taught to look at African American people in his community, as well as at issues of hetero- and homosexuality. As he put it, the workshop challenged him so that "I really began to look at the baggage that I was carrying." It offered him, he said, a new way of looking at what he had learned while growing up, and how it had affected him. After the workshop, he began to feel, "Boy, if I can learn this, and I can change, I want to help other people do the same thing." The further experience of entering a men's group at the advice of his psychotherapist led him to meetings with men who were, as he put it, "of a whole variety of ethnicities, a whole variety of classes."

John's world thus changed quickly over the next few years. New daily life experiences in context of the men's group entailed recognizing much more about his own socialization into hostile and hierarchical ways of thinking about gay people and people of color, and the deleterious effects of these on others and on himself. Shortly thereafter, new workplace responsibilities entailed applying what he had learned at the five-day workshop.

This, in turn, confirmed and enhanced his newfound experiences at the Episcopal Church. For, he said:

> [The workshop] happened at the same time that I'd been going for three years to my men's group. [In it,] we'd been doing a lot of things around ritual. I'd begun to get what the Episcopal Church was all about, that it was very rich with its liturgy and its history. Most people don't understand and can't articulate it. But somehow just being in the environment with this ritual really nourishes the soul. So I was clued into that part of it. And so it all kind of connected for me.

I have already proposed that the dream, John's interpretation of it, and the possibility of weekly communion, moved John toward a more collective sense of self, soul, and lifeblood. The men's group and the five-day workshop broadened his sense of who was, correctly, a part of that collectivity. Thus, as he put it, the soul was "nourished" by church participation, and at the same time other events told John that the collectivity that comprised the Body of Christ was diverse in a way that was, for him, radically new.

The third critical resource was John's introduction to the Diamond Heart Path, again through the counselor to whom he had gone for marriage and family related guidance. The Diamond Heart Path is Kuwaiti-born A. H. Almaas's synthesis of Sufism with psychology, and centrally involves the practices of meditation and contemplation or self-inquiry. John perceived no contradiction between this relatively new, syncretic, meditation-based practice and the Episcopal Church. As he put it, "I keep seeing them as being not only compatible but adding to each other." Especially important for him in the Diamond Heart path, John said, was that "we spend a lot of time with meditation and working in pairs, asking and repeating questions, and responding, to begin to strip away those superficial parts of the personality to get at the true essence of who we are. As I've burrowed down into that, I've become more grounded and have learned more about who I am in a more fundamental sense." The Episcopal Church had offered John one mode of self-interpretation anchored in a long, communal history. The dream had then hitched John personally into that history. The work undertaken through Diamond Heart offered John yet another entry point into the process of self-examination in a way that was conscious (rather than dream-like), collective and readily repeatable, yet as personal as the dream itself had been.

While there was compatibility in method, here, there was also, for John, compatibility in the content of what John was finding out. The upshot of all of this was that (as John remembered, at exactly forty-eight years old) he became clear that "I wanted to make a difference in the world," and that he could not do so in his work situation of the time. As he explained: "Three years in [the men's group] helped me tremendously in terms of growth, personal growth. And then it said, 'Boy, if that's where I was, I know a lot of other people who are in the same place. We need to have some conversations.' So this became very meaningful and purposeful work for me to be doing." At that moment, John's company asked him to take up a position in its head office back on the East Coast, moving away from his current California location. John responded by requesting early retirement, and investigating the possibility of entering a new line of work, that of "diversity consulting and training. What I've actually been doing is facilitating diversity awareness and skill-building workshops . . . working with corporations and nonprofits to make culture changes, to change their policies and procedures so that the workplace is fairer for everybody coming into it."

John's spiritual practice was key to his capacity to do this work. As we discussed this, he laughed as the "two ways" in which he said that this was so, gave way to three, then four, and his decision that "I'd better stop counting!" First, a sense of community came with church membership, along with the feeling that an immense power, inherent in the ritual of the church, as he put it, "fed his soul." As well, as noted, his work in the men's group and in diversity workshops had widened his sense of community and belonging. However it was the Diamond Heart techniques that had enabled him to actually design and implement workshops on diversity. Of this he said: "It's really helped me break that paradigm that I grew up with of life being logical and rational. [It has shown me] that other ways of looking at the world, other realities, may exist, that we have powers of intuition, that feelings count, and we can make decisions based on feelings." In John's view, what had happened here was a stepping away from rational and logical thought toward an intuitive approach. But I would argue that, in fact, one can, with equal appropriateness, propose that the new, feeling-based and intuition-based mode of thinking was in fact also a new mode of nothing other than rationality and logic. This was clear as John further explained his thinking process. He said: "Diamond Heart is all about staying in the present, but being with the feelings that are going on and using whatever is happening in the moment as a way of furthering your understanding of reality." This, he continued, had enabled him—even pushed him—toward greater self-awareness. It was also a crucial resource in the workshop setting. He offered me an example of this:

> The kinds of things that come up in workshops—people might want to avoid issues around sexual orientation. Now, I think a long time ago, I would have said, "Well, that's not part of the curriculum here. We're not going to talk about it. Let's do what we're supposed to do." And then there was a time when I would have said afterwards, "You know, it seemed like there was something going on around sexual orientation, but we just didn't get there." Now it's like, "Okay, let's put it on the table and let's talk about it, folks. What's going on here?" Or sensing it and even if I can't name it, saying, "You know, I'm not sure what's going on, but I'm feeling a lot of resistance from the group. Help me!"

This kind of "groundedness," as John named it, was premised on the courage to know himself. It made it possible for John to achieve his goal—extending to others an invitation to investigate the making of their own consciousness in the workshop setting. For John, as we have seen, the journey toward self-consciousness anchored in the particularities of his sociocultural history was premised on specific tools from one spiritual path. Also essential was the rich mixture of his sense of belonging to a church and its practices, with that connection itself further refined by the work of sociocultural critics and educators who had opened the way for John to begin "re-understanding" himself. Finally, the inexplicable—John's vivid dream of a horse bleeding and dying, but later resurrected—was crucial here. It was key to John's own understanding of his story, and thus also as an instance of the complex interplay of human agency and its excess, in the making of individual lives and spiritual journeys.

⚖

In Buddhism, one talks of the three poisons—passion, aggression, and ignorance. Aggression is pushing something away. So, in meditation, if something comes up and you want to push it away, that's the aggressive response. If it's something wonderful and you feel, "Wow, I want to have this for the next hour!"—it can be a meditative state or a fantasy, or whatever—then that's the passion. And then there's the most difficult state, which is ignorance. When ignorance is up, how do we know it's there? And unfortunately, that one seems to be so wrapped up with white liberal racism. The more right-wing racisms are much more wrapped up with aggression.—ROBERT HORTON

ROBERT HORTON'S INVOLVEMENT in educational work against oppression had come later in his life than had his religious practice. Yet, as might be guessed from the quote above, the two were at this point interwoven with one another. Robert was a practitioner of Vajrayana or Tibetan Buddhism. And he had also worked on an antiracist pedagogy, one particularly aimed at what he called "The Untraining" of white, liberal men and women from the racism that was, in his view, an inevitable aspect of growing up in a white dominant society. Alongside his Tibetan Buddhist training, it was the thinking and analysis of a diversity educator, Rita Shimmin, from which Robert had benefited in crafting "The Untraining." The result was a framework that drew on both classical Buddhist thought and on Shimmin's skills. This generated an approach that engaged the whole individual rather than treating racism as an isolated problem.

Robert had grown up in a working-class town, although his father's job as an engineer working for local government made their family wealthier than many others there. Robert was raised Unitarian Universalist. But early on, he said, he had felt that "something was missing [in] what was being taught to me. [It] missed the fundamental natures of things. It didn't satisfy me." When Robert was in the eighth grade, his school had offered a class on the world's religions. He remembered listening closely: "I felt like I was contemplating each one. And something just resonated with Buddhism." He then began reading books on Buddhism (he is now conscious from the retrospective purview of an antiracist educator of the privileges that had given him a relatively adequate public library).

Thus it was that, Robert said, "by tenth grade, which would be about sixteen, I actually knew who my teacher was, even though I had not met him. I read one of his books. And I just put the question down. It felt like a whole part of me relaxed." That teacher was Chogyam Trungpa, a Tibetan Buddhist master who had lived and taught in the United States since 1970. In fact, Robert said, when I asked him who his teacher was, "even though it was tenth grade, I actually remember exactly what I read that so inspired me. He said that you don't throw anything away, that all your emotions, neuroses, etc., are necessary. They were needed, Robert continued, for what is most frequently translated into English as the attainment of "enlightenment." Robert is here referring to a key Vajrayana teaching that all aspects of self, whether believed to be good or bad, were to be considered the raw material of one's spiritual practice and thus to be systematically engaged. However, drawing on his later critical questioning about the traces of racist and colonialist thinking in language, Robert proposed a different expression of Chogyam Trungpa's idea: "All your emotions, neuroses, and so on are necessary if you are to become a whole being in the world."

But whatever the translation, Robert emphasized that this single sentence had at the time, "made sense on some level that was way deeper than intellectual. I just thought, 'This is the first real observation that I've encountered.' " And interestingly enough, just as he had learned then that *all* of one's self must be engaged with in order to awaken spiritually, he realized much later that in order to engage racism one must see it as inextricably enmeshed with *all* other aspects of daily life and consciousness.

When he finished high school, rather than heading to college, as might have been expected of him by his family, Robert said: "I just put on a backpack and left. And the first place I went was Boulder, to

Chogyam Trungpa's school, Naropa. I stayed there a month and went to a few classes and decided that the next summer I would go there again. The next summer I went there and, you know, it was like coming home. I was still very young. I was twenty years old." After that year, Robert settled in San Francisco. In the years that followed he mainly earned a modest living and meditated. There were some periods of cessation of meditation practice, sometimes for health and at other moments to experiment with some of the ideas and life choices that, as a young Buddhist practitioner, he had set aside—the punk rock music movement, anarchism, Marxism, among other things. Still, he continued to be drawn back to meditation practice.

For example, during a long break from active practice, Robert had a job in a print-shop where work assignments were few. His supervisor, rather than laying him off, had offered him the option of simply relaxing or reading while on the job. But instead, Robert said, he found himself returning to meditation. Robert remained in touch with Chogyam Trungpa until his death, contacting him by mail when he needed advice on medical or other matters. Robert was, at the time of the interview, still involved with this spiritual community, attending the local *dharmadhatu* or meditation center.

Robert said his health had very often been the site or trigger of transformation in his life. And it was in search of clarification for a health problem that he went to a workshop led by Arnold Mindell, a Jungian analyst and originator of process-oriented psychology. According to Robert, Mindell argued that:

> Body symptoms are dreams trying to happen. He works with illness as a sense of life unfolding . . . There's no judgment that "if you do this, you'll get well." [Although] sometimes you unfold what's trying to happen and you do get well. And that was very important in my life. I had an illness caused by parasites. I went to that work and it helped me as I went through my own personal healing process, and it opened up lots of different parts of my life.

Thinking back over that health challenge Robert said, "From my viewpoint now, my health interrupted my spiritual practice because it was too focused on only my own individual salvation." Indeed one might argue that one important event that the work with Mindell opened was his first meeting with the person Robert named as his current teacher, Rita Shimmin. Shimmin, whom Robert described as "a powerful teacher, of African American and Filipino ancestry," had participated along with Robert and eighty-three others in a six-week training program. There, Robert began learning from Shimmin why in her view it was important to incorporate the critical analysis of race hierarchy into any work intended to engage sociocultural issues, whether for individuals or communities.

For a long period after that workshop ended he continued to visit with and learn from Shimmin. In the end, he said, "I was learning a tremendous amount and began to just get this nagging feeling I should do something. Then one night I had a dream. And in that dream I started an antiracist group. When I woke up, I remembered who each of the people were. And I wrote it down and I said, 'Why don't you just call these people?' Maybe I can start to do this. So I just called—there were four people in the dream." Three out of the four were excited to concur. From there, he said, he started a group. It met for nine months and afforded him the possibility of, as he put it, "developing an approach and a program and a way of presenting what I'd learned from Rita."

As Robert explained "The Untraining," it seemed evident that it bore the traces both of Rita Shimmin's ideas and those of his long-standing meditation practice. Thus for example, he explained that a central aspect of Shimmin's thinking was that individuals' relationships with racism would always be interwoven with that which Shimmin referred to as "core issues," which is to say the repetitively difficult areas of their lives. This meant, in turn, that it was important for individuals to become more consciously aware not only of their relationships to racism but also of their own core issues.

The goal of the work was not the resolution of core issues, so much as the cultivation of a witnessing relationship to them. Thus Robert said that the participant was requested to "become familiar with [the core issue] and let yourself know it's there, so that you can begin to have awareness when it happens. Also it seems that if you enter those places voluntarily, that when you're thrown there, you have a tiny bit more choice about where it's going to go, how long you're going to be there, and what you see while you're there." Although he did not say so, this approach also clearly owed much to Robert's practice of Vajrayana Buddhism. To begin with, one could argue that The Untraining made "the emotions and neuroses" of racial formation the very site of its work. Second, The Untraining shared with Vajrayana teaching the injunction to investigate one's formation with a view to deepening awareness. Finally, both undertook such a process with the intention not of "getting rid of" mind-states but of becoming an observer of them in such a way that they no longer dictated one's responses.

It should be noted that, in the context of The Untraining, the core issue was primarily significant as a place where racism would be expected to be present. For as Robert put it, "if you're [from a] community that's largely white, individual racist training [means] that, unless it's dealt with, is going to come out." He added, "[It is] just naturally just going to manifest." Thus, learning to cultivate a deeper awareness of one's core issues and of one's relationship with the racism endemic to the culture were conceived as interconnected processes.

It followed that discussion of personal lives in the group setting was crucial. Robert said:

> An important part of it is for people just to tell their stories around how they first encountered race. Just that—one of the unwritten rules of white supremacy is you don't talk about this. And so, that's becoming more important, just giving the space for people to tell their stories, and hear other people's stories. And I basically try to encourage people to look at their own lives and to see what they may have been not wanting to look at. And, an important piece is the tying in of the core issues or difficult spots in a person's life. Those spots will be intimately related to how racism is expressed through the person.

One sees here points of connection between Robert Horton's/Rita Shimmin's approach and that described by John Potts. For in both instances, self-knowledge turned out to be crucial if one were to transform one's relationship to oppressive systems. Robert saw the intentionality of one's engagement with core issues as a distinguishing feature of this approach, although one could argue that the commitment to self-examination that John Potts describes was an equally intentional process. What was specific to this approach, however, was the idea that one's personal, individual areas of pain or concern inevitably articulated with race and racism such that the latter could not be challenged without addressing this link. Buddhist practices converged with a secular, psycho-social analysis, to offer an approach with the potential to serve individual and community alike.

᯽

MICHAEL BELL had grown up in an upper-middle-class, African American family that was strongly rooted in three branches of the Christian tradition. These included, he told me, the "robust, rural, passionately engaged" Southern Baptist practice of his maternal grandmother, his father's more staid and urban version of the same, and his mother's

Episcopalianism with its "very conservative and rigorous engagement" with the social issues of the day. Michael added that, growing up in the 1960s and 1970s, such issues had included the Vietnam War, the Civil Rights movement "and the changing landscape for African Americans in both the church and the larger community." From the beginning, he said, his parents had served as role models for their children, "illustrating how their spirituality informed their community work."

One might indeed surmise that it was in part this early guidance that led Michael to his current work, which invited individuals and organizations to transform their thinking about social diversity and its impact in the world. Michael and his female business partner ran two linked organizations. He explained: "I work with organizations on change and planning, [helping them] plan for their future, effectively changing systems within organizations, and [discovering] how to value difference." This work took place, he said, in a variety of settings: churches, community groups, businesses, universities, educational institutions. "On the nonprofit side," he said, "we develop models of adult learning and change, using video as a catalyst."

For Michael, this work had arisen out of his earlier job in upper management in the hotel and restaurant industry. There, he had quickly discovered that "people of color were where you 'expected' to see people of color—in housekeeping, in the kitchen washing dishes, and in low-level jobs. I created opportunities for women and people of color to be at all levels at the organization. And in order to do that without the process being sabotaged, I had to start really engaging people with how to value difference." In short, as Michael sought to create diverse workplaces, he realized that he needed to help those in the workplace realize why diversity was a positive rather than a negative thing. Quickly a success, Michael's work was recognized by others in what he described as "the hospitality industry." And soon thereafter, he realized that he would have more flexibility in this area of activity if he became self-employed.

However, even though there was a relatively clear congruence between the religious context of his childhood and his work as an adult, the same was not the case for other aspects of his life. For, as he put it, "I really had a crisis of conscience about religion as I embraced my gay identity. I felt that there were proscriptions around gay identity that didn't give me a happy home in the Christian tradition. I left spiritual practices for a while." This was so "except," he emphasized, "for prayer. I never stopped praying."

The challenge to find a new spiritual context took him first to Nichiren Shoshu Buddhism. In contemplating making a connection to that practice he said, "The turning point was when I went to an event sponsored by that tradition, where there were eight hundred gays and lesbians being welcomed into the practices by the folks from Japan. I felt like we were leaves on a tree of a religious practice where we were welcomed for our different shades and hues and colors." Still, he said, spiritually "it wasn't quite right" for him. Soon thereafter a friend (now his business partner) introduced him to Siddha Yoga, and to the woman who is now his teacher, Gurumayi Chidvilasananda. As he expressed it, although his prayers still "really transcend any religious tradition," he has "found a home" in that spiritual community.

One can argue that the Siddha Yoga path (a distillation of Kashmiri Shaivite Hinduism brought to the United States in the 1970s by Gurumayi's own teacher, Swami Muktananda) echoes, in its structure though not its content, some aspects of the Episcopalian church in which Michael grew up. For example, every Sunday he attended the communal worship service that in fact took place daily for those able to be present. He also participated in a year-round calendar of festivals, each of which symbolized one or more aspects of the path and its philosophy. Finally, he said that Siddha Yoga community's "strong commitment to service to others is congruent with how I was raised, and with my own learning style and aptitudes."

At the same time—and also deemed positive rather than negative by Michael—the path lacked the proscriptions and institutional pressures that had, one might say, driven Michael away from his childhood church. Instead, he said, in *this* path, "much of what they consider to be essential is focused on one's relationship with one's self." Michael is referring here to practices of self-reflection and examination that are a key aspect of the Siddha Yoga path. In the end, Michael said, "when you make the decision to leave the African American church, and move from Western to Eastern religion as practiced in America, you're not going to see as many people [of color] as you would in other settings. And I think you have to reconcile yourself to that fact." Still, he continued, "I think what's very satisfying and important to notice with Siddha Yoga is the really careful attention on the part of the leadership to placing people of color, and a variety of people in terms of looks and orientation, in leadership positions, men and women." In the final analysis, Michael seemed satisfied with the particular mix of the old and the new: engagement with a religious calendar, the cultivation of a faith community, and of service to others, alongside a less proscriptive sexual code and serious efforts to create a diverse organizational hierarchy.

Very different from his earlier life and practice, however, was the place in it of a teacher who was not just respected as an interpreter of the Siddha Yoga path. She was also acknowledged to be more than that—one whose capacities at times moved into the realm of the inexplicable, and the lexicon of whose speech and action demonstrated her fluency in more than one realm. It should be remembered from chapter 1 that Gurumayi had personally welcomed Michael Bell into her community by introducing him to these capacities. She achieved this by first, despite her physical absence, assailing his nostrils with the strong fragrance of a gardenia flower. Then a year later, with no explanation, and this time in her presence, she had presented him with an actual gardenia blossom, saying, "I believe you've been waiting for this."

Michael felt nourished by his relationship to his guru and expressed that his current path enabled him to build bridges between self and other, self-improvement, and sociocultural healing. He offered as an example the conversation between Krishna and Arjuna in the Hindu text, the *Bhagavad Gita*. In it Krishna, a divine teacher, is instructing his devotee, Arjuna, on the ethics of life, all the while heading into a battle zone. Michael said: "It's a lovely metaphor for the way in which most of us experience our lives—trying to develop consciousness and self-engagement as we live our lives. You know, as we battle all of our battles of living to be present for the pain, the joy and the mystery, all of it. So that's why I find it such a satisfying practice. It's really helped me experience life in a much richer tapestry." As Michael translated his spiritual path into his workplace, the philosophy and symbols of his practice were all present. His office was full of images of Gurumayi and her own teacher, Baba Muktananda, as well as of other Hindu deities signaling important and necessary resources, among them Ganesha, the deity deemed protector of the gods and remover of all obstacles. Very often, Michael said, he and his business partner began their workday with a ceremony of prayer to that particular being.

But the connections made between spirituality and daily work activity were not just confined to ritual and symbol. He said:

> There are certain capacities that my practice of Siddha Yoga has given me: a capacity for critical self-reflection, a capacity for hanging out with not knowing, a capacity for, if you will, living with ambiguity, a capacity for moving away from calculated judgment into questioning in the broadest sense of the word. And a capacity for deep listening, *really* listening, and creating spaces for silence in that listening. These, I think are capacities needed in valuing difference.

In his workshops, Michael strove to invite participants to cultivate these same qualities. Although, for him, they had emerged in context of his spiritual practice, he was clear about their relevance to the work of "valuing difference" in a broad and nonsectarian sense. Michael's approach to his work centrally involved asking clients to ask *themselves* new questions about relationships between self, environment, and activity. As much as anything, he hoped that his clients would leave with the capacity to draw on his company's approaches rather than with specific answers deemed correct or "better than others." Thus the idea that self-inquiry must be applied in daily life remained present and important.

Michael was also very clear that there would always be temporal limits to his and his colleagues' impact on any situation. And at that point another key dimension of his spiritual frame came to the fore. In this regard, he said: "We think about our work as planting seeds and inviting new ways of being that we probably won't see the fruits of, with the people that we work with. So what we're counting on is grace stepping in to do the next steps once we've gone. That's a very intentional part of our formula. We anticipate that grace will step in because we can't do it all." He added, "It's interesting to arrive at a place where an essential component of your business practice is grace. [*Laughs.*] It's very interesting."

All of these ideas—questioning and self-questioning; "sitting with ambiguity and uncertainty"; deeming process as important as product if not more so; trusting grace to support the process; and all of this in the name of honoring diversity—are easy enough to grasp in the abstract. Yet, when I asked Michael how this worked in practice, he shared with me one experience that had exemplified all of these dimensions of his approach to his work. The event, which was, as he put it "one of the most remarkable experiences around difference that I've ever had," took place during a national study group on spirituality and diversity of which Michael was a member. In it, he was asked to lead a two-day discussion of lesbian and gay issues. From the outset, Michael knew this to be a contentious area, that he was "in a place with people whom I respected and from whom I had learned, that had very traditional, conservative, or even rejecting ideas about gay and lesbian identity."

Even in the planning stages of this two day event, Michael had depended on more than his analytical and pedagogical skills. He told me, "I did a lot of prayer in preparation for that experience." And indeed one might argue that this approach was wise. For, he said:

I remember we were going into the really gnarly part of our differences around sexual orientation. This tremendous sense of peace came pouring over me, and a tremendous sense of confidence, not in the outcome, but in my ability to be there in that moment. There were two days of difficult conversation with no resolution. Still, I kept the belief in my heart that there was a mystery, that there was something there for all of us that had yet to be revealed.

In this moment, one might argue, what Michael had earlier called "grace," what was inexplicable and even counterintuitive given Michael's situation, came into play. Michael felt himself to be protected, with regard to the process and his capacity to survive within it. Although not able to be confident with regard to the outcome of things, he nonetheless felt able to stay with his own methodology—that derived from his spiritual practice—and to live with the uncertainty of that moment.

Part of the challenge of the situation, Michael said, was that a sizable number of the group, men and women, white and of color, held to the positions derived from their own religious frameworks, that the most they could and should do was to "love the sinner but not the sin," when it came to gay men and lesbians. In that context, Michael had no choice but to emphasize that for him, "anything less than a willingness to be an advocate, an ally for my life, was just a subtler form of violence and rejection. Just because they didn't have the stick in their hand beating me to death, they were still part of a system of rejection that put my life and my well-being at risk."

Thus, living with ambiguity and uncertainty did not mean a shift to relativism, or a watering down of Michael's principles. Rather, one might argue, he remained committed to the content of his argument while accepting the uncertainties associated with process and context. Once again, "grace" stepped in to enfold him. Where he had expected pain and even tears to overwhelm him, something different happened. He said: "The deeper we got into it, I cannot describe to you—it was like golden light raining down all around me. There was a palpable feeling of love for them and for me that I was surrounded by. It was a difficult conversation, but I never felt lost or in danger. And I had this sense of knowing at the deepest level that there was something as yet not uncovered in our conversation, particularly with the man who was most virulently homophobic."

Eventually a good number of participants did shift in their perspective around gay and lesbian issues. One exercise that became a turning point asked all participants to take turns playing out three roles—those of "victim," "oppressor," and "ally," whether with respect to gay and lesbian identity or another aspect of self or identity. This, Michael said, was beneficial in opening up the terrain of the discussion, and making more fluid and more flexible all individuals' relationships to the subject at hand. He commented: "It was so revealing for us to know that all of us had been in all of those roles at one point or another, and that around all types of 'isms,' that we're not one or the other, but we're all of those things. We are all victims, oppressors, and allies at some time in our lives." Finally, he said, what he had surmised had not been "uncovered" emerged, when the most insistently homophobic member of the group asked Michael for a private meeting after the workshop ended.

This man "confessed," as Michael put it, that his gentle, introspective, and kindly demeanor had, in his younger days, led to his being frequently "accused of being gay." In other words, Michael said, "underneath his rejection of *my* identity was a whole pool, a whole well, of distress around being rejected for who *he* really was." However, Michael said, "because of the compassion he experienced that weekend, because it was OK for him to not need to change, and because we were all willing to just be with the question, he started to question himself. That whole process of bringing the question into oneself led him to understand the path that had caused him to reject gays and lesbians. And so there was a huge shift for him, for himself."

One may now examine in detail the ways in which Michael's work put into action much that was learned from his spiritual frame. First, having initiated discussion of a conflictual social issue in all its ramifications, he did so in a way that prioritized process. Indeed as things turned out, the very democratization of the process (for example in the exercise on who is a victim, an oppressor, or an ally) made way for a broadening of content with respect to all three categories. This in turn made possible some critical awakenings. Thus the man with whom Michael had spoken separately at the end had himself benefited from a deepened understanding of the painful origins of his own homophobia and, one might suggest, his own relationship to it as both target and oppressor. Further, and central to the relationship between Michael's spiritual practice and workshop design, it was key, not merely for him to be able to listen and work in a place of "unknowing," but to invite participants to do the same.

It was important to this approach that, just as all individuals might at different moments find themselves "victim, oppressor, or ally," all workshop participants were deemed able to learn about others and selves. Likewise, binaries were blurred as participants and facilitator alike were encouraged to pose and answer questions about self *and* other. Questions and answers themselves remained open-ended, and all questions were seen to be potential resources for change. Here, workshop participants were offered a taste of the rigorous self-examination that was key to the Siddha Yoga path. However, one must also note that Michael was not alone in calling for this, whether on his own or his clients' part—as has been seen, the same was true for John Potts and Robert Horton.

At the end, Michael emphasized the critical connection between his spiritual practice and his ability to stay the course in the workshop. He said: "I don't think I would have been able to sit through what I heard with such a sense of calm if it wasn't for a strong spiritual practice. So, it was really the culmination of a lot of work on my part, and a lot of belief that something greater than just us in the room was with us in the conversation." For Michael, "grace" and his spiritual training and practice were crucial, interwoven resources. Yet one must also note that the operation of grace as he saw it was not evidenced in others' changes of heart (although these did, it seems, occur). Rather, evidence of grace was, for Michael, signaled by his capacity to hold to the process, encouraged by signs of its presence (peace, confidence, golden light) that, as far as one could discern from Michael's telling of the story, may well have been witnessed by Michael alone. If grace did pave the way for changes of heart, then, one might suggest that this was, as much as anything, because Michael's awareness of it enabled him to be present and act in ways that made room for others to open to fresh ways of thinking. Indeed, this analysis might provide a means to understand Michael's seemingly ambiguous comment that, "It's interesting to arrive at a place where an essential component of your business practice is grace . . . very interesting."

※

BORN IN 1956, Akaya Windwood is African American and lesbian. She had two ways of explaining how she had entered her current work. The work was a consultancy in organizational development, focused especially on creating workforce inclusiveness alongside, as needed, conflict resolution, team building, and leadership training. In both tellings of the story, Akaya was clear that for her, work, politics, and spiritual practice were interwoven to the point of inseparability.

In the first description of her entry point into this kind of work, childhood experience was key. Up until the age of seven, she had lived at the Air Force bases (in Panama, Germany, and Kansas) where her father was assigned. Next, the family had moved to an African American neighborhood in southern California. There, her father's military status and both of her parents' high school diplomas had given her family a relatively high social status and economic standing. In stark contrast, when Akaya's parents moved the family into a nearby white neighborhood (in order to "provide the best opportunities" for their two daughters) the family was "welcomed" into the neighborhood with a cross burned on their lawn. All of this taught Akaya that privilege and status were relative and variable, and had given her what she called a "personal commitment to end systems that would put folks in a one-down position."

In a second mode of accounting for her current commitments, a sudden crisis had, according to Akaya, reinforced her understanding of the workings of privilege and power, and sent her firmly and forcefully into this line of work. Having, as she put it, been "wooed" with "fabulous fellowships" into graduate study in clinical psychology at an elite West Coast university, Akaya spent three years on preparatory course work. But then, on sharing with her faculty mentor her proposal for doctoral research (the investigation of modes of conflict resolution among lesbian and heterosexual women) she was bluntly told that her project was "soft, uninteresting, and not worthy of graduate study." On first hearing this, Akaya decided, "Maybe he's right. Maybe I'm not very bright. Maybe I'm not smart enough. Maybe I'm not right for this."

Over time, Akaya revised this conclusion. In the end, this experience became grist for the mill of a critique of privilege and power based on identity (gender, race, age, sexuality) in universities and other institutions. Thus in the end Akaya could say, "It was a big lesson and a bitter one. And yet it was the best lesson that I've gotten, in some ways, because it brought me to here. I started my social justice work as a result of getting clear about what that [experience] meant. So I really do honor that time." By the time of the interview, Akaya had developed an approach to working against oppression that was, she said, "the everyday practical application of my spiritual practice." Her spiritual practice, in turn, was "a sense of connectedness with all that there is . . . the part of me that I can get in touch with when I know I am right in line with the universe."

But where did Akaya's spiritual practice come from? As noted previously, Akaya grew up with no religious training or involvement. What she now practiced was thus the result of her own work to make meaningful spiritual connections for herself. She had, she told me, had to wait until her thirties to realize that there were religious and spiritual frames available to her beyond the kinds of Christianity with which her parents had been raised. At that point, thanks to her introduction to the tradition by her partner, she was initiated and trained in "Wiccan Paganism." But, in the end, she concluded, "while I really appreciated the immanent, ongoing, and vibrant relationship with spirit, something was missing for me culturally. The tradition that I had found myself walking in was Celtic, which I'm not—I'm not Celtic." From there, Akaya had taken the next logical step—"I started looking at African-descended spiritual traditions." Here, she said, she was not comfortable with the kinds of hierarchy that she found to be present in her explorations. A third stopping point had been the primarily African American "East Bay Church of Religious Science," rich in spiritual wisdom and committed to connecting social with religious questions. (We return to a fuller discussion of this church in the next chapter.) This church was the closest Akaya felt she had come to an ideal religious institution. Yet, it left her wanting: she wished for her faith, sense of belief, and practice to be articulated in a less masculinist and Bible-centered frame.

Thus, said Akaya, "Where I am now is, I'm feeling a need for—and I need a new word—fellowship. I really need a new word for that. Because we aren't fellows, you know! But [I need] that sense of communion." Today, with or without a religious community of which she might call herself a member, Akaya nonetheless had a strong sense of the meaning of spiritual practice to her. To begin with, she said, "my spirituality is very active, present, concrete, tangible. I read an article a couple of years ago called, 'Praying Unceasingly.' It was just the notion that we're always in contact with God or spirit. And I decided it was easier for me to be in immediate contact as opposed to doing it once a week or at my altar. And I have found that I get immediate answers when I pay attention." This sense of ready access to "God or spirit," one might argue, made something workable, indeed positive, out of Akaya's "extra-institutional" spiritual practice, despite the disappointment she expressed that she now found herself in that situation. One must notice too that Akaya sensed no necessity for an intermediary of the sort that might be connoted by the idea of a "once a week" immersion in one's practice in the context of church membership. Instead, Akaya felt that her proactive agency, her willingness to "pay attention," was crucial to her success in sustaining her relationship to God or spirit.

As Akaya continued to describe to me her understanding of spirituality and her relationship to it, I saw how she conceived "God or spirit" and its relationship to humans in radically egalitarian terms. For when she responded to my question about the meaning of the word *spirituality* with the answer, "A sense of connectedness with all that there is," she continued in the following terms:

> It's a sense that there is something of which I am a part—of which we are all a part—and is therefore much more vast than any one of us, and yet is not greater than any one of us. It's the part of me that I can get in touch with when I know I am right in line with the universe. Every once in a while, I get a sense of, "I am right in line. I am exactly where I need to be." Which I know is always true but every once in a while, I get aware of it. And I realize that that hierarchy doesn't exist, and yet, I do believe in a universal consciousness, if you will. I call it Spirit. Others call it God, or Goddess, or any number of names. But it's that notion that I'm in the mix. I'm connected. And we're all connected.

Egalitarianism is expressed in several ways here. First, there is her sense that "God or spirit" is not "greater than any one of us," and that "hierarchy doesn't exist." As Akaya expresses it there is no "power" that is "higher" than other beings in and of itself. Rather, it is the collectivity of that power that makes it "vaster," or a "universal consciousness," though still not inherently "higher." Second, as she had put it earlier, only the willingness to listen was required for one to consciously experience "God or spirit." And third, diverse names for "God or spirit" were all equally appropriate.

Fourth, the possibility of connectedness with "God or spirit" had little or nothing to do with one's individual behavior or status, as might be the case in a more conventional Judeo-Christian, Muslim, Hindu, or Buddhist framework. Rather, it was all about "being in the mix," recognizing oneself to be "connected." Finally, one might note that while aspects of Akaya's thinking about individuals' relationships with "God or spirit" might be shared with each of the three religious institutions that she described as stepping stones on her journey, for the most part she departed from them.

Akaya was by no means unique in doing this. As Catherine L. Albanese, historian of U.S. religion, has argued in analyzing the history of the term *spirituality*, the recent period is one in which individuals have felt empowered to articulate and rearticulate for themselves the meanings of the word.[1] Albanese argues that the term has gathered into itself a variety of features. These include personal connection with God, the sense of connection with others, and ways "of thinking not based on conventional religious foundations."[2] All three elements were to be found in Akaya's own discourse.

Akaya's anti-oppression work was a direct outgrowth of her spiritual framework. Indeed as she explicated the way in which she conceptualized it and carried it out, it too evinced a recognition of all humans' connection to one another and thereby, one might argue, to spirit or God also. Describing the basis on which she worked with clients, Akaya said: "I think about what the world would look like if it were a place where everyone was celebrated and every child was born with a sense of, 'I belong in this world, and everyone is happy to have me, and all of my "stuff." ' " She continued: "That's what I think is our potential as human, and therefore is what I consider spirit or God. So it infuses what I do. I work from that vision knowing that it's just a matter of time." Akaya articulates here her sense of people's relationship to "spirit or God" as an individual one. Yet at the same time, since she understands God and spirit as nothing other than the collectivity of all beings, any individual's connection with spirit must by definition be one shared with all others. It follows that individuals' connections with one another and with God are complexly interwoven.

Moreover, as we have also seen, Akaya understood humans' connection to spirit as a matter of course—something that the individual might or might not be aware of, but a reality in any case. By analogy it made sense to her that when people chose to celebrate and value their fellow beings, they were simply recognizing what followed from the conditions of their very existence within the collectivity of spirit. Appreciation for others was not, then, something that individuals "should" or "must" cultivate. Rather it was the bringing to consciousness of what already was in place: their existence and their relationship to "spirit or God" were founded in celebration of self and other.

The end point, or what was "just a matter of time," was thus the moment when more beings, even *all* beings, would see themselves and others as inherently valuable people. And this state of consciousness was, Akaya proposed, the one in which all human beings are born. I would argue that it was from this a priori construct that Akaya entered her workshops. For as she worked with groups of individuals, she said:

What I know is that when a child is born, that child is born without hate or fear or bigotry . . . You know, little white kids, little black kids, or little Asian kids, or little Latino kids, all come out with this sense of, "I'm alive! Here I am! Aren't you excited? Isn't that great?" You know, "I'm about being connected and loved and I'm ready to do that. So let's go!" And I know that it isn't until somebody tells them and says, "This is who you are, this is who we are, this is who they are. We like us, we don't like them." So part of my work is to remember that that little bitty, lovely, alive, excited child is still there.

In the end, one might suggest, for Akaya the work of fostering diversity was not so much a matter of change or adjustment but one of readjustment, restoration, or return.

While this process might not, on the surface of things, seem to be a simple one, in Akaya's experience the opposite was the case. For, she said, she experienced those men and women with whom she worked as caring rather than uncaring about connection and communication with others, and uncertain about how to achieve this rather than unwilling to try. Thus, she said, it was enough at times to simply "give permission," reassurance, and encouragement that communication was possible and, as she put it, "they always rise. As long as I remember that I'm talking to delightful folks who have been taught to fear, then I tend not to lose people." Taking this one step further, Akaya said that she in fact shared with her clients the way of recognizing the inherent goodness of humans that she had shared with me. This too, she said, was useful and meaningful in the training session: "If I put that context on it, folks can go, 'Oh yeah, that's right. I know that I am whole and wonderful and I know that [there is], you know, stuff in history that tells me that I'm not, but that's a lie. Okay, I'll struggle. Let's work.' And they will. And not everyone moves as far as I want them to move, but they move." Here, then, one sees Akaya putting directly into action the a prioris of her thinking about humanness and its relationship to spirit. As I noted, from her point of view spirit or God was nothing more and nothing less than the aggregation of our collective existence, and that existence was at its point of origin loving and oriented to its connectivity to all other beings. In the workshop setting Akaya applied this mode of thought, as it were, in reverse order. By inviting participants to recognize their loving and cooperative nature, she found that in fact they "remembered" or "recognized" both and acted on them.

This is not the kind of naive or optimistic approach that it might appear to be on first glance. For one thing, Akaya cautioned that there were limits to what might be achieved, saying that "not everyone moves as far as I want them to move." As well, the individuals she described expressed willingness to engage in a process ("I'll struggle. Let's work"), rather than just spontaneously altering their ways of seeing, thinking, and feeling. Akaya presented her foundational beliefs about humanity and spirit in the workshop setting in order to initiate dialogue.

There was more than one step to this pedagogical process. For example, when I asked what might happen if a participant raised the familiar thorny questions of affirmative action or sexual orientation, it became clear that there were additional steps that needed to be taken, but that they built on Akaya's premise about human connection.

> RF What do you do with, "Well, you know, it's all very well and good what you're saying, but I know that my kid didn't get a place at Berkeley because affirmative action kept my kid out"? Or, "Well, it's all very well and good, but I know that God does not want homosexuality to be practiced"?
>
> AKAYA What I don't do is engage folks in conflict. So if somebody said to me, "My kid didn't get into Berkeley because of affirmative action," then I would say, "And I bet that was really hard for you." [If s/he then said,] "Well, yeah, it was really hard because we've worked hard and she'd worked hard and it was a very big disappointment," I could say, "Yeah, I bet it was. And why do you imagine there was affirmative action?"

Akaya concurred when I observed that in the situation just described, her approach had been to remain connected with the participant, rather than positioning herself as, in response to their words, separate or different from them. She had done this by, first, acknowledging their grief, pain, and discomfort. She reaffirmed it when, in the hypothetical interaction, the participant had named her/his efforts toward providing for their child. Then she included the participant as coanalyst when she shifted the terms of the discussion from the personal to the social or institutional ("Why do *you* imagine there was affirmative action?"[emphasis added]). As her imagined discussion continued, she opened it out to the larger group, again avoiding any "us/them" classification, and seeking instead to draw upon all present as colleagues. Thus she said:

> So then we can start to discuss, "You know, folks, what that person is saying to me is, 'I'm really hurt.'" And I can go, "Yeah, of course you are. And now what?" You know, "So then how do we then build a society in which your child, every child, who wanted to go to college

went? How can we make that happen?" And I can say, "You know, for generations, folks who have been disempowered or disenfranchised from the system have been feeling the same thing you are feeling now. And I know that it felt like shit then, and it feels like shit now, so what are we going to do—you and me—to create a system where nobody's child gets told no?" Then we can work.

As Akaya alluded to the history of exclusion she once again emphasized three kinds of sameness—that of suffering, that of rights, and that of the capacity to help make changes toward greater inclusion.

Striving for sameness did not, however, exclude the possibility of disagreement. Disagreement, in turn, did not exclude the possibility of continued connectivity. Addressing my question regarding sexual orientation she said:

> The issue of homosexuality, that's a little different. I've had people say, "My God tells me that it's an abomination against the Lord, and it's a sin." And I say, "Well, you know, my God tells me it's not, because I was not born for no reason. So this is where we're going to have to disagree. And we're going to have to be in relationship. So, how do you suppose we're going to get on?" And folks then can go, "Well, okay." So then the conversation isn't about whether or not one of us should exist. The conversation is about "How do we both exist, given the fact that we have very different ways of looking at the world?" So I'm always going for the connection. That's my work.

At this point, Akaya turned once more to two important a prioris: humans are all part of God or spirit; and humans are distinctive, particular rather than homogeneous. This set up a framework into which Akaya could invite her interlocutor to become the analyst in the situation, opening the door to that person to use her capacity to address the "problem" that she herself had placed on the table. Yet in doing so, Akaya reframed the terms of the discussion such that binarisms had been dissolved and "connection" (her term) had been reasserted. Thus this last example proposed that it was possible (even expected) for persons to cope with differences between them, precisely by turning to an overarching connectedness between them as coanalysts.

As has been seen, Akaya drew on a set of ideas about the relationships between "spirit or God," individual men and women, and human beings as a collectivity in her workshops on issues of social justice, leadership, and team building. Thus the sessions sought to actualize all of those relationships as she conceived them. This was evident both in the design of the workshops and even more forcefully so in step-by-step retellings of specific interactions between Akaya and her clients. Within that overarching framework, Akaya drew on specific aspects of her "spiritual tool kit" to engage with particular places of difference and diversity, hitherto seen as sites of conflict, offering instead the means of transforming them into opportunities for collective reconsideration.

Like Michael Bell, Akaya sought to create nonhierarchical and non-binary methods for the exploration and analysis of the issues at hand. Yet their commitment to positioning their clients as coanalysts did not lead them to relativism or to blunting their arguments, whether about race or sexuality. The two had divergent approaches to engaging with difference, however. Michael had, as we have seen, invited all to recognize that each might easily be deemed "other" at some point and that their potential similarity lay therein. Akaya emphasized instead that, different or not, humans' connectivity might be seen to override or at least make complicated individuals' differences from one another. Nevertheless, both shared with John Potts and Robert Horton the recognition that they, just as much as their clients, were a part of the sociocultural context in need of transformation. As Akaya phrased it, they were all "in the mix."

⚕

RYUMON ZENJI is an Afro-Cuban Soto Zen Buddhist. Her spiritual name, which was given to her at her initiation, comprised four characters that she explained might be translated as "Dragon Gate of Total Compassion." As this book neared completion, in September 2002, Ryumon Zenji was ordained a Soto Zen Priest at the San Francisco Zen Center. Prior to her spiritual training, Ryumon had for many years also worked in Re-evaluation Counseling, specifically with the "Unlearning Racism" teaching system developed by Ricky Sherover-Marcuse.[3] Ryumon's own cocounseling work as a student and later as a teacher had focused in particular on what Re-evaluation Counseling calls "internalized oppression." But her work today as an anti-oppression trainer and educator addressed, as needed, all three of the (shifting) positions within systems of domination identified by many in that field as "target," "oppressor," and "ally."

Born in 1953, Ryumon moved at nine years old from Cuba to New York City. She lived, from early childhood until the end of high school, primarily with her paternal grandmother. Her family was, she said, "definitely working class—the men, busboys, restaurant workers, and porters; the women, factory workers. Monolingual Spanish households. Pretty much to this day, thirty-five years or more." Ryumon's grandmother was her caregiver, and a key influence, as she put it, "my main hero, the central figure, the myth creator in my life." Of her grandmother, Ryumon said: "She went [only] to second grade and she was a maid and all this, and yet, to me, she was the smartest person in the world. She was brilliant. So somehow that created this construction at a very early age that education or schooling did not go with being smart. This has been confirmed through my life."

Ryumon also remembered sleeping each night next to her grandmother and hearing her pray aloud before she slept. That prayer, Ryumon said, still influenced her meditation practice. She said:

> If I refer too much to my childhood, you let me know. But it's from those early times that I see meditation as being internal prayer. [In zazen meditation] I'm being quiet and looking at this wall and watching my breath—it's a prayer to myself. And prayer was something I learned when I was very little, even before I learned how to read. Even from Cuba my grandmother would pray out loud every night in bed—we all slept in the same room. I hadn't remembered this in years, [and then] my lover loaned me this book on angels. It included a prayer in English that was very familiar. And then I realized this was the prayer my grandmother taught me as a child, with a couple of variations, about guardian angels. So meditation is like this internal prayer, whereas to me, the ones that are taught in religious environments are sort of an external kind of prayer.

If one can surmise that Ryumon's internal spiritual journey began beside her grandmother, "even before [she] learned how to read," her quest for an external religious context also started young. Looking back on the process that led her finally to Soto Zen Buddhism, she said:

> It was an evolving path. It probably began when I was eleven or twelve years old. [At that time] I started going to Catholic school because my mother was Catholic. She was a Communist and stayed in Cuba. She's never left. And when we were sent out of the country, she told my father's family that she wanted my sister and I to be raised Catholic. My father's family were not Catholic, they were spiritualists. So at home, what I saw practiced was spiritualism, but I went to Catholic school and went through the whole thing.

The atmosphere in church, she remembered, felt special: "The incense and the vestments these priests wore, the stained glass windows in the church and the candles. At that time, the masses were in Latin, and the priests had their back turned to the people. It all looked omnipotent. And coming from a working class background, where my day-to-day environment was somewhat chaotic at times, this was like such a refuge." Ryumon was shocked when, on confiding to one of the priests that when she grew up she would like to "be like you. Do what you do," he smiled and said, "Oh, that's very sweet, but little girls aren't born to be priests." This was, she knew in hindsight, one of her first experiences of what she now named *sexism* and *adultism*. However, even in that moment, she said, she had not really believed his statement: "It didn't make sense because my grandmother told me at home I could be anything. So I just thought he was misinformed or something." Key truths that Ryumon would carry with her and apply later on had thus arrived early in her life. These included the actuality that one might distinguish between spiritual life within and without; that religio-spiritual systems were diverse; and that public and private sources of authority might differ from one another.

Ryumon continued to seek religious sanctuary throughout her childhood and young adult life, learning tai chi, yoga, and various forms of meditation practice. At the same time, however, as she told it, she had continually "forgotten" that this was the case and was often surprised when others noticed. Thus, for example, she said that a lover had given her Suzuki Roshi's book, *Zen Mind, Beginner's Mind*. She added:

> Just recently I asked her, "Why did you ever give me that book?" and she said, "Because you've been talking about that for so long. You were looking, you were searching. You were searching for something." I don't remember that. I don't remember having discussions or talking to friends that I was searching for anything. But she said, "Yeah, you'd always talk about it." And when I was initiated [at the San Francisco Zen Center] I called some people to tell them I was doing this. And a couple people said, "We're so happy because I know that a spiritual path has always been important to you."

It was in 1980, between periods of seeking spiritual guidance, that Ryumon was introduced to Re-evaluation Counseling. Its theory of healing was premised on the argument that revealing old injuries, through partner-based counseling, would enable the practitioner to recover her or his full intelligence and wisdom otherwise lost thanks to these early, untended wounds. Although Ryumon did not agree with the theory in whole cloth, she found the work that she undertook in the people of color Re-evaluation Counseling group of which she was a member to be transformative. "What *we* worked on was internalized oppression, internalized racism."

This mode of thinking through racism and other forms of oppression enabled Ryumon to link the external systems with their internal effects on her and all others. She said the study of internalized oppression was "the biggest tool and gift that the universe could have given me." Ryumon had already undertaken "sociological readings in Marxism on an academic level, and [had] come from Cuba, [where] the whole thing of politics was very big in my family." Still, she said, seeing it "as personalized to me, that's where it gelled. Yes, there is this system out there that is set up to take people like me out, you know. And I'm very up-front about how I see oppression. I don't make excuses for it, I don't have soft words. It's a system that's set up to maintain white supremacy." The group also became aware that even issues which seemed on the surface to be personal, familial, or community-based were frequently also linked to life in an oppressive society.

Ryumon had, she said, been able to do a great deal of emotional healing through cocounseling. She explained that the Chinese American friend who introduced her to it said: "It's simple. This theory says we're all born extremely brilliant, loving, cooperative, zestful, curious, and then we start getting hurt and we're not allowed to do our healing. And our intelligence gets occluded. Through cocounseling we do healing and reclaim our child." Subsequently Ryumon saw analogies between this mode of analysis and the idea of humans' "Buddha nature": "The fact that I know all of us to be very powerful and good, and have inherently all these qualities goes hand-in-hand with [the idea that] we're all Buddhas. So that's very concrete for me. And, all being Buddhas, we still do some inappropriate things, you know. So you gotta take responsibility for the things you do. I still recognize your Buddhahood. But just because I believe you're a Buddha doesn't mean I'm going to let you off the hook." By now, Ryumon was able to continue working with some of the premises that she had learned as a child while also making them more complex. Thus, Re-evaluation Counseling had affirmed that one might receive "misinformation" from the outside world—information that might be injurious to one's self-esteem if one was not able to question it. And as with spiritualism and Catholicism, in linking together the insights of Re-evaluation Counseling and Buddhism, she was simultaneously living and working in different worlds, each with its own tools. But now, as an adult, she was in a position to work consciously within, against, and between those diverse frameworks.

By the time of the interview, Ryumon was active around the nation as an anti-oppression workshop leader and trainer. She held to the ideas that she had learned back in her graduate student days about the structuring of systems of domination and individuals' complex relationships to them. But if anything, she said, the more she practiced Buddhism, the more she felt able to challenge those systems. As well, the more strongly she was moved to argue that people must turn inwards in order to challenge oppression. She explained:

> What motivates me when I do my work is how to get people of color, or women, or target groups, to work on our internalized oppression. And I believe that that's not what has happened, historically, in attempting to do antiracism work. The focus has been how to get white people to change. So when I do my talks and I tell people, "I don't really care what white people do," there's this reaction—"What do you mean?" I say, "On one level, yes, there's white supremacy and white power, but the issue of dismantling the system is for us to heal ourselves as people of color, to not continue to collude with how to maintain the system of power." Because whites don't keep it in power by themselves.

Ryumon argues here that internalized oppression has a significant impact, not just on the state of consciousness of oppressed people but also on their capacity to challenge systems of domination. It is not that Ryumon does not want white people to do antiracist work. Rather, she argues, that can never be enough by itself, either for systems to change, or for people of color to be healed from the injuries of racism.

As Ryumon continued to build bridges between the internal and the external effects of systems of domination, it became clear that both zazen meditation and Re-evaluation Counseling were crucial resources. As she pointed out, the two approaches have in common the idea that all men and women have an inherently whole and joyful nature. Indeed, both in their different ways call on the individual to look within and find out how that nature has been changed, or disrupted. And this applies to those who were oppressed as well as to those positioned as oppressors: it would surely not make sense for one group but not the other to return to full consciousness of their "Buddhahood" or original completeness. However, as Ryumon continued speaking, she made it clear that this journey was not an easy one. She said: "Through my Zen practice, I've become more clear that as a woman, as a lesbian, as a person of color, I contribute to maintaining the system, and that is a lot of grief. And to get to that place of realization, I think we need to become very raw, very vulnerable. This is where I see the two intersect, the political practice and the spiritual practice."

How Ryumon conceived of this intersection between inner and outer, the political and the spiritual, and the interrelationship between oppressor, the oppressed, and the potential ally became clear toward the end of our meeting. I asked Ryumon to respond to the following incident, which brought to the fore many of the issues that had been integral to the interview.

RF I would like to ask you a question, but it involves telling you a story. I recently had a conversation with my friend, Helena [*pseudonym*]. She had just gone to a two-day meditation retreat at an East Coast Zen Center. They were pretty strict about not moving the body when sitting.

The fact that she was not allowed to move her body brought up slavery for her. Whether from an ancestral memory or because, as an African American, one has social and cultural memory of enslavement, what was coming up for her was the middle passage. She really went through a lot. After a point she was able to say to herself, "Okay, now, you are an adult. You are who you are. You can move your body right now if you want to." So she did move her body.

RYUMON Good for her!

RF Halfway through the two-day retreat Helena had a conversation with one of the teachers, a white woman. This teacher's response was, "I feel really lucky that I didn't grow up with the kind of things that you grew up with." Helena told me, "That wasn't really enough for me as a response." Then, at the very end, she talked to another teacher about it, also white. He said he was really sorry that she had experienced so much pain during the sitting. So Helena said to him, "Well, it wasn't really physical pain, it was psychic pain." The teacher said, "Yes, species pain." Again, for Helena, that was not a supportive response.

So here's my question. On the one hand, I agree with what Helena was saying. And yet, when someone said to her, "species pain," that reminded me of the way in which to be human is indeed to suffer and sometimes it's the suffering of your ancestors. So then, how do we not lose the particular in the general? But how do we avoid—how do we make sure that we don't get stuck in the particular?

RYUMON It has to be both/and. I get scared when universality is used to erase particularities and the specific situations of people. It makes me think that in that case, universality is not seen in a holistic way, it's seen as an either/or. Because then I need to separate myself from my experience and my history and just focus on this unity that I have with all beings around the planet, because we have a human form. That's what I get from the story you shared, and that's the experience I get from some spiritual practice. That either/or flavoring—it's a Eurocentric cultural paradigm, which is why I say that we need to be very diligent and aware that everything that we practice in this human form is tainted through oppression, even when I'm wanting to talk about a spiritual practice.

Because if we truly practice the Buddhist view of interrelationship, my *particular* experience is very much part of the universality. I can't separate it. And why would I want to separate it? Because that's what has encased the self. That's what created this ego that I'm attempting to extinguish when I sit on my *zafu* [meditation cushion]. So it can't be separated. And the both/and approach is a very much more Afrocentric or indigenous tradition's way of seeing the world. So that's what comes to me when you ask that question. Within the context in which we are doing this pure practice, the pure practice is coming through a white dominant paradigm.

Ryumon's response placed her firmly within the frames of her Soto Zen Buddhist spiritual practice. Her analysis of Helena's situation proceeded by reference to ideas at the heart of Buddhist philosophy: sustained meditation practice as holding the potential for ego dissolution, the interrelationality of all beings; and the universality as well as particularity of the human experience. To describe this more simply, Ryumon Zenji could see that for Helena and the two teachers an important question had been whether her suffering in this instance had been the same as, or different from, that of other people, why, and how. For Ryumon this mattered because the teaching as given had failed to support a practitioner on her journey. Also critically necessary here were the fruits of her years of analysis of systems of racial domination. Thus her interpretation of Helena's experience took her immediately to a critique of the "Eurocentric flavoring" of "some practice" including, she implied, that which Helena had encountered. It was, she proposed, Eurocentrism that had left the two teachers unable to engage with the specificity of Helena's experience.

Ryumon proposed that *both* sides of my question about Helena's situation—should one address what was specific about it or should one recognize its similarity to what other humans also faced?—must be addressed. Both were true and both were important. Hence her immediate response that a "both/and" approach must be taken. As we saw, the female teacher treated it as an unfortunate experience, but one that she did not seem able to address as an integral aspect of Helena's meditation journey. On the other hand, the male teacher moved in the opposite direction, toward the ways in which one might universalize the memory of slavery as a more general "species pain."

Adding to Ryumon's analysis, one might argue that the female teacher had overly particularized Helena's experience in stating, "I feel really lucky that I didn't grow up with the kind of things that you grew up with." By contrast, the male teacher had overly generalized the experience, suggesting it be conceived as "species pain." Thus, one might suggest, one instance of what was particular (the white teachers' life experience) was masquerading as universal. This led them to exceptionalize on one hand, or blur on the other hand, the particularity of Helena's experience. And in either instance there was no straightforward way for them to see Helena's "particular" as self-evidently something to be examined within the meditation journey. Thus a second problem is revealed: the absence, in this "particular version of the universal" to avoid a binary way of seeing everything as *either* particular *or* universal.

As she continued to examine this question, Ryumon made a further point. She suggested that in fact the teachers, as well as Helena, were losing the opportunity to fully comprehend and learn from the situation that Helena had faced on that day. She said:

> If in that moment the white teacher removes himself or herself and becomes "the teacher," then the teacher is no longer there. See what I mean? In other words, if the teacher says, "Let me remove what's coming up for me as a white person and talk about the universality of the suffering," s/he has already lost sight of that student that's sitting in front of her/him, because s/he's not responding. I don't care who they are, when a person of color talks about their history with racism, white people have stuff come up for them.

Here, as earlier, one is reminded that whether by reference to Buddhist practice or to Re-evaluation Counseling, no one is left outside, either as student or as teacher—in fact everyone is both of those things.

Ryumon agreed when I stated one of the many implications of the events we had just discussed:

> RF  So then for you a key question is, "Well, teacher, what's up for you right now?"
> RYUMON  Exactly.

REWORKING MEANINGS of self, difference, and sameness, of identity, identification, and acceptance; applying spiritual frameworks and at times remaking them; acting on the basis of particular, recognized truths about the relationships among humans and for most, between humans and God, grace, or spirit. Different, yet readily comparable versions of these ideas were at stake in the work of John Potts, Robert Horton, Michael Bell, Akaya Windwood, and Ryumon Zenji. For all five, two premises were fundamental: first, that the human community is diverse, and second, that this is a positive rather than a negative thing. However, and again for all five, there was a third recognition, not a premise precisely because it was seen as naming what was unnecessary rather than inevitable: the degree at this time in history of hostility, hatred, and inequity organized around the entire range of human differences.

If one were to take the work of these five down to its simplest level one could conclude that it was undertaken for the first two premises, and committed to challenging the third recognition. However, even the clearest of goals can turn out to be difficult to attain in actuality— thus the care and subtlety with which these three men and two women needed to craft their work. For each of these men and women, particular spiritual resources were critical to their work against oppression and for diversity. Yet neither those resources nor these individuals' relationships with them were static. Rather, anti-oppression work was at times formed and re-formed by spiritual practice. But very often that work of necessity required revision or adaptation of the spiritual practices themselves.

John Potts's history offers a clear example of this cyclical process. His entry into anti-oppression work drew on parts of two religio-spiritual frames—the Episcopal Church and the Diamond Heart Path. Within Christianity, the Communion service first helped John to revise (or perhaps revive?) his sense of self and agency. As events outside of the church further altered that sense of self they also revised his understanding of the "Body of Christ." One might argue that it was thanks to that process that John decided to honor that collective body through pro-diversity work. Work with the Diamond Heart Path facilitated that change, helping him (alongside secular anti-oppression teachings) to unpack the "baggage" (his term) that he had carried with him from childhood. Through this multifaceted process, John's prior enmeshment in what I called "hostility, hatred, and inequity organized around the entire range of human differences" could be set aside.

For Robert Horton, a recognition fundamental to Tibetan Buddhist teachings of Chogyam Trungpa—that everything about oneself must be engaged on the path to one's liberation—turned out to be startlingly relevant to his later work against racism. But as with John Potts, it was outside of that path that Robert learned about the kinds of inequity that he would then be moved to challenge through the Untraining workshops developed on the basis of work with another teacher, Rita Shimmin. Particular religious or spiritual resources needed to be re-worked in order to be fully applicable to anti-oppression work. But, they remained crucial to his approach.

Michael Bell's connection to the Siddha Yoga path was central to his work in diversity education. He drew on and taught skills learned in meditation, including comfort with ambiguity and cultivating willing-ness to wait and listen rather than hasten toward conclusions or judge-ment. Besides this "skill-sharing," for Michael there existed a distinc-tive relationship between himself and grace, a potent presence that was not in any way in his control.

Akaya's description of what she named *spirit* was not entirely analo-gous to what Michael called *grace*. Still, as was demonstrated, spirit both inspired and provided the logic, structure, and rationale for Akaya's work encouraging men and women to accept, honor, and work with the differences among them. And in her experience, spirit, and Akaya's work from within its frame of reference, was consistently effective.

Ryumon Zenji's work against oppression was based in two sets of resources, Soto Zen Buddhism and Re-evaluation Counseling, each reinforcing and extending the other. Both distinguished between the potential of humans to be whole or free and the actuality of human suffering. And although their understanding of the reasons for this diverged, both worked with the individual and his or her formation and each, through its particular practices, invited individuals to be-come free of such suffering. Ryumon's consciousness of oppressive structures extended to the very teaching of Zen. In her view, Zen teachers needed to open to the same processes of introspection in the arena of race and other differences if they wished to realize the full potential of the tradition, as well as appropriately assist a diverse set of practitioners on their spiritual paths.

*Spirit*, among its several meanings, suggests for these interviewees both the notion of an extrahuman entity and the recognition that all activity is undertaken with a particular set of ideas, values, and goals in mind. Thus for Michael, grace held him while he undertook his work. And as he also stated, he fully expected grace to continue and complete his work once a given event was over. Thus one might argue that for Michael this was grace's work and activity as much as it was his own.

By contrast, while grace was a force very much conceived to be "over and above" Michael, for Akaya it was just as important to emphasize the "sameness" of spirit with earthly, ordinary human beings. Spirit was for her immanent rather than transcendent. Nonetheless it was clear that when spirit worked it achieved what she, Akaya, could not accomplish alone. One might argue that here spirit rejoins grace as a potency over and above the individual. Critically, though, spirit, for Akaya, was what signaled both the potential and actuality of humans' connectedness with one another.

For both individuals there was a dialogue in play between the spiritual philosophy on one side and spirit/grace, on the other. For both, a philosophical system was essential to processes of planning and even making sense of the work. Yet in their different ways one might argue that spirit/grace were critical as active forces in the process, whether as that which was immanent or that which was transcendent.

Another way of noting a force other than the quotidian consciousness of the individual arrived in the context of dreams and other messages. Thus, Robert Horton's dream of an antiracism workshop pushed him to begin designing The Untraining. Likewise, looking back on the events that led him to Arnold Mindell and thence to Rita Shimmin was a health crisis that he subsequently read as a message that he needed to make some changes in his life. As well, John Potts's dream was key to his telling of the story of his transformation both into prodiversity work and into spiritual practice.

Regarding the second, as it were, spirit in which the word *spirit* is used, there was much commonality across the five interviews. If a single word covered all aspects of "the spirit of the work" in this sense, it would be *egalitarianism*. But as we have seen this did not mean a turn toward a "lowest common denominator" of expectations. Rather the spirit of the work entailed cultivating recognition that all humans could, as Akaya put it, "rise" to the highest common factor of their humanity. And as we have seen, as stated explicitly by Michael, Akaya, Ryumon, and implicitly by John, it was God, or the "Buddha nature" of humans that underwrote this possibility.

Also in the spirit of egalitarianism, for all, it was deemed crucially important for teachers and workshop leaders to come to understand themselves before they could consider themselves ready to lead workshops. This commitment honored the central recognition that the issues under consideration were socially constructed ones. That meant, in turn, that anti-oppression teachers needed to see themselves as students as well as educators. As well, it should be remembered that several named in detail the tools and resources that they continued to use on and for themselves, even during workshops, to ensure that they remained present to the work, the practice, and in some cases to divinity in one or another named form.

As seen, egalitarianism also meant that in workshop design boundaries were intentionally blurred between categories of oppressor and oppressed and, at times, teacher and student also. Instead, the processes by which individuals became one or the other of these, the possibility of being both, and the option of change were focused on. Yet as before this did not mean a compromising of goals, but rather an invitation to all to open their consciousness to transformation.

What were the outcomes of all of this expected to be? Here, one might argue that the two senses of the "spirit of the work" were reunited. For as we have seen, egalitarianism meant that, in critical ways, the workshop leaders declined to assume any hope of complete control over the outcome of any work session. Rather, as was stated at different times, they hoped to offer new questions rather than new answers, processes rather than finished products, transitions and directions rather than arrivals. However, if this felt like enough, it was, I suggest, precisely because the Spirit of the work in the uppercase, be that named God, Spirit, or Buddha nature, was trusted by all five of these men and women to be present in this work. As such, all saw themselves as extending to those present an invitation to consider seriously and accept wholeheartedly the diversity that is constitutive of human society.

## CONSCIOUS SEX, SACRED CELIBACY

*sexuality and the spiritual path*

This chapter is about sexualities, spiritual journeys, and the interweaving of the two. Sex is a potent site in most contemporary cultures. The policing of sexuality and sexual practices in religious contexts at times made spiritual journeys into agonizing ones for the men and women interviewed here. Some struggled over the relationship between sexual life and spiritual life in ways that mapped neatly onto the normativity of heterosexuality that still characterizes most mainline Christian congregations, and one must add, almost all Jewish, Muslim, Hindu, and Buddhist institutions as well. For others sexuality was a matter of little significance, precisely because it was a locus of, so to speak, "no conflict" vis-à-vis religious or spiritual life. Meanwhile, beyond the coercive division of sexual practices into the forbidden and the acceptable, the "sinful" and the "legitimate," the social, spiritual, and religious ordering of the sexual led at times to the effort to make sex consciously into a sacred act. And it led also toward sexual renunciation and celibacy as chosen dimensions of spiritual life. For some of these people there was an effort to redesign relationships between selfhood and sexuality in the context of celibacy. For still others celibacy itself made of sexuality a rather trivial topic.

Much that was distinctively local, current, and new gave form to the sexual environment in which this group of interviewees resided. Yet there was a longevity to the issues faced here, one that seemed frequently to cross religious and spiritual lines. These included large and challenging questions. Among them were the meaning, conduct, and ethics of interpersonal relations; the legitimacy, rationality, and religious acceptability of forms of sexual practice; relationships between sexuality, nature, and culture; the acceptability, normalcy, or God-givenness of particular forms of sexuality; and lastly the question of whether there is a place in human life above or beyond sexuality. Rather than seeking to resolve these questions, this chapter explores the means by which interviewees strove to understand them and make sense of them, in order to live in accordance with their spiritual systems of understanding.

A key challenge faced here by interviewees was, in fact, how to separate the religious and spiritual from what is deemed normative in secular, sociocultural terms. As John Boswell argued in his groundbreaking effort to resituate gay (his term) people in Western, Christian history:

> Hostility to gay people provides singularly revealing examples of the confusion of religious beliefs with popular prejudice. Apprehension of this confusion is fundamental to understanding many kinds of intolerance, but it is not usually possible until either the prejudice or the religious beliefs have become so attenuated that it is difficult to imagine that there was ever any integral connection between them. As long as the religious beliefs which support a particular prejudice are generally held by a population, it is virtually impossible to separate the two; once the beliefs are abandoned, the separation may be so complete that the original connection becomes all but incomprehensible . . . Only during a period in which the confusion of religion and bigotry persisted but was not ubiquitous or unchallenged would it be easy to analyze the organic relation of the two in a convincing and accessible way.
>
> The modern West appears to be in just such a period of transition regarding various groups distinguished sexually, and gay people provide a particularly useful focus for the study of the history of such attitudes.[1]

The challenge faced by lesbian and gay interviewees seeking spiritual safe haven was a particularly difficult and poignant one. Yet, as all of them told me, degrees of repression and flexibility were to be found in both secular and spiritual/religious environments. And questions about sexual form, practice, and ethics were not raised only with regard to what one might name (awkwardly) nonheteronormativity. Rather, a "bundling" of issues about sexuality including, but going beyond, heteronormativity per se, meant that interviewees' sense of sexuality and relationship was connected at almost all times with a range of questions ostensibly beyond it—for some, those of wedlock and childbirth, for others those of psychological health, well-being, and even full "humanness."

It is not difficult to agree with John Boswell's assessment of the contemporary period as one of conflict, commentary, and transition, in both secular and religious settings, in the realm of things sexual.[2] These interviewees' sexual sensibilities tell us something about the sociocultural contexts in which they live, as well as about what sex and relationship meant in practical and ethical terms.

☙

THESE INTERVIEWEES KNEW that, for better or worse, they inhabited a sexually diverse world. It was also clear to them that this could mean a range of things from the standpoint of religion and spirituality—again at times for better and at times for worse. The possibility of enacting particular sexualities and sexual practices, as well as individuals' sense of agency and self-worth (or the lack thereof) were marked by locations in time, space, and sociogenerational culture. And all of the above was made harder or easier by interviewees' sense of God, their spiritual path, and the religio-spiritual communities with which they were connected. Thus at times the fluidity of the sociocultural moment made available a sense of sexual flexibility and choice. At other times it made possible individuals' insistence or self-acceptance as being *this* kind of sexual subject, rather than that one. It was in this context that Nancy Nielsen, fifty-three, white, and heterosexual ally for the Lutheran Church's movement for the respectful inclusion and acceptance in the church of people of all sexualities, could say: "It's a struggle within all of the mainline [Christian] denominations, this whole, from my perspective ludicrous, debate over sexuality and our inability to see sexuality as not a choice but simply who we are as created beings."

In Nancy's insistence that humans are "*created* beings" (emphasis added), one gets immediately to what is for many religious practitioners, Christian and otherwise, at the heart of the matter. Once one sees oneself as created, one has access to a lynchpin of self-understanding and self-recognition. Love of the divine and/or of particular spiritual paths makes possible and indeed inevitable the interconnection of one's spiritual practice with particular modes of sexual practice (including celibacy). But, meanwhile, for many the refusal of organized religion to accept all forms of sexuality causes anguish, as well as becoming the locus of activism and efforts to transform religious institutions.

Early in every interview, I asked, "How would you name your sexuality?" In cases where there was an appearance of confusion, there would be follow-up prompts: "Sexual orientation—gay, lesbian, heterosexual, bisexual?" Far later in the interview I asked whether celibacy had ever been a part of an individual's spiritual/religious practice, and how each understood the relationship between sexuality and spirituality. For most, these matters were taken up in the order in which I presented them. But for a few, issues of sexuality were clearly at the very center of the spiritual journey. While it could be argued that the experience of this latter group of individuals cast most light on the matter of how sexuality, religion, and spiritual practice are interrelated, this would be a naive reading. For that which is taken for granted, unmarked from the purview of the speaker, is also crucially telling.

As men and women responded to my request to identify themselves in terms of their sexuality, the positions of individuals within the hierarchies and debates around sexuality current in the United States became clear. Most (although, importantly, not all) were willing and able to name themselves in terms of sexuality or sexual orientation. Gloria Williams, almost forty-seven, African American, devotee of Sri Sri Ravi Shankar, a guru in the Hindu tradition, said the following about herself and sexuality:

GLORIA Which category would I put myself in?

RF What would you like me to do?

GLORIA I'd have to be one of the people [in your sample] who doesn't choose. It's really horrifying to think of being straight. It's like, no, no, no, no, no, that's not who I am. And bisexual—the way that I see it used, again it's like more boxes. I don't like having to choose. If, you know, for some reason push was coming to shove, and I don't know why it would have to, I would choose bisexual before I would choose anything else. It gives me the most freedom to connect with any spirit in any way that I choose to do that. But I never think of myself that way. And I often do think, "Oh, I'm not anything. I'm not really anything any more."

RF And is that a positive thing? I mean, you kind of made a face when you said that.

GLORIA Well, it's not a bother to me, but it's sort of—it's a wonder, you know.

For Gloria the conventions associated with her temporal and spatial location seemed unacceptable, even insurmountable. She had seen my question coming, before it was even posed. For she had said, "I've gotten very tired of all the things that create separation. Ruth, I know you're going to [ask] the sexuality question." But whether or not she liked it, it must be noted that, first, Gloria was all too aware of her categorical options. Second, she was able to come up with a self-naming, albeit one that was only provisional and contextual. Lastly she was aware that her options included *not* choosing, which is to say choosing transcendence or evasion of the sexual categorization system as a whole.

All of these men and women, including Gloria, were aware of themselves as residing in a sexually alert, sexually hierarchical society. All recognized that they were expected to be able to come up with a "sexual ID" for themselves. All knew at least a little about protocols of sexual self-naming and knew also which conventions were necessary or at least apposite to their own positions within the sexual landscape. This was so even as individuals checked on language choices: L'dia Omari Mohammed, forty-two, African American, member of the Nation of Islam responded to my "How would you describe your sexuality or your sexual orientation?" with, "In regards to heterosexual or homosexual? Um, heterosexual. That's straight, right? Yeah, heterosexual."

For some, heteronormativity (heterosexuality deemed normal, normative, to be "expected," and the discursive and material ordering of society around those ideas) was at the center of self-naming. Yet whether heteronormativity really remained intact was a question. For example, Derek Jones, white, British immigrant, fifty-eight, deacon in the Episcopal Church, said, "Oh, definitely heterosexual." Derek was, then, firm in his insistence that he is a heterosexual man. I had, indeed, interviewed him in the home that he shares with his wife and five children. His statement might thus simply underscore the obviousness (as he saw it) of his answer to an apparently redundant inquiry. But any forceful statement raises the question of context—what was it, for instance, that he thought I *might* be searching for instead of heterosexuality? Here the idea of a sexually diverse society is brought forward.

Misha Ashoorian, sixty-nine, Orthodox Christian, born in Iran, similarly insisted on the obviousness of the answer to my question. Misha said, "I'm very naturally a man. I mean, not sexual other. I'm married. I have two children." One can again comment on what Misha's context has made possible: this man has somehow at his disposal the concept of sexual "otherness." For Misha, it was self-evident that being married and having children were proof positive that he was straight, not gay. (While true in his case this is, of course, not always a correct assumption.) But be that as it may, he was also clear, in his mind, that to be straight rather than gay is to be "very naturally a man." And here is heteronormativity in play.

Others besides Misha described their sexuality relationally. Nancy McKay said, "Heterosexual. Married thirty-seven years." Sita, forty-eight, a female renunciate in the ashram of Mata Amritanandamayi said, "Well, I used to date men quite a bit. But I never felt that I wanted to get married." Michael Yamamoto, forty-nine, Japanese American, practicing Tibetan Buddhist, said, "We're, uh, you know, hetero." He then laughed nervously, possibly at a question about sexuality being raised at all so early in our acquaintance.

One could argue that, when men and women described their sexuality relationally, this was a simple, factual message about how their own worlds were lived, rather than the proffering of spouse, partnership, or offspring as signs that all was, as it were, sexually in good order. But whether or not there was anxiety or insistence inherent in any of these utterances, they were indicative of fluencies in sexual self-naming. Moreover their language choices in fact shift the terms of the discourse from essentialist modes of identification to performative ones. Thus one might transcode Sita's response to read "I date [men,] therefore I am [heterosexual]." Likewise one implication of Nancy McKay's answer could be, "I have been married to my husband for thirty-seven years. That is *how* heterosexual I am." But I do not claim that either woman is naming her sexuality in a way that is judgmental of the "nonstraight." Indeed, both Sita's and Nancy's life paths have in different ways disrupted heteronormativity: Sita is now a renunciate and Nancy has sought to sexually integrate her Christian congregation.

For many, the question and answer was a straightforward checking off of a category. Thus Tariq Naficy, Muslim, thirty-two, simply said, "Um, heterosexual." Barbara Monsler, fifty-two, white, Episcopalian, psychotherapist in private practice, offered "Heterosexual—female, attracted to males." Charlotte, fifty-five, white, longstanding participant in Alcoholics Anonymous, said, "Heterosexual." Mushim Ikeda-Nash, forty-six, Japanese American Sansei, Zen Buddhist said, "I'm heterosexual."

Tom Wagoner's playful and almost sarcastic response to my forewarning that I was about to ask him a list of questions about gender, sexuality, socioeconomic, and racial location, and so on—"Okay. I'm forty-seven years old. Um, uh, I'm white, uh, I'm heterosexual"—

makes explicit his awareness of the expectation that all U.S. residents cultivate skills in "self-demographizing." However, it does so in a way that in turn signals his locatedness, perhaps in California, certainly in a "sexuality-savvy" context. For while the need to provide name, gender, and age are standard, it is rare, past college years (at least outside of the Department of Motor Vehicles and the census) to be asked to identify oneself racially. And it is almost unheard of to be asked to supply sexual orientation in any public or official space.

Thus far (other than Gloria) I have intentionally mentioned only heterosexual interviewees: their self-naming was different from that of nonheterosexuals precisely because of their positioning as "unmarked" in the sexual world of the United States. Because we are in a "post-Stonewall" time, which is to say, because movements for gay, lesbian, and transgendered people's rights have been a part of the United States's discursive landscape for several decades, albeit unevenly dispersed, some gay and lesbian interviewees named their sexual orientation in simple, factual terms. Thus Aditya Advani, thirty-four, Hindu, an Indian resident in the United States since university, said simply, "I'm gay." Likewise Emerald Matra, forty-six, white, and a priestess in the Wiccan tradition, responded to my question, "And how would you describe your sexuality?" with one word—"Lesbian."

The responses of some gay men and lesbians took the same form as those of heterosexuals. For example Pearl Werfel, forty-one, who described herself as a "Jewish pagan" committed to prepatriarchal Judaism, described her sexuality relationally: "I am a lesbian. Probably more towards the bisexual side, but I'm in a committed relationship that I've been in for over thirteen years, so I'd say that qualifies me as lesbian." Arinna Weisman, South African–born immigrant who has practiced and taught Vipassana meditation for sixteen years, spoke in a way that mimicked, but also subverted and supplemented the census-like list of "vital statistics" that I had begun to request from her: "I'm forty-six. I came from a Jewish home that was culturally identified but not spiritually identified as Jewish. And I'm a lesbian, pale-skinned, able-bodied." For Arinna, the term *pale-skinned* substitutes for *white*. *Able-bodied* served as a reminder of an axis of privilege most often forgotten. *Lesbian,* it seemed in that moment, could be simply slotted in as one more characteristic in a list. But Arinna's lesbian identity was critical in her spiritual life in several ways.

For lesbian women and gay men, however, a simple one-phrase response was not usually enough in their own eyes. Emerald Matra, for example, immediately added to her single-word answer a brief autobiographical note: "I came out as a lesbian—I was very happily married, really in love with my husband . . . My sexual orientation changed in the course of our marriage." Michael Bell, African American, thirty-nine, devotee of Gurumayi Chidvilasananda, also answered my question with a brief annotation: "Gay. I'm gay. And I've been out for seventeen years now."

As is well known to all those who do not fit the heteronormative mold, if one's sexuality is "unmarked," which is to say, deemed normative in the culture in which one lives, it seems somehow less necessary to account for its formation. By contrast the accounting process is one that people whose sexuality is *non*normative cannot easily escape. In this regard a small clustering of heterosexuals who were examining the etiology of their sexuality signaled the new sexuality-consciousness of the contemporary United States. Diana Winston, twenty-eight, European American, practitioner of Vipassana, expressed complexity rather than simplicity about her sexual orientation: "I generally would say, 'straight-identified bisexual.' I'm in a heterosexual relationship right now and I'm primarily involved with men . . . I would say my sexual orientation is probably the newest piece informing my spiritual life. I never really saw it as a piece of why my spiritual practice is as it is. But I now, as I get to a place where I don't want to cut off pieces of myself, I have to figure [it] out." Diana emphasized that she was not yet clear how her spiritual practice might inform her sexuality, or vice versa. Indeed she told me in some frustration, "I just think the question, 'What is your sexual orientation,' is incredibly confusing. It's hard for me at this point in my life to be strictly identified into one category. So that's why I sort of made it oblique. I could say bisexual, but I would say I'm kind of not completely. You know what I mean? But what is bisexuality?"

Meanwhile, in the Tibetan Buddhist tradition, Robert Horton, white, forty-one, had perhaps traveled some of the same paths of inquiry as had Diana. He said of his sexual orientation: "I would say it's bisexual, but mostly active in heterosexual. But I've definitely—I'm aware of both bisexual tendencies and the culturally imposed homophobia towards those in myself. That's actually been up over the last few years, just being really interested in how desire is kept in a box within our culture and how that box gets put inside oneself as well." Here, perhaps, Robert Horton summarizes what Diana is grappling with: a sense of nonexclusive sexual desire that is accessible only if and when one is able to be conscious of it. I do not wish to argue, here, that spiritual practice alone accounts for these individuals' questioning of sexual categories and (in

Diana's and Robert's cases) their emplacement in them. Diana *did* state that these were spiritual questions for her. While Robert did not say that explicitly, he did say that he had been "inspired" by a 1997 discussion in San Francisco between the Dalai Lama and a group of gay and lesbian Buddhist practitioners. In it, the spiritual leader had suggested that it might be necessary to examine the cultural and spiritual roots of anti-homosexual sentiment.[3] But in any event, I suggest that these individuals' spiritual practices come together with the cultural context(s) in which both live.

SEX AND SEXUALITY are sites of activity rather than only identities: naming one's sexuality by no means exhausts the terrain of sex and sexuality as a realm of practices. And, more than one might imagine, the conscious choice not to have sex—whether as a temporary or a permanent decision—is also very much connected to contemplation of the meaning of the sex act itself.

As interviewees spoke to me about what sex is, what it is about, and what it is "for," whether for them personally or more generally, it was almost impossible to separate what might be deemed "religious" or "spiritual" from that which one might consider "sociocultural." To put this differently, neither sex/sexuality, nor religion/spirituality are separable from their cultural contexts. Neither of these pairs is pure, pristine, or natural, and neither stands apart from other sets of issues or representational systems. Examining on one hand the "culturalness" of religion and spirituality and on the other hand the cultural formation of notions of sex and sexuality revealed the intersections and disjunctions between these.

The words of the youngest interviewee, Hana Neilsen Kneisler, begin to make clear what I mean. Hana is European American and heterosexual. At the time of this interview she was twenty-two years old. In discussing sex and sexuality, Hana drew on the teaching of her religion, Bahai. As she did this it was clear to her that she had to do so in a sexually diverse society. And for me it was evident that she needed to work through the cultural imperatives placed on her by her religion and by the other context in which she currently lived—the university where at the time of this interview she was a student.

Hana's parents had become members of the Bahai faith when Hana was seven or eight. Hana remained active as a Bahai leading workshops on "family life" and "preparing for marriage," and joining discussion meetings with other Bahai students on such topics as "the equality of men and women."

When I asked Hana how in her view sexuality and spirituality were related, she turned directly to her religion. Hana told me that Bahaullah, the founder of the Bahai faith, "talked about the natural and spiritual aspect of sexuality. One does not need to avoid sex in order to be spiritual." But, she added, "sexual practice is, however, confined to marriage between a man and a wife." Hana also explained that preparation for marriage entailed thoroughly investigating the character and personality of a potential mate. Also, she added, one could not do that before one had also deeply examined oneself.

Bahai thus placed sex within another set of practices and logics. Sex was limited to heterosexual union, and contained within a legal/cultural structure called *marriage*. Both of these were in turn emplaced within rigorous processes of self-inquiry. Thus despite the assertion within Bahai teaching that sex is "natural," "spiritual," and "a necessary part of human nature," culture in a specific, religious mode overrode nature in setting parameters around both the timing and the form of sexual activity. Sex did not stand alone but rather within a discursive and practical terrain that generated appropriate and inappropriate sex acts.

A generalized and informal sociology of sex followed as Hana continued, "At this present age, humans struggle with it . . . in the form of excessive promiscuity, marital infidelity." Hana is not, of course, the first to make this observation about sexual practice in the contemporary United States, nor did she claim that hers was an original statement. Rather, to her it was if anything a statement of something so obvious that it did not need to be defended nor supported with data. Speaking on a more immediate level about her workshop leadership with Bahai youth, Hana said, "One of the sticky points for young people . . . is that balance between finding somebody and investigating their true character, and balancing the expectations of this social Western culture. It's very hard. It's very hard to resist the dating practices, the sexual involvement, and be pure. And 'pure' is not to say devoid of mistakes or anything, but a purity of motive in one's actions." Here one meets the array of "good" and "bad" spiritual actions that travel along with "good" and "bad" sex acts. Hana and other young Bahais faced what one might call the politics of their location: the challenge of making "Bahai sense" of the very same environment that they shared with their non-Bahai peers. Sex became a site of contention and sociocultural clash. While striving for "balance" (her term) Hana acknowledged that the situation is a "sticky" one. Again, sociocultural forces overrode "nature." Of these forces one set is emergent from, as she named it, "Western culture," and another set articulated within the Bahai faith. The playing field was not seen to be even: rather, Hana says, young Bahais faced expectations that were difficult to "resist." Thus on one side were "expectations" about "dating practices," and on the other side the quest to find somebody and investigate their true character, in a way that remained "pure." These two roads to the sex act were, clearly, different from one another. As had been the case for others discussed in earlier chapters, Hana was aware that there were many competing ways of seeing the world in which she lived, and that her framework (Bahai in this instance) was not the dominant one. Whether one supported "the pressure to date" or "the effort to be 'pure,'" sexual practice was revealed here as embedded within competing sociocultural imperatives, some coded "Bahai" and "spiritual" and others coded "Western culture." In the end, Hana tagged the pressures that were difficult to resist as cultural, not natural, ones.

The same issues were present vis-à-vis nondominant, nonheteronormative sexualities. Hana was concerned as she faced the apparent contradiction between Bahai teaching and the visible presence of gay, lesbian, bisexual, and transgendered peers at her campus:

> Homosexuality is a result of—I don't know exactly what. It's sort of a sticky issue, and especially for me for being in [college] and trying to figure out what the Bahai faith says and what is right. Bahais come from all walks of life. No one is discouraged from becoming a Bahai because they're homosexual or because they drink alcohol or because they take drugs. [These] are all things that are not condoned in the Bahai faith, but everybody has their own struggles that pertain to this earth. And those struggles enhance or detract from our spiritual life, which is the ultimate purpose of our life.

The politics of location are critically important here. For it is, as Hana said, her presence in a university setting with a simultaneous presence of gay, lesbian, bisexual, and transgendered people (my terms, not Hana's) that pushed Hana into a place of questioning "what the Bahai faith says and what is right."

As she contemplated "homosexuality" (her term) Hana did not—perhaps, sensibly, could not—cite social pressure as leading individuals toward such practices. Rather it remained a mystery, "the result of—I don't know exactly what." But even if the etiology of the practice(s) was unclear it was easy enough for Hana to link "homosexuality" with other acts deemed problematical. Thus homosexuality was linked with other practices not self-evidently related to it—drinking alcohol and taking drugs. If these three kinds of activities have anything in common in this instance it is, perhaps, that they are not "condoned" by Bahais, and that the renunciation of them may as a result be the site for spiritual growth. Although Hana did not say so explicitly, both of these things would, presumably also be true of sexual issues named earlier, promiscuity, infidelity, and the desire for sex outside marriage. She said, in fact, that she had very recently separated from a non-Bahai boyfriend keen for premarital sex. This had, she said, led her to question the appropriateness of the partner rather than that of Bahai teaching. Thus while Hana did not claim to have final answers to these questions, she *did* seek answers to questions of sexuality that were Bahai ones rather than any other kind, finding in Bahai sufficient authority to feel comfortable with one particular mode of reading and structuring sexual practice.

Despite superficial differences, another young interviewee, Enigma (her chosen pseudonym) mapped and commented on sexual practice in some similar ways. Enigma, twenty-four, was raised Muslim and still practiced the religion. Enigma shared with me a video she made about U.S. Muslim women's choice to wear the veil. Her feelings about United Statesian views of veiling were strong ones:

> What inspired me to do this film . . . was a reaction of, "I've had it with all of you telling me what I am. Do you even give a damn about what I think, what I feel?" . . . [And] watching TV you hear about these stupid, stupid stories done by *60 Minutes* or NBC, CBS—who already have the intention to go to Afghanistan, to go to the Middle East, knowing that, "Oh God, these women have to wear these draggy black outfits. The poor souls! We should do a documentary."

She added: "I mean, I could just go out in California and videotape a bunch of women wearing bikinis and then do a documentary saying, "These poor souls, they have to go out wearing underwear and bra all the time. I feel so sorry for them. Look at them. They're wearing these things." Is that really real? Am I doing [them] justice?" These comments are not about sexuality per se. But they are about modes of performing femininity. Enigma had very definite views about the relationships between femininity and Islam as she saw them. It is clear too that Enigma was aware that she was positioned as "object," as "objectified," more often than as full subject, within the gaze of media and everyday U.S. culture.

Enigma's response to my question about her sexuality was, "Oh, heterosexual, I suppose. I mean, that's—I think all the monotheistic beliefs have that. Nothing out of the ordinary." Linguistically complex as these sentences are, they may nonetheless be analyzed. The statements, "all the monotheistic beliefs have that" and "Nothing out of the ordinary" are central here. The word *that* in the first fragment might be read in two ways. *That* might mean "heterosexuality." Here the claim would be that all the monotheistic religions "have," practice, or believe in, heterosexuality alone. Or *that* might mean "rejection of homosexuality." But in either instance Enigma is pointing to the idea that "all the monotheistic beliefs" support, enforce, and deem normal and "ordinary," heterosexuality. In asserting a place of commonality among "all monotheistic beliefs" Enigma reminds her listener that Islam, her own religion, often made "other" in the United States, shares ground with Christianity and Judaism.[4]

Enigma's self-description also dismisses out of hand any other possibility besides heterosexuality with regard to herself. Her language proposes that she is answering in a way that is almost offhand—"Oh," "I suppose," and "Nothing out of the ordinary" giving the impression that the question is a trivial one. Yet immediately following the statement on sexuality it became clear that Enigma had strong feelings around sex, sexuality, and relationships. Having learned that she was unmarried, I sought to reconfirm something that I had already thought was the case, asking, "And you don't have children?" Enigma responded with increasing passion:

> No. We don't get involved in things like that. We are strict, you know, with the old values . . . As years pass by, people feel the need that, "Oh, as the new generation, we must come up with the new rules and regulations. The old, that's old-fashioned." You know, as far as I'm concerned, values do not change. Moral values do not change. If stealing is wrong, it's going to be wrong until the day of judgment. I'm sorry, I'm not going to believe—you know, change my concept. I don't believe in, you know, whether—things regarding gender issues of sexuality. I'm sorry—people are going to be proud of coming out of the closet—I'm not going to apologize and go back in my closet. I'm going to be outspoken in my views. If I see it's wrong, it's wrong, and I'm going to stick with it. I'm not going to force my views on other people but I'm also not going to shut up and hide away my views if someone asks me.

Enigma invokes a "we" here in order to inhabit it, and contrasts it with another group, a "new generation" that is ready to reject old values. It should be remembered that Enigma began this statement in response to my asking whether she had children, even though I had already ascertained that she was unmarried. For Enigma it was a moral impossibility for marriage and parenthood to travel separately. As was true for Hana, culture and religion overrode nature.

Likewise Enigma, like Hana, connects a set of issues not inherently linked, including childbirth outside of marriage, stealing, and a set of behaviors less exactly named, "gender issues of sexuality." In naming them, it is interesting that Enigma draws on the discourse of gay/lesbian/bisexual rights. For if there is a single metaphor associated with that movement and its discourse, it is "coming out of the closet." In that moment Enigma became the one who might, she feared, be forced into the closet. As she positions herself as a person determined to be outspoken, one sees again her own struggle not to "shut up and hide away" as a Muslim woman. One witnesses too the familiarity with sexual diversity available to all those interviewed. Lastly, although Enigma invokes the "monotheistic religions" and the "judgment day," she also forcefully asserts *herself* as speaker and analyst in this situation—"If *I* see it's wrong, it's wrong" and "*I'm* not going to shut up" (emphases added). I would argue here that Enigma carries with her a religious underpinning for her argument but foregrounds an individualism that is, ironically enough, quintessentially United Statesian.

Both Hana and Enigma set out, on the surface of things, to speak about sex and sexuality in religious terms. Both sought to swim against the tide of cultural practices and expectations different from their own religious or spiritual beliefs. Both struggled with the politics of their campus location and against a set of expectations, even pressures that they felt their own generation faced and/or tried to assert. Yet as they did so they almost inevitably drew on ways of seeing the world around them that did not originate in their religion alone. For of course Islam and Bahai are by no means the only places, the only institutions, from whence this very particular set of comments and concerns has emerged. They are present in some of contemporary Christian, Jewish, Buddhist, and Hindu discourse as well.

Adding a further layer of confusion is that both women contrasted their own views with that which they deemed "Western," "modern," or "new." These distinctions do not fully hold true, however, once one remembers the Westernness of many opponents of each of the practices named by Hana and Enigma. Again while it is true that all the practices named by the two women *do* take place in the West in the contemporary period, each of them has its own complex timelines. (It is not, for example, as though stealing is new. Nor is the use of alcohol or even, despite arguments to the contrary, homosexuality.)

Both women packaged together a range not only of sexual practices but of other nonsexual activities also. Thus two sets of protocols were put into place simultaneously, one prescribing and proscribing particular routes toward sexual activity (and results of the same), and the other engaging with other prohibitions on the use of alcohol and drugs, as well as on stealing. The discussion of the sexual thus became not so much about sex but about social practices more broadly. The implication was that all of them were similar or at least worthy of analogy.

While interesting in sociological and perhaps even historical terms, the articulation of these proscriptions into sets would perhaps be lacking in great significance but for one further effect. This process of categorization leads toward a series of binaries wherein there are two major categories: "godly sex versus ungodly sex"; "godly activity versus ungodly activity"; and "godliness versus ungodliness" in general terms. As I have stated before, I do not seek, here, to comment on the "godliness" of any particular form of sexual practice, nor for that matter any approach to the use of alcohol or other substances, legal or not. But what is of great interest here is the emplacement of sex and sexualities within particular cultural frames, and the assertion that these frames are religious ones that are themselves transparent renderings of what is natural.

While other interviewees did not express the same attitudes about sexuality and sex as the two women just named, it would be entirely erroneous to suggest that others' spiritual maps of the sexual world were unanchored in the politics, perils, or promises of any social, cultural, or political location. In other words, if those who leaned towards caution and conservatism were clearly located in time and space, so were those whom one might label "progressive," or "permissive."

For some sex was deemed inherently valuable, healthful rather in the same way as are other aspects of a balanced diet. or beneficial in the way that a daily run in the park balances a desk job. David Jacobson, fifty-three, European American, heterosexual, osteopathic physician and practitioner of kundalini yoga, said that for him human spiritual life must entail full engagement with all human capacities, including sexuality. Akaya Windwood, forty-one, an African American lesbian whose spiritual practice was extra-institutional said of sex: "sexuality in its best sense is a joyous hoot and holler, a way of saying, 'I think you're pretty spiffy.'" And Pearl Werfel said: "It's a celebration of my body . . . It's connection with my partner, it's enjoying myself. It's pleasure and enjoying myself and a recognition that this is something that I have that I can use."

For all three of these people sex was self-evidently connected with one's spiritual life. Thus for Akaya:

> I can't understand how [sex] could be devoid of spirit, any more [than]—you know, I love to cook. Is there a sense of sacred in that? Absolutely. So when I'm making love with someone, or being in a place of sexual excitement with someone, is spirit there? Of course! But you know, spirit is there when I'm brushing my teeth, and when I'm using the bathroom, and when I'm washing my car, and when I'm patting my cat, or even when I'm watching a video. I mean, spirit is always present. So why—I just don't—I can't understand a spirit that wouldn't incorporate sexuality.

Pearl said: "I believe that sex and sexuality is a gift. It's something that was given to me, as well as it is given to anyone who chooses to accept this gift. And it's something that I can appreciate like any gift that is given to me. Experiencing sexuality is a celebration—it's a celebration of the goddess, it's a celebration of my body. And it's very beautiful and it's very sacred." As his words about spirituality, humanness, and sexuality made clear, David also saw a clear connection between sexuality and spiritual practice.

In Akaya's, Pearl's, and David's eyes sexuality is a site of the valuable, the permissible, even the necessary, rather than a place that must be contained or controlled. Yet for all three of these people sexual practice unconsciously undertaken lacked an ethical dimension that was in their view crucial. Thus Pearl warned: "As with really appreciating good food or, for me, because I'm not an alcoholic, appreciating a glass of champagne in a celebration, it is a wonderful thing as a gift. It's from the vine. If I abuse it, then I'm stepping off my spiritual path. So, you know, if it's only about sex, if it's not about connection, purely about pleasing myself, then I'm off, and I'm abusing the gift. It ceases to be a gift." Again David Jacobson's view of things was consistent with Pearl's: "I think humans have a spiritual life when they're fully human, meaning their heart is open . . . and when they conduct, have a spiritual—a sexual life that's appropriate. You know, neither excessive nor celibate. Or, you know, when it's managed in a sane way." Akaya did not describe the ethics of sexual practice quite so directly. But she did tell me of a time when her guiding spirits had interrupted her as she and another woman initiated a relationship:

AKAYA I had an affair with this woman about three and a half, four, years ago. And we had no business having an affair. We should have been on opposite sides of the room. But, you know, there was all this sexual attention and it was lovely and we both decided to move on it. So we set this date . . . I left work early, driving. It was the first time we were going to do this thing. And a woman turns left and totals my car, puts me in the hospital, briefly. I was fine. But I obviously did not get [there] . . . And I knew that this was not anywhere I needed to go.

RF So when you got in that horrible car accident, you knew that was why?

AKAYA No, no, no. I'm not going to do the cause and effect thing. But I did take it as a sign that perhaps I needed to rethink this decision.

As for Hana and Enigma, a set of protocols for sexual practice (albeit different from theirs) emerges from the voices of Akaya, Pearl, and David. For all three sex is to be expected, is part of humanness. It is simultaneously part of "spiritualness." For David, sex must take place because it is part of one's full humanness—sexuality and spirituality thus become mutual guarantors of one another's authenticity. Indeed in a slip of the tongue David accorded the very same criteria to spiritual life as he accorded to sexual practice, saying that humans are fully human and fully spiritual "when they have a spiritual—a sexual life that's appropriate." But, as for Hana and Enigma, sex must be contained, organized, planned. Thus for Pearl, sexuality must be about human connection, not only self-interest. In Akaya's experience sexuality was inherently spiritual. Yet mistakes could be made and if they were made, they would be brought to one's attention. For all three management strategies were in place. Indeed David literally used the word *manage* as he described an ideally ordered sexual world as he saw it. For all three the human *spiritual* being and the human *sexual* being were coconstitutive.

Richard Chu shared much with David, Pearl, and Akaya. But although familiar with a range of approaches to the integration of spirituality and sexuality in the gay community, a more important goal for Richard was linking renunciation to sex, within his life and spiritual practice. It was not, he explained, that affirming sexuality was a problem. Rather, sex had come to occupy a particular place in the spiritual mapping of his world.

Richard, forty-five, gay, and Chinese American, practiced Vipassana meditation. Richard said about the relationship between spirituality and sexuality: "As my sitting practice has deepened, this quality of renunciation I have experienced just arises. There are things that I just don't want to do any more that used to, I thought, give me pleasure." He had not renounced sex. But still, he said: "I can see, even though I'm not there, how [for] people in deep practice, like monks or people who take vows, sexuality can fall away in that process of renunciation as well. As opposed to pushing away sexuality, it just falls away as one explores this place, whether one calls it emptiness or whatever." Richard's practice was already applied to sexual relationships in a different way:

> RICHARD I'm in the early phases of a relationship right now. The person is not a practitioner. So there is this contrast between our views around sexuality. I hold it in a sacred space as opposed to an identity space.
> RF What does it mean to hold sexuality in a sacred space as opposed to an identity space?
> RICHARD To be as conscious and as intentional as I can be. Am I really doing what I want to do? Do I hold my own experiences of pleasure and boundary of experience with integrity or do I compromise them? And in the moment of actually being sexual, am I really feeling the feelings that are coming up or am I only worried about the other person, or a certain event that's going to occur? Am I not completely in the moment? And then at the end, to treat it with respect. That it's not something trivial that just happened. That may not make or break a relationship, but it's not something inconsequential. That's how I would define holding it in a sacred space.

Richard, like Pearl, David, and Akaya, was clear that sexual practice must be consciously engaged. But unlike David, he was not certain that being sexually active was an inevitable, necessary dimension of one's humanness. Rather for Richard if one was sexual one should be so in a way that was continuously as conscious as possible of the full dimensions of oneself and one's partner. But if at some point one's sexual desire fell away, this was not a sign that one was no longer fully human. Here perhaps his voice is united again with David's commitment to engaging one's full humanity in one's sexuality; to Pearl's insistence that for sex to be spiritually meaningful it cannot be only self-interested; and to Akaya's view that by definition all human actions, including sex, cannot not be spiritually engaged. For all four of these individuals sex becomes a sacred activity. And from Richard's point of view this is the case whether one renounces it or engages in it.

Pearl, Akaya, David, and Richard have more in common with Hana and Enigma than one might notice at first sight. All six of these individuals have a spiritual frame in mind for sexual practice. All six claim that sexual practices and spiritual/religious practices are connected with one another. All six assert that spirituality/religion can provide guidelines for sexual practice. All six name both prescriptions and pro-scriptions, albeit different ones. Lastly, whether or not they are conscious of this, their readings of sexuality are both social and spiritual.

A common social context (at least as much as commitments to religion and/or spirituality) led toward what was shared by these individuals in the spiritual/sexual arena. All six lived in a sexually diverse world. This was so both in the sense of the visibility of diverse sexual orientations, and that of diverse sexual mores. Thus all six needed to grapple with that *social* reality. We can note, though, that while the first two voices on which I focused here emphasized the proscription of certain behaviors and orientations, the other four engaged the ethics of practice but did not raise any concern about *whom* one might have sex with. This was as true of David, heterosexual, as it was of Pearl and Akaya, lesbian, and Richard, a gay man.

All six lived in a social context in which, in their view, sexual activity was relatively unrestrained. They thus turned to their religious and/or spiritual practices as sites for the application of sexual order to what might otherwise be sexual chaos. But the mode of that turning was different for the two younger women on one hand, and the four older interviewees on the other. Pearl, David, Akaya, and Richard described themselves as well able to practice the sexual mores that came with their spiritual paths—even to make mistakes, be reminded of them, and self-correct. Hana and Enigma, though, spoke of social pressure from non-Bahai and non-Muslim peers to conform to different modes of sexual practice. It is possible that, in fact, youth was as much a factor as anything else in accounting for this difference. For arguably Pearl, David, Akaya, or Richard were equally likely to encounter demands, expectations, or invitations to violate their own sexual norms. So-ciogenerational differences may, then, be as significant as religious and/or spiritual factors in shaping how these individuals applied their sexual protocols.

⚘

THE LAST GROUP sought to regulate sexual practice in an apparently sexually complex world. With the partial exception of Richard Chu, all were "for" sex, albeit within limits. I now turn to the organization of *not* having sex—conscious, intentional celibacy. Celibacy, like sexual activity, is not a homogeneous site.[5] Individuals turned toward it for a range of reasons. But for all of them, sex was displaced from its location as an essential part of identity and life activity in order for other modes of organization and self-understanding to come into play.

Donna Gonzaga, fifty-two, mother of two and grandmother of three, is European American. She is a community organizer working as an advocate for homeless people. Donna's spiritual practice centered in the Twelve Step recovery movement. Donna identified herself as the adult child of an alcoholic family. She told me, "I'm ACA. As that, you come back to a cornerstone of not feeling like you fit in anywhere."

Donna said, and laughed as she did so, "My sexuality is ambiguous. Having been celibate for almost nine years, it's a moot question sometimes." She continued, "I feel, I suppose, most closely identified with bisexual . . . although the majority of my adult and political life has been primarily with lesbians." But an aspect of her life far more salient to her sexuality, Donna said, was that "I have been celibate for the last eight, nine years in the period that I would define as my healing years. I've had nine years of a concentrated and fairly focused spiritual practice . . . I believe my sexuality, my sex drive, my sex interest have been somewhat sublimated in order to do this work, and to face into all that I've needed to face into." Simply put, for Donna, healing had taken priority over sexuality for the nine years prior to this interview. More than that, she said, healing enabled her to more clearly see what her authentic sexual desires might actually turn out to be. For, she said, "My childhood was difficult and complicated. I think I developed a lot of defenses that caused me to create identities that I don't even know were really mine." In this process sexuality was by no means all that was at stake. Rather a broader sense of selfhood in the world could be assessed and reorganized in these "healing years." At issue were, for example, her identities as white, as working class, and as politically radical, as well as her sexual orientation. The question of what, from her past, she might bring unconsciously to a sexual partnership also became clearer in this process (one that at the time of the interview was not yet over with).

For Ana Gamboa, Latina, heterosexual, and thirty-six years old, celibacy was a choice centered precisely around the social construction of sexuality in her sociocultural world. Indeed Ana's choice of celibacy stemmed from an effort to refuse the sexual order that she saw around her. As Ana told me, "[Celibacy] is an experience that shapes my sense of who I am more than sexual orientation." She added: "It's kind of a contradiction because being a celibate is certainly having an identity based on your sexual practice . . . I don't go out there in the world feeling I need to identify myself as a celibate person and make a stand for the rights of celibate people or whatever. However, it's a conversation that I have with the people who are closest to me." As such, she added, her practice did initiate rethinking on the part of those around her on the meaning of sexuality in the present time.

Ana had first been drawn to the political/spiritual work of Vietnamese Zen Buddhist master, Thich Nhat Hahn, but then she realized the centrality to her spiritual path of Mata Amritanandamayi whom she now names her guru. As she said, "That was a whole earthquake. Because I wasn't expecting to end up with a Hindu guru." Political activism in fact predated Ana's spiritual seeking. Ana had been a feminist from the 1970s onward. As Ana described her journey toward celibacy it became clear to me that these two sides of her life path had contributed to it. On one hand, she said:

> [For] most people who came of age around that same time, in the seventies, there was so much social pressure and, I think, [a] misunderstood kind of feminism. There was a sense that men had gotten the right to be sexual. So now in order to be equal we had to be able to be as sexual as we wanted. There was this thing of "If it feels good, do it. And if you're not doing it then you're repressed or neurotic or frigid." And so there was all this pressure for sexual experimentation and sexual acting out to prove how liberated you were.

On the other hand her celibacy did not reflect a desire for lifelong sexual renunciation. As she put it, had she wanted that, she would have looked seriously into a monastic path. But as a woman desirous of a meaningful life-partnership it was, she felt, crucial to proceed toward that partnership in a way that conformed with her spiritual path. Thus: "Part of the work is letting go of attachment . . . I mean, sure I can go and answer a bunch of personal ads or whatever. But it's not that one can say, 'Well, okay . . . I'm going to be in a partnership.' I feel like that's something that is an opportunity that is given to one by the universe, or not. And so there's a lot of letting go involved in the process." Letting go also meant accepting the possibility of not having a life partner. Ana's practice of celibacy was thus, she said "for the purpose of getting myself more ready for whatever my best form of service is. Whether it's life-partnership or to just do my work as a single person." One might note here that, for Ana, the sexual self was inextricably connected with spiritual practice, even to the extent that she was willing to set aside the former for the sake of the latter. And rather forcefully one sees, as in earlier chapters, the relationship between cultivation and spontaneity. In this instance, the cultivation of self-healing in spiritual, sexual, and psychological terms, will, Ana suggests, lead toward the spontaneous unfolding of her spiritual future.

On the road to celibacy, Ana had thought carefully about the relationships between sexual practice and spiritual paths. To begin with, she noted, there is, in relation to women's bodies in particular, "that huge separation in patriarchal religions where spirituality is on one side and sexuality is on another side." She did not support that binary. If anything she felt a converse calling, "to do some work revaluing the sacred nature of sexuality." Later, she encountered Mata Amritanandamayi (Ammachi) and felt deeply moved by her. But when others told her that Ammachi's closest devotees were renunciates, she worried whether that might make it impossible for her to fully follow that path. Over time, though, as she learned how many nonrenunciates also worked closely with Mata Amritanandamayi, she realized that there was room for her in that community.

In the midst of all this spiritual exploration and self-examination, two things became clear. The first of these was that she did, in fact, wish for a life-partnership. The second was that it was crucially important to make sexuality sacred. She said of the latter, "It seems like a winding path, but I still feel like that's where I'm going to go." As she put it:

> Sexuality is still something people have a lot of addictions and a lot of stuff around. For example, I had a lot of stuff around using sexuality as a way of trying to get [a] man to fall in love with me. So I wanted to purify all of the obsessive or wounded, dysfunctional stuff around my sexuality, as part of this process of really being able to manifest—a partner. And, in that process, I got it that I don't think that you can say "yes" unless you can also say "no." In order to have a really sacred, positive, wonderful sexuality, I think it's really important to be able to say no to compulsive and sort of mindless and "stuck" kinds of sexuality. And at that point I became very interested in exploring the process of being a celibate person.

At the time of the interview, Ana had practiced celibacy for ten years. This had not meant, however, having no intimate relationships. Rather, such relationships had not been sexual. About this, Ana said, "It's so freeing to just be not a sexually available person and still have [a potential partner] be interested in me; still have them want to get to know me and still have them value the opportunity to be emotionally close to me. It's just such a wonderful, wonderful, wonderful feeling,

I can't tell you. It's just great." Here Ana separated processes often conflated—sexual desire and attachment, emotional desire and connection, attraction and attractiveness. To put this another way, Ana learned that her own desirability was not only dependent on her sexual availability. And for her this was an enormous gift and a great pleasure—"a wonderful, wonderful, wonderful feeling."

Furthermore, Ana viewed her spiritual and sexual practices as being in communion with each other through this process. Referring to the process of freeing herself from previous "stuck" patterns of sexual behavior and the shift to something different, she said: "That [may look] more psychological than spiritual. But, see, for me, it's kind of a similar thing. Because I think that really healing, and really learning to love oneself, and really learning to come into one's strength, is a real part of the whole spiritual process." One can rather easily link Ana's words with those of Donna. For both women celibacy was conceived as a space and practice that would enable healing of old wounds. Indeed, equally, although David Jacobson was explicitly in disagreement with celibacy, Ana's commitments to self-love and "learning to come into one's strength" are not fully separable from David's definition of spiritual practice as the quest for experience of one's "full humanness."

Sita, renunciate at Mata Amritanandamayi's ashram, said that she had dated men prior to leaving secular life. But, Sita said in a way not unrelated to Ana's thinking, the reasons for those relationships had been other than sexual ones:

> I primarily would get involved because I enjoyed the experience of love . . . But I thought, "This is not quite the right way to go about getting this experience of love." So, I was relieved finally to discover a spiritual community so that I could finally discover the source of that. Mother can provide all that and more. I don't have to think about those issues anymore. I remember the very first time when I discovered, "That's it with relationships. I just don't want to do this anymore," I had such an increase of energy, just so much energy came up.

Archana, fifty-two, European American, is also a renunciate or *brahmacharini* at Mata Amritanandamayi's ashram. With qualification, Archana also placed her sexuality in the past tense, and made clear that her spiritual practice and her spiritual master had displaced sex:

> ARCHANA I was—uh, was, is—it's funny to say homosexual, because I am, but I'm not. It's kind of like, it doesn't mean anything anymore.
> RF You're not because you've renounced sexuality?
> ARCHANA Yeah, as much as one can, until you're enlightened, and

what does that mean? . . . It's not really an issue. And the beauty of Mother and the beauty of the spiritual work has sort of swallowed all that up.

Both women were conscious of sexual identifications and identities. Yet, each was certain that sex might be displaced, replaced by other kinds of love and beauty. Further, for both, it was clear that setting aside sexual activity had led to gain rather than loss. As Sita put it, "I had such an increase of energy."

Brother Camillus Chavez, member of the teaching order of La Sallian Brothers, is also a sexual renunciate. Having taken religious orders at the age of eighteen, Brother Camillus later faced the challenge of falling in love and contemplating marriage. He left the order for two years around 1969. But the relationship did not work out. Looking back, he said: "That relationship fell apart. I was trying to save somebody . . . [But] there's only one Savior, you know, the Lord of life! [*Laughs.*] That was a very hard lesson for me to learn, and I actually had to learn it many, many times over in many other ways." At the time of the interview Brother Camillus, now sixty-seven, was professor of psychology at a college founded and run by the La Sallian Brothers in the San Francisco Bay Area. Brother Camillus commented on the terms on which one can *really* support others, about the value of celibacy, and about how the two may be interwoven. For one thing, he said, a celibate person can be available as a resource for more individuals, as long as he/she remembers that he/she cannot be a savior. He said of his work with students and clients that it was crucial always to know that "I can't make their life work for them. I can only be a channel for the divine, whether it's through wisdom, or through energy. They have to find their own way."

He also argued that there was more than one way to understand sexual partnership. The desire for it, he suggested, may from a Jungian perspective be understood as a hunger for otherness, alterity. Thus he said, sexual renunciation might have more in common with heterosexual union than is obvious at first glance. For, he said, "it's the marriage of the opposites, but within [oneself]. Nobody from the outside can really do it for you. Ultimately it becomes divine work." This did not mean, though, that a celibate path was easy. As he put it, "Some people get frozen. It's the easiest way to devalue your sexuality, deny it, not even look at it, accept it, acknowledge it . . . What's hard is, how do you do it in a grounded, human way . . . [not] short-circuiting the human by going into the divine."[6]

There are commonalities among the voices of this group. For all, sexual renunciation was only one practice among others on their spiritual paths. Each had recrafted the place of sex and sexuality in their lives. As a result sex and sexual identities were accorded places more marginal than had been the case before their turn to celibacy. Thus Donna had joked that her sexual identity was "a moot question sometimes," And Ana felt that her celibacy was more meaningful than any other aspect of her sexual identity. Both Ana and Donna, who did not plan on a lifetime commitment to sexual renunciation, were clear that other aspects of their relationships with self and others were for now more important or at least equally so.

For these men and women celibacy was part of a whole—one piece in a spiritual or religious system that was satisfying on its own terms as well as offering grounds for healing. In no case did celibacy imply lack or signal loss. Rather other activities—recovery from growing up in an alcoholic family, seeking partnerships not driven only by sex—were made possible. Likewise energies were released or received in the very same contexts that celibacy was cultivated. It must be noted, too, that these other activities should not be read as "compensatory" ones, such that "despite" the lack of sexual activity one was blessed with healing, time for other activities, or even the possibility of encountering the other within. Such a reading of the practice of celibacy would entail catachresis—the reversal of cause and effect. For in these individuals' view, celibacy offered precisely what had previously been sought in the "wrong" place via sexual relationship. For each the gift was a different one—self-love no longer sought via sexual partnership; the possibility of sexuality made sacred by its interweaving with self-valuing; a sense of one's full humanity as joyfully premised on one's indebtedness to the divine.

᯼

ALL OF THE INTERVIEWEES discussed so far knew themselves to reside in a sexually diverse society. All were capable of naming their own sexual identity. All expressed the wish and the willingness to craft and name their own sexual practice. For all those who discussed it, it was clearly preferable to make one's sexual practice consonant with one's spiritual practice. All sensed that these two sites were not unrelated to one another. But a critical point of differentiation was that between those who felt they had easy access to living their sexual choices in a supportive spiritual/religious context, and those who did not.

Here the issue is which forms of sexuality are unmarked, deemed normative or acceptable and which are considered problematic. For it was not that heterosexuals very consciously felt supported in their sexuality by their religious institutions or spiritual houses. It was rather that it was not a question that needed to be discussed at all. I will not here engage with all the marked or prohibited sexual practices named above—childbearing outside of wedlock, marital infidelity, sexual activity frequent enough for some to name it "promiscuity." Rather I focus in ending this chapter on that form of "marked" sexuality that has come most strongly to the fore in recent debates in Christianity, Judaism, and Buddhism—gay and lesbian sexuality.[7]

Interviewees who were gay and lesbian needed to achieve, balance, and harmonize three things. The first of these had to do with the self: self-acceptance and self-love as a gay or lesbian person. Perhaps not surprisingly, individuals varied in the degree to which love of the gay/lesbian self came easily or was harder to achieve. The second was connection with the divine or—in the case of those whose practice was nondeistic—the path toward oneness or the absolute. For most a connection with divinity and/or path was striking in its spontaneity and durability. The third factor, and in fact the most difficult of access, was a site—whether sangha, synagogue, congregation, guru house, or otherwise named religio-spiritual community—that would honor and value the individual, sexual identity and all.

The quest for any simple convergence of self, God or path, and place of spiritual practice was complicated, not because there was no possible convergence of these. Rather the effort to achieve it entailed a clash of marked sexualities with heteronormative institutions. This meant either that it was necessary to avoid such institutions altogether, work to transform them, or to create alternative institutions that did welcome men and women of all sexualities.

Arinna Weisman had, at the time of the interview, been a teacher of Vipassana meditation for over a decade. But besides that, she said, "I'm the only lesbian teacher in the United States in this tradition." This minority status together with her efforts to politicize her teaching in other ways had given her the reputation of "troublemaker" in the community of her fellow teachers. She explained: "I bring my understanding of Marxism, feminism, what it means to be a lesbian in this culture, and also of training with a Native American Indian elder for two years, with me to this tradition, and it definitely infuses it . . . I teach the dharma, but I—it comes out differently. [*Laughs.*]" Arinna had always taken great pleasure in teaching heterosexual as well as lesbian and gay students. Nonetheless, she said, "one of the most exciting things for me is the sense of community that's growing out of the gay and lesbian retreats. A very special energy happens when we come together, sit together, and share together. And out of those retreats, sitting groups have started to form . . . [My coteacher] and I started doing it four years ago, and it's really taking seed and sprouting." As Arinna explored this experience further, she commented that "every mind has the qualities of ignorance and every mind has the potential for freedom and liberation." The particularity of one's very being was what provided the "gateway" into spiritual practice. Thus in her view what added to the dynamism of a lesbian and gay retreat was not only shared experience of oppression or of homophobia. She said, "We're not lesbians because, you know, our fathers hated us. We're lesbians like apples and oranges are apples and oranges. I think just that experience of being that way is the gateway. So it's beautiful to be able to meet that, to offer a spiritual practice [in that context]." As well, Arinna's dharma teaching took particular direction in those retreats where she worked with gay and lesbian participants precisely because "a lot of my talks originate in question and answer periods or in personal interviews, when I talk with people about their difficulties in practice." She continued:

> Often my talks are related directly to what people are experiencing. For example . . . at the last retreat, people brought up homophobia. One woman said, "What do I do with my anger? I'm working with the Christian fundamentalist churches in my community work. And there's such intense homophobia" . . . So both my talks asked, "What does it mean to be happy and not happy? And where and how do we choose to work with our anger and hatred? And how does political activism come in?"

As a teacher, Arinna worked with individuals as beings in the world—beings who happened to be gay or lesbian, and who therefore faced particular pain on encountering hatred and hostility towards what their being in the world represents to others. Thus, as Arinna explained, being lesbian or gay *and* facing homophobia became gateways, sites wherein the dharma can be explored and practiced. As Arinna and retreat participants built contexts that brought together the dharma with gay and lesbian existence, one might suggest that the application of the dharma was enriched and transformed, as was the experience of being gay or lesbian.

Arinna noted that although deemed a "troublemaker" in her lineage, she was, nonetheless, not prevented in any way from continuing her work. As a practitioner she was able to craft an institutional context that brought together her lesbian selfhood with her spiritual path as teacher and as practitioner. Arinna's dream, though, was to find a residential community in which to live full-time—not something available within the U.S. Vipassana community. And although she had been approached as the potential founder of such a community, she was clear that she was not yet spiritually strong enough to undertake that task. Given this, Arinna had made inquiries into taking up long-term residence at a community in a different lineage, whose founder and head was perhaps closest in style and spirit to her own practice of Vipassana in the United States: Thich Nhat Hahn's Plum Village in rural France. Thich Nhat Hahn, Vietnamese Zen Buddhist monk in exile, is known as one of the leaders of the international Engaged Buddhism movement. Thich Nhat Hahn is also reported as having said in an interview with Alan Senauke in *Turning Wheel: Journal of the Buddhist Peace Fellowship,* "God is a lesbian also."[8] Arinna had spent six weeks in retreat at Plum Village, and following that period, she and her partner had applied jointly to take up residence. But their application was summarily turned down, not by Thich Nhat Hahn but by the lead teacher in the "women's hamlet." Arinna said:

> The head teacher said that we had to reapply separately. In no way could we infer that there was any sexuality between us, that the Viet-namese didn't understand about this kind of stuff, did we understand that the precepts were operative, and that she hoped I would recon-sider my application . . . It was totally homophobic, because she knows I'm a teacher, and she knows I understand the precepts. I mean, I've been working with the precepts for sixteen years! I was there for six weeks. Of course I knew the precepts . . . She would never have said that to a heterosexual couple.

The head teacher's response was rooted in a heteronormative concep-tion of sexuality. It implied that all Vietnamese were heterosexuals. As well it suggested that one aspect of nonheterosexual identity (lesbian-ness) would lead to other problems, including the imputed incapacity to exert sexual self-discipline and the inability to comprehend sexual protocols. Arinna was saddened, and very conscious that whether or not Thich Nhat Hahn was individually supportive of lesbian and gay practitioners, this did not mean that he was in a position to exert full control over the community.

In this context Arinna had reached a point where she could proceed no further. She said:

I watch myself thinking about going to Plum Village for a little bit, and actually standing up in one of the community gatherings, and talking about it . . . There's gay people in Vietnam like there's gay people everywhere. And if the monks or nuns don't understand it, then they have to understand and learn about it, because they're going to go back to Vietnam and they're going to be working with the Vietnamese. And [even] if they don't, they're going to be working with all the Westerners who come to Plum Village, many of whom are gay and lesbian. I mean, it's just plain homophobia. That's why, you see, that's why I say, there's nowhere to go. There's nowhere to go! That means I have to do it, but I'm not ready, so that's the scene, you know. [*Laughs*] . . . It's sad. It's really sad.

Given these challenges it is hardly surprising that the possibility of connecting with a spiritual community that supports and shares one's sexuality is a treasured gift. In this regard, Patricia Lin counted herself fortunate to be a member of Sha'ar Zahav, Lesbian, Gay, Bisexual, and Transgender Synagogue of San Francisco. Patricia, who is twenty-seven and Asian American (the daughter of Taiwanese immigrant parents), is a graduate student studying history. She converted to Judaism as a young adult. For her, coming out was crucially connected with coming out to God. She put it this way:

For a long time I knew I was gay, or had gone to gay bookstores. But I think for me being lesbian is not enough . . . I needed to have some other meaning for my life . . . Only a couple of weeks before my formal conversion ceremony I sort of had this crisis and I came out. And there was a sense, not totally intellectually, [that] before I could formally "present myself to God," I had to be totally honest with who I am . . . This wasn't rational, but I think that you sense that there—there's also this idea that God makes you, sort of symbolically, but makes you as you are and accepts you as you are. And so that gives you a sort of confidence to say, "Okay, then maybe I'm okay the way [I am]." And also having those role models around me of Jewish leaders who are gay and lesbian really gave me a sense of "Oh, okay, so this is okay."

Patricia was very clear that in the process of formal conversion she needed to be totally honest about herself. This meant a move from someone whose sense of gayness had been previously confined to "going to gay bookstores" to someone who needed to state her identity more directly both to herself *and* to God. In other words, honesty to self and to God needed to take place simultaneously. And, she learned in that process, they were mutually reinforcing. For as she accepted that God had made her "as you are" she could then accept, "Okay, then maybe I'm okay the way [I am]." It is an irony that although Patricia said, "This wasn't rational" the opposite was in fact the case. For it was precisely as the result of inductive reasoning that Patricia reached a newfound self-acceptance. Patricia reasoned like this: (1) "God made me"; (2) "God made me lesbian"; (3) "God must feel OK with how He made me"; and (4) "It must be OK that I'm lesbian."

Patricia emphasized that the presence of gay and lesbian rabbis and other gay and lesbian Jews had been critical to her. Further, she was not one to go to bars, clubs, or other social spaces wherein she might meet other lesbians or gay men. Thus she did not demur when I said, "Am I pushing words on you to say that Sha'ar Zahav gives you a place in which to be gay?" She said: "Yeah, I guess so. Because, yeah, my most important community is my synagogue, which is a gay and lesbian synagogue. I mean, I've gone to other things, but that's where I found my home. It's where I feel most comfortable in terms of gay and lesbian issues. I mean, I'm out generally but, you know, that's where I feel sort of [a] purpose as opposed to a label, you know?" Patricia was well aware of differences within Judaism, one of which among the Orthodox would be nonacceptance both of her conversion and of her gayness. Yet for her, a Reform Jew:

> The key thing is that you choose to do this, as opposed to the Torah's making you. You say, "Okay, I want to pray every morning, I want to wear *tzi-tzid* all the time, I want to keep kosher." The essence of Reform Judaism ideally is that you go through all of the *mitzvot* and you make a decision—is this meaningful in my life? . . . Reform Judaism I think in many ways can be more difficult if you take it to its utmost and say, [rather than] just accepting what the Torah is saying, "I am doing it because it's meaningful to me."

And as we have seen, part of what enabled Patricia to find this meaningful for her was the presence of other gay and lesbian men and women who, before her, brought together Judaism, God, and gay and lesbian identity.

🖉

THE EFFORT TO BRING TOGETHER God, gayness, and religious community has perhaps been most visible in Christianity, still by far the largest religion in the United States. Four Christians—two heterosexual women and two gay men—demonstrate from different places and from different denominations the meaning and challenge of that struggle.

Both of the heterosexual women are European American and active in mainline Christian denominations. Both are parents of grown daughters. Nancy McKay, fifty-nine, is married, and Nancy Nielsen, fifty-three, recently divorced. Both of them had found themselves taking strong stands in support of the struggle, now well-publicized, to open the doors of the church wide, welcoming men and women of all sexualities.

Nancy McKay had received the call to seek ordination unexpectedly following the death of her father. She entered the seminary at the age of thirty-nine. Once her ordination was completed she served as pastor in the United Church of Christ in a small San Francisco Bay Area town, in a congregation where she had previously served as student minister. As Nancy looked back she remembered the warmth with which she had been welcomed, appreciated, and loved. But midway through a decade of ministry, she began to urge her congregation to contemplate the feminine aspects of the divine. Nancy had sought to complement rather than to replace images of the masculine face of God (after all, her deep connection with Jesus will be remembered from chapter 2). Yet some began to object. She remembered with pain "people who I have pastored, people who I have loved, who loved me, screaming at me that I was taking away their God, that I had turned against them, all kinds of stuff like that. People leaving the church trying to vote me out. Others just scared and saying, 'What's going on? Why is this important?'" Although that "uproar," as she named it, took place in 1985, Nancy did not leave her congregation until five years later. What finally drove her out was her congregation's reaction when Nancy sought to start, "what in our denomination is called the open and affirming process—moving a congregation into looking at sexual orientation, [examining] attitudes towards all kinds of sexuality and really affirming everything."

That process, she explained, entailed not only self-examination but also reassessment of existing interpretations of scripture. It involved asking, for example, whether it was really homosexuality or sexual abuse that was being castigated in particular texts, and pondering the effects on scripture of contemporaneous culture and later translations. Unfortunately, Nancy said, her congregation was less than pleased with her idea. She said, "One, they had their own feelings and for the most part they were afraid the church was too small and it would really split the church . . . They said, 'You really don't want to do this.'" But whether or not Nancy wanted "to do this," clearly her congregation did not. Nancy said, "It was time for me to leave. I loved them and I couldn't communicate with them on the deepest levels anymore. And so, I left. And that's been a hard healing process."[9]

Nancy is no longer a full-time minister although her pastoring work is hardly over, since she is a spiritual director, leads healing work groups with the seriously ill, and teaches at a San Francisco Bay Area seminary as well. Her grief about the end of her time at the church is palpable. Yet she said: "That's part of being a witness. To say, 'This I see. I see the suffering. I see the scriptures. I see the love of God. This is the interpretation I see.' To say it and to live it, to stand in solidarity with someone is an enormous witness. Just to stand and be present. Terribly important."

Another Nancy, Nancy Nielsen, has never been a minister, but rather is an elected member of the governing board for the denominational structure of the Lutheran Church. As such she was well aware of two congregations in San Francisco "that were kicked out of the body because they ordained gay and lesbian clergy." Nancy Nielsen, much like Nancy McKay, was committed to standing as witness and supporter in the effort to create an inclusive church. She said, despite these congregations' expulsion, "many of us within the [denominational] structure have worked [with them], continued the relationships as we struggle for change within the system." This meant that on relocating from a city a hundred miles south, into the San Francisco area, "my ethical decision was, when I started visiting congregations in San Francisco, I had to start there. As part of support and part of recognizing. They have wonderful exciting ministries going on, but it was also that part of being faithful to what they stand for and what I believe in is to be physically present with them. It's not enough to just say, 'Yes, I think they're doing well.' You have to go there and be part of that." Nancy's home congregation, in San Jose, had gone through the process that Nancy McKay had sought to initiate—in Nancy Nielsen's words "a very in-depth, intentional study . . . to where that congregation made a conscious decision to be what is called in [our] tradition, a 'reconciled in Christ congregation,' which simply is publicly open and welcoming of gay and lesbian people." Nancy's own support of gay men and lesbians had stemmed partly from personal experience with "one man in particular who was a friend, who was married. And who at age forty finally came out. He had been struggling internally, and then went public and ended up divorcing. I knew him and his wife and his daughter. We were all part of that process for him. I mean, I know what he went through." She added that over time she came to know more and more gay men and lesbians. In the final analysis, though, she said it was important to reach a point when the sexuality of any new member of a congregation could become a "nonissue":

> If someone new comes in and they're gay or they're a couple and gay or lesbian, it's like, "Okay, now what else are you going to do? Are you going to be a teller, a deacon, sing in the choir? . . . What's your faith journey, where are you?" But at the same time to be supportive of their journey, in the reality that their journey is in many ways more difficult. [It's important] to honor that and to hold that where we can. But I guess I'd have to say I don't see that particular area being separated out. It's a journey with someone that would be done for anyone coming in with particular concerns in their life.

Witnessing, to draw on Nancy McKay's word, thus meant offering support, recognizing that the path of lesbians and gay men might be harder than that of heterosexuals in relation to sexuality, but perhaps no harder than the paths others might journey along, for very different reasons. For neither woman, however, was there any sense that non-heterosexuals should occupy a place in the church different from that of their heterosexual fellow Christians. And thus the work of support and bearing witness was triggered not by gayness or lesbianness but rather by churches' hostility to those persons, those sexual orientations.

Nancy Nielsen resisted my suggestion that this was a political matter when I asked her, "Is this just a political process or is it also a spiritual process?" Nancy said, "It's spiritual and it's justice. It's standing with people. So recognizing that it is a justice thing and it's also recognizing the gifts they bring . . . If you're going to be about healing the brokenness in our world then the way you do it, is standing with and next to someone. And connecting at a very human level." Nancy had "cringed" as I put it, when I asked whether this was only a political issue because, she said, "my involvement on any political level is spiritual. I don't do it where it isn't. I'm trying to think of some political issue that wouldn't be a spiritual issue. The gay and lesbian issue is a particularly spiritual issue because it's being fought more in the faith community than in the wider culture." By this, Nancy meant that in her view other areas of the United States had *already* moved further toward acceptance of non-heterosexual sexualities:

> The corporate community is ahead of the faith community. Domestic partners legislation is going through in many places. Visibility of gay and lesbian people in television is far ahead . . . You know, I think that

sooner or later, the church will be dragged kicking and screaming into being in-line just as in issues of slavery or women's rights or any of those things. The church has always lagged behind, unfortunately. The prophetic voice within the faith community does not lead the way most of the time.

Given this, Nancy argued, it was critically important for those who considered themselves part of a faith community to "push" the issue forward. For this is, she reiterated, "a justice issue." Here Nancy describes in her own language and from a different standpoint what I earlier argued was true of all interviewees: whatever their sexuality and whatever their view of this, there was an awareness that the United States is a sexually diverse place. And this meant for Nancy that anything other than full inclusion of gay and lesbian people in the church was simply "trying to exclude another group of people. It's not right."

☙

LAST IN THIS CHAPTER, I describe and analyze in some detail the work of two gay men to bring together that triad of God, gay self, and church. When I interviewed Eric Thomas, he was thirty-six years old. For around ten years he had been a member of the East Bay Church of Religious Science. During that decade he had preached in the church on questions of gay identity, at the request of the Reverend Eloise Oliver. That service and the "Reverend E's" openness to learning from Eric, his partner, and other gay men and lesbians had in turn led to the church establishing annual participation in the San Francisco Lesbian, Gay, Bisexual, Transgender Pride Parade. Eric had cofounded a men's group in the church, comprising, he said, heterosexual men and some gay men. In it, he told me, "I've been letting the heterosexual men know they have got to do more outreach for gay men, and letting them know that this is an East Bay Church, Religious Science function here. You can't . . . isolate yourself from other things."

For the church, Eric is also a prayer partner and counselor. Most recently, a year after he benefited deeply from the loving support of the entire congregation after the death of his partner, Severic, from HIV-AIDS, Eric accepted responsibility for coordination of the congregation's efforts to reach out to individuals and families on the deaths of "significant others." About himself, Eric said, "I'm the most loved person I know." And of his relationship with the divine, "As long as I have God in my life, I am God, God is me. We are one. And I—it's a blessing that I'm a gay man. It's a blessing that God made it so I can want to be gay."

Eric's description of his relationship with God, draws directly on the philosophy of the East Bay Church of Religious Science: the inseparability of the human and the divine and the sense that oneness with the divine is always there if only one could feel and see it. And his description of being gay is a subtle one. For in thanking God for being made gay, Eric made clear that in his view he had been, as Nancy Nielsen put it, *created* as such. His gayness was not, then, merely a contingent but rather an essential part of who he was—not a choice, but God's act, and not just an act, but a blessing. And going even further, it is as though God has addressed the social construction of his sexuality also. For in the additional "blessing," that of God having "made it so [he] can want to be gay," it is not stretching the point too far to propose that in Eric's view, God is countering the realities of life in a homophobic society, too. Eric's self-description proposes, then, that the integration of love for the self, love of God, and access to a spiritual house that will accept and honor all aspects of the self, including one's gay sexuality, is in fact a possibility. But, for Eric, the journey to that place had not been a straightforward one.

Eric, an African American, grew up in a working-class, mainly Latino and African American city south of San Francisco. About his sexuality, Eric said, "I had a little boyfriend when I was five. His name was Mark." And from an equally young age, Eric somehow made a point of finding and attending the nearest church. Eric said:

> My family did not go to church. I was the only child who really would go, and I would go and visit the different churches. We always lived across the street from someone's church. The house that I remember most of all in my childhood . . . was right across the street from the Catholic Church. Early in the mornings I would get my two younger friends, and we would go and visit. I didn't know what the Catholic Church was about, I just wanted to go . . . I always wondered if God had a purpose for me, what was my reason for living . . . So I always was very comfortable being around anything that had to do with God.

Eric's terminology is striking here—the church was always "someone's," not his own. But for Eric, it seemed that whatever the institution, it was God's house, and thus Eric "just wanted to go." One cannot guess, unfortunately, why Eric asked the particular questions about God that he did—whether God had a purpose for Eric, and why he was living. But one can note that these were not, as far as one can discern, fearful questions, nor were they questions that seemed to be addressed toward a punishing God. Rather they led, said Eric, to a feeling of comfort, even familiarity.

Throughout Eric's childhood and adolescence he continued to have boyfriends his own age. And simultaneously he continued to feel close to God, with or without membership in a church. But his connection with the divine did not take place in a sociopolitical vacuum. For Eric was aware of the debates over sexuality and religion unfolding around him as he grew up. In the late 1970s, when Eric was in high school, "Anita Bryant, and her hatred for people who are gay, was a big thing." (Bryant campaigned assiduously for the exclusion of gay men and lesbians from the teaching profession.) But, Eric said, "I knew that something was not right about this. How can you hate somebody because they are gay? It *didn't* make any sense. And I knew that God loves me. And it was like, something was just—just wrong." One sees here a noninstitutionally anchored relationship with the divine. That instinctual connection was, it seems, powerful enough that love of God and love of the self remained intact and mutually supportive. It was not until Eric encountered a religious institution through his mother (with whom he was then, and remains, very close), that there was any disruption to this early certainty. Eric said of his high school years: "I was still walking around knowing that God was okay with me and I was okay with God. And then my mother decided that she would start going to a Pentecostal church, which she was raised in."

Eric and other family members now began attending that church. This opened the doors to self-questioning on Eric's part:

> I began to visit this church more and more and more. And then hearing things about [how] being gay was a sin. It just didn't make any sense. But I didn't want to do the wrong thing. So I was confused a little bit . . . [by] what they were saying about gays, about homosexuals. And they would never say "homosexual," they would say "homo-*sexuals*," you know. Make it sound horrible, to the point where you might see saliva coming out of their mouths, or foam.

By the time he turned eighteen, Eric said, "I didn't have a lot of positive self-esteem. So I remember we would go to the bathhouses. And sometimes I would be wrestling with, 'Should I go and have sex with these men or should I go over to the church?' Because some of this stuff wasn't making any sense."

In the end, a range of stands taken by that church, besides its excoriation of "homo*sexuals*" meant that Eric had less and less faith in that church. For one thing, the church argued forcefully that women should not answer the call to preach. Yet a former neighbor was, Eric knew, a wonderful, wise, and talented preacher. Next, this church said that women should not wear pants, makeup, or cut their hair. But as he began training in fashion design and learning the complex history of female and male attire around the world, it made little sense to him when the church insisted not only on particular dress codes but claimed that such codes had originated in the Bible.

Then, Eric got a job as assistant caregiver for a local woman who had suffered a stroke. His supervisor, Marva (pseudonym), was known to Eric as a woman. He then learned that she had, previously, been a man and was in fact transsexual. Eric commented, "When I was . . . getting to know Marva and knowing what a beautiful person Marva was, it didn't make any sense that God could dislike her for being such a sweet person." In this context, family tensions began to run high, with Eric questioning the church and being criticized for doing so, by his mother and his siblings alike. Finally, he said, "it became very clear to me to move. I needed to make some money. I needed to find a job. I got a job at a department store. I started making some money . . . And then I got another job that made me a lot of money. Then I had my mind focused: I'm getting out of here!" Eric was by now twenty-two. He and a friend moved to Oakland, following their dream: "I'd always loved Oakland . . . I think one of the things that made me want to move here is that there was such a large community of black gay men, beautiful men, and I was always fascinated with that. And also just seeing a community of black people, African people, living here who were— who had all different types of outlooks on life, who did things in a different way."

But this did not mean leaving behind a connection with God. Rather, it provided the context for reunification. For even before the move to Oakland, Eric said, Marva had taken him to Hope Central Church (pseudonym), a large African American Christian congregation renowned for its gospel music. Of his first visit to the church, Eric said,

> I'm in Hope Central. And I had already believed that if you are saved
> you cannot be a gay person. All of a sudden, I was seeing gay folks . . .
> I'm in there and I seen all these folks shouting, these gay people
> running and shouting. And I know that they are gay men. I'd been
> taught that if you are a gay man, you can't have the power of God. You
> can't shout. You can't do this. And I'm looking at this—and the music

is taking me . . . It's just great. It's just wonderful. And then, I'm looking at Marva, and Marva is talking to me about her relationship with God and I'm saying, "Something has got to be wrong here. She is too loving, too kind. How could God dislike her?" That didn't make any sense. How can you not inherit the Kingdom of Heaven? It didn't make any sense. So I knew then and there that you could. So I moved up here.

In this moment, Eric was once again able to reconcile gayness and the love of God. More than that, he now witnessed gay men and one transsexual woman as feeling God's force in a way that he had been told, at the Pentecostal church in his hometown, was by definition impossible. In this sense it appeared that all three aspects—self, God, and religious institution, were in alignment with one another. What had previously been the site of painful confusion was now set aside. As he said very clearly, he now knew that one could be gay and "inherit the Kingdom of Heaven."

Eric continued to belong to Hope Central Church for several years. But after some time cracks appeared in what had once seemed an easy and unproblematic linkage of gayness and Hope Central Church membership. Several events contributed to Eric's growing unease. First, Eric sought counseling from a minister at the church about a love relationship that was going awry. In the context of all that he knew about the church and its large number of gay members, Eric was stunned by the minister's response to him: "Well, Eric, you know, being gay is against God's accordance." Eric was, he said, "hurt," and "confused." Yet he said, he was "feeling really disconnected in a small way, but still going there, with all these herds of gay folks."

Then, he said, larger events took over as a "couple of men pass away at Hope Central Church . . . This is in 1984 or '85 . . . By that time, you were already hearing about the big 'A,' AIDS. [But] then black people didn't get AIDS, only white people got AIDS. That's what the media put out." Hope Central Church tried to gloss over and "hush-hush" the cause of death of these men. One such man was Robert, fifteen years Eric's senior, very briefly his lover but more importantly and in an ongoing way his friend, mentor, and protector. Robert was, Eric said, the first "gay father I ever had." And the Hope Central Church's handling of Robert's sudden death was the next blow to Eric's relationship to that church. Eric said that when Robert died, "my whole world crumbled." His friends rallied to his side but the church did not, despite the fact that their connection was well-known: "I didn't get any type of notes or letters or cards [from the church], no acknowledgment of any kind . . . I was going through so much pain, but Hope Central Church was not a support. I was very clear about that." At the funeral, Eric sat with Robert's family, who acknowledged the closeness of his connection with Robert. (Robert's father even checked with Eric that Robert's face, as his body was prepared to be laid in the casket for viewing, had been made up to look as Robert had looked before he passed away.) But still, the church neither acknowledged Eric's loss nor sought to name it in any way. There was, as it turned out, a "don't ask, don't tell" orientation to gay sexuality, relationship, and community at Hope Central Church.

Time passed. The HIV-AIDS epidemic deepened. Eric became co-founder of BMX—Black Men's Exchange—an organization that sought among other things to support African American men through the HIV-AIDS epidemic. As BMX planned a major convention in San Francisco, they realized that it was necessary "to get a religious leader who was not homophobic [to address the convention]. [Thanks to a member of BMX] a Religious Science minister by the name of Reverend Ahman came and spoke to the group. He talked about love and self-love. He was not a gay man, he was just a man who talked about love." Eric was intrigued to hear, for the first time, a minister preaching about self-love. Even more exciting, he learned from a BMX coactivist that "in this type of church [one] can be gay. Because Hope Central Church wasn't making too much more sense to me." Eric added, "And then that's when [my] Science of Mind journeys started." Although Reverend Ahman left the area for Los Angeles, a Religious Science Church opened in Oakland, headed by the Reverend Eloise Oliver.

Here was a church where Eric felt safe to pray aloud with others and for others and to share in the nurturing of a religious community. After a long telephone call with Reverend E., Eric was asked to preach about the meaning of being gay on the following Sunday. "The topic of the sermon was, 'Getting by in Spite of Yourself.' So I said that being gay, being overweight, having dyslexia, stuttering, being black—with all these things, God loves me. I really just put it out there. And the shock on the people's faces, in the church! I had made up my mind. I refused to be in a church where I can't be a gay man! Something is wrong, if I can't be who God made me to be."

From that moment, Eric became clearer than ever before that God and prayer could and should be present in every part of his life. This was so even in preparation for the practice, time-honored in gay life, of cruising in search of sexual encounters. Eric said: "I would pray that I would be covered, and God would protect me—I would have a great night. Even praying that I would get the right and perfect man to have sex with in a safe way. And truly, it happened just that way. And there were times I would meet a guy and he would turn his face away from me. I knew that was God. I knew that!" Eric was forthright and systematic here about his needs and about his desires. Thus pleasure and safety were both prayed for. And, Eric says, "it happened just that way." One sees also, then, faith in God to handle cruising with the same efficacy that others might pray to God to handle an exam, an interview for a job, or any other kind of life activity. Eric also describes the same kind of "divine intervention" that others referred to earlier in the book—the provision of drivers at Mata Amritanandamayi's retreat, for example. The only difference here is that Eric brings God into a kind of life activity that others might eschew. Thus if a man whom Eric approached turned away, Eric took that as God's decision, as much as that of the individual concerned. God may, then, give, or God may withhold but will do so on the basis of what is good for Eric. But as he had said when he spoke to the congregation at the East Bay Church of Religious Science, "Something is wrong, if I can't be who God made me to be."

Eric continued, stating forcefully that which, he acknowledged, would be anathema to many Christians:

> I couldn't get all that I wanted. I'd been very clear about this in my life, [that] if I could have got every man I wanted, I would have. But that wouldn't have been the healthy thing for me. So that's when it was so clear to me, and I would share it with people, "Take God into every part of your life, especially the part that you think is the worst, or you think has no light in there. Because God is there anyway! If you acknowledge God is there, you can get an understanding of why that is."

It is important to note here another aspect of the structure of faith as Eric described it: what was desired and what was "healthy" were not always the same thing. Eric, because of his faith, was willing to give over to God that decision-making process and trust that it was being undertaken in a "healthful" way. Yet simultaneously the a prioris of what "makes sense" or "didn't make sense" and Eric's strong trust that self and God must be in harmony were in play here. He did not, then, believe that God could be against his gayness or that of others. As we have seen, excepting his confusion while at the Pentecostal church, God's rejection of gayness "did not make sense" to him. Further, one must remember the many moments described above in which Eric witnessed the kinds of "sense" made by gay and transgendered people in cultivated and spontaneous epiphany with God. These, one might suggest, confirmed Eric's a priori belief for him.

The next step in Eric's thinking was the argument that God is in all parts of one's life, so that it would be literally impractical to try to compartmentalize it. Moreover, Eric said, if one acknowledged God's presence, one would be able to learn from that presence. Thus, Eric felt clearly that God would organize and design the ways in which he practiced his gayness—keeping him in safe and healthy relationships and encounters.

We have moved very far from that statement uttered by the minister at Hope Central Church, one far more familiar in the discourse of contemporary Christian institutions: "Being gay is against God's accordance." Eric acknowledged this discursive disjunction when he reminded me that for many, sex is a site wherein there is little or no (divine) light. But, as Eric described his practice and belief, God's accordance clearly and forcefully included gayness. And more, in Eric's view, God supervised one's gayness just as much as any other aspect of one's life activity. Eric's practice intentionally had no boundaries. He said: "Some people would [say] they could only be a gay person outside of the church. They couldn't bring God into the clubs, couldn't bring him to a party, couldn't bring God into certain things because it was just like, 'Oh, no, no, no, no.' I mean, please! God created all this stuff—let's just get with it! God created sex, okay?"

✎

PAUL WOOLEY is a European American gay man. Now fifty-three, he grew up in Louisville, Kentucky, the ninth of ten children. His family was Catholic. For Paul, as for Eric Thomas, a deep sense of the presence of God and an equally strong sense of self as not being heterosexual, were fundamental, a priori. Paul had been aware of his sexual orientation "from the first sexual inklings when I was a child." He went on: "The homosexual orientation is probably one of the most profound experiences of who I am. Growing up in a fairly homophobic society . . . having no language to name it, no models or people to look at, and feeling there was something wrong with it had a very profound effect on . . . my developing a relationship with God." He continued: "The original understanding of that relationship was, as some kind of person outside of me, and [of] regulations that I was supposed to learn and figure out. So, that's what my spirituality really was as a child—just learning the rules and doing what I'm told to do."

As Paul contemplated the "rules" and "regulations" one was supposed to follow, it was clear that his own sexuality did not fit with them. He said, "I can remember at night, praying as a child . . . I remember frequently crying myself to sleep at night, wondering—'I have done something, what did I do wrong?' "[10]

Like Eric, Paul's first church was a Catholic one. But for Paul the Catholic Church was not "someone's church" but rather his own and that of his family. Fear and concern framed Paul's questions to God. Without pushing the comparison too far at this point one might notice that it was not until he was almost through his teens that a church drove Eric to ask, "Am I doing something wrong?" One might note here too that while for Eric the question was whether his sexual orientation was wrong, for Paul the feeling was, rather, that homosexuality was *punishment* for doing something wrong. Paul said:

> I think it was a real obstacle to the growth of my spirituality. I couldn't get out of guilt that there was something wrong. [I felt] there was something that would keep me from—[Yet] it was part of who I was and I had no choice, and I couldn't—I have been through this so many times but I still—Even recalling it, I mean, I understand no more now. But looking back at that time, I can become somewhat inarticulate about it. I think it's because that's what the experience was at the time.

What one witnesses here most forcefully is pain and an imprisonment between two certainties. One of these was the sexuality that Paul emphasized was inescapable. The other was guilt and the sense "that there was something wrong"—with him rather than with God or church. And as Paul looked back he returned, he said, to the very difficulty of expression, the impossibility of reconciling the irreconcilable that confronted him at the time. For some, if sexual orientation could not be altered, any thought of God might be set aside. But for Paul, the "growth of my spirituality" remained a goal. And lastly, we might notice that Paul "understands no more now." Paul continued, even after half a century of living, questioning, self-examination, and religious and spiritual practice, to ask whether "something" is "keeping [him] from—" what? God? By the time of the interview, he worked with his recognition of internalized homophobia and sought to move past the "guilt that there was something wrong."

The contrast between Paul's struggle and Eric's teenage sense that all was well between himself and God is a forceful one. While Eric's sexuality was—more by accident than by any human intent—able to flourish relatively unhindered, Paul's was a site of dread from the start. Yet Paul and Eric both spent much of their lives seeking to make congruent their relationship to God and self-recognition as "homosexual."

Given the socioreligious setting into which Paul was born, he faced the challenge of bringing into harmony an uneasy triad—God, gayness, and the Catholic Church. The last member of the group was, as might be expected, the most unwilling of these. Paul's first step toward engaging this challenge was to leave his hometown in order to join a religious teaching order. (Paul, as had Brother Camillus Chavez, gently explained to me that the term *monk,* although once the correct one for such men, is now deemed old-fashioned. But naming aside, Paul did join a residential teaching order, taking vows of poverty, chastity, and obedience.) Paul lived in that community from the age of seventeen until forty-five, just two years shy of three decades.

In retrospect, Paul said, "I now know that the reason I did this was because I liked men. It was partly also to escape. A lot of young men joined religious communities, I'm sure, because they were gay." Paul's point was not that he believed, then or now, that religious orders were sites wherein one could enact one's gayness—rather they were places where one might be able to "delete" it or otherwise live with that which felt unlivable. But on a different level, as someone who felt very much drawn to men, Paul recognized that it made sense to have sought life in an all-male religious community simply because he "liked men."

It was in fact at the religious community that Paul was able for the first time to tell another living being about his attraction to men. Paul said:

> I can remember my first year there, thinking I had to tell somebody this. So I did go to confession and I can remember thinking this man was going to tell me I had to leave. And I was prepared to do that and very frightened, very terrified. And he didn't. He just told me to practice custody of the eyes, which was not a very practical piece of advice for a young gay man surrounded by young men . . . And I said, "Well, that's what he said, so I'm going to hang in there."

"Custody of the eyes" meant, simply, not looking at those to whom one was attracted. Paul now had had something to "do about" his sexuality in the context of the religious tradition to which he felt closest, in the realm of keeping "rules," conforming to "regulations." This was, rather obviously, a case of corralling his sexual feelings rather than anything else. However, as Paul hinted, "custody of the eyes" was not necessarily a useful or effective instruction.

In fact, this strategic admonition was not one given only to gay men. Rather, said Paul, "that was pretty common advice. It was part of the religious life culture . . . It was one of the ways they taught you how to deal with celibacy, [although] not necessarily the healthiest way of dealing with it." This approach was perhaps even more draconian than the "don't ask, don't tell" atmosphere that had pervaded official culture at Hope Central Church. And indeed as time passed, Paul said, some (heterosexual) brothers sought to push the envelope further, proposing that it was possible to develop "celibate sexual relationships" with women. But on further questioning about what that entailed, Paul said, laughing wryly, "A celibate sexual relationship—boy, that's a good question."

In practicing "custody of the eyes" one is merely "dealing with" a celibacy imposed from without, rather than actually engaging it as choice and/or from within. But at least in Paul's case the issue was not so much with the pros and cons of celibacy but with his sexuality. Given this, the very question of celibacy was a detour, a turn away from the journey to create peaceful coexistence between one's sexuality, one's relationship to God, and the religious context in which one sought to anchor these.

For Paul the three vows central to his chosen path—poverty, celibacy, and obedience—were in principle deeply meaningful ones, tools or contexts within which spiritual faith might be nurtured. He explained that "when I joined the religious community, poverty served me well. I was the kind of person who grew up simple. Simple living, [I] got into it, it fed me . . . helped me not be distracted with a lot of physical stuff. It was really good for me and I enjoyed it." Paul did not, in other words, only "deal with" poverty. Rather it was both practice and site for learning. The vow of celibacy, though, did not work well for him. Rather than anything else, he said, "I was running away from my sexuality." "Custody of the eyes" replaced all contemplation of sexuality's—or celibacy's—spiritual potential, meaning, and benefits or challenges. In other words, Paul had not so much cultivated celibacy as a path toward God but rather as a path *away from* a fundamental aspect of himself. The contrast between the vow of celibacy and that of poverty for Paul was significant. Of the former, he had little confidence in his description of its benefits since, he noted, "I think I'm trying to explain something I may not entirely agree with, [although] I do respect those who for whom it is a reality." He added: "There are some men whom celibacy did serve, very much as poverty fed me, helped me grow. And if the vows really don't do that—if one would say them but you don't really have a gift for it, you don't belong here."

Paul had, then, been able to practice one of his three vows, poverty, and feel it as a location for spiritual growth. At the same time, however, he suffered from the effects of another vow—a "celibacy" that did little other than provide scant cover for his homosexuality. And as a result of this contradictory situation he came to learn that the third vow, "obedience," made less and less sense.

In the context of these last words it was hardly surprising that in 1989 Paul took a leave of absence from his religious community, finally leaving it in 1994. It was during that period, he told me, that he "came out"—acknowledged himself as a gay man. Paul rejected my suggestion that this transition had been a courageous one: "I resist that word. I don't know why. Maybe it was. It might have been."

Courageous or not, however, the move was painful, and possibly, in his own mind, not yet fully completed, given his phrasing: "[if] you don't really have a gift for it, you don't belong *here*" (emphasis added). Coming to honor and practice his sexuality was, it turned out, no simple matter. For one thing, beginning to seek sexual relationships and partnerships when one is already past forty-five is difficult. Paul also discovered that articulating a living relationship with God outside the religious community was very hard. He said:

> Having left religious life, where by profession, I'm supposed to—*was* supposed to—have been a person who would spend more intentional time praying, more intentional time developing an inner kind of spirituality, and even what I would call the inner to the outer journey of spirituality in relationship to the world—which is part of the spiritual journey, too—[*Here, Paul paused.*] I ask myself, "What's going on right now with myself, in terms of my spirituality?"

In retrospect, it appeared that despite everything that had been problematic about it, life in a religious teaching order at least provided a context for the cultivation of spiritual practice, and the application of that practice in the world. It looked, in short, as though Paul had, in fact, moved from the proverbial "rock" to the apocryphal "hard place." Paul told me, "I have found that my spirituality has to be fed in the community, hearing other people's faith stories."

The organization that came the closest to providing a religious and spiritual context for Paul was Dignity, described by him as "a faith community, a worshiping community of gay, lesbian, bisexual, and transgendered Catholics."[11] Paul said, "Dignity is a place where I can stand, it's a prophetic voice in the community." Founded in Los Angeles, in 1969, Dignity has members who, Paul explained, "have never seen ourselves as some sort of schism. We're Catholic folks. We're raised in that. It's just in our bones and blood and there's nothing we can do about that . . . It has chapters throughout the country . . . Increasingly it has a large membership that doesn't worship with us but that supports our agenda." At the time of this interview Paul was cochair of the San Francisco Dignity chapter. It met each Sunday for worship service, a time that, as is true of all other churches, served a social as well as a purely religious function. And although Paul did not note this in the interview, Dignity had also for many years carried its banner at the Pride parades, in San Francisco as well as elsewhere in the country.

Paul was frustrated, though, that at times Dignity faced the conservatism, or possibly the caution and realism, of its own membership:

> PAUL Six years ago [Dignity] developed a rite of committed relationships as sort of a statement to people in our community about respecting the relationships, but also to the broader church, [about] what we're doing, who we are. [But] not a single couple in this community has stepped forward to do that.[12]
> RF Not a single couple has come forward to get married?
> PAUL We were careful not to call it marriage, I should point out. It was more a rite of committed relationships. Actually, we're not quite willing to take that on, though it is taking place elsewhere. But we wanted to at least recognize committed relationships and bless them.

Unfortunately that caution might have been well placed. For when Dignity finally sought, as it were, to call the Vatican's bluff, the response was swift:

> I think it was about six years ago Dignity finally just made this statement about—we always tiptoed around it—our sexuality and our spirituality. [We said], "These are holy relationships. They're blessed by God, we believe that." That was the beginning of a real conflict with the Catholic Church . . . Rome spoke, and spoke very loudly and very cruelly. There was a letter produced by the Department of Catholic Doctrine . . . And that was the beginning of Catholics being kicked out of the Catholic churches. Gay people, Dignity, being kicked out of the Catholic churches so we were no longer allowed to physically have our worship spaces in the Catholic church.

Importantly, from Paul's point of view, Dignity saw itself as Catholic. Catholicism was in "the bones and blood" of its membership just as

Paul said that his homosexuality was unmovable. Here was a place where Paul might remain in his birth religious community and stay gay. Yet the circumstances in which he might do this were immediately circumscribed: "Catholics [were] kicked out of Catholic Churches" symbolically, and literally—"We were no longer allowed to physically have our worship spaces in the Catholic Church."

The third member of the triad of self/sexuality, religio-spiritual institution, and the divine was very much at issue here as well. The Catholic Church saw (and sees) itself as intermediary between individual and God. Thus if the church disputes one's Catholicness, one's right to act as a Catholic and as a gay person simultaneously, then the authenticity of one's relationship with the divine is automatically called into question. Moreover as we have seen, Dignity was not, and is not, satisfied with the "custody of the eyes" approach to nonheterosexual orientations. Rather, such sexualities and relationships are to be honored as "holy," "blessed by God." In other words, they were to be understood in the same ways as heterosexual relationships. Clearly, the disputed coin and currency here is in fact God's word, God's will, God's blessing. The questions of who is permitted to be in a church, and of who is truly Catholic, ultimately lead into questions about "what God thinks" and therefore what the institution(s) self-designated as arbiters or intermediaries can, will, or must do.

Given this stranglehold it is hardly surprising that Paul continued to ask himself what God's word on homosexuality actually might be. Thus late in the interview Paul returned to his first statements about his sexuality and followed them up: "[A] lot of old tapes and guilt around homosexual behavior and whoever this God is, and the guilt around that. Even though, intellectually, I can talk the talk . . . I think, at some deeper level, it's really nagging at me. There's no question about it . . . It's almost as confusing as when I was a child." Paul's frankness about his continuing internal struggle is striking, and given his history perhaps unsurprising. But extrapolating from his prior adult experience as a Catholic gay man, one might suggest that he is no longer practicing "custody of the eyes." Rather he is looking directly into the face of his childhood question, "What did I do wrong?"

Having described his self-doubt, Paul went on to explain to me how scripture and indeed the very concept of God had changed for him over the years. He noted the more recent scholarship on the Bible and homosexuality that argues that cultural biases in belief, interpretation, and translation are responsible for much of what, in the Bible, is apparently critical of homosexuality. And when possible, he avoided any contact with the kinds of extreme hostility to nonheterosexuality associated with some preachers.

But more important than those things, he said, was asking what God *is* about, rather than what God is not. In that regard, Paul said, teaching a course on spiritual renewal, he had told his audience, "Spirituality is about establishing a relationship with God. You can't have a relationship with God if you don't have a relationship with the things that God cares about." For Paul, what God cared about centered on social justice. Thus referring to the book of Exodus in the Old Testament of the Bible, Paul said:

> The times in which God breaks through are really profound moments . . . In the understanding of the Jewish people, God really broke through in their lives and liberated them from slavery . . . This isn't some spiritual pie in the sky, it's getting them the hell out of slavery . . . That's got to have a profound influence on who I think God is and whatever God is in this world—this spirit which moves the human spirit to free itself from being enslaved. Call it a will—there's this piece of us that doesn't want to be enslaved and just says no to it. The Jewish people named that God. I guess I'm getting more and more in touch with that little part of it.

Here, clearly, God within each human and God as external force are no longer separable as they had been during the "rules and regulations" period of Paul's spiritual journey. The idea of God as "spirit breaking through" and the notion of humans as the vehicle for "breakthrough moments" were crucial for Paul. He felt the moment of Dignity's foundation was one such time. Remembering those moments, "reading those stories, understanding those stories [and] the spirit that comes from those stories . . . helps me understand God as a caring God."

The "caring God" and the "caring human" were increasingly connected in Paul's thinking, just as were the vision of God within the human self and that of God as an external force. Paul added, "I think spirituality is getting in touch with that humanity inside of us, that just wants to get out, that has to be there, getting in touch with it and expressing it in some way." He continued:

> PAUL I'm realizing it as I talk—if it's true for Jesus, why is it not true for me and if it's true for Martin Luther King, why is it not true for me? And if it's true for Gandhi . . . I really believe, you know, that the spirit just jumps out in small ways, for all of the rest of us.
>
> RF So, presumably, just as soon as you can ditch the idea that because

you're queer you can't really be godly, then you're all set and then you'll be all put back together.

PAUL Right. I hope. [*Laughs.*] Well, in dealing with my own homophobia, which is pretty profound, it really is, I've become much more aware of it.

Paul's triad was now revealed as process rather than stasis—dependent on rich reinterpretation of God, scripture, and the relationship between divinity and humanity. And although Paul insisted that his own journey was still incomplete, he was more certain now that it might be his own fear of himself, not God's rage toward him, that was keeping him in bondage.

And he was clearer that even his Catholicism could be revised and yet retained. He said: "My spirituality can no longer be tied to an institutional church, parts of which feed it and parts of which don't. The sacramental life of the church feeds it. The pastoral life of the church feeds it . . . Proclamations from Rome about homosexual people, rules and regulations and kicking us out of churches don't feed it." As before, Paul noted that his issues around sexuality were on one level similar to those of heterosexuals: "Ninety-five percent of Catholic couples made up their own mind years ago about birth control, divorce, and remarriage. Generally in the area of sexuality I think American Catholics are just profoundly out of sync with the institutional church."[13]

Just as Paul's sense of the relationship between God and self is changing, so is his sense of a spiritual home base. Now, it entailed "finding those places where it's safe, with people who are of the same mind, little groups of people who are willing to pray and to talk together. Like a church in exile if you will. I happen to think that the church is more than just what's in Rome." It might just be possible, then, for the triad to be reconfigured yet remain intact. For Paul said, "Rome has consolidated its power for years . . . I just think that's bad theology . . . I don't think that they're all what it means to be Catholic. So I can be a Catholic even though I don't believe all of what they teach."

❧

DIVERSE AS THEY WERE, the men and women in this chapter had much in common. To begin with, all shared key premises about the meanings of sex and sexuality in the worlds in which they lived. They shared the recognition that they lived in a sexually diverse world. And they also lived in cognizance of something that stood in contradistinction to sexual diversity: the awareness of themselves as living in a heteronormative context. Heteronormativity was defined above, as will be remembered, as heterosexuality deemed normal, normative, to be "expected," and the discursive and material ordering of society around those ideas.

This pair of mutually contradictory premises was dealt with in a range of ways by interviewees, although all were conscious of their salience. Thus, for some, while heteronormativity was taken for granted it was still somehow to be named emphatically when a "sexual nametag" was requested. For others heteronormativity was what must be forcefully reasserted. For still others, it was what could rather easily be disregarded although, as noted, many whose sexualities were "marked" ones needed to account, autobiographically, for themselves. For a final group, heteronormativity was what had to be explicitly challenged and worked against.

These, though, are statements about society and culture, not about religion or spirituality. What, one might ask, did the first pair have to do with the second one? In fact, they had a great deal to do with one another. For everyone it was both possible and necessary to name sex and sexuality in relationship to religion and spirituality, or to put this more strongly, to imagine, organize, or "manage" sexuality in religious or spiritual terms. There was much commonality, at least in principle, in how this process was understood. All agreed that sexuality and religion or spirituality *were* connected with one another. And, for all, it was critically important for self, sexuality, and spirituality to be in concordance with one another. For everyone, even sexual renunciates, sexuality could in principle and should in practice be lived in ways that worked alongside rather than apart from a spiritual or ethical code. Stating the point even more forcefully it seemed, very often, as though spiritual practice was the necessary resource by means of which to corral sexuality, as socially organized activity and identity, into some kind of order.

Thus we saw interviewees describing sexual practice as that which could and must be received and undertaken in ways that would harm neither self nor other, and in ways, importantly, that were consonant with God and/or path as understood by each interviewee. One can note critical differences here too, though, since particular modes of sexual practice deemed reasonable for some were beyond the bounds of acceptability for others. Again the contradiction between heteronormativity and sexual diversity was a critical issue.

It seemed, indeed, as though sites of organized religion were the places in and against which those struggles needed most immediately to be waged. As we have seen it was at times possible to transform such institutions from within (Nancy Nielsen's Lutheran congregation and the East Bay Church of Religious Science were key examples). And elsewhere religious institutions like Dignity, Sha'ar Zahav, and indeed Arinna Weisman's gay and lesbian Vipassana retreats, had been created with the specific intention of supporting and ministering to gay, lesbian, bisexual, and transgendered practitioners. But we also saw six individuals, Paul Wooley, Eric Thomas, Nancy Nielsen, Nancy McKay, Arinna Weisman, and Patricia Lin facing directly the religious institutions and religious forms that could, in effect, make or break their sense of the "rightness" and the possibility of living by their spiritual belief and ethical code.

I argued earlier that gay, lesbian, bisexual, and transgendered people of faith often struggle to create and sustain situations in which self, God/path, and religious institution can harmoniously coexist. Elsewhere in this book I have discussed the interplay of spontaneity and cultivated practice, as well as the triadic relationship between form, practice, and surrender. These issues are of relevance here also. In Eric's case, for example, a spontaneous relationship with God emerged, it seemed, from no particular place and weathered many of the storms wrought by conservative institutions. And indeed Eric's surrender to that inner sense of God carried him, finally, to a religious institution wherein it was possible to create safe haven for people of all sexualities. And Patricia learned suddenly that her sexuality and her religious life should and could be brought into harmony with one another. The same was so for Paul, albeit with more difficulty. And Arinna was able on one hand to build such a space and on the other to be excluded from an institution that, it turned out, would not support her sexuality at the same time as her practice.

Excepting Eric's childhood, *spontaneity* may not be the correct term with which to describe these individuals' encounters and experiences with God and path. Nonetheless, for each the spiritual journey was characterized by an inner relationship that was determined, durable, and deeply committed to the idea that path and/or God were not acceptable unless they recognized and valued all aspects of the self, including sexual orientation. The inner journey here takes the lead over the external form of path or God, and over its attendant institutions also. It is not, then, that the practitioner expects the path or divine to surrender to him or her. Rather, the practitioner strives, through the cultivation of her or his practice, to call into question the institutions that seem to fail to live up to what body, heart, mind, *and* spontaneous relationships to path and God bring forward.

It may take a long time for the contradiction between heteronormativity and sexual diversity to be resolved in houses of worship and practice. Even so, as has been seen, most of the men and women interviewed here were well aware of a contradiction that needed to be addressed, either within religious institutions or in the context of their own private spiritual practices. As Nancy Nielsen remarked, "If you're going to be about healing the brokenness in our world, then the way you do it is standing with and next to someone . . . The prophetic voice within the faith community does not lead the way most of the time." One could, however, argue that "prophetic voices" are present and may be witnessed through the journeys of the men and women described here, whether they strive to transform institutions or just to honor sexual diversity as they see it.

Any interview-based study of human subjects encounters individuals at a particular point on their life path. Yet something other than that which is momentary or transitory has been presented here. For what has been revealed, above all, is an exploration and elaboration of the means by which a set of lives was crafted, created, and thus continued to flow and evolve. As this book neared completion, I had occasion to contact Sadiqa once again to ask her a practical question about her interview. Returning my telephone call, she said, "I assume that you are calling me to ask about the impact of '9/11.'" I had to admit that, no, I simply needed to clarify when Sadiqa wore a head covering, when she did not, and why. I did explain, though, that in one of the chapters I had discussed the challenges of living as a Muslim in the United States at this time in history, challenges that had, we both agreed, greatly intensified since 11 September 2001.

Shortly thereafter, I received a call from another interviewee, John Potts. Returning his call, I learned that he and his son were considering a new line of activity—developing resources for the integration of spiritual practice into the workplace. In this context, he had telephoned to see whether I might recommend any local graduate programs to provide the scholarly undergirding that he felt he needed. This new venture marked a transition from his involvement in cultivating workplace diversity at the time of our interview. Still, clearly the spiritual resources crucial to that earlier work remained at the center of his life activity. I also had occasion to return to the home of Nancy McKay (still in good health and now a proud grandmother). Her work as a health counselor and spiritual director continued. I learned from her that she was delighted that, in the church of which she is now a member, she more frequently heard celebrations of the feminine aspects of the divine in music, poetry, and prayer.

Some time after that, I approached Chochmat HaLev, the Jewish Meditation Center of which Avram Davis was founding director, requesting use of their building for an event that I was organizing. Things had changed for Avram, too. With Chochmat HaLev now in a far larger space with a bigger staff, I learned that it would not help, especially, that I had "worked with" Avram on a book I was finishing. For, it was explained, Avram was more involved in the visioning and guidance of the center than with its day-to-day activity. Next, I had the good fortune to meet once again with Arinna Weisman. She informed me that since the interview she had coauthored a book on Vipassana meditation.[1] More than that, she had cofounded a nonresidential meditation center, the Dhamma Dena Meditation Center, in Northampton, Massachusetts. One might, then, propose that some of Avram's goals, hopes, and dreams, and Arinna's also, were being realized.

All of this signals, among other things, that the men and women interviewed for this study continue to undertake the work of living in spirit, and living through practice, demonstrating as well that the contexts for their practices continue to thrive. The spiritual and religious lives of these fifty men and women have continued well past my own direct dialogue with them. In closing this text, I visit once more some of the key terms by means of which I have gathered together these voices.

*Living Spirit, Living Practice*: a central argument of this book has been that one must understand this pair of terms as dialectically related to one another by means of a second pair—*spontaneity* and *cultivation*. These four terms are in dynamic relationship with one another. As well, all four are supportive of one another. Thus, as has been seen, that which has manifested spontaneously about living spirit has been supportive of, and supported by, living practice. Likewise, spontaneously arising experiences of living spirit have been more readily repeated, understood, and lived as practice by means of the cultivation of both.

*Poetics*: the voicing of one's sense of that which resides, in the end, at the boundaries of language and beyond. The term *poetics* has been used here to refer to individuals' effort to name, in the clearest way possible, the places, forces, form, and, above all, the experiences of religion and spirituality. Here, artistry, particularity, creativity, and even idiosyncrasy, tautology, and grammatical slippage were present and, one might argue, necessary, as individuals sought to voice what needed to be explained. It is precisely because of the beauty of these voicings that it has been impossible to resist offering, throughout this book, story upon story about the living of spirit and the practice of practice.

*Politics*: this word has been used broadly here to signal all that creates context for relationships to spirit and practice as these are experienced in the social world. Thus, national location, race, gender, sexuality, and class as interwoven systems of categorization, domination, and culture were variously critical to the forming and transforming of spiritual and religious practices. Interviewees were at times bricoleurs who crafted their practice in relation to sociocultural settings. At other times knowledge about particular spiritual resources and histories helped interviewees to make cognitive sense of spiritual or religious experiences.

*Epistemology*: this word, like all other "ologies," refers to the study of something—literally, the articulation of *words about* something. And if an episteme is a system of meaning, understanding, or comprehension, epistemology examines (makes words about) the meanings, the making, the implications, and the effects of meaning systems themselves. In this case the question has been how, for a group of fifty men and women, spiritual and religious meanings were formed, and how they were understood. The answers to those questions at times returned us to the category of politics as just defined. As well, the poetics of expression were crucially important, as individuals explained how meanings had been made for them. Each chapter has returned to this set of epistemological questions, engaging at times with particular institutional religious frames, and at other times with extra-institutional modes of thinking and analysis.

*Particularities and commonalities*: networks of meaning were crucial for all, as spiritual and religious meanings were made, or perceived, or discovered. These networks were specific ones. Thus, Christian men and women were cognizant of that religion's texts, its key discursive turns, and also, crucially, the debates and choices that made space for spiritual learning, decision-making, and transformation within it. And as well as offering room to maneuver, that religious form provided what many have termed a *sacred container*, designating a space of shelter, structure, and coherence of meaning. The same was true for Jews, Muslims, Buddhists, and Hindu or Hindu-derived practitioners, as well as practitioners of Twelve Step, Bahai, and Diamond Heart. Moreover, even extra-institutional practitioners whose practices were less readily categorized could explain clearly the logic and framework of what they knew, and referred to, as spirit, life force, or divinity. In short, across the diversity of practices and forms, the actuality, indeed the practicality and necessity, of sense-making formed the sine qua non of religious and spiritual life.

While the notion of a sacred *container* might signal the marking of a boundary line, in this text at least interviewees were not interested, for the most part, in creating hierarchical or hostile distinctions between one religious form and another. More frequently, interviewees named other religious or spiritual forms as they sought to "translate" their own practice into one that might seem more familiar to a listener. At other times, individuals' own practice entailed working within more than one mode of practice or comprehension. As often as those kinds of bridge-building, one witnessed interviewees' effort to situate or explain their spiritual and religious practices in relation to linguistic, discursive. and cultural environments coded as secular rather than in any way spiritual. However, this did not indicate doubt or concern about their practice—rather in those moments interviewees simply verbalized their awareness that their modes of thinking, being, and seeing might not sit well with the dominant culture of the United States as they saw it.

*No borders*: spiritual and religious practices, one might argue, in-evitably took place in sociocultural contexts. However, sociocultural contexts were not merely backdrops within and against which such practices took shape and place. Rather, the practice and its episteme transformed context itself, making the relationship between practice and context dialectical, dynamic, and processual. The complexity of these relationships was evident in each chapter of this text. As will be remembered, a spiritual episteme shaped Sita's approach to dealing with the expected arrival of a large number of devotees at the ashram where she lived and worked. It formed not merely her inner conscious-ness in relation to this situation, but also her outer experience of it. Blanche Hartman's understanding of self, other, and world changed radically and forever as she sought, and found in Buddhism, the means of understanding the moment in her life in which she had spontane-ously experienced her oneness with another being.

Enigma's and Tariq's commitment to Islam remained intact as they began, as adults, to practice it in an environment where theirs was a minority, marginalized, and for the most part unappreciated religion. Practicing Islam in this sociocultural setting necessitated a constant process of renegotiation of the terms *Muslim* and *American* and the living of the compound identities American *Muslim* and Muslim *American.* To offer one final example, men and women contemplating their sexualities and sexual lives found that these could and should be understood to be a part of spiritual life, rather than separate from it. Once again, there was a commitment to bringing all aspects of one's daily life and selfhood into one's spiritual practice.

There was, then, no division of worlds into arenas where the religious and spiritual applied, and where they did not. By intent, and for purposes of analysis, what *is* spiritual, *is* religious, about daily lives has been drawn out in this text. But for those living the practice, such separation was, as we have seen, not meaningful. Religious and spiritual practice continually informed, suffused, reformed, and transformed interviewees' experience of the social, and even though the social frequently exerted its disciplinary pressure, it could not, in the final analysis, terminate their spiritual journeys.

APPENDIX 1

*biographical summaries*

ADITYA ADVANI, born 1963. Immigrant from India. Raised and remains a Hindu. Landscape architect. Gay.

AKAYA WINDWOOD, born 1956. African American. Raised in nonreligious home. Current practice extra-institutional. Diversity educator, living simply by intent. Lesbian.

ALAN LEW, born 1943, Jewish by birth. Nuclear family secular, but extended family practiced Judaism. As an adult, practiced Soto Zen Buddhism for ten years and then returned to Judaism. Rabbi of a conservative synagogue. Heterosexual.

ANA GAMBOA (pseudonym), born 1961. Latina. Migrated to United States at age eight from a Latin American country (name withheld to preserve confidentiality). Raised Roman Catholic. Adult practice, devotee of Mata Amritanandamayi, guru in the Hindu tradition. Also drawn to teachings of Thich Nhat Hahn. Social worker. Heterosexual, practicing celibacy.

ARCHANA (pseudonym), born 1944. European American. Grew up in nonreligious home. Current practice, renunciate (brahmacharini) resident at the ashram of Mata Amritanandamayi; formerly a devotee of Sri Maharishi Mahesh Yogi, founder of Transcendental Meditation (TM), both in the Hindu tradition. Nurse when not working at the ashram. Gay (her term), celibate.

ARINNA WEISMAN, born 1950. White immigrant from South Africa via Britain. Jewish by birth (nonpracticing). Current practice Theravada Buddhism. Vipassana teacher living by dana (donation). Lesbian.

AVRAM DAVIS, born 1951. Jewish by birth. Childhood religion and current practice Judaism. Religious teacher and founder and codirector of Chochmat HaLev. Heterosexual.

BIRGIT WOLZ, born 1954. White German immigrant to United States. Raised Catholic. Current practice Diamond Heart Path, a synthesis of Sufism and psychology. Marriage, family and child counselor. Heterosexual.

(BROTHER) CAMILLUS CHAVEZ, born 1929. Chicano. Raised Catholic, now a La Sallian renunciate. College professor, also grief counselor and reiki healer. Heterosexual, celibate.

CHARLOTTE (self-chosen pseudonym), born 1942. European American. Regarding childhood religion, stated only, "I grew up with Christianity." Current practice Twelve Step. Living with the disability of environmental illness brought on by work as a printer. Heterosexual.

DARSHAN (pseudonym), declined to give age, but given age of her children was probably in her early 50s at the time of the interview. Canadian-born immigrant to United States. Sikh by birth. Current practice, devotee of Sathya Sai Baba and Mata Amritanandamayi, gurus in the Hindu tradition. Artist. Heterosexual.

DAVID JACOBSON (pseudonym), born 1944. Jewish by birth. Childhood religion Judaism. Current practice Kundalini yoga. Osteopath. Heterosexual.

DEREK JONES, born 1939. White immigrant to United States from Britain via Canada. Raised Church of England (Episcopalian); current practice Episcopalian (deacon). Retired businessman, now full-time unpaid director of meals program for homeless and impoverished persons in a large county in the San Francisco Bay Area. Heterosexual.

DIANA WINSTON, born 1966. Jewish by birth although not raised within Judaism (her mother was a devotee of the Hindu guru Baba Muktananda and later a Gurdjieffian). Current practice Theravada Buddhism, · Vipassana. Lives simply by intent and works with Buddhist Alliance for Social Engagement, of which she was a founding member. Heterosexual.

DONNA GONZAGA (pseudonym), born 1944. European American. Raised in nonreligious home. Current practice Twelve Step. Works in the non-profit sector with a homeless coalition. Described sexuality as "ambiguous," "most closely identified with bisexual."

EMERALD MATRA (spiritual name), born 1951. European American. Childhood religion Protestant (chose not to name denomination). Current practice, priestess of the goddess in the Wiccan tradition. Healer and counselor. Lesbian.

ENIGMA (self-chosen pseudonym), born 1975. Migrated to United States from Saudi Arabia. Of South Asian (Indian) descent. Childhood and current practice Islam. Had just graduated from a university in the Bay Area at time of interview. Heterosexual.

ERIC THOMAS, born 1961. African American. Raised in nonreligious home, although as a child insisted on attending neighborhood churches. Joined family in attending Pentecostal Church as a young teen. Current practice, member of East Bay Church of Religious Science. Clothing designer. Gay.

GLORIA WILLIAMS (pseudonym), born 1952. Black (her preferred description). Childhood religion Catholic. Current practice, devotee of Sri Sri Ravi Shankar and prior to that a devotee of Maharishi Mahesh Yogi, the founder of Transcendental Meditation (TM), both in the Hindu tradition. Chiropractor, living simply by intent. Regarding sexual orientation, she said she would prefer "not to choose" but if pressed, "I would choose bisexual."

HANA NIELSEN KNEISLER, born 1974. European American. Raised in the Bahai tradition. Current practice Bahai. Undergraduate student at a university in the Bay Area. Heterosexual.

HAPPY CAROL WININGHAM, 1953–1998. European American. Childhood religion United Methodist. Adult practice, minister, Ananda Church of Self-Realization and resident at Ananda Village, spiritual community founded by J. Donald Waters (Swami Kriyananda) disciple of Paramahamsa Yogananda, a guru in the Hindu tradition. Instructor in yoga, pranayama, and (self-)healing practices. Was living with HIV-AIDS at time of the interview. Heterosexual.

HOMER TENG, born 1969. Hong Kong Chinese immigrant to United States. Raised and remains Catholic. Graduate student in religion at a university in the Bay Area. Heterosexual.

JOHN POTTS, born 1947. European American. Childhood religion Presbyterian. Current practice primarily Episcopalian but also practices the Diamond Heart Path. Took early retirement as corporate executive to undertake his current work in diversity education. Heterosexual.

JUDY SMITH, born 1960. European American. Raised Catholic but her family broke with church after Judy broke her neck and became physically disabled. Current practice Soto Zen Buddhism. Program director of Axis Dance Company. Also teaches self-defense and is an educator in relation to disability issues. Lesbian.

L'DIA OMARI-MOHAMMAD, born 1956. African American. Childhood religion Baptist. Current practice, member of Nation of Islam, and also identifies herself as a "universalist spiritualist." Douala coach and health educator. Heterosexual.

LIÊN SCHUTT, born 1964. Asian Pacific American of Vietnamese descent. Adopted at eight years by European American parents and moved to the United States. Pre-adoption childhood religion Buddhism. After adoption was baptized in the Presbyterian Church. Current practice Buddhism—practices Vipassana and is part of the San Francisco Bay Area People of Color Sangha. Graduate student at a university in the Bay Area. Lesbian.

MARGARET MAJORS, born 1943. European American. Childhood religion Episcopalian. Current practice Episcopalian. Marriage, family and child counselor and faith healer. Heterosexual.

MARILYN MCCLAIN, born 1963. African American. Childhood religion Baptist. Adult practice, a member of the East Bay Church of Religious Science. Health and fitness instructor and personal trainer. Lesbian.

MERCEDES MARTIN, born 1962. Afro-Cuban immigrant to the United States. Raised Catholic but also influenced by father's practice of Afro-Cuban spiritualism. Current practice syncretic and extra-institutional, drawing on spiritualism and including meditation. Diversity educator. Heterosexual.

MICHAEL BELL, born 1957. African American. Raised Episcopalian, but with Southern Baptism strongly present in the family. Current practice, devotee of Gurumayi Chidvilasananda, in the Hindu tradition. Self-employed consultant in organizational growth, change, and planning. Gay.

MICHAEL YAMAMOTO (pseudonym), born 1951. Japanese American. Raised in nonreligious nuclear family but close to practicing Buddhist extended family. Current practice Tibetan Buddhism (name of teacher withheld on request to ensure confidentiality). Self-employed environmental planning consultant. Heterosexual.

MISHA ASHOORIAN, born 1929. Migrated to the United States from Iran (his preferred term is *Persia*) in late 1970s. Childhood and current practice Assyrian Orthodox Christian. Also a dream-seer. Semi-retired accountant. Heterosexual.

MUSHIM IKEDA NASH, born 1954. Japanese American. Nonreligious childhood home, although grandparents and close extended family practiced Buddhism. Adult practice, initiated into Korean Zen lineage, still practices Zen but no longer in that lineage. Poet and writer. Heterosexual.

NANCY MCKAY, born 1938. European American. Childhood religion Protestant with Congregational and Presbyterian upbringing but rarely attended church. Health counselor, spiritual director, and minister in the United Church of Christ. Heterosexual.

NANCY NIELSEN, born 1944. European American. Raised in primarily nonreligious home but sent by mother to local Sunday schools, and baptized Lutheran at behest of relatives. Current practice Lutheran. Program director on health and interfaith issues for a Catholic nonprofit organization. Heterosexual.

NICK MUELLER, born 1957. European American. Childhood religion Catholic. Current practice self-taught Buddhist unaffiliated to any specific tradition. Car salesman. Gay.

PALOMA TAN (pseudonym), born 1969. Biracial Chinese American/European American. Raised in nonreligious home. Current spiritual practice Twelve Step and extra-institutional. Temporary "pink collar" office worker, living simply by intent. Heterosexual.

PATRICIA LIN, born 1970. Asian American of Taiwanese descent. Raised in nonreligious home. Converted to Judaism in her early twenties. Doctoral student. Gay (her term).

PAUL WOOLEY, born 1944. European American. Childhood religion Catholic. Remains Catholic; from ages seventeen to forty-seven, a member of a renunciate teaching order, which he had left six years prior to the interview in order to make space for his sexuality. Works for Catholic Charities in the social justice and community education division. Gay.

PEARL WERFEL, born 1955. Jewish by birth. Childhood religion Judaism. Described her current practice as that of a Jewish Pagan, committed to prepatriarchal Judaism. Psychologist and health educator. Lesbian.

RICHARD CHU (self-chosen pseudonym), born 1955. Chinese American. American Baptist until early teens. Current practice Buddhism, Vipassana. Psychotherapist. Gay.

ROBERT HORTON, born 1956. European American. Childhood religion Unitarian Universalist. Adult religion Tibetan Buddhism, student of Chogyam Trungpa. Self-employed antiracist educator. Heterosexual.

RYUMON ZENJI (spiritual name), born 1953. Afro-Cuban immigrant to the United States. Childhood practice spiritualism and Catholicism. Current practice Soto Zen Buddhism. Antiracist educator. Lesbian.

SADIQA (spiritual name), born 1971. Palestinian American. Raised Orthodox Christian culturally, with little religious practice. Became Sufi in her early twenties. Self-employed in henna product sales and as a henna artist. Heterosexual.

SALLY MAGNUSSEN, born 1960. European American. Raised in a non-religious home. Current practice syncretic: "Deep Visioning" taught by Diane di Prima, cofounder of San Francisco Institute of Magical and Healing Arts, and Tibetan Buddhism as taught by Chogyam Trungpa. Student. Heterosexual.

SITA (pseudonym), born 1948. European American. Childhood religion, mainline Christian (chose not to name denomination). Adult practice, renunciate (brahmacharini) resident at the ashram of Mata Amritanandamayi, guru in the Hindu tradition. Formerly member of Ananda Church of Self-Realization and resident at Ananda Village, spiritual community founded by J. Donald Waters (Swami Kriyananda) disciple of Paramahamsa Yogananda, a guru in the Hindu tradition. Works on site at the ashram. Heterosexual, celibate.

TARIQ NAFICY (pseudonym), born 1966. Iranian immigrant to United States. Childhood and current practice Islam. Software engineer. Heterosexual.

TOM WAGONER, born 1950. European American. Grew up in non-religious household, although confirmed Presbyterian. Current practice Tibetan Buddhism, student of Lama Yeshe. Self-employed in housing construction business. Heterosexual.

WILMA JEAN TUCKER, born 1945. African American and Native American, although identifies as African American. Childhood religion Pentecostal Christian. Returned to spiritual practice after long gap, in the wake of receiving terminal cancer diagnosis. Prefers to describe herself as spiritual rather than religious and said, "I'm still very drawn to going to churches, and I'm actually in search at this moment in my life." Registered nurse and healing practitioner. Doctoral student. Heterosexual.

ZENKEI BLANCHE HARTMAN, born 1927. Jewish by birth. Raised in non-religious, leftist household. Current practice Soto Zen Buddhism, abbess of the San Francisco Zen center. Heterosexual.

*demographic profile*

*(Total Number of Interviewees = 50)*

RELIGIOUS OR SPIRITUAL PRACTICE IN ADULT LIFE

| | |
|---|---|
| Christian | 12 (24%) |
| Buddhist | 12 (24%) |
| Hindu/Hindu-derived | 9 (18%) |
| Jewish | 4 (8%) |
| Muslim | 4 (8%) |
| Twelve Step | 2 (4%) |
| Bahai | 1 (2%) |
| Diamond Heart | 1 (2%) |
| Wicca | 1 (2%) |
| Syncretic and/or extra-institutional | 4 (8%) |

| RACE OR ETHNICITY | |
| --- | --- |
| White, including Jews of European descent | 26 (52%) |
| African American | 7 (14%) |
| Chicana/o or Latina/o | 4 (8%) |
| East, South, or Southeast Asian American | 9 (18%) |
| Middle Eastern | 3 (6%) |
| Mixed heritage | 1 (2%) |

Note: Three respondents noted their biracial heritage but did not identify themselves as primarily biracial.

| U.S.-BORN OR IMMIGRANT STATUS | |
| --- | --- |
| U.S.-born | 37 (74%) |
| Immigrant | 13 (26%) |

| AGE | |
| --- | --- |
| 21–30 | 7 (14%) |
| 31–40 | 11 (22%) |
| 41–50 | 17 (34%) |
| 51–60 | 12 (24%) |
| 61+ | 3 (6%) |

| GENDER | |
|---|---|
| Male | 18 (36%) |
| Female | 32 (64%) |

| SEXUALITY | |
|---|---|
| Heterosexual | 32 (64%) |
| Gay | 6 (12%) |
| Lesbian | 10 (20%) |
| Bisexual | 2 (4%) |

## SOCIOECONOMIC STATUS

| | Childhood | Adulthood | Shift |
|---|---|---|---|
| Upper middle class | 16 | 8 | −8 |
| Middle class | 7 | 10 | +3 |
| Lower middle class, Upper working class | 14 | 15 | +1 |
| Poor, Lower working class | 13 | 5 | −8 |
| Disabled | n/a | 2 | +2 |
| Dana, Renunciate, Living simply | n/a | 10 | +10 |

INTRODUCTION

1  For a useful discussion of the history and current popular usage of the word *spirituality*, see Catherine L. Albanese, "Introduction."

2  The marketing of religion and spirituality is a wider phenomenon. Susan Friend Harding analyzes the ways in which Jerry Falwell and televangelists like Pat Robertson, Jimmy Swaggart, and Jim and Tammy Faye Bakker "marketed" their missions in *The Book of Jerry Falwell*, especially chapters 4, 6, and 10. For a trade press book that simultaneously criticizes and participates in the new connection between consumerism and spiritual or religious seeking, see Richard Cimino and Don Lattin, *Shopping for Faith: American Religion and the New Millennium*. As the cover matter for this book puts it, "American religion flourishes in a consumer culture and presents us with a bewildering array of choices as we navigate the shopping mall of faith . . . *Shopping for Faith* is full of practical information for anyone interested in what influences modern American religious practices . . . Its companion CD-ROM is sure to keep you apprised of the latest offerings in America's spiritual supermarket into the next century."

3  Here one sees in play a shift noted by some scholars of religion in the United States—the greater possibility and legitimacy, in recent decades, of individuals choosing and crafting their own religious paths. See for examples Robert Wuthnow's *After Heaven: Spirituality in America Since the 1950s* and Wade Clark Roof's *Spiritual Marketplace: Baby Boomers and the Remaking of American Religion*. As Sadiqa moves between one religion and another she also "gives herself" permission to stay within the religious system of her choice. For she rejects the idea that without the legitimate "entry card" of a teacher,

she must deem herself excluded from belonging. Also visible here is another theme that Roof identifies: the bricolage of modes of naming spiritual and religious themes available to many thanks to new patterns of globalism (*Spiritual Marketplace*, 73; 75).

4 Lopez, "Belief."

5 For a disturbing study of this process, see Lopez's examination of the history of the reception (or rather the construction and distortion) of Tibetan Buddhism in the West, *Prisoners of Shangri-La: Tibetan Buddhism and the West.*

6 Wittgenstein, *The Blue and the Brown Books*, 42.

7 Throughout this book, I will use *United States* rather than *America*, and *United Statesian* rather than *American*, in recognition of the actuality that countries in both the North and South American continents, not just the United States, can justifiably lay claim to that name.

8 Becker and Eiesland, *Contemporary American Religion*, 15.

9 Marty, "Revising the Map of American Religion," 14; 25–26. Marty begins here with the words of self-described artist/sculptor/storyteller Brian Andreas, whose voicings of everyday wisdom-seekers bring to the attention of his audience ways of seeing that are at times new, at times old, frequently quirky, but always provocative. Marty cites Andreas's quote as appearing in *Strange Dreams*. In fact, the statement, which is part of an untitled artwork, appears in an earlier collection, *Mostly True*. The pages in the collection are not numbered.

10 Roof, *Spiritual Marketplace*, 3.

11 Marty, "Revising the Map of American Religion," 17.

12 Roof, *Spiritual Marketplace*, 37.

13 Ammerman, *Congregation and Community*, 3.

14 Note especially Roof's subtitle, *Baby Boomers and the Remaking of American Religion.*

15 Herberg, *Protestant-Catholic-Jew.*

16 For example, Marty, "Revising the Map of American Religion," 24; Roof, *Spiritual Marketplace*, 135.

17 McNamara, "Introduction," xi.

18 Ammerman, *Congregation and Community*, 1.

19 Roof, *Spiritual Marketplace*, 77–110; Harding, *The Book of Jerry Falwell*, chapters 4, 6, 10. The role of the media is a sustained theme in Cimino and Lattin, *Shopping for Faith.*

20 For example, Eiesland, "Contending with a Giant."

21 Among others see Wuthnow, "The Political Rebirth of American Evangelicalism" and *The Restructuring of American Religion.*

22 Ammerman, *Congregation and Community;* Roof and McKinney, "American Mainline Religion."

23 See, for example, Kamenetz, *Stalking Elijah.*

24 See for example Wuthnow, *After Heaven;* Roof, *Spiritual Marketplace,*

7. Roof also notes the eclectic, multifaith materials in the living room of one of his interviewees, but does not comment on it beyond its existence (32).

25 Cimino and Lattin note: "According to a survey of 113,000 Americans by the City University of New York, an overwhelming 86 percent consider themselves Christian. Jews represent 2 percent, whereas Muslims, Buddhists and Hindus have smaller representations. Figures were even smaller for followers of nonconventional religions, such as the New Age movement" (*Shopping for Faith*, 2). While there are weaknesses in this mode of listing, it at least makes clear the numeric predominance of Christian identification in the present-day United States.

26 Elsasser, "Religious Pluralism."

27 Tweed and Prothero's *Asian Religions in America: A Documentary History* offers a thorough engagement with this history. However it must be noted that Islam is not addressed in it, given that the region "West Asia" is known to many, perhaps most, in the United States as the "Middle East."

28 Note here, for example, the much-discussed appearance of then–Vice President Albert Gore at the Hsi Lai Buddhist Temple, Hacienda Heights, California, in April 1998. Less often remarked on in the media, although nonetheless relevant, was the presence at that same reception of several Republican Party officials and the then-mayor of Los Angeles, also a Republican. Here see Chandler, "Placing Palms Together."

29 Moore, "Muslims in Prison"; Dannin, "Island in a Sea of Ignorance"; Parkum and Stultz, "The Angulimala Lineage"; Masters, *Finding Freedom*.

30 Tweed, *Retelling of U.S. Religious History*, 10.

31 Albanese, "Exchanging Selves."

32 Ibid., 224.

33 For a forceful discussion of anthropological engagements with rationality, see Stoller, "Rationality."

34 *The Compact Oxford English Dictionary*, 2nd edition (Oxford: Clarendon Press, 1991).

35 See also Stoller, "Rationality."

36 McClenon, "Spiritual Healing and Folklore Research," 65.

37 Ibid., 65.

38 Brown, "Telling a Life."

39 Sarris, "Telling Dreams."

40 Brown, "Telling a Life," 23–26; Sarris, "Telling Dreams," 63–76.

41 Orsi, *Thank you, Saint Jude*, xxi.

42 Rochford, *Hare Krishna in America*, 9.

43 Harding, *The Gospel of Jerry Falwell*, 33.

44 Ibid., 34.

45 Ibid., 36.

46 Ibid., 155–56.

47 Brown, "Telling a Life," 24, 25.

48 Ibid., 33–34.

49 Ibid., 34.

50 An interesting collection of essays on ethnographic practice, religion, and the positioning of the researcher is James V. Spickard, J. Shawn Landres, and Meredith B. McGuire's *Personal Knowledge and Beyond: Reshaping the Ethnography of Religion.*

51 Mechling, "Rethinking (and Reteaching)."

52 Ibid., 65, quoting James, *The Varieties of Religious Experience,* 31.

53 Ibid., quoting Berger, *A Rumor of Angels,* 2.

54 Ibid., quoting Berger, *The Sacred Canopy,* 43.

55 Ibid., 66–67.

56 Ibid., 67.

57 Ibid., quoting Geertz, "Religion as a Cultural System," 90.

58 Ibid.

59 It must be noted that, unfortunately but perhaps inevitably, this group of interviewees does not comprise a comprehensive reflection of the religious landscape of the United States. It should especially be noted that the study does not include any individuals practicing Native American spiritual traditions. Nor is there anyone here involved in the Yoruba-derived practices of the African diaspora.

60 The exception here is former Bay Area resident Arinna Weisman, a regular teacher at Spirit Rock Meditation Center, outside San Francisco. At the time of this research, Weisman was the only openly lesbian teacher of Vipassana in the United States.

61 For more on the subject, see Linzer, *Torah and Dharma;* Kamenetz, *The Jew in the Lotus;* Boorstein, *That's Funny, You Don't Look Buddhist.*


CHAPTER 1 : TALKING TO GOD

1 Schmidt, *Hearing Things,* vii; see also Schmidt, *Holy Fairs.*

2 Ibid., 15.

3 Ibid., 21–22.

4 Ibid., 28.

5 Ibid., 30. Philip A. Mellor and Chris Shilling, in *Re-forming the Body: Religion, Community and Community,* argue in a related fashion that the "re-formulation" of the body through three periods—first, the medieval period, second, the Protestant reformation, and, third, what they term "baroque modernity" [not postmodernity]—has been protracted and is by no means complete.

6   Wolterstorff, *Divine Discourse*, 262–63.

7   See especially ibid., 261–80.

8   Ibid., 261.

9   As will be discussed later in this chapter, the term *guru* is a complex one. In this text I do not use the word to signal "teacher" in the general sense. Rather my focus is on specific spiritual teachers emergent from the Hindu tradition, some of whom are deemed "avatar" or incarnation of the divine, and all of whom are recognized for their *siddhis* or unusual spiritual skills and qualities.

10  Strikingly enough, Homer's approach here seems firmly Lockean in the ways that that approach is articulated by Wolterstorff, *Divine Discourse*, 262–73.

11  Wuthnow, *After Heaven*, especially chapters 1, 7.

12  Frankenberg, "The Poetics of Healing."

13  Taken from material produced by the Institute for BioSpiritual Research, PO Box 741137, Arvada, CO 80006-1137.

14  *Sophia* is a name for the divine in its aspects as female and for the linking of divinity to wisdom. On the history of this name, and traditions and practices associated with it, see for example Schaup, *Sophia*.

15  Frankenberg, "The Poetics of Healing."

16  The first Hindu teacher to come to the United States on an official basis was Swami Vivekanananda. He spoke at the Worlds' Parliament of Religions, Chicago, 1893.

17  Gold, "Guru's Body, Guru's Abode," 231.

18  Mani, "An Empty Quest?"

19  My difference from Gold stems from the way *tradition* is construed here. Gold tends to see such reformulations of traditional practice as "modern." But such reworkings are integral to Hinduism's history. As Arvind Sharma has pointed out, "The principle that though moral laws are eternal, their actual application is mutable is important for understanding Hinduism" (*Our Religions*, 28). This, he argues, is characteristic of a religion that is "definitional without being definitive" (26).

20  For a discussion of the guru's role and functioning in relationship with devotees, see Gold, "Guru's Body, Guru's Abode."

21  For comparable descriptions, see ibid., 233, 238.

22  For a succinct introduction and commentary on Hinduism, see Sharma, "Hinduism."

23  Orsi, *The Madonna of 115ᵗʰ Street* and *Thank you, Saint Jude*.

24  *The Compact Oxford English Dictionary*, 2nd edition (Oxford: Clarendon Press, 1991), 471.

CHAPTER 2 : MIND EMBODIED

1 See for example Kasulis, "Editor's Introduction," especially 2–5. Neither Kasulis in his succinct discussion of Yuasa Yasuo, nor Yuasa
himself, insists that bodies might initiate mental activity, or usurp
minds' status. Rather, Yuasa argues for bodies and minds as working
inevitably and necessarily in conjunction in order to enhance selfhood
and subjecthood. Thus there is in Yuasa's analysis a body that is the
holder of knowledges and that applies those in a relatively autonomous fashion. As well, the experience and indeed daily work of spiritual healers such as Mama Lola and Mabel McKay, discussed very
briefly in the introduction to this book, require the presence and
praxis of bodies acting in ways beyond the sole control or "forward
planning" of minds. See Brown, *Mama Lola;* Sarris, *Mabel McKay:*
*Weaving the Dream.*

2 LaFleur, "Body," 37; reference to Feyer with Nadaff and Tazi, *Frag-*
*ments.*

3 Turner, "The Body in Western Society," 17.

4 Ibid., 15–16.

5 Scheper-Hughes, "Embodied Knowledge," 231.

6 Bynum, "Bodily Miracles," 69.

7 Ibid., 68–69.

8 Ibid., 68–106; for a reading of the European medieval body's continuing relevance to the contemporary period, see Mellor and Shilling, *Re-*
*forming the Body.*

9 Asad, "Remarks," 48, n. 10.

10 A project more ambiguous in its results is that of Thomas Csordas's
"Embodiment as a Paradigm for Anthropology." His examination of
the place of bodies in Christian charismatic healing events proposes to
develop a "paradigm of embodiment." Yet it quickly gives way to
conclusions that explain away at least some of the fieldwork findings
by means of semiotic analyses of maladies, as well as to hypotheses of
group pressure, in analyzing group responses to healing situations. My
point here is not, it should be emphasized, to assess the efficacy of
these group healings. Rather, I note the difficulty of developing and
retaining a "body-centered" frame of analysis.

11 Coakley, "Introduction: Religion and the Body," 2.

12 Yuasa, *The Body,* 24–25.

13 Ibid., 25.

14 Kasulis, "Introduction."

15 For a discussion of the rich symbology of the dove across a range of
religions and cultures, see Rubin, "The Dove."

16 For a brief summation of a study of Soto Zen practice in the United
States drawing on the Berkeley Zen Center, see Coleman, "The New

Buddhism"; see also the longer and fuller version, *The New Buddhism: The Western Transformation of an Ancient Tradition*.

17 A useful introduction to and review of the contemporary state of Vipassana practice in the United States is Gil Fronsdal's "Insight Meditation in the United States: On Life, Liberty and the Pursuit of Happiness"; see also Coleman, "The New Buddhism" and *The New Buddhism*.

CHAPTER 3 : PLACE AND PRACTICE

1 Several books are helpful in providing introductions to, and analyses of, Islam and Buddhism in the contemporary United States. Two valuable collections on Islam in the United States are Yvonne Yazbeck Haddad's *The Muslims of America* and Haddad and Janet Idleman Smith's *Muslim Communities in North America* (here, see in particular Haddad's "Muslim Communities in North America: Introduction," xvii–xxx); also Barbara Daly Metcalf's *Making Muslim Space in North America and Europe*, especially her "Introduction: Sacred Words, Sanctioned Practice, New Communities," 1–30. For a rich survey collection on Buddhism in the United States, see Charles Prebish and Kenneth Tanaka's *The Faces of Buddhism in America*. Prebish's "Introduction" (1–10) and Tanaka's "Epilogue" (287–98) map the field and speculate on its future. See also Prebish's *Luminous Passage: The Practice and Study of Buddhism in America* and James Wellman Coleman's *The New Buddhism: The Western Transformation of an Ancient Tradition*. Beyond specifically Buddhist and Islamic studies, see also R. Stephen Warner and Judith G. Wittner's *Gatherings in Diaspora: Religious Communities and the New Immigration*, which examines the relationships between immigration and religion in the United States (especially pertinent to the themes of this chapter is Warner's "Immigration and Religious Communities in the United States").

2 In this regard, see for example Warner's "Immigration and Religious Communities in the United States," 9; 16–18; 20–22.

3 Haddad notes that one key theme in the burgeoning U.S. Muslim world is the effort to honor and build bridges across the diversity *within* that community (Haddad, "Muslim Communities").

4 See for example Dillon, *Catholic Identity*; Roof, *Spiritual Marketplace*; Wuthnow, *After Heaven*.

5 As Haddad puts it, "One of the significant and motivating factors in the communities under consideration is the necessity of understanding their identity and role within American society and culture in the context of a long-standing and continuing atmosphere of prejudice and misunderstanding" (Haddad, "Muslim Communities," xxvii). These interviews took place prior to the 11 September 2001 attacks on

the World Trade Center and Pentagon, attributed by the U.S. government to al-Qaeda, a militant Muslim political group. These events have increased the anti-Muslim sentiment and worsened the situations of Muslims in the United States.

6   For example, as Charles Prebish points out, it was during the years of internment that the Buddhist Mission of North America, which accounted for the majority of Japanese American Buddhists, changed its name, becoming the Buddhist Churches of America (*Luminous Passage*, 22).

7   For analysis of this process in a predominantly immigrant setting, see Numrich, *Old Wisdom;* for a study of such changes in predominantly white convert Buddhist institutions, see Coleman, *The New Buddhism.*

8   See for example the multiracial collection Adams et al., *Making the Invisible Visible;* also, Fields, "Divided Dharma."

9   See for example Takaki, *Strangers.*

10  T. Liên Shutt, "Vietnamese American Thoughts on Being a Buddhist in America," in Adams et al., *Making the Invisible Visible,* 23.

11  See chapter 5 for further discussion of retreats of this kind.

12  Examples of the effort to integrate Buddhism and Western psychotherapy include Epstein, *Thoughts without a Thinker;* and Wilbur, Engler, and Brown, *Transformation of Consciousness.* For a contrastive perspective on the subject see Imamura, "Buddhist and Western Psychotherapies."

13  For discussion of the ongoing process of negotiating authority as Tibetan Buddhist practice moves to the United States, see Lavine, "Tibetan Buddhism in America"; for a discussion of processes of "democratization" in a range of Buddhist orders in the United States, see Tanaka, "Epilogue."

CHAPTER 4 : THE SPIRIT OF THE WORK

1   Albanese, "Introduction."

2   Ibid., 1.

3   Ricky Sherover-Marcuse's approach to antiracist pedagogy built on her own research on Marxism and the Frankfurt School of sociocultural criticism, put together with the theory and method of Harvey Jackins, founder of Re-evaluation Counseling. Sherover-Marcuse designed and conducted Unlearning Racism Workshops throughout the United States and abroad in the 1980s. These workshops invited participants to draw on their own life experience as a basis for understanding how structures of oppression constructed individuals' own subjectivity. Sherover-Marcuse proposed, and the workshops demonstrated, that altering one's consciousness was a tool that could help challenge both external systems of domination and one's unwitting

reproduction of them. The method was quickly expanded to engage other forms of domination, including those based on anti-Semitism, sexism, and homophobia. See Sherover-Marcuse, *Emancipation and Consciousness.*

CHAPTER 5 : CONSCIOUS SEX, SACRED CELIBACY

1  Boswell, *Christianity, Social Tolerance, and Homosexuality,* 5–6.
2  In this regard see also Olyan and Nussbaum, *Sexual Orientation and Human Rights.*
3  The Dalai Lama's position was a complex one that appeared to give with one hand what it took away with the other. See "Dalai Lama Meets with Lesbian and Gay Leaders," *Turning Wheel: Journal of the Buddhist Peace Fellowship* (fall 1997): 25.
4  For discussion of the complex status of same-sex sexuality in Islam (mainly focused on men) see Murray and Roscoe, *Islamic Homosexualities.*
5  For a cross-cultural collection of essays on the meanings of celibacy, see Sobo and Bell, *Celibacy, Culture and Society.*
6  Of relevance here is Southgate, "A Swallow in Winter."
7  Related work in this area includes Alpert, *Like Bread on the Seder Plate;* Balka and Rose, *Twice Blessed;* Boswell, *Christianity, Social Tolerance, and Homosexuality;* Corless, "Gay Buddhist Fellowship"; Dillon, *Catholic Identity;* Glaser, *Uncommon Calling;* Hartman, *Congregations in Conflict;* Holtz, *Listen to The Stories;* Leyland, *Queer Dharma;* Nugent, *A Challenge to Love;* Shallenberger, *Reclaiming the Spirit;* Shneer and Aviv, *Queer Jews;* Tigert, *Coming Out While Staying In.*
8  Alan Senauke, "Interview with Thich Nhat Hahn," *Turning Wheel: Journal of the Buddhist Peace Fellowship* (winter 1998): 33–34.
9  Nancy McKay's experience was hardly singular. See for example Hartman, *Congregations in Conflict,* especially 1–24.
10  Several men and women interviewed by Michele Dillon also spoke of the pain and confusion of growing up gay or lesbian and Catholic (*Catholic Identity,* 128–29).
11  Ibid., especially 85–95.
12  Dignity/Boston is a contrary case—there, Holy Unions *have* been celebrated (Dillon, *Catholic Identity,* 135–37).
13  Substantiating Paul Wooley's point here, see Dillon, *Catholic Identity,* 79–82 and elsewhere.

EPILOGUE

1  Weisman and Smith, *The Beginner's Guide to Insight Meditation.*

Adams, Sheridan, et al., eds. *Making the Invisible Visible: Healing Racism in Our Buddhist Communities* (Berkeley, Calif., 2000) [self-published: available through Buddhist Peace Fellowship, Berkeley].

Albanese, Catherine. "Exchanging Selves, Exchanging Souls: Contact, Combination and American Religious History." In *Retelling U.S. Religious History,* edited by Thomas Tweed, 200–226. Berkeley: University of California Press, 1997.

———. Introduction to *American Spiritualities: A Reader,* 1–15. Bloomington: Indiana University Press, 2001.

Alpert, Rebecca. *Like Bread on the Seder Plate: Jewish Lesbians and the Transformation of Tradition.* New York: Columbia University Press, 1997.

Ammerman, Nancy Tatom. *Congregation and Community.* New Brunswick, N.J.: Rutgers University Press, 1998.

Andreas, Brian. *Mostly True: Collected Stories and Drawings.* Decorah, Iowa: StoryPeople, 1993.

———. *Strange Dreams: Collected Stories and Drawings.* Decorah, Iowa: StoryPeople, 1996.

Asad, Talal. "Remarks on the Anthropology of the Body." In *Religion and the Body,* edited by Sarah Coakley, 42–52. Cambridge: Cambridge University Press, 1997.

Balka, Christie, and Andy Rose, eds. *Twice Blessed: On Being Lesbian, Gay, and Jewish.* Boston: Beacon Press, 1989.

Becker, Penny Edgell, and Nancy Eiesland, eds. *Contemporary American Religion: An Ethnographic Reader.* Walnut Creek, Calif.: Alta Mira Press, 1997.

Berger, Peter L. *The Sacred Canopy: Elements of a Sociological Theory of Religion.* New York: Anchor/Doubleday, 1962.

——. *A Rumor of Angels: Modern Society and the Rediscovery of the Super-natural.* Garden City, N.Y.: Anchor/Doubleday, 1969.

Boorstein, Sylvia. *That's Funny, You Don't Look Buddhist.* San Francisco: HarperSanFrancisco, 1998.

Boswell, John. *Christianity, Social Tolerance, and Homosexuality: Gay People in Western Europe from the Beginning of the Christian Era to the Fourteenth Century.* Chicago: University of Chicago Press, 1980.

Brown, Karen McCarthy. *Mama Lola: A Vodou Priestess in Brooklyn.* Berkeley: University of California Press, 1991.

——. "Telling a Life through Haitian Vodou: An Essay Concerning Race, Gender, Memory, And Historical Consciousness." In *Religion and Cultural Studies,* edited by Susan L. Mizruchi, 22–37. Princeton: Princeton University Press, 2001.

Bynum, Caroline Walker. "Bodily Miracles and the Resurrection of the Body in the High Middle Ages." In *Belief in History: Innovative Approaches to European and American Religion,* edited by Thomas Kselman, 68–106. Notre Dame: Notre Dame University Press, 1991.

Chandler, Stuart. "Placing Palms Together: Religious and Cultural Dimensions of the Hsi Lai Temple Political Donations Controversy." In *American Buddhism: Methods and Findings in Recent Scholarship,* edited by Duncan Ryuken Williams and Christopher S. Queen, 36–56. Richmond, Surrey: Curzon Press, 1999.

Cimino, Richard, and Don Lattin. *Shopping for Faith: American Religion and the New Millenium.* San Francisco: Jossey Bass, 1998.

Coakley, Sarah. "Introduction: Religion and the Body." In *Religion and the Body,* 1–12. Cambridge: Cambridge University Press, 1997.

Coleman, James William. "The New Buddhism: Some Empirical Findings." In *American Buddhism: Methods and Findings in Recent Scholarship,* edited by Duncan Ryuken Williams and Christopher S. Queen, 91–99. Richmond, Surrey: Curzon Press, 1999.

——. *The New Buddhism: The Western Transformation of an Ancient Tradition.* New York: Oxford University Press, 2001.

Corless, Roger. "Gay Buddhist Fellowship." In *Engaged Buddhism in the West,* edited by Christopher S. Queen, 269–79. Boston: Wisdom Publications, 2000.

Csordas, Thomas J. "Embodiment as a Paradigm for Anthropology." *Ethos* 18, no. 1 (1990): 5–47.

Dannin, Robert. "Island in a Sea of Ignorance: Dimensions of the Prison Mosque." In *Making Muslim Space in North American and Europe,* edited by Barbara Daly Metcalf, 131–46. Berkeley: University of California Press, 1996.

Dillon, Michele. *Catholic Identity: Balancing Reason, Faith and Power.* Cambridge: Cambridge University Press, 1999.

Eiesland, Nancy L. "Contending with a Giant: The Impact of a Megachurch on Exurban Religious Institutions." In *Contemporary American Religion: An Ethnographic Reader,* edited by Penny Edgell Becker and Nancy Eiesland, 191–221. Walnut Creek, Calif.: Alta Mira Press, 1997.

Elsasser, Glen. "Religious Pluralism is Newest Theater for Military Action." *Wisconsin State Journal,* 13 May 1999, 7A.

Epstein, Mark. *Thoughts without a Thinker.* New York: Basic Books, 1995.

Feyer, Michel, with Ramona Nadaff and Nadia Tazi. *Fragments for a History of the Human Body,* 3 vols. New York: Zone Books, 1989.

Fields, Rick. "Divided Dharma: White Buddhists, Ethnic Buddhists, and Racism." In *The Faces of Buddhism in America,* edited by Charles Prebish and Kenneth Tanaka, 196–206. Berkeley: University of California Press, 1998.

Frankenberg, Ruth. "The Poetics of Healing: A Sociocultural Perspective." Paper presented at the Conference on Health, Healing and Spirituality, Indian Society of Health Administrators, Bangalore, India, 13 December 1999.

Fronsdal, Gil. "Insight Meditation in the United States: On Life, Liberty and the Pursuit of Happiness." In *The Faces of Buddhism in America,* edited by Charles Prebish and Kenneth Tanaka, 163–80. Berkeley: University of California Press, 1998.

Geertz, Clifford. "Religion as a Cultural System." In *The Interpretation of Cultures.* New York: Basic Books, 1973.

Glaser, Chris. *Uncommon Calling: A Gay Man's Struggle to Serve the Church.* San Francisco: Harper and Row, 1988.

Gold, Daniel. "Guru's Body, Guru's Abode." In *Religious Reflections on the Human Body,* edited by Jane Marie Law, 230–50. Bloomington: Indiana University Press, 1995.

Haddad, Yvonne Yazbeck, ed. *The Muslims of America.* New York: Oxford University Press, 1991.

Haddad, Yvonne Yazbeck, and Janet Idleman Smith, eds. *Muslim Communities in North America.* Albany: SUNY Press, 1994.

Harding, Susan Friend. *The Book of Jerry Falwell: Fundamentalist Language and Politics.* Princeton: Princeton University Press, 2000.

Hartman, Keith. *Congregations in Conflict: The Battle over Homosexuality.* New Brunswick, N.J.: Rutgers University Press, 1996.

Herberg, Will. *Protestant-Catholic-Jew.* Garden City, N.Y.: Anchor Books, 1955.

Holtz, Raymond C. *Listen to The Stories: Gay and Lesbian Catholics Talk About Their Lives and the Church.* New York: Garland Publishing, 1991.

Imamura, Ryo. "Buddhist and Western Psychotherapies: An Asian American Perspective." In *The Faces of Buddhism in America,* edited by Charles Prebish and Kenneth Tanaka, 228–37. Berkeley: University of California Press, 1998.

James, William. *The Varieties of Religious Experience*. 1902. Reprint, New York: Penguin, 1982.

Kamenetz, Rodger. *The Jew in the Lotus: A Poet's Rediscovery of Jewish Identity in Buddhist India*. San Francisco: HarperSanFrancisco, 1994.

——. *Stalking Elijah: Adventures with Today's Jewish Mystical Masters*. San Francisco: HarperSanFrancisco, 1997.

Kasulis, Thomas P. "Editor's Introduction." In *The Body: Toward an Eastern Mind-Body Theory*, by Yuasa Yasuo, translated by Nagatomo Shigenori and T. P. Kasulis, 1–15. Albany: SUNY Press, 1987.

——. Introduction to *Self as Body in Asian Theory and Practice*, edited by Thomas P. Kasulis with Roger T. Ames and Wimal Dissanayake, xi–xxii. Albany: SUNY Press, 1993.

LaFleur, William. "Body." In *Critical Terms for Religious Studies*, edited by Mark C. Taylor, 36–54. Chicago: University of Chicago Press, 1998.

Lavine, Amy. "Tibetan Buddhism in America: The Development of American Vajrayana." In *The Faces of Buddhism in America*, edited by Charles Prebish and Kenneth Tanaka, 99–115. Berkeley: University of California Press, 1998.

Leyland, Winston, ed. *Queer Dharma: Voices of Gay Buddhists*. San Francisco: Gay Sunshine Press, 1998.

——. *Queer Dharma: Voices of Gay Buddhists*. Vol. 2. San Francisco: Gay Sunshine Press, 2000.

Linzer, Judith. *Torah and Dharma: Jewish Seekers in Eastern Religions*. Northvale, N.J.: Jason Aronson, 1996.

Lopez, Donald S. Jr. "Belief." In *Critical Terms for Religious Studies*, edited by Mark C. Taylor, 21–35. Chicago: University of Chicago Press, 1998.

——. *Prisoners of Shangri-La: Tibetan Buddhism and the West*. Chicago: University of Chicago Press, 1998.

Mani, Lata. "An Empty Quest?" *Humanscape* (January 2001): 20–22.

Marty, Martin E. "Revising the Map of American Religion." In "Americans and Religions in the Twenty-First Century," edited by Wade Clark Roof. *Annals of the American Academy of Political and Social Science* 558 (July 1998): 13–27.

Masters, Jarvis Jay. *Finding Freedom: Writings from Death Row*. Junction City, Calif.: Padma Publishing, 1997.

McClenon, James. "Spiritual Healing and Folklore Research: Evaluating the Hypnosis/Placebo Theory." *Alternative Therapies* 3, no. 1 (1997): 61–65.

McNamara, Patrick H. Introduction to *Religion: North American Style*, edited by Thomas E. Dowdy and Patrick H. McNamara, xi–xii. New Brunswick, N.J.: Rutgers University Press, 1997.

Mechling, Jay. "Rethinking (and Reteaching) the Civil Religion in Post-Nationalist American Studies." In *Post-Nationalist American Studies*, edited by Jon Carlos Rowe, 63–83. Berkeley: University of California Press, 2000.

Mellor, Philip A., and Chris Shilling. *Re-forming the Body: Religion, Community and Modernity.* London: Sage Publications, 1997.

Metcalf, Barbara Daly, ed. *Making Muslim Space in North America and Europe.* Berkeley: University of California Press, 1996.

Moore, Kathleen. "Muslims in Prison: Claims to Constitutional Protection of Religious Liberty." In *The Muslims of America,* edited by Yvonne Yazbeck Haddad, 136–56. New York: Oxford University Press, 1991.

Murray, Stephen O., and Will Roscoe, eds. *Islamic Homosexualities: Culture, History and Literature.* New York: New York University Press, 1997.

Nugent, Robert, ed. *A Challenge to Love: Gay and Lesbian Catholics in the Church.* New York: Crossroad, 1989.

Numrich, Paul David. *Old Wisdom in the New World: Americanization in Two Immigrant Theravada Buddhist Temples.* Knoxville: University of Tennessee Press, 1996.

Olyan, Saul, and Martha C. Nussbaum, eds. *Sexual Orientation and Human Rights in American Religious Discourse.* New York: Oxford University Press, 1998.

Orsi, Robert. *The Madonna of 115th Street: Faith and Community in Italian Harlem, 1880–1950.* New Haven: Yale University Press, 1985.

———. *Thank You, Saint Jude: Women's Devotion to the Patron Saint of Hopeless Causes.* New Haven: Yale University Press, 1995.

Parkum, Virginia Cohn, and J. Anthony Stultz. "The Angulimala Lineage: Buddhist Prison Ministries." In *Engaged Buddhism in the West,* edited by Christopher S. Queen, 347–71. Boston: Wisdom Publications, 2000.

Prebish, Charles. *Luminous Passage: The Practice and Study of Buddhism in America.* Berkeley: University of California Press, 1999.

Prebish, Charles S., and Kenneth K. Tanaka, eds. *The Faces of Buddhism in America.* Berkeley: University of California Press, 1998.

Rinpoche, Sogyal. *The Tibetan Book of Living and Dying,* edited by Patrick Gaffney and Andrew Harvey. San Francisco: HarperSanFrancisco, 1993.

Rochford, E. Burke Jr. *Hare Krishna in America.* Newark, N.J.: Rutgers University Press, 1991.

Roof, Wade Clark. *Spiritual Marketplace: Baby Boomers and the Remaking of American Religion.* Princeton: Princeton University Press, 1999.

Roof, Wade Clark, and William McKinney. "American Mainline Religion: Its Changing Shape and Future." In *Religion: North American Style,* edited by Thomas E. Dowdy and Patrick H. McNamara, 66–80. New Brunswick, N.J.: Rutgers University Press, 1997.

Rubin, Norman A. "The Dove." *The Holy Land,* online edition, 1999.

Sarris, Greg. "A Culture under Glass: The Pomo Basket." In *Keeping Slug Woman Alive: A Holistic Approach to American Indian Texts,* 51–62. Berkeley: University of California Press, 1993.

———. "Telling Dreams and Keeping Secrets: The Bole Maru as American Indian Religious Resistance." In *Keeping Slug Woman Alive: A Holistic*

*Approach to American Indian Texts*, 63–76. Berkeley: University of California Press, 1993.

——. *Mabel McKay: Weaving the Dream*, Berkeley: University of California Press, 1994.

Schaup, Susanne. *Sophia: Aspects of the Divine Feminine, Past and Present.* York Beach, Maine: Nicholas Hays, 1997.

Scheper-Hughes, Nancy. "Embodied Knowledge: Thinking with the Body in Critical Medical Anthropology." In *Assessing Cultural Anthropology,* edited by Robert Borofsky, 229–39. New York: McGraw-Hill, 1994.

Schmidt, Leigh Eric. *Holy Fairs, Scottish Communions and American Revivals in the Early Modern Period.* Princeton: Princeton University Press, 1989.

——. *Hearing Things: Religion, Illusion and the American Enlightenment.* Cambridge: Harvard University Press, 2000.

Shallenberger, David. *Reclaiming the Spirit: Gay Men and Lesbians Come to Terms with Religion.* New Brunswick, N.J.: Rutgers University Press, 1998.

Sharma, Arvind. "Hinduism." In *Our Religions,* 3–67. San Francisco: HarperSanFrancisco, 1993.

Sherover-Marcuse, Erica. *Emancipation and Consciousness: Dogmatic and Dialectical Perspectives on the Early Marx.* Oxford: Basil Blackwell, 1986.

Shneer, David, and Caryn Aviv, eds. *Queer Jews,* New York: Routledge, 2002.

Sobo, Elisa J., and Sandra Bell, eds. *Celibacy, Culture and Society: The Anthropology of Sexual Abstinence.* Madison: University of Wisconsin Press, 2000.

Southgate, Paul. "A Swallow in Winter: A Catholic Priesthood Viewpoint." In *Celibacy, Culture and Society: The Anthropology of Sexual Abstinence,* edited by Elisa J. Sobo and Sandra Bell, 246–63. Madison: University of Wisconsin Press, 2000.

Spickard, James V., J. Shawn Landres, and Meredith B. McGuire, eds. *Personal Knowledge and Beyond: Reshaping the Ethnography of Religion.* New York: New York University Press, 2002.

Stoller, Paul. "Rationality." In *Critical Terms for Religious Studies,* edited by Mark C. Taylor, 239–55. Chicago: University of Chicago Press, 1998.

Takaki, Ronald. *Strangers from a Different Shore: A History of Asian Americans.* New York: Penguin, 1989.

Tanaka, Kenneth. "Epilogue: The Colors and Contours of American Buddhism." In *The Faces of Buddhism in America,* edited by Charles Prebish and Kenneth Tanaka, 287–98. Berkeley: University of California Press, 1998.

Tigert, Jeanne McCall. *Coming Out While Staying In: Struggles and Celebrations of Lesbians, Gays and Bisexuals in the Church.* Cleveland: United Church Press, 1996.

Turner, Bryan S. "The Body in Western Society: Social Theory and its Perspectives." In *Religion and the Body,* edited by Sarah Coakley, 15–41. Cambridge: Cambridge University Press, 1997.

Tweed, Thomas A., ed. *Retelling U.S. Religious History.* Berkeley: University of California Press, 1997.

Tweed, Thomas A., and Stephen Prothero, eds. *Asian Religions in America: A Documentary History.* New York: Oxford University Press, 1999.

Warner, R. Stephen. "Immigration and Religious Communities in the United States." In *Gatherings in Diaspora: Religious Communities and the New Immigration,* edited by R. Stephen Warner and Judith G. Wittner, 3–34. Philadelphia: Temple University Press, 1998.

Warner, R. Stephen, and Judith G. Wittner, eds. *Gatherings in Diaspora: Religious Communities and the New Immigration.* Philadelphia: Temple University Press, 1998.

Weisman, Arinna, and Jean Smith. *The Beginner's Guide to Insight Meditation.* New York: Bell Tower, 2001.

Wilbur, Kenneth, J. Engler, and D. P. Brown. *Transformation of Consciousness: Conventional and Contemplative Perspectives on Development.* Boston: Shambhala, 1986.

Wittgenstein, Ludwig. *The Blue and the Brown Books.* New York: Harper and Row, 1958.

Wolterstorff, Nicholas. *Divine Discourse: Philosophical Reflections on the Claim That God Speaks.* New York: Cambridge University Press, 1995.

Wuthnow, Robert. "The Political Rebirth of American Evangelicalism." In *The New Christian Right,* edited by R. Liebman and R. Wuthnow, 167–87. Hawthorne, N.Y.: Aldine, 1988.

———. *The Restructuring of American Religion.* Princeton: Princeton University Press, 1988.

———. *After Heaven: Spirituality in America Since the 1950s.* Berkeley: University of California Press, 1998.

Yasuo, Yuasa. *The Body: Toward an Eastern Mind-Body Theory.* Edited by Thomas P. Kasulis. Translated by Nagatomo Shigenori and T. P. Kasulis. Albany: SUNY Press, 1987.

consciousness and mind embodiment, 77–78, 130
conversion, 16–17
counterculture, 162
Csordas, Thomas, 286 n. 10
cultivation vs. spontaneity, 232–33, 262–63, 266
cursillo, 41, 42, 43–44

Dalai Lama, 220, 289 n. 3
dana (payment by donation), 27
Darshan, 55–56, 272
Dass, Ram, 99
Davis, Avram, 90–93, 94, 96, 128, 131, 266, 272
Desert Fathers, 48
Desert Storm, 98–100
Dhamma Dena Meditation Center (Northampton, Mass.), 266
*dharmadhatu* (meditation center), 183. *See also* meditation
Diamond Heart Path, 24, 174, 179, 180, 208–9
Dignity, 256–58, 259, 262, 289 n. 12
disability and spiritual practice, 118–27, 129
diversity, sexual, 214, 216, 225, 230, 236, 245, 260–61, 263
diversity and anti-oppression work, 174–211; church membership and, 176–78, 208; community and belonging and, 179, 180; connectedness and collective existence and, 195–200, 210; Diamond Heart Path and, 179, 180, 208–9; dreams and, 176–79, 183–84, 210; egalitarianism and, 210–11; gay and lesbian identity and, 189–92, 198–99; goals of, 208; grace and, 189–91, 192, 209, 210; internalized oppression and, 200, 203, 204; intuition and feelings vs. rationality and logic, 180; meditation and, 183, 184, 209; men's groups and, 178,

180; process-oriented psychology and, 183; through Re-evaluation Counseling, 200, 202–4, 209, 288 n. 3; secular analyses of oppression, 175, 183–84, 185; self-knowledge and self-inquiry and, 179, 180–81, 184–85, 189, 191–92, 210–11; Siddha Yoga and, 187–89, 192, 209; Soto Zen Buddhism and, 201, 204–7, 209; spirit as presence in, 175, 194–95; Tibetan Buddhism and, 181–82, 184, 209; universality and, 205–7; through Unlearning Racism Workshops, 200, 288–89 n. 3; through Untraining (racism) workshops, 181, 184–85, 209, 210; Wiccan Paganism and, 194; through workshops on diversity, 178, 179–81, 186, 189–92, 196–200; zazen meditation and, 204
divine guidance and intervention, 44–46, 54, 64–65, 68–69, 73–74, 251
Divine Mother, 64–65
divine rationality (sacred reason), 46–47, 48, 53–54, 70, 73
dreaming: diversity and anti-oppression work and, 176–79, 183–84, 210; lucid, 101–2; prophetic, 93–103, 129, 131

East Bay Church of Religious Science (Oakland), 194, 245–46, 250, 262
eating disorders, 83–86, 129
ecstasy, 20, 22
egalitarianism, 210–11
Eiesland, Nancy, 5
embodiment of mind. *See* mind embodiment
Engaged Buddhism, 239
Enigma, 55, 135–36, 138–42, 148–49, 223–26, 228–30, 268, 273
enlightenment, 182

*hejab* (head cover), 140
Herberg, Will, 6–7
heteronormativity, 212, 213–14, 216–17, 219, 224, 237, 239, 261, 263
Hildegard of Bingen, 48
Hinduism: anklets' significance in, 62–63; *Bhagavad Gita*, 188; Christianity vs., 71–76; decenteredness of institutions and practices in, 72; Divine Mother in, 64–65; Ganesh in, 66–67, 68, 70; Godtalk in, 55–63, 70; gurus and teachers of, 55–65, 285 n. 16; in India, 55–57; Kashmiri Shaivite, 187; Parvati in, 66–67, 68, 70; Shiva in, 66–67, 68, 70; traditional vs. modern practice in, 57, 285 n. 19; U.S. presence of, 8, 283 n. 25
HIV-AIDS, 249–50
homophobia, 189–92, 198–99, 219–20, 238–40, 252, 253
homosexuality. *See* gays and lesbians
Hope Central Church, 248–50, 252, 255
Horton, Robert, 174–75, 181–85, 192, 208–9, 219–20, 275
Hsi Lai Buddhist Temple (Hacienda Heights, Calif.), 283 n. 28

immigration, 67–68
Immigration and Naturalization Service (INS), 67
Indian Hinduism, 55–57
Insight Meditation Society (Barre, Mass.), 114–15
interviewees: biographical summaries of, 271–76; demographic makeup of, 25–28, 277–79, 284 n. 60; harmonization of daily and spiritual lives of, 28–32; religious makeup of, 22–25, 277, 284 n. 59; self-questioning by, 32
intuition and feelings, 180

ISKCON (Krishna Consciousness) movement, 15
Islam: alcohol and drugs avoided in, 135; Americanism and, 268–69; clothing of women in, 135–36, 140, 142–43, 223; converts in United States to, 142–45; diet in, 140; diversity in United States among, 136, 148, 287 n. 3; fasting in, 135; femininity and, 223; immigrants' place, 134–42, 149; as marked and other, 133, 142, 148–49, 287–88 n. 5; prayer in, 136, 140–41; scholarship on U.S. presence of, 8–9, 283 n. 25, 283 n. 27; September 11 attacks and, 265, 287–88 n. 5; sexuality in, 224. *See also* Nation of Islam

Jackins, Harvey, 288 n. 3
Jacobson, David, 58, 226–30, 234, 272
James, William, 19–20, 21
Jerrahi Order (of Sufism), 146–47
Jesus, 52–54, 71–72
Jones, Derek, 40–48, 54, 72, 74, 216, 272
Judaism, 7–8, 240–41. *See also* Chochmat HaLev Center for the Study and Practice of Jewish Meditation
Jude, Saint, 14
Judeo-Christian tradition, in United States, 6–8, 283 nn. 24–25
Jung, Carl, 74

Kali, 62–63
Kashmiri Shaivite Hinduism, 187
Kasulis, Thomas P., 82, 286 n. 1
Kneisler, Hana Neilsen, 220–23, 225–26, 228, 229–30, 273
knowledge: belief vs., 4; mind embodiment and, 81, 85–87, 131; self-knowledge and self-inquiry and, 179, 180–81, 184–85, 189,

modernity, 34, 284 n. 5
monastic vows, 254–56
Monsler, Barbara, 217
Mother (Amritanandamayi, Mata),
    55–56, 58, 59, 60, 62–65, 73–74,
    232, 233
Mueller, Nick, 27–28, 275
Muktananda, Swami, 187, 188
multiply mediated and connected
    events, 74, 75, 100
Muslims. See Islam

Naficy, Tariq, 135–36, 137–39, 142,
    148–49, 217, 268, 276
names and forms of divine beings,
    35–38, 54–55, 70–71, 262
naming of spiritual and religious
    belief, 3–4, 11, 21, 281–82 n. 3
Naropa (Boulder, Colo.), 182–83
Nash, Mushim Ikeda, 24, 150, 152–
    54, 161–67, 170, 172, 217, 275
Nation of Islam, 8, 144–45, 149
Nichiren Shoshu Buddhism, 186–
    87
Nielsen, Nancy, 24, 214, 242, 243–
    45, 262, 263, 275
Nityananda, 58
non–Judeo-Christian practices, 8–
    10, 283 nn. 24–25, 283 nn. 27–32

oa (Overeaters Anonymous), 83,
    85, 86
Oliver, Eloise, Rev., 245, 250
Omari-Mohammad, L'dia, 135–36,
    142–45, 149, 216, 274
oppression, challenging. See diver-
    sity and anti-oppression work
Orsi, Robert, 14
Orthodox Christians, 145–46, 149
Overeaters Anonymous (oa), 83,
    85, 86
Oxford English Dictionary, 11

parenting, as spiritual practice,
    164–67

Parvati, 66–67, 68, 70
Pentecostal Church, 247–49
Perrin, Stuart, 58
place, 133–73; adult vs. childhood,
    134, 154, 156–61; Americanization
    of, 138–39; Buddhism as Ameri-
    can and Americanized, 151, 152–
    53, 157–58, 167–71; Buddhism as
    marked and other, 151; Bud-
    dhism from childhood to adult-
    hood, 156–61; Buddhist drug use
    and, 162–63; of Buddhist immi-
    grants, 152; of Buddhist monastic
    practice, 163–65, 167; of Bud-
    dhist sanghas, 150–51, 158, 160–
    61, 172, 288 n. 6; Buddhist tradi-
    tionalism vs. Americanization
    and, 168–69, 171–72; countercul-
    ture and, 162; inner and outer,
    133–34, 141; Islam as marked and
    other, 133, 142, 148–49, 287–88 n.
    5; language for expressing re-
    ligious concepts and, 134, 142–
    43, 154; meanings of, 133, 172–73;
    memories and, 150, 154–57; of
    Muslim converts in United
    States, 142–45; of Muslim immi-
    grants, 134–42, 149; old vs. new,
    134, 145; of origin, 133, 145, 149; of
    Orthodox Christians, 145–46,
    149; political and cultural, 148,
    157–59, 162–63; race and eth-
    nicity and, 150–52, 159, 160–61;
    religious vs. secular life and, 134–
    35, 139–40, 142–43, 145, 147–49,
    164–65, 172; sexuality and, 159–
    60; of Sufis, 146–47; temporal
    complexities of, 151–52
Plum Village (France), 239–40
poetics, 266–67
politics, 267
Potts, John, 24, 174, 176–81, 185,
    192, 208–9, 265, 273
poverty, vow of, 255–56

212, 214–15, 221, 261–62; sacredness of sex and, 229, 233; selfhood of gays and lesbians, 237–41, 246, 258, 262; social practices and, 225–26; Vipassana meditation and, 237–39, 262; Western and modern views of, 224–26. *See also* gays and lesbians
Sha'ar Zahav, Lesbian, Gay, Bisexual, and Transgender Synagogue (San Francisco), 240–41, 262
Shankar, Sri Sri Ravi, 58
Sharma, Arvind, 285 n. 19
Sherover-Marcuse, Ricky, 200, 288–89 n. 3
Shiism, 139
Shilling, Chris, 284 n. 5
Shimmin, Rita, 181, 183–84, 185, 209, 210
Shiva, 66–67, 68, 70
Shutt, Liên, 150, 151, 152, 155–59, 274
Siddha Yoga, 187–89, 192, 209
Siddha Yoga Meditation foundation, 174
Sikhism, 8, 55, 56
Sita, 58–59, 63–65, 71, 75, 217, 234, 268, 276
sitting meditation, 110–11, 114–17, 158
Smith, Judy, 118–27, 129, 273–74
sociology, 14. *See also* ethnography
Sogyal Rinpoche, 156, 157
Sophia. *See* feminine aspects of the divine
Soto Zen meditation: diversity and anti-oppression work and, 201, 204–7, 209; mind embodiment in, 110–18, 122–27, 132 (*see also* Zen Buddhism)
spirit, meanings of, 1, 2, 3
spirituality and spiritual practice: academic vs. practitioner, 10–19; Americanness and, 82–83; compartmentalization of, 11, 13–15,

17, 21; as connectedness, 195; dismissal of, 11, 17; marginalization of, 11, 13, 21; marketing of, 3, 281 n. 2; meanings of, 2–3, 195–96, 209–10; place in (*see* place); spontaneity vs. cultivation in, 32. *See also* religion
spontaneity vs. cultivation, 32, 232–33, 262–63, 266
subjecthood and mind embodiment, 132
Sufism, 146–47. *See also* Diamond Heart Path
surrender, 36–37, 38, 45, 54–55, 262
synchronicity, 44–46, 74–75, 101

talking to God. *See* Godtalk
Tan, Paloma, 82–90, 94, 96, 127, 128, 129, 131, 275
Tanaka, Kenneth K., 9
Taoism, 153
teachers, 3. *See also* gurus and teachers
Teng, Homer, 36–40, 48, 54, 55, 71, 273
Theravadin Buddhism, 111, 116, 150, 159
Thich Nhat Hahn, 58, 158, 232, 239
Thomas, Eric, 245–52, 253–54, 262, 273
*Tibetan Book of Living and Dying, The* (Sogyal Rinpoche), 156, 157
Tibetan Buddhism, 162–63, 168–69, 181–82, 184, 209
transmission, 154, 169–70, 171
Trungpa, Chogyam, 175, 182–83, 209
Tucker, Wilma Jean, 276
Turner, Bryan S., 79
Tweed, Thomas A., 9–10, 283 n. 27
Twelve Step, 23, 83–84, 85, 86

United Church of Christ, 242–43
United States vs. America, 282 n. 7
universality vs. particularity, 205–7

Ruth Frankenberg is a professor
of American studies at the University
of California, Davis.

*Library of Congress Cataloging-in-Publication Data*
Frankenberg, Ruth.
Living spirit, living practice : poetics, politics,
epistemology / Ruth Frankenberg.
p. cm.
Includes bibliographical references and index.
ISBN 0-8223-3257-4 (alk. paper) — ISBN 0-8223-3295-7
(pbk. : alk. paper)
1. Spirituality—United States—Case studies.
2. Syncretism (Religion)—United States. I. Title.
BL2525.F73 2004
204—dc22        2003019463